Advocacy

Authors

Evan Ashfield, Barrister, Lincoln's Inn
Susan Blake, Barrister, Associate Dean, The City Law School
Colin Bobb-Semple, Solicitor, Senior Lecturer, The City Law School
Elizabeth Cassie, Independent Voice and Communication Skills Adviser
Paul Corben, Barrister, Gray's Inn
David Emmet, Barrister, Senior Lecturer, The City law School
Judy Harris, Independent Voice and Communication Skills Adviser
Frances Hastings, Barrister, former Senior Lecturer, ICSL
Debbie Lithman, Barrister, former Principal Lecturer, ICSL
Robert McPeake, Barrister, Principal Lecturer, The City Law School
Conor Quigley, Queen's Counsel, Gray's Inn
Suzanne Reece, Solicitor, Lecturer, The City Law School
Charles Scott, Barrister, Middle Temple
Stuart Sime, Barrister, BVC Course Director, The City Law School
Margot Taylor, Solicitor, former Principal Lecturer, The City Law School

Editor

Robert McPeake, Barrister, Principal Lecturer, The City Law School

Series Editor

Julie Browne, Barrister, Senior Lecturer, The City Law School

Advocacy

The City Law School, City University, London

OXFORD
UNIVERSITY PRESS

OXFORD
UNIVERSITY PRESS
Great Clarendon Street, Oxford OX2 6DP
Oxford University Press is a department of the University of Oxford.
It furthers the University's objective of excellence in research, scholarship, and education by publishing worldwide in
Oxford New York
Auckland Cape Town Dar es Salaam Hong Kong Karachi
Kuala Lumpur Madrid Melbourne Mexico City Nairobi
New Delhi Shanghai Taipei Toronto
With offices in
Argentina Austria Brazil Chile Czech Republic France Greece
Guatemala Hungary Italy Japan Poland Portugal Singapore
South Korea Switzerland Thailand Turkey Ukraine Vietnam
Oxford is a registered trademark of Oxford University Press in the UK and in certain other countries
Published in the United States
by Oxford University Press Inc., New York

British Library Cataloguing in Publication Data
Data available
Typeset by Laserwords Private Limited, Chennai, India
Printed in Great Britain on acid-free paper by
Ashford Colour Press Limited, Gosport, Hampshire
ISBN 978–0–19–956846–8

FOREWORD

I am delighted to write this Foreword to the manuals which are written by practitioners and staff of the Inns of Court School of Law (ICSL [now The City Law School]).

The manuals are designed primarily to support training on the Bar Vocational Course (BVC). They now cover a wide range, embracing both the compulsory and the optional subjects of the BVC. They provide an outstanding resource for all those concerned to teach and acquire legal skills wherever the BVC is taught.

The manuals for the compulsory subjects are updated and revised annually. The manuals for the optional subjects are revised every two years. To complement the Series, the publishers will maintain a website for the manuals which will be used to keep them up-to-date throughout the academic year.

The manuals, continually updated, exemplify the practical and professional approach that is central to the BVC. I congratulate the staff of The City Law School who have produced them to an excellent standard, and Oxford University Press for its commitment in securing their publication. As my predecessor the Hon. Mr Justice Gross so aptly said in a previous Foreword, the manuals are an important ingredient in the constant drive to raise standards in the public interest.

Lord Justice Etherton
Chairman of the Advisory Board of the Institute of Law
City University, London

OUTLINE CONTENTS

DETAILED CONTENTS

Part I

Introduction

1 Introduction

1.1 Why should you read a manual on advocacy?

Advocacy is one of the skills that form the core of the Vocational Course for the Bar. It is actually composed of several disparate skills which, when merged, produce the person recognisable as 'the competent barrister'. When you begin reading this manual, and especially this chapter, you may have little idea what constitutes this 'competent barrister'. You will have seen actor/barristers in films, in plays, on television and heard them on the radio. Do not confuse dramatic effect with reality. These players are addressing themselves to audiences measured in hundreds, thousands or even in millions. As a real barrister, you will address your words to an audience often as small as one and rarely larger than a dozen. Furthermore, these films and plays can never show the constant consideration, and rejection, of alternating courses of action and even of words which precede the final performance of the barrister. You should spend some time in a barristers' chambers and the courts on a mini or a full pupillage. Then, you will start to experience for yourself the effort and planning that goes into producing what the public sees in court. Until you do this, you may find it difficult to judge whether a barrister is competent or not.

The early parts of the manual are designed to introduce you to those skills which are necessary in order to perform competently as a barrister. Many of them are really 'everyday' skills, but thinking about them in that context should help to get you started on this course. The manual takes you first to the preparatory skills that any good advocate depends upon. Following on from those, we consider how to open and close a case. These important aspects should always play a significant part in your planning and preparation for advocacy. Then we move onto working with witnesses, another fundamental part of the advocate's armoury. Finally, you will find a toolbox of how-to-do-it guides, covering a broad range of applications and submissions that you might make to a court or tribunal. These guides meld the advocacy skills and the practical know-how to give you a thorough insight into what will be expected of you in each of these hearings. When you have grasped the skills successfully, you will be better equipped to 'think on your feet', to maintain your composure and fluency when a witness gives a 'difficult' answer to one of your questions, or to recall at the end of a trial exactly what a witness said three days earlier. These are skills that the competent barrister has and which, if you do not possess them already, can be acquired through hard work and practice.

1.2 What this manual cannot do

It is not expected that this manual alone can render you competent to represent someone in court (it would be nice if things were that easy!). Armed with the manual and having completed the Vocational Course, you will have some experience and understanding of the practices and procedures that constitute the professional life of the barrister. You will then be going into pupillage, and that offers something that no classes or manual can—daily access to a practising barrister, with the chance to read all the case briefs that your pupil supervisor receives, perhaps to do some 'devilling' work on them and go into court and observe what goes on, fully informed about the issues in each case and its background. It is likely, though, that if you have worked through this manual diligently, your experience of pupillage may be enhanced by the awareness you have already of certain techniques or practices; equally, pupillage should improve and sharpen your understanding of what is demanded of an advocate. The sooner you start to visit courts and see how the rules are used and what the advocates do, the sooner you will accelerate your own development.

1.3 How to use the manual

As stated above, a competent performance by a barrister draws on a variety of skills and abilities. It would be possible to write a manual that simply told you about those skills but that would not be particularly helpful. Experience has shown us that you will understand and acquire these skills more easily if you can do two things. First, obtain some criteria by which to assess your own performances and those of others that you see (whether fellow beginners or practitioners in court). It is not enough to watch someone who is an acknowledged leader—you must have the ability to evaluate what you see. To say that a speech was 'compelling' or 'obviously persuasive' does not really help you to see what made it so. We have developed a set of advocacy training criteria, which we use as the basis for feedback in all of our advocacy classes (see **Chapters 4** and **19**). If you read them carefully now, and always try to apply them later, you will be able to learn a lot more when you observe others or review your own performances. It should be noted that, while these training criteria are written with advocacy skills in mind, they largely represent transferable skills which are extremely useful in many areas of an advocate's practice (and beyond).

Second, it should help comprehension if you see the skills presented in the practical situations where they are likely to occur in reality. This manual has several chapters which deal with the typical transactions in a courtroom—making speeches and questioning witnesses—see **Parts 4** and **5**. **Part 4** looks at opening *and* closing speeches. This has been done because, although in the courtroom they would be separated by all of the evidence in the trial, you would start to plan both how to start and how you intended to end the trial within a short time of receiving the papers in the case. As planning for the two should not be viewed as two separate processes but as a single coherent approach to the case, we have put them in the same section. **Part 5** looks at witnesses and the evidence they give. The chapters there explain, with practical examples, the techniques and objectives of questioning witnesses. Also, in **Part 6**, **Chapters 39** and **40** deal with the more 'mechanical' aspects of two applications or submissions which are often made to courts and are directly relevant to the evidence (either actual or potential) in the trial—namely, the *voir dire* and the submission of no case to answer.

After the Parts that mix skills and tasks to show you the skills in commonplace or recognisable situations, comes **Part 6.** This has several short chapters which are more like guides to specific transactions, telling you how to do it. They reinforce and repeat the skills that are involved in the earlier chapters but the emphasis has shifted so that you are learning as much about the transaction as about the skill. These chapters look at particular applications or submissions that you could make in court, or particular procedures that you might use. The objective when selecting topics for inclusion here is to show those matters which the junior advocate (or pupil) will encounter most often in practice. Many of these applications will require a skeleton argument, so **Part 6** begins with a guide to these.

Please remember to refer to this manual **throughout** the course. It is always useful to refresh your memory or even rework a topic in the light of experience. Soon, practice should ensure that many of the techniques and skills become more familiar and almost habitual. In particular, **Part 3** deals with some ancillary skills without which we will never succeed in gaining competence as advocates. Whenever you want a case to practise with, turn to the Appendix and use *R v Heath*.

1.4 The importance of thorough preparation

You should note now that preparation is as important as the 'performance' in court. Your objectives and how you may achieve them will differ from case to case and even within a single case. You need to identify what you are being asked to do at the outset—only then will you be able to plan the means of fulfilling those objectives. In particular, your lay client's needs and wishes are paramount. You must be able to discover what they are as efficiently and effectively as possible, then agree on an appropriate solution and the means of achieving it. To do all of this competently, you should become as familiar with other essential skills as you are with those in advocacy. Important examples are those of legal research, fact management and conference skills. Without a fluency in these sorts of skills to assist you in preparing for an appearance in court, you will always be working in court 'flying by the seat of your pants'. For any barrister this is an uncomfortable position to be in—anything that you can do to avoid it should be done. You must appreciate that when you make your first few appearances in court for real clients, you are bound to find these moments both nerve-wracking and intimidating, as well as very exciting. There are some simple steps that you can take in order to minimise the worst effects of your nerves. Arrive early at court, go into the courtroom in which you will be appearing. Stand where you will be standing when acting as an advocate. Make yourself as comfortable as you can. Try your voice out. Arrange your papers as if you are beginning the case. When the court is sitting and you are due to begin, take two or three deep breaths to counteract the breathlessness you will feel. If you can, arm yourself with a glass of water to deal with the dryness in the mouth you will experience. The pounding in the chest, the roaring in the ears, the loss of your stomach to an area adjacent to your shoe laces you can do nothing about. You are not odd. You are not alone in experiencing all this. Everyone does.

But do not add to your problems by a sudden realisation that you have not mastered your brief thoroughly. If you do, then you will be adding to the problems of your client, the very person you are in court to assist. You ought to use this manual (and its companions) as a guide during the Vocational Course and to help you make a more comfortable transition from student to practitioner.

1.5 A cautionary note

Please remember that certain practices and procedures used by barristers are governed by rules. Sometimes these are legal rules, sometimes they are customary in origin (for example, wearing a wig and gown in open court). Whatever their basis, the rules mean that these procedures always occur in the same manner (until the law is changed or someone thinks up a better method which then becomes the custom).

It is not the function of either this manual or the advocacy course to challenge accepted practices at the Bar but you should note that, sometimes, there is more than one way of doing something. The aim may be the same but two barristers may differ, quite properly, on how best to achieve that aim. So long as you abide by the legal rules and the rules of professional conduct, you are able to develop your own style and preferences as an advocate. If the method that you choose suits you and the particular situation, then that is acceptable. Do not do something in a particular way simply because someone else has told you to. They may know better than you—if so, you should follow their advice. Never do so unquestioningly.

Oxford University Press has a website for this manual—the current address is shown on the back cover. We would welcome your thoughts, comments and suggestions as to the content of this manual and your own ideas about advocacy, especially advocacy training. Our aim is to build up this website into something really useful for everyone involved in advocacy—whether as a trainer or someone undergoing training or from practitioners reflecting upon their own practices.

1.6 Objectives and teaching theory for the advocacy course

It may be helpful for you, when reading this manual, to understand what The City Law School is doing on its advocacy course because this manual exists primarily to support that course. What we aim to do, for everyone on the advocacy course, is as follows.

1.6.1 Training objectives

(a) to demonstrate that competence in advocacy can be understood by reference to skills-based criteria;

(b) to familiarise students with the essential criteria by which competence in advocacy should be judged;

(c) to enable students to observe performances of advocacy and judge what is and is not competent;

(d) to allow students as much practice of advocacy skills in the classroom as can practically be arranged;

(e) to encourage students to practise their advocacy skills as much as is reasonably practicable;

(f) to offer students criteria-referenced feedback on their performances of advocacy skills, whether in the classroom or on DVD;

(g) to demonstrate to students various practices and procedures encountered by an advocate, either on video or through live performance;

(h) to familiarise students with basic techniques for advocacy, including questioning techniques and preparation for court;

(i) through all of the foregoing, to enable students to perform one or more advocacy tasks with a degree of competence that shows they are ready for pupillage and are likely to benefit from pupillage through their continued practice and observation of advocacy.

1.6.2 Teaching theory

Our teaching theory for advocacy, although it also applies to the other legal skills, is:

> People learn skills best through practice. Such practice is most useful if it is preceded by thorough preparation and followed by specific and informed feedback.

This theory leads us to abide by the following guidance, for the purpose of course design:

(a) Preparation should be as thorough as circumstances allow. Particularly, one should know the facts or allegations in the case and understand the relevant laws, substantive and adjectival, in order to determine which facts, allegations and evidence are material to the present task. By the end of the course, a student should be able to analyse factual material and have such existing knowledge of substantive and procedural law that an informed decision can be taken as to any appropriate advocacy tasks that may be undertaken.

(b) Preparation may be general and, in the early stages of learning advocacy skills, may need to be repeated often. Examples might be control over breathing and nerves, the ability to speak clearly and fluently and the ability to construct a logical argument. At a less general level, examples are the ability to use different questioning techniques in appropriate situations, to empathise with witnesses or judges and to listen with eyes as well as ears. Preparation may also be specific (that is, related to a particular case or task) and this type of preparation should complement general preparation during the early stages of learning. By the end of the course, the competent student should have mastered the basic skills needed for general preparation and be able to demonstrate them, whenever called upon to do so.

(c) Unless very basic skills are to be practised or demonstrated, it is best to practise or demonstrate in the context of a specific advocacy task, using a particular set of case papers. This should assist in showing the relevance of the exercise and may encourage an insight into the application of an individual basic skill in many varied situations, that is, transferability.

(d) Learning may occur through a variety of ways. It may be through performance, or observation of oneself on video or of one's peers or of experienced demonstrators. Such observation may take place in class or through video but will always be of maximum benefit when the performance is accompanied by feedback and explanation. Learning may also occur through reading a book or working through a computer-led lesson, but neither format is likely to be as effective as observing others or performing a skill personally, with explanation and feedback.

(e) A student will learn best how to improve their skills, as well as identifying strengths and weaknesses, if he or she performs a skill (usually in the context of an advocacy task) and that performance is reviewed (either instantly or later) by an observer who is able to apply skills-related criteria to the performance and articulate the degree to which that performance satisfied each of those criteria.

(f) Any skill **may** be learned through sheer repetition alone and untutored. It may not be learned well, though. Many of the greatest advocates were effectively self-taught but it may now be agreed that early learning is done best with supervision. The student should be guided by an instructor who can demonstrate and observe, provide explanation and feedback. Self-tuition should be left until later, when the advocate's own professional experience, and familiarity with the criteria that should be used to judge competence, can replace the instructor.

(g) Students learn best in small groups with one or more instructors. While they learn most about their own abilities by performing in groups of one or two plus an instructor, they should experience larger groups as these will expose them to a variety of methods and thinking, as well as examples of good and bad practice. The student sometimes needs to see bad practice since it may be that only by being told it is bad, and why, will the student know and understand that some aspect of the performance was faulty. The group has become too large when one or more students are denied the opportunity to perform and to discuss a particular skill or task in the class, for whatever reason.

(h) Feedback should be based on clear and objective criteria which are relevant to the skill and/or task, and are made known to the student in advance. Giving useful feedback is itself a skill which can be learned and should be practised often. An infrequent instructor may not have great familiarity with the relevant criteria and may not refer to them at all when giving feedback. New instructors (or occasional instructors) should be trained to give feedback and, if resources permit, be accompanied in classes by experienced instructors.

(i) In the course of offering feedback, an instructor should have an opportunity to illustrate certain points by a brief demonstration. It should be possible to check that the feedback has been understood by observing an improvement when the student next performs.

(j) Feedback may be limited to a single issue, for reasons of time or because the student is at a very early stage on the course. Single-issue feedback will work best when the student has many further opportunities to perform and those will occur in a short space of time. If future performances will be separated by a considerable period (say, a week), it may be better to offer 'multi-issue' feedback to the student, indicating a variety of strengths and weaknesses as the student will have ample time to reflect on each issue.

1.7 General bibliography

You may find helpful information and techniques in the following books:

Bergman, P., *Trial Advocacy in a Nutshell,* West Group, 4th edn, 2006.
Du Cann, R.L.D., QC., *The Art of the Advocate,* Penguin, 1993, revised.
Evans, K., *Advocacy in Court,* Blackstone Press (OUP), 2nd edn, 1995.

Foster, Gilliatt, Bourne and Popat, *Civil Advocacy: A Practical Guide,* 2nd edn, Cavendish, 2001.

Fridd, N. and Weddle, S., *Basic Practice in Courts, Tribunals and Inquiries,* Sweet & Maxwell, 3rd edn, 2000.

Hyam, His Honour Judge Michael, *Advocacy Skills,* Blackstone Press (OUP), 4th edn, 1999.

Lubet, *Modern Trial Advocacy: Analysis and Practice,* NITA, 2004.

Morley, I., *The Devil's Advocate,* Sweet & Maxwell, 2005.

Murphy, P., and Barnard, D. *Evidence and Advocacy,* Blackstone Press (OUP), 5th edn, 1998.

Nathanson, S., *Non-trial Advocacy: A Case Study Approach,* Cavendish, 2001.

Pannick, D., *Advocates,* OUP, 1993.

Shaw, N., *Effective Advocacy,* Sweet & Maxwell, 1996.

Stone, M., *Cross-Examination in Criminal Trials,* Tottel Publishing, 3rd rev. edn, 2009.

Stone, M., *Proof of Fact in Criminal Trials,* W. Green & Son, 1984.

Welsh, Bevitt and Stanton, *Advocacy in the Magistrates' Courts,* Cavendish, 2003.

(Other books and articles may also be referred to within the following chapters.)

2 The qualities of the advocate

2.1 Introduction

The barrister is known as a person of integrity, someone whom judges can trust. The best barristers are also known for the qualities they display in the courtroom. They have mastered their briefs—they know the evidence and the contentious issues in each case, how to handle a 'difficult' witness and, perhaps above all, how to get the triers of fact to see the case from the standpoint of their client.

These practitioners have accumulated several of the disparate qualities that make up the able barrister. Some of these qualities are to do with personality and this course is unlikely to change that. Either you are the sort of person who will stand up to an unpleasant judge to safeguard your client or you are not—all that can now be attempted is to encourage you to use your latent strength of character. Similarly, no one can make you behave in an honest fashion, they can only stress the vital importance of doing so. Honesty is important—to you professionally; to your client in a case where your dishonesty might harm his or her interests; and to ensuring public confidence in the judicial system.

Other qualities can be acquired or improved, for example, eloquence and detachment. There are others. Although opinions may differ as to the entire spectrum of such qualities or as to their relative importance, those qualities or skills set out in the rest of this chapter are particularly important. Considerable reliance has been placed on Richard Du Cann, QC's excellent book *The Art of the Advocate.*

2.2 The essentials of advocacy

2.2.1 Practice and hard work

You may not currently have much experience in public speaking. The idea of being the only voice heard in a courtroom may fill you with a sense of dread as well as great anticipation. Two things are certain though. First, you should get better with practice, so never miss a chance to gain experience—debates, moots or mock trials, for example. These opportunities may occur infrequently. All your fellow students will, at least should, read this manual, so you may encounter some competition. So practise with your friends, better still, with your relatives for they will be more long-suffering. Force yourself to listen to what you are saying. Force yourself to criticise yourself as you are speaking. Ask yourself all day and every day: 'Was that the best word, was that the best way of expressing myself?' Never be content with the answer: 'Well, that's how I always do it.' In due course, your performance is going to be judged by the audiences you are to face and address. Their opinion will be based on their assessment, not yours.

Second, you must be prepared thoroughly for every case you take. The need for solid preparation and planning is emphasised in every skills manual for this course, but it is important to stress that the conduct of an application or trial, the handling of an examination-in-chief or a cross-examination, in a competent fashion will not happen by some magical process. It is the product of hours of hard work or, as Richard Du Cann puts it, industry.

The advocate, as Lord Hewart said, must 'claw the facts'. If he or she does not, all the virtues and brilliant improvisations will not help him or her. The facts must all be retained in his or her memory, so long as the case lasts: dates, names, times, exhibit numbers. Then as fast as they were mastered they must be forgotten so that others in the next case he or she does can take their place. Memorising facts of this kind is sheer drudgery. To do it properly the advocate must be prepared to forgo the pleasures of private life at the most inconvenient moments and for indefinite periods.

2.2.2 Tenacity, courage and self-control

Tenacity and self-control are two distinct but related qualities—both depend upon you having the strength of character necessary to do a good job in adverse circumstances. Tenacity is needed when you encounter a difficult witness—perhaps one who is out to show the court he or she is smarter than you or is just wilfully contrary. As Richard Du Cann says:

> Counsel must expect to cross-examine many witnesses whose evidence he will fail to destroy. He must also expect to come across a number who believe that attack is the best method of defence and who will do all they can to embarrass him . . . Two qualities are required on these occasions more than any others: tenacity and a form of question which allows no opportunity to the witness to score.

You also need self-control in such circumstances—the advocate who is readily embarrassed or angered into an obvious flush will show signs of losing control of himself or herself and the case. The position is worse if your reaction is more than a mere blush; one of the most unpleasant sights in a courtroom is to see a barrister and a witness engaged in a row (unless, of course, to do so is part of a deliberate plan on your part). To quote Du Cann again:

> Control of his feelings there must be, in particular of his temper. If he cannot, he will not keep control of his tongue and he will not keep control of the case. Forensically simulated emotion should be one of the armaments of the advocate. Personal sensitivity is not.

Finally, you will require courage. You will sometimes find that those in a position of authority seek to test you, occasionally to dominate or bully you. On such occasions make sure of your position. If it is untenable, abandon it. As stated in Du Cann:

> It is always right to be seen to admit wrong. To fail to do so can do immense harm.

But if, on checking, you are satisfied that you are right, press on and stick to your point even if it means confronting a judge. You should be fearless in promoting or defending your client's interests. Remember, though, that judgement is also a quality possessed by the competent advocate. As Du Cann says:

> There is a time to stand and a time to sit for every advocate, and unless he can solemnise some form of marriage between courage and judgment he will never reach the first rank of the profession.

Your point may have been made the first time. To persist in pressing a matter may do more harm than good. Such judgement cannot be taught, it must be acquired through experience and reflection. Never be afraid to ask your colleagues, especially senior ones, for advice on such matters.

2.2.3 Honesty

The rules of professional conduct require the barrister to maintain a sense of etiquette in court but the quality of honesty is one which is essential. If you have made a mistake—for example, referred inaccurately to some evidence in your closing speech; forgotten to put a point in cross-examination—never be too egotistic to admit your error. Also, never mislead the court. If you have said anything which may have done so, always retrieve the matter before anything irremediable occurs. This must be adhered to no matter what the cost to one's reputation or self-esteem and sometimes, regardless of the cost to your client. Richard Du Cann gives a memorable example from the libel action brought by Harold Laski. (Note that Slade is the QC appearing for the [claimant], Laski; Hastings and Wentworth Day are leading and junior counsel for the defence.)

> In the Laski case Slade contended that the plea of justification (the claim that the words printed in the newspaper were true) included the claim that Laski had been guilty of cowardice by remaining in America during the First World War since this was the suggestion made by Wentworth Day's question to Laski. If this was right it meant that Hastings also had to prove that Laski was a coward. If he did not, Laski was bound to succeed. During Slade's final speech to the jury Lord Goddard interrupted to raise a matter of law, then Hastings intervened:
>
> > HASTINGS: . . . I distinctly recollect hearing Mr Slade say that he was not making a substantive claim in respect of that [ie. that Laski was a coward] and therefore I have not even addressed my mind to it.
> >
> > After further legal argument Slade left the point saying:
> >
> > SLADE: . . . I shall be very astonished to find that . . . I have allowed this case to proceed on a footing that the jury could find the whole of these words to be true, which would mean that Mr Laski had been guilty of cowardice.
>
> Half an hour later Hastings intervened again. He had found a passage in the transcript when Sir Valentine Holmes, Slade's junior in the case, had said during an exchange with the judge: 'We are not asking the jury as regards the part relating to cowardice to give Mr Laski damages . . .'. In that possibly ill-considered sentence, which was not vital to the argument then taking place, the whole of Slade's point, one upon which he believed he could win the whole case, was swept away in the middle of his final speech. Whatever the obligations to his client and whatever the personal feelings he had himself, Slade recognised the most important single fact of the situation: Hastings had already addressed the jury on the basis that the point was abandoned. So he told Goddard:
>
> > SLADE: . . . I am not going back on anything Sir Valentine Holmes said, any more than I should go back on anything I said myself; and I therefore prefer to err on the side of fairness, and I shall not ask the jury to deal with that part of the libel at all.

2.2.4 Language and humanity

Given the possession of the qualities of tenacity, courage, self-control, judgement and honesty, the advocate requires an understanding and a love of language, and the trial advocate requires also an understanding of and love for humanity. These latter qualities cannot be taught. You have either got them or you have not. But you can be alerted to the need to value both. You can be taught the need to demonstrate that you value both. Take language first.

Throughout your future professional life, words will assume a dominant position. Some, boringly, will be inflexible because the practice of law and human affairs has made them so: *'mens rea',* 'bills of exchange', 'charterparty', 'Scott schedules', 'maliciously', the list is endless. From these you will be unable to escape. It is not so with the rest of the natural English vocabulary. But you will find when you are on your feet that you use one word and can then become a prisoner of it. Words like 'situation' and 'relationship', once used, become traps. This can only be avoided if you train your mind concisely to be a movable *Roget's Thesaurus,* alert to the use of alternative words apt both for the occasion and the different clients, witnesses and audiences that you will face. Your language, as Lord Chesterfield said in 1750, must be 'the language for them all'. Take the simple example used by Du Cann from *R v Gardiner.* Ernest Wild, QC is cross-examining a labourer who claims to have seen the accused entering a building with the victim.

WILD: Where did you see him [the defendant] first?
WRIGHT: Against Church Lane.
WILD: So he saw you?
WRIGHT: Yes.
WILD: You were loitering about.
WRIGHT: No, I was going down the road.

But the youth was leaning against the edge of the witness-box, his hands in his pockets. 'Loitering' was what the jury were going to remember. Wild continued:

WILD: When did you see him the second time?
WRIGHT: He came down the road.
WILD: He saw you then?
WRIGHT: Yes.
WILD: And the third time too?
WRIGHT: Yes, he spoke to me.
WILD: He must have seen you all the time?
WRIGHT: Yes.
WILD: And he must have known you were about?
WRIGHT: Yes, he spoke to me.
WILD: Do you represent that, knowing you were about, he went into the chapel and behaved in the way you state?
WRIGHT: Well, he did.

When striving to hit your target in this fashion, it is essential to keep one eye on the judge/jury/magistrates to see if they have taken your point. Also, try to observe the witness as much as possible—something in their demeanour may be very useful. In short, be alert and be observant.

Finally, always remember to whom you are talking. In the first instance, this may be the witness but, through him or her, you are talking to the triers of fact. Try to see whatever you do in terms of how they will see it and understand it. Almost the last word goes to Richard Du Cann—this time referring to Marshall Hall.

He had an understanding of human frailty which enabled him to catch the throats of all who heard him speak. When he was quite young he defended a prostitute charged with murdering one of her clients. She was forty-seven, her former attraction devoured by the life she had been forced to lead. At the end of his speech as he was about to sit down, he caught sight of her sitting hunched in the dock. On the spur of the moment he added these words:

Look at her, gentlemen of the jury. Look at her. God never gave her a chance—won't you?

You might note that this style of advocacy seems a little dated now—indeed that has sometimes been said to the writer. A more recent example of a celebrated advocate is George Carman, QC. He was criticised by opposing counsel in a libel trial (*Mona Bauwens v The People Newspaper*) for:

> . . . painting a rather crude picture of Mr Mellor [then the Government's Heritage Secretary] behaving like an ostrich and putting his head in the sand 'thereby exposing his thinking parts'.

Maybe rather than consider whether styles of advocacy have 'dated', one should simply ask at the end of each case, 'did it work?'.

3

Ethics, etiquette and cross-cultural communication in the courtroom

3.1 Introduction

There are various rules of professional conduct that must be observed by any advocate, breach of which will lead to serious consequences. There are also certain conventions of etiquette to be observed in the courtroom and guidelines relating to cross-cultural communication of which you should be aware. The following sections cover the main points but are not exhaustive.

3.2 Rules of professional conduct

3.2.1 Duties to the court

You must:

- bring to the attention of the court all relevant decisions and legislative provisions of which you are aware, whether or not their effect is favourable to your case;
- assist the court in the fair administration of justice;
- bring any procedural irregularity to the court's attention during the trial itself and not reserve such matter to be raised on appeal;
- take all reasonable and practical steps to avoid unnecessary expense or waste the court's time;
- observe the rules relating to disclosure of documents/information.

You must not:

- deceive or knowingly or recklessly mislead the court. For example, if your client tells you that he or she has committed a similar offence in the past for which he or she was never caught, you cannot tell the court in mitigation that this was the 'only time' your client has done such a thing. Equally, if your client tells you he or she is guilty but insists on pleading not guilty, you may continue to represent him or her and make the prosecution prove their case against him—but the ways in which you can test the prosecution case against him or her will be limited. You can test and probe the view that the witness had of the alleged perpetrator, exposing the fact that the lighting conditions were poor or the witness was quite far away from the scene, but you cannot assert that which you know to be false, eg, you cannot suggest to a witness that your client was elsewhere at the time;

- misquote the evidence;
- make assertions of fraud without clear instructions to do so and without reasonably credible material which establishes a prima facie case of fraud;
- manufacture or assist your client to manufacture a defence or other explanation for his or her conduct;
- devise facts which will assist in advancing your lay client's case;
- make statements or ask questions which are merely scandalous or intended or calculated only to vilify, insult or annoy either a witness or some other person;
- express your personal opinions, view or belief to the court unless invited by the court to do so;
- by assertion in a speech impugn a witness whom you have had the opportunity to cross-examine unless in cross-examination you have given the witness the opportunity to answer the allegation.

3.3 Conventions of etiquette

These derive from custom, and can be divided into dos and don'ts.

Do:

- dress and robe appropriately;
- use the correct mode of address for the judge or tribunal;
- stand when the judge enters and leaves the courtroom. He or she will normally bow before being seated and you should return the bow. You should also bow to the judge when leaving court and, if the judge is already in the courtroom, as you sit down;
- sit down if your opponent rises to object. Only one advocate should be on their feet at the same time unless the judge is addressing you both;
- show courtesy and respect to your opponent and the other personnel in the courtroom;
- accept blame when you are at fault and apologise.

Don't:

- leave the judge 'unattended', ie, if there is no other advocate present in the courtroom, wait for a signal from the judge before leaving;
- speak or shuffle papers while a witness is taking the oath;
- comment on the evidence as it is being given;
- make faces/sigh to show a jury your incredulity of an opponent's witness;

- show your emotions at a verdict or a judge's ruling;
- continue to argue a point after the judge has heard the arguments and ruled upon it: the proper place for this is an appeal.

3.4 Cross-cultural communication in the courtroom

It is not suggested that any advocate will intentionally cause offence to any party in the courtroom. However, working in a multi-cultural society often requires sensitivity to the ways in which norms and customs may differ from one community to another. It is important to recognise the influence of your own cultural background on your unconscious perceptions and behaviours and to bear in mind that:

- no matter how well intentioned, use of racial and ethnic terms (such as coloured or oriental) are liable to give offence;
- cultural differences in body language can contribute to misunderstandings and conflicts between members of ethnic minorities and, for example, police officers;
- on the other hand, stereotyped notions about the body language of particular cultures should be avoided;
- there may be differences in language—jargon, slang and metaphors—which may not be familiar to all witnesses/jury members, and so on;
- words may not have the same meaning in all cultures, for example, descriptions of family relationships (eg, uncle, cousin) and times of the day (afternoon and evening);
- just because someone responds to questions in English in court, that does not mean that person necessarily understands fully what has been said;
- in some cultures, looking away rather than maintaining eye contact is not necessarily a sign of dishonesty or disrespect—it may be the opposite! Equally, raised voices do not necessarily equate with loss of control or aggression.

3.5 Preconceptions

A preconception is an opinion or idea which is conceived or framed prior to *actual* knowledge. It is important to recognise your own preconceptions and how these may affect your judgement in your work as a barrister.

- Is a client more likely to be guilty because he or she is unemployed?
- Do you believe what a client tells you more easily if he or she is well dressed, articulate, educated?
- Do you listen less easily to what a client has to say because he or she is inarticulate or poorly educated?
- Does the fact that a client has a previous conviction for dishonesty mean that he or she is more likely to have committed a crime of violence?

- Do you believe your opponent is trustworthy because she is attractive and initially friendly?
- Do you assume your opponent is less competent than you because she looks younger than you? Or because she confides that she has not done a lot of this type of work before?
- Do you believe your opponent is more competent than you because he looks older than you?
- Do you let your opponent's bragging of her experience undermine your confidence so that you advise your client to compromise on less favourable terms?

Of course, the answer to all these questions is 'no'; yet, in practice, many barristers forget this. They fail to recognise their own preconceptions and the manner in which they may affect their conduct of the case.

As a barrister you cannot pick and choose your clients so that you only represent those whom you like to believe in. You are bound to observe the 'cab-rank principle'. Unless you recognise your preconceptions about the client, they are likely to affect your judgement; the way in which you approach, prepare and present the case; the way you communicate with the client, your opponent, the court; the way in which you advise, negotiate or argue the case. By relying on premature assumptions or beliefs, you will be less able to communicate effectively with the client; you may lose the confidence of the client and your solicitor; you are likely to convey to your opponent and the court, by gestures or body language, your apathy towards the client. With the growth of conditional fees the art of assessing the possible success of a case is growing. Make sure all your judgements are objective.

The most important factor in dealing with preconceptions is to recognise them, either in ourselves or in others. You must learn to differentiate between assumptions and actual knowledge, so that you can identify where you have anticipated without justification. You must be careful not to prejudge a client, an opponent or a tribunal.

Once you learn to recognise preconceptions you can then determine their possible effects and uses. Ask yourself:

- Have they affected my judgement or approach to the case in any way?
- To what extent?
- Are they more/less/equally likely to affect my opponent/the court's approach/judgement?
- Is my opponent proceeding on the basis of an assumption I haven't made?
- Is it likely to undermine or support his or her case?
- Is the court likely to proceed on the basis of any preconception?
- Is it likely to influence the jury?
- Can I use it to my advantage?
- Do I need to dispel it?

It is only by being alert to these possibilities that you can ensure that you recognise the existence of preconceptions, their dangers, uses, advantages and disadvantages.

Part II

The basic components for applications and submissions

4 Recognising competence—advocacy skills criteria

4.1 Introduction

Isn't this a rather strange chapter to put in a book of this sort? After all, any time that you go into a court or tribunal, you should see people acting as advocates and (usually) being paid to do so. Aren't they all competent advocates? And isn't it safe simply to mimic their techniques and style? Well, 'No' is the answer. When you see an advocate in court, it may be their first time in such a court, or it may be that they have good points and bad points (regardless of how much experience they have). The latter is more likely to be the case.

The point is that you cannot afford simply to adopt wholesale and uncritically whatever you see being said and done by advocates in court. It would be fantastic if you could do so but that is not the case. As a novice advocate, you will be tempted to regard all other advocates as more experienced than you (probably true) and therefore better advocates (not necessarily true) and highly competent in everything they do (almost always not true). All of us have strengths and weaknesses, things we do well and things we do badly. It is a fact that when advocates appear in court, they very seldom receive any feedback on the quality of their performance. You might say that they learn whether they are potential silks or should start looking for another job by the amount of work they are sent to do. Unfortunately, that may depend on a number of factors, only some of which are connected to the advocate's ability. Even then, there may be things that the (soon-to-be-ex-) advocate does well. There is no formal system for helping advocates to monitor the standards of their advocacy, more is the pity. Indeed, most practitioners would look aghast if you (or anyone else) offered them some constructive criticism after seeing them in court.

So until there is some such monitoring system in place, the best that can be done is to look out for yourself the best way you can. How can you do this? One of the best methods is to have a set of criteria that you can take into any court or tribunal. Then, when you watch other advocates in action, you can judge for yourself how well (or otherwise) they are performing all of their functions and be confident that you have identified those functions and the proper standards to be attained.

4.2 How should we define competence?

4.2.1 Different things to different people?

It is plain nonsense to suggest that the degree of expertise that we should expect from an experienced advocate is the same as that which we are likely to find in a beginner. Nevertheless, it is a fact that professional advocates must be capable of achieving a certain minimum level of competence, no matter what their experience. This is an essential requirement; one need only point to the public interest in litigation being conducted by competent advocates (for the avoidance of miscarriage of justice and achieving an efficient and effective system for litigation, for example) to see that there must be a basic level of competence that must be achieved before it is safe to employ someone to be an advocate in court.

4.2.2 A basic level of competence

What should we expect of any advocate, regardless of expertise or experience? This could be defined in terms of knowledge, perhaps.

4.2.3 Knowledge

We might say that any advocate should know and be able to make effective use of the rules of procedure (ie, those rules which govern the way that the relevant court functions). We should not expect an encyclopaedic familiarity with all such rules but the advocate should know all those rules of general, common relevance—on costs, for example. The competent advocate should also know when he or she is confronted by a more unusual rule, where to find it and how to apply it. The same goes for the rules which govern the evidence that can be put forward in court. So we can say that a competent advocate should have a good accurate knowledge of the rules of evidence and procedure, those matters which are adjectival to the subject matter of the litigation.

In a similar fashion, we can say that any competent advocate should have a good working knowledge of various, commonly met, bodies of substantive law. Examples might be the criminal law, the laws governing contracts and the laws governing liability for negligence. In addition, the advocate should have a thorough knowledge of the laws that are relevant to the particular matter that is before the court (ie, the subject of the present litigation). That knowledge may have been acquired through previous experience of such litigation, it may have been acquired through post-qualification study or it may have been acquired specifically for the purposes of this litigation. Any competent advocate should know (and have the ability to research, if necessary) the substantive legal rules which are or may be relevant to the current litigation.

It is a fact that professional advocates in this country (that is, barristers and solicitors) will have spent a considerable amount of time in learning a large body of law, before they ever obtained their professional qualification. The vast majority of advocates will have law degrees and the rest will have a non-law degree and have gone through a shorter, intensive law course. There are certain core law subjects in which all would-be professional advocates must have passed examinations (there is no need to rehearse them here). Furthermore, during their training period for their professional qualification, they must have passed examinations on the rules of procedure and evidence (see the BVC and

LPC requirements). We might be safe in assuming a basic level of competence as far as legal knowledge is concerned. How about the application of that knowledge? And what about factual knowledge? Advocates must be familiar with the allegations in the litigation, the available evidence and, combining legal and factual knowledge, the advocate must know in every case what facts need to be proved in order to achieve the outcome which their client seeks.

These intellectual qualities must be gained **in advance** of the hearing where the advocate is to perform. How the knowledge was gained is irrelevant although we can learn effective techniques for both the law and the facts. What we need, as an observer in court, is a criterion that relates to **preparation.** Often, we will not know exactly what the advocate has had to do in order to be prepared for this piece of litigation (although a trainee or pupil connected with the advocate should have observed the advocate's preparation). What we can do is observe what the advocate says and does in court, and judge whether those words and deeds are appropriate and relevant to the laws and allegations in this particular piece of litigation. That relates to the **content** of the advocate's performance and we should have a criterion to judge that, too. Since we are beginning to look at this in terms of what the competent advocate should be able to say and do, we can see it as the definition of a skill. Or rather, as the definition of a collection of skills which might be summed up as advocacy skills.

4.3 Advocacy skills

This part of the chapter follows the standard City Law School philosophy of separating out the bundle of related but disparate skills which typically are used together to produce a competent performance in the courtroom. The City Law School has spent a great deal of time looking into what makes for a competent piece of advocacy. We have looked at those skills which are required for a submission or application to a court, as these are the tasks on which most advocates cut their teeth. We have also analysed the skills that advocates use when questioning witnesses; we think that slightly different skills are used or objectives set, depending upon whether one is engaged in examining one's own witness or one called for the opponent. We have produced sets of criteria which can be used to produce an objective critique of an advocate's work, whatever the context.

We should note here that we regularly review our advocacy criteria and make any changes which we consider to be necessary. There are of course many other providers of advocacy training, both in the UK and further afield, who may set out their own criteria in a different way or who perhaps use additional or different criteria. No criticism of these other criteria is intended by the focus on our own here. Indeed, if you think that we should amend any of our criteria, we would be glad to hear from you with the reasons for the suggested change. You can contact us via the web address shown on the back cover of this manual.

The training criteria for making (or opposing) an application to a court are set out in **4.3.1**; those for submissions in the course of a hearing are in **4.3.2**. The criteria for handling a witness are set out in **Chapter 19**. Some criteria are always relevant—such as the ability to speak clearly and fluently—others are relevant either to making a submission or to questioning a witness but not to both (for example, the use of appropriate questioning techniques). In the main, we are looking at *transferable skills,* that is, skills that can be used in more than one context.

4.3.1 Advocacy training criteria for applications

In order to be regarded as competent, the advocate should show his or her ability to do the following:

SKELETON ARGUMENT

1 *Style and structure*

Draft a skeleton argument in an appropriate style with a clear and logical structure.

2 *Law and analysis*

Summarise your submissions on the main issues to be resolved, referring to law and evidence to persuade the judge to grant the order(s) sought.

ORAL PERFORMANCE

3 *Structure*

Structure the application in a clear and logical way.

4 *Delivery*

Deliver the application clearly and fluently, using appropriate language and manner.

5 *Law and analysis*

Present submissions on the main issues to be resolved, referring to law and evidence to persuade the judge to grant the order(s) sought, referring where appropriate to relevant documents, including your skeleton argument and responding appropriately to the interventions of the judge.

Remember that the rules of professional conduct should always be observed.

4.3.2 Advocacy training criteria for submissions

After the court has heard oral evidence, counsel will make a submission (akin to a closing speech at the end of a trial). Because it is impossible to predict with certainty what evidence will be before the court following testimony, it is difficult to submit a skeleton argument which can deal comprehensively with the issues and arguments before the court. Frequently, for this reason, such closing submissions will be made without a skeleton argument. It is also likely that the judge will not intervene while counsel is addressing the court. The training criteria which would otherwise apply (for applications to the court) need to be recast as follows, to meet this situation.

In order to perform this task satisfactorily, you must show your ability to:

(a) Prepare the case effectively, by understanding the relevant law, facts and procedure and planning your submission.

(b) Make a submission which is appropriate, relevant and legally and factually sound, and in which you respond appropriately to points made by the other side.

(c) Structure your submission in a clear and logical way.

(d) Deliver your submission clearly and fluently, using appropriate language and manner, referring to notes when necessary or desirable.

(e) Make a submission which is effective and persuasive.

Remember that the rules of professional conduct should always be observed.

4.3.3 The training criteria in more detail

Those criteria are explored in more detail in the following five chapters, with one exception. Professional conduct and ethical behaviour is the subject of the separate ***Professional Conduct*** manual and it is better to look at that manual for expert coverage of the topic. For present purposes, we might say that the advocate is bound by a code of conduct established by the legal profession. A simple understanding of (and adherence to) the standards that the courts, clients and the public are entitled to expect from an advocate should enable you to do the right thing in most situations. Further guidance and the current copy of the Bar's Code of Conduct can be found on the new website of the Bar Standards Board at <http://www.barstandardsboard.org.uk>.

5 Preparing for court

5.1 Introduction

This is a job that has to be done sometime and by someone; you can only hope that it is you doing it in plenty of time before you are due in court. Of course, life doesn't always work out like that and you may be heavily reliant on someone else's notes of interviews with the client, background research on the law and the evidence, etc. That does not mean that you can simply breeze into court with little preparation. A classic example of how things can suddenly go wrong is when you are asked to go to court on some simple matter and ask the court to make 'the usual order'. Somehow, courts have a knack of discerning those advocates who are working to someone else's script and when you stand up and ask for 'the usual order', you may be asked, 'And what is that then?' or 'Why do you say you should have it?'. The competent advocate has considered these points in advance and has a reply ready; the incompetent advocate will become flustered and begin searching among their papers in the vain hope that the answer will magically appear there.

Of course, there is a third category of advocate, too. Neither wholly competent nor wholly incompetent, this category is perhaps best described by the label 'beginner'. Anyone just starting out on their career as an advocate will be only too well aware of the high-profile nature of the job. It matters not that there may be only three people in the room to witness your performance—you, your opponent and the district judge, perhaps—in your eyes, that's two too many! You will prepare the case to the best of your ability, devoting far more time to it than your more experienced colleagues seem to spend on their preparation. When someone passes you a file or brief and says, 'Just ask him for the usual order, and don't worry, he's a pussy cat', you won't accept that. You will read books, ask people to explain, try to be prepared. Then you go to court and everything falls apart; that great point you discovered at 2 am last night is never argued in court because:

- you were too nervous about it; or
- you were too intimidated by the judge or your opponent or the situation to raise it; or
- you couldn't find it in your notes; or
- you forgot it.

This has happened to every advocate at one time or another but it happens to some more than most and it happens to beginners more than to experienced advocates. What can you do to stop it from happening to you?

There are three basic lessons to learn. First, prepare thoroughly for your appearance in court. Second, deliver the performance that you have prepared. Third, be prepared to adapt in court to a fluid situation. Let's consider these in a little more depth.

5.2 Thorough preparation

When you go into any court or tribunal, in fact whenever you want to speak on someone else's behalf, you should be prepared. You should be familiar with the relevant procedure and rules that apply in that court; you should be familiar with the law that is relevant to the case; you should be familiar with the evidential material that is (or might be) available for this hearing.

For example, you are sent to argue for summary judgment in a hearing before a Master in the Queen's Bench Division in the High Court. Before entering the room, you should know the procedural rules set out in Part 24 of the Civil Procedure Rules, together with any related rules, for example those dealing with the possible costs orders that may be made. You should be familiar with any rules governing the evidence that you (or your opponent) wish to use, for example, has your client's affidavit been served on your opponent in good time? If not, are there any rules that you can use to seek extraordinary permission to use that evidence? You should also know the relevant substantive law, that is, the law which deals with the claim. Since your claim is for summary judgment, more likely than not your client alleges that the defendant has no defence to the claim. In order to substantiate that allegation, if required to do so, you should be familiar with the relevant legal principles, first, as to why the claim should succeed and second, why there is no viable defence to it.

It follows that you must be familiar with the factual allegations made in the case (for which you will need to know the statements of case and your client's affidavit in support), because it is the synthesis of the legal framework with the specific factual allegations in this case which produce the argument that your client's claim must succeed and there is no reason why the case should go to a full trial.

Once you have gone through all of this preparation, you will need to write a skeleton argument to submit to the court in advance. These are increasingly used, both in civil trials and interim applications. What you put into a skeleton argument will depend partly on your style and preferences and partly what you learn suits the court. However, it should cover the following matters:

- The nature of the application or submission.
- What the case is about (where necessary).
- The issues between the parties (if necessary).
- The argument in the form of a series of legal propositions and submissions supported by authority and evidence (with references to pages and paragraphs as necessary).

The skeleton argument should also:

- Assist the court to assimilate your argument easily.
- Persuade the court to grant the order that you seek.
- Identify precisely what you are asking the court to do.

It may also be appropriate to hand in a separate chronology to the court. More detailed guidance on skeleton arguments can be found in **Chapter 25**.

Is that all you need to do in order to be fully prepared for this application? I'm afraid it is not that easy. Let's go back to the first two of our three basic lessons. First was thorough preparation and second was deliver the performance that you had prepared; in sporting parlance, don't leave your performance in the dressing room! It makes little difference to the outcome whether you prepared the case poorly or prepared yourself poorly for court. What you have done with your preparation so far is to work on the content of your advocacy performance; the necessity to do that will never change from one case to another. What you must do now is to prepare the delivery of your performance.

5.3 Prepare your delivery

Delivery will be the subject of an in-depth exploration in **Chapter 8**, so what you have here is a summary of the points that you will need to work on.

For many people, the ubiquity of the video camera, the camcorder and even mobile phone camera has meant that many of us now know what we look like to others, much more realistically than we would by simply looking into a mirror. Video footage shows us what we look like when we move, stand or sit, it reveals our gestures to us and it tells us how we sound to others. You may have already seen the picture that you present to others, the value of which was once described by Robert Burns, in 'To a Louse', as follows:

> O wad some Pow'r the giftie gie us
> To see oursels as others see us!
> It wad frae mony a blunder free us,
> An' foolish notion.

If you have seen yourself, you may have been minded to make some changes but that is unlikely to have been done if the video was shot on a social occasion. What you need to do now is record yourself delivering a piece of advocacy. Try to create the sort of conditions that will be present in court. For example, dress in formal court clothes, and deliver a straightforward speech or submission to the camera. Five minutes' worth should be enough to start with! Then review it. How do you look? Are you standing up straight or slouching? Are your hands in your pockets or fiddling with a pen? Can you hear yourself? Are you speaking too fast? Are you looking at the camera or away from it?

All of these points, and others, will be addressed in **Chapter 8.** For now, it is enough that you appreciate that, for many lawyers, preparing the law and the evidence for each case is relatively straightforward. After all, you have a law degree, are used to working on researching legal points in a law library, have a fund of basic legal knowledge; you have read the statements of case in this case (and maybe many others during your training), you have seen the evidence (in witness statements, affidavits and the like) and can remember it. If you can't remember it, now is the time to read **Chapter 11** of the manual. What is not straightforward is the transition from **lawyer** to **advocate.**

5.4 From lawyer to advocate

On the face of it, this transition should be simple. After all, don't we all advocate almost every day of our lives? When you are at the supermarket and debating with your partner which brand of breakfast cereal to buy, if you want the cornflakes you will argue in favour of buying them and your objective will be to persuade your partner of the merit of your choice. What is so different about 'advocating' something in a courtroom?

Perhaps it is the fact that you are now arguing for someone else, so there is a sense of responsibility. Perhaps it is because you are now being judged on the quality of your argument by someone who has power, over both you and your client. Perhaps it is the public nature of the advocacy; whereas you may be happy and relaxed to debate points on a private level and at a private volume, when called on to do so with an audience and at much greater volume, the situation becomes less familiar and more uncomfortable. It should be clear that the more appearances that you make as an advocate, the more familiar and less uncomfortable it should all become. How do you survive until then?

Practice is the answer. You will find things becoming easier as you get more and more appearances under your belt. What you need to do is to increase your number of performances artificially, by using the video camera and working with others in a similar situation, as well as with more experienced advocates who can point out things that you may have overlooked. In the same way that pilots train on a flight simulator, so you can clock up more hours by working on advocacy simulations and getting more experience that way.

In the Appendix at the end of the manual, you will find an entire case to use as a vehicle for some advocacy work.

5.5 Being adaptable

The third basic lesson that has to be grasped is that you must retain the ability to adapt and respond to a changing situation. It is sometimes said that advocates are quick-witted and have the ability to 'think on their feet' in court. What that really means is that the advocate is sufficiently well versed in the relevant law and evidence that, even if something unexpected happens, the advocate can cope with it. The unexpected may be just being asked a question by a judge in the middle of your submission to the court; the judge wants to know about a particular point and wants to hear your answer now. For all the judge knows, you were just about to deal with that point. If so, it should be no problem for you to tackle it now. If you were going to deal with it later on in your submissions, you should know the answer even if you have to think about it a little more carefully. When that happens, you then have to make a judgement on whether to go back to the topic you were dealing with before the question or carry on from the point that your answer has now taken you to. The choice you make depends on what points you had to skip past to get the answer: were any of them important to your case, or contentious? If so, it's probably better to go back and deal with them. If not, carry on from the point which interested the judge.

It is a little different when you are questioning a witness. Here, the witness is meant to be under your control inasmuch as they are in the witness box to answer your questions. There is more chance that something unexpected will emerge from a witness than there was with the judge (at least we can expect the judge to appreciate concepts like legal relevance, admissibility and know the relevant legal framework for the case). So when the unexpected, and possibly inadmissible, answer is given, you should be prepared with your response. First, don't let your mouth open wide with surprise, don't flush with embarrassment and don't start stumbling over your words. If the answer was irrelevant to the issues in the case, you might ignore it or perhaps admonish the witness to listen carefully to your questions and simply answer them (this is likely to draw more attention to the unexpected answer). If the answer was relevant to the issues in the case, you may want some time to consider your response, in which case say something like:

> Perhaps we will return to that later, Mr Jones. For now, perhaps you could tell the court . . .

Having bought some time, you may want to leave the subject well alone but, if the answer came from a witness you were cross-examining, you might decide it has to be squashed. You could do that by attacking the credibility of the answer, for example, why is this the first we've heard of that? Is it something the witness has just made up? If they have made written statements some months (or even years) ago and the subject is not raised in the statement, why not? An alternative is to challenge the witness's memory of events that may have happened a long time ago; another might be to suggest that the witness, however innocently, is enhancing their account in a bid to help the court.

The central point is that you should be ready with an array of possible responses to the unexpected, like a collection of arrows in your quiver, so that you can calmly select the appropriate one to use in any given situation. Problems start when you don't expect the unexpected; you approach the trial or hearing with the mental equivalent of blinkers on and you are so focused on your own case and how to present it that anything that upsets your planned strategy pushes you completely off course. If you can remember that things seldom turn out exactly the way you anticipated before going into court, then you won't be so shocked when that prediction comes true.

5.6 Planning a route to your destination

We have looked at the need to understand (and perhaps research) the relevant law, to acquire a thorough grasp of the allegations, the evidence and the areas of dispute between the parties. We have also looked at the need to present yourself clearly in court and to be adaptable. The last hint is that before you finally start out on your journey through this case, you must have a clear idea of where you want to be at the end of it. You have to identify your client's objectives: what does he or she want out of this litigation? A judgment that they are not liable to the claimant? An award of damages? A verdict of not guilty? Then, what might you need to do in order to achieve those objectives? To answer these questions you will need to predict the arguments that you want to present to the court at the end of the case. Only then can you start to work backwards to consider how you can best guarantee that those arguments are in fact available to you at the end of the case.

It is often said that the advocate needs to start planning the closing speech for a trial before setting foot in the court. Really, you need to have a very clear picture in your mind of how the hearing will work—who will be there, what they are likely to say—so that you can start to see the time spent in court as a whole, rather than a series of isolated events. In a trial, what counsel says in opening the case may present a certain version of the case; the opponent needs to know whether that version might be challenged. As each witness appears in the witness box, the advocate cannot ignore what preceding witnesses have said, their answers will help to determine the questions that **this** witness is asked. At the start of a trial, a judge's notebook is blank, apart from the names of the parties perhaps. By the end of the evidence and speeches, it will have been filled up; the advocates cannot change its contents but they had a large role in determining what was written in it. During the course of the hearing, the thorough advocate has to keep in mind what he or she wants to have in the notebook, what is **actually** going into it, and what **might** still be put in.

5.7 A work plan for a criminal trial and conference

5.7.1 Introduction

The remaining paragraphs of this chapter contain a short, simple plan to use when preparing for a trial in the Crown Court, either as the prosecutor or for the defence. It is intended to act partly as a checklist of the things you should cover in your preparation and also as a guide to organising your materials.

There is also a plan for a conference with the defendant in a criminal case and some points to consider when questioning witnesses in court and making speeches. Some of these will be covered in greater detail in other chapters.

You could try to create your own checklists after studying a particular situation; perhaps add your points to the one given here for the defence conference. Remember, what you find here is always open to improvement or adaptation. This section of the chapter provides a start for you—build on it!

5.7.2 Work plan

On receiving the brief:

Read the instructions: What am I being asked to achieve?

5.7.2.1 Defence brief

(a) Look at the *indictment.* **Never** prepare a case without the indictment. Compare the counts with the charges on which the case was sent for trial. Are they the same? If they differ, ask yourself why. Always consider what alternative convictions could be recorded.

(b) Read prosecution statements and exhibits: do the papers disclose a prima facie case?

(c) Are my instructions a plea of guilty or not guilty?

Not guilty

(a) Is that supportable on my instructions? If not, conference/advice.

(b) Is a conference required in any event? (Desirable in all but the simplest of cases.)

(c) Are my instructions adequate? If not, request further and better particulars.

(d) Points of law: PACE 1984; CJA 1988; CJA 1991; CJA 2003. What additional evidence may be needed, eg, custody record and relevant police officers; medical reports of any examination of victim/defendant?

(e) Additional evidence required generally: eg, proofs to be taken from potential witnesses; plans; photos.

(f) What is in the defence statement? Has proper disclosure been made?

(g) Expert evidence: must be served on prosecution if intended to be relied upon at trial.

(h) Alibi:

  (i) is it an alibi case?

  (ii) if so, has anything been done about it—defence statement?

(i) Notices of additional evidence: do we require the witnesses to attend?

(j) Unused material. Has this been served? Is an application necessary?

(k) As a result of my instructions/conference can I offer any sensible pleas to the prosecution? If so, solicitors should write at once.

Note: most of the above points are far better covered in a written advice than in a chat over the telephone.

Guilty

(a) On my instructions is that a proper plea or is it equivocal?

(b) On my instructions is a *Newton* hearing likely on issue(s) of fact? If so, consider a discussion in advance with prosecution to try to agree a 'basis of plea' and put it into writing. Failing that, witnesses can be warned to attend, thus avoiding need for adjournment.

(c) Any evidence required in support of mitigation, eg, proof of job?

(d) Any character witnesses, references, service records, etc?

(e) Request extension to public funding for psychiatric/medical report (if appropriate).

(f) Research authorities on sentence for type of offence and assess likely range, or talk directly to the prosecuting advocate to find out what, if any, pleas of guilty might be acceptable to the prosecution, or possibly if the prosecution would be willing to allow the court simply to bind the defendant over to keep the peace.

(g) Advise solicitors to inform court of fact of guilty plea. Always prepare for a best and a worst result. If best, an acquittal, be ready to argue costs. If worst, be ready to make a speech in mitigation of sentence **and** to advise on appeal.

5.7.2.2 Prosecution brief (not guilty)

(a) *Indictment:*

draft it if requested;
if already drafted, check it is correctly drafted and that there is evidence to support it.

(b) *Advice:*

additional evidence if needed and photos;
disclosure/non-disclosure in accordance with the Criminal Procedure and Investigations Act 1996 and relevant case law and Protocol; disclose any previous convictions of any prosecution witness.

(c) *Opening note:*

contents must be borne out by reference to admissible evidence;
plan structure: enough law/fact to help the jury, not confuse them;
visual aids: OHP, video, graphics, schedules—will they help?

(d) *Preparation of jury bundle:*

only what's really necessary;
make sure it's legible;

include plans, agreed schedules, glossaries, etc;
folders/binders, etc.

(e) *Order of witnesses:*

defence (and judge) always want to know this.

Tight preparation = Strong presentation.

5.7.2.3 Defence conference

(a) Keep requisite degree of formality: avoid use of first names with client and (during conference) with solicitor (often difficult to do!).

(b) Put client at ease: explain what you are going to discuss: be prepared to **listen** and not just **talk.**

(c) Explain what the charge means.

(d) Explain strengths/weaknesses in the defence } be frank: this avoids the 'why

(e) Explain possible sentence upon conviction } didn't you tell me?' afterwards.

(f) If this is the defendant's first Crown Court trial: explain what will actually happen at court.

The idea of points (a)–(f) is that they remove uncertainty in the client's mind and help to make the client confident that:

(i) you understand the case; and

(ii) you are in charge and capable of running it.

5.7.2.4 Examination-in-chief

(Much harder than cross-examination in many ways because you are not allowed to lead the answers from the witness.)

In advance

(a) Be clear in your own mind what it is that you want to adduce from the witness.

(b) A statement is often badly put together and you may well not want to follow its sequence. As a result a plan/checklist of sequence and content may be helpful. (Note: if you are going to ask questions on matters not covered at all, then a further statement should be taken and served on the defence.)

(c) Try to put the witness at ease—courtrooms can be very intimidating. A relaxed witness is far more likely to come up to proof.

(d) 'Difficult' witness: **Don't** rush to make him **hostile** in law: try 'going round again'; if it's a memory problem, seek a short adjournment so that he can refresh his memory—a trial is not a memory test (Note: there will almost always be an argument over this in the absence of the jury.)

5.7.2.5 Cross-examination

(a) You have a duty to put your main challenges to the witness during cross-examination, eg, 'it never happened'; 'you've made it up'; 'you're mistaken', etc.

(b) From the statement and your instructions, **plan** what you're going to ask in order to try to **assist** your case: ie, are there obvious areas where the witness is vulnerable and you can make a good point? Are there obvious areas where the witness is strong and will simply be 'firmed up' if pressed by the defence?

(c) Don't try to get the witness to make comments: he or she is unlikely to want to help you and you can make the comment in your closing speech without fear of getting the wrong answer.

(d) When you have got a favourable answer: **stop**. Many cases have been lost by pushing a question too far.

(e) Don't be frightened **not** to ask questions: if a witness has been favourable to you or failed to identify/mention your client, **leave well alone**, however tempting to try to score a few points.

Both in examination-in-chief and cross-examination:

(a) make sure that the witness is keeping his voice up;

(b) don't go too fast: follow the judge's pen;

(c) let the witness answer before asking your next question;

(d) try to keep questions short: nothing is worse than when your clever but convoluted question is met by blankness and 'Sorry, I don't understand what you're getting at'.

5.7.2.6 Speeches

(a) Speeches should be as short as possible: juries do not need 20 minutes on the burden and standard of proof, for example.

(b) Make your good points and sit down: don't spoil them by waffle and numerous bad points.

(c) If you are concerned that your client won't feel you have 'had a good go' if you make a very short speech, explain to him or her beforehand why you're doing so—they normally understand.

(d) Prosecution:

(i) fair presentation and comment on evidence;

(ii) no duty to secure conviction at all costs;

(iii) no duty to 'sum up' case to them by rehearsing all the law and facts (again).

6 The content of your application

6.1 Introduction

To a certain extent, the answer to the question implied in the title of this chapter must be found in **Chapter 5**. It is unlikely that you will be able to say the right things at the right times unless you have prepared for your appearance very thoroughly. So, hasn't the job been done? Well, the proof of the pudding comes when it is eaten and even the best preparation in the world is just wasted effort if you cannot say the right things and take the right decisions once you get into the courtroom. Every advocate has to make use of their knowledge of the law and put it together with their analysis of the evidence and issues in dispute to produce what the court requires, namely a performance which is (i) appropriate, (ii) relevant, (iii) legally sound and (iv) factually sound. It is worth looking in more detail at these requirements, in particular to see how they might apply to the range of tasks which the advocate may be asked to perform.

6.2 The content of submissions

In a sense, the four essentials for content are set out in **6.1** the wrong way round: if the advocate does not put forward arguments on a submission which are 'legally sound and factually sound', there is little chance that the arguments will be 'appropriate and relevant'. Although the twin requirements of appropriateness and relevance are more important than simply being sound on the law and facts, the advocate must first know the 'facts' and the necessary law in order to construct the legal and factual framework within which it becomes possible to gauge whether an argument is appropriate or relevant.

6.2.1 Appropriate and relevant

6.2.1.1 Your submission

Whenever you are called on to make an application or submission to a court, one of your earliest steps in preparing will be to digest exactly what appears in the statements of case. Of course, it is a little different in criminal cases but there will still be a charge sheet, summons or indictment to consider. Looking at these will help you to discover the issues between the parties, who alleges what, when, and who bears the burden of proof. It will also be the start of your legal analysis, when the causes of action are disclosed or the elements of the offence revealed.

'Relevance' denotes some sort of relationship between things; what you say in court must be directed to identifying the issues in the case and how they should be resolved. When you dissect a set of papers prior to going into court with them, you have to learn a lot of things which you did not know before. Someone else may have been through a sorting process already, so that if you are instructed on behalf of Mr Smith in his careless driving prosecution, you don't suddenly find a lot of documents to do with his pending divorce. Similarly, when you open your mouth in court, you should not just say anything that appeared in the case papers (or your instructions). You must regularly gauge whether what you are about to do, whether it be drawing the court's attention to some factual allegation or addressing an argument to the court, is connected to the issues that are of concern to the court.

If 'relevant' means that you should talk only about matters that are likely to be (and should properly be) considered by the court when adjudicating in the case, what does that leave for 'appropriate' to do? Appropriate means that you are sensitive to your surroundings, the context in which you are operating. For example, in a prosecution for grievous bodily harm it may be clear that the victim has suffered nasty injuries. A defence advocate who has to allege that in fact the 'victim' was the protagonist and the accused was simply acting in self-defence must appreciate that the court is likely to feel a considerable sympathy for the injured person. That may make it necessary to (a) adopt certain tactics or arguments which acknowledge that sympathy and (b) appreciate that, when putting forward the defence case, there may be a lot of resistance. Again, it may be 'appropriate' in a hearing seeking an interim payment of damages for personal injury to tell the court what the claimant requires the money for, even though the legal test for making the interim payment doesn't require you to do so. A piece of factual information or an argument may be 'appropriate' without strictly being 'relevant' in a legal sense.

6.2.1.2 Opposing a submission

When a court hears a submission or application, it is generally the case that the advocates and the judge all have the same documentary information (affidavits and statements of case have been served on the opposing party in advance). No one is usually taken by surprise at the hearing. However, just because the advocates have access to the same information it does not follow that they will make the same use of it. Different people see different arguments, disagree over what is a strength and what is a weakness in the case. When you are opposing a submission or application, your task is twofold.

First, you must prepare to respond as best you can, so you should try to anticipate your opponent's arguments. What will the other side be emphasising? Which of the weaknesses in your case will they seek to exploit? When preparing to respond, it is tempting to plan for every eventuality and that has some sense to it. But you must be ready to adapt your strategy or your arguments to meet the situation on the day; you must not present your case like an automaton, blithely assuming that everything is going just the way you thought it would. Suppose that you spotted a weak point in your evidence while preparing the case, then you should work out a tactic to deal with it, but you must still listen in court. If your opponent does not raise that topic, for whatever reason, you should consider very carefully whether you now need to say anything about it when you respond. If you do, you may just remind your opponent of a forgotten argument or alert your learned friend to the existence of a weakness (they may not have seen the point in those terms until now). Thus, what is relevant and appropriate can change quite rapidly in the course of competing arguments on a submission. The second part of your task, then, is to monitor constantly what the other side is saying and the response of the court, and to tailor your arguments to suit the circumstances as they are at the moment.

6.2.1.3 Skeleton arguments

In a civil case, your application or submission may be supported by a skeleton argument. This document will be prepared by you in advance of the hearing and supplied to both the court and your opponent. Assume that both have read it before the application starts. Clearly, the content of your skeleton argument should fulfil the same criteria as your oral argument—it should be appropriate, relevant and sound in fact and law. It may be that there is adequate coverage of a point in your skeleton and you can therefore either take it very shortly in addressing the court orally, or perhaps simply refer the court to the passage in the skeleton. For further guidance on skeleton arguments, see **Chapter 25**.

6.2.2 Legally and factually sound

Whatever you say in court as an advocate, it must be a fair and accurate representation of the facts in the case and the law relating to the case (or the particular hearing at least). You should never knowingly mislead the court on the law or the evidence (whether going to a disputed fact or not). If you do so innocently and in good faith, then as soon as you realise your error you should draw the court's attention to it and correct yourself.

Let's look at how your submission might be legally and factually sound. In an application for summary judgment, the test is to be found in the Civil Procedure Rules (CPR), r 24. No judge will need you to tell him or her that but they will expect you to base your arguments, for or against summary judgment, on an accurate understanding of what the criteria are for summary judgment. For that, you need the current text of CPR, r 24, to hand. As this rule is interpreted and applied by the courts over time, some elements may assume greater or lesser significance. You will need to be as up to date as you can be on how the courts are using CPR, r 24, and be able to use that knowledge as the basis of your arguments to the court.

As for being factually sound, you should know the number of affidavits or statements in the case, who swore them, when they were sworn and, most importantly, what they say (and don't say). Anything you say to the court of a factual nature must be accurate: don't say the unpaid debt is £12,500 if it is £15,200, for example. On a more mundane level, if one of the witnesses is named John Tyler, don't refer to him as Jack Taylor. We all make little slips like that from time to time but the important thing is to listen to yourself. Even if you know the witness is called John Tyler, it may not always come out like that. As stated, that slip is probably quite inconsequential but for one thing—it may plant a seed of doubt in the court's mind whether you know what you are talking about. If you can make an error over something as simple as a name, especially when it is on a document in front of you, what else might you be mistaken about?

6.2.3 Reference to legal sources

On most applications or submissions, your court will probably be legally qualified (a judge, a district judge, a Master) and the last thing such people want is a lecture on the law. After all, they are likely to know it as well as you, if not better, and use it more frequently too. What the court wants, then, is not copious references to the legal sources for your arguments, it wants you to have extracted the legal principle from the case of

Smith v Jones, say, and apply it to the allegations and evidence in the present case. On an application by the defence advocate in a Crown Court trial to exclude an interview between the police and the accused from being heard by the jury, the judge will not want to hear from counsel about the legal history of the Police and Criminal Evidence Act 1984, s 76. The judge will want the advocate to have identified the relevant part(s) of s 76—maybe 'oppression'—and then present the arguments, based on a synthesis of the relevant law and evidence.

7 Structuring your application

7.1 Introduction

The subject of structure needs to be seen in two distinct ways. First, you can deal with structure in the context of applications or submissions made to a court or tribunal. These may be applications at an ad hoc hearing (eg, application for summary judgment) or in the course of a trial (eg, *voir dire*). The second context is in the examination of witnesses, whether called by your client or by other parties in the litigation. This chapter looks at structure within these two contexts but it is important to note, at the outset, that there are three basic requirements that are relevant to structure, whatever the context.

7.1.1 Three basic requirements

The three basic requirements for structure are:

- be clear;
- be logical; and
- be responsive.

Remember, **clarity** is everything, obscurity is nothing. Your ultimate aim is to persuade and, to do that, you must communicate accurately with the tribunal. You are most likely to do that if everything you say and do is clear in its meaning. A clear structure is a good guarantee for that. Coupled with clarity is the need to be **logical**. Despite the critiques of the human reasoning process that have been made (see eg, the works of Edward de Bono), it is a fact that the most common process for reaching conclusions relies heavily (although not solely) on logic.

When devising a structure for your work, you should choose one that 'makes sense'. To achieve that, it should make sense to others, too. That is not to say that there can only be one logical structure, although there may be a 'normal' or common structure to particular applications. One might present information on the basis of a chronological order, or a geographical order, or even 'best point first'. Perhaps the best general description is that individual points should flow clearly from one to another, rather than appear as a motley collection of unrelated data.

Finally, **respond** to the other players in the drama. Even when there is only you and the judge (maybe on an application when no one appears for the opponent), you may still face questions from the court. Deal with them as they arise if at all possible. If you really cannot provide an immediate response, indicate that you will be doing so shortly. Whether making an application or questioning a witness, you cannot afford to stick to preconceived notions or a particular structure *regardless* of what others are saying or thinking. A script is almost useless in court for many reasons but here it hampers good advocacy by imposing a straitjacket on the advocate. You must have a clear and logical structure certainly, but you must never adhere to it just for its own sake. If there is no need to amend or adapt it while you are in court, so much the better, but your planning should have enabled you to be flexible in your work. You should be alert to what the tribunal or your opponent or the witness are saying, doing or thinking. They are communicating with you and each other either directly or indirectly and you cannot afford to ignore what they are saying.

7.2 Applications to a court

7.2.1 Clear and logical: your application

Your first consideration is, what stage of the proceedings are we at? Has the hearing been arranged primarily for the purpose of the application you are to make, or is the application merely incidental to a more wide-ranging hearing? For example, is this an application for summary judgment or is it an application, during a trial, to exclude evidence?

In an ad hoc hearing, introductions are required. The court needs to know who the advocates are and courtesy dictates that you tell the court, even if it clearly knows their identities already. The court also needs to know who the parties are to the litigation and which advocate represents which party. The court may require you to tell it something about the case itself, before you launch into the application. Where the application is made during the trial, on the other hand, such introductions would be unnecessary at best and bizarre at worst.

7.2.1.1 The ad hoc hearing

A general structure for such a hearing could look like this:

(a) Introduce advocates, parties, the case, the application, all very briefly.

(b) Check that the court has all of the relevant documents. Be specific, don't just say, 'Have you got the papers in this case?'.

(c) Briefly state the order in which you propose to present the rest of your application.

(d) Explain the background to the application, if appropriate.

(e) The substance of the application:

- (i) Set out the arguments in support of your application, combining the specific evidence in this case with the relevant legal rules. Don't lecture the court on the law, or spend time stating what you understand the law to be in some abstract way. Always apply the law to the evidence and remember that the court has probably heard a great many of these applications; it does not need to receive the benefit of your legal research!
- (ii) If necessary, anticipate and deal with the arguments of your opponent. If these counter-arguments will be on points that you need to establish to succeed in the application, deal with the point as you interpret it first and then indicate why the counter-argument has no merit.
- (iii) For any application, there may be several legal requirements on which the court needs to be satisfied before your application can succeed. You should have an argument designed to deal with each such point.

(f) Summarise your strongest arguments, by way of a conclusion, and offer to assist the court with any questions that it may have.

(g) Allow your opponent to make his or her arguments to the court.

(h) Ask to be allowed to reply to those arguments, if necessary.

(i) The court announces its decision.

(j) You raise any supplementary points which are relevant now that the main decision has been reached.

That is fine as a framework but it may not turn out that way in practice. For example, suppose your opponent keeps interrupting your arguments? Or the judge keeps asking questions, none of which seem relevant to the point you are dealing with? The answer is to be flexible and responsive. You might suggest that it would be simpler for all concerned if you could present all of your arguments first and then give the floor to your opponent. That is responsive as it does not require you to carry on as if your opponent was saying nothing. If the judge asks a question, you should deal with it. You might then return to your previous point, or you could skip to that part of your plan which follows on from the judge's question. If in doubt, ask the judge.

7.2.1.2 The application within a trial

Typically, this type of application will arise after the beginning of the trial, perhaps concerned with an issue of evidence. Here, one can afford to be much more specific as the court should be fully aware of the context of your application. So, a general plan might work like this:

(a) State that an application now needs to be made. In circumstances where questions of law are decided by different people from those who decide questions of fact, this is all you should say at present, then wait for the triers of fact to leave the court.

(b) State what the application is (eg, an application pursuant to s 76 of the Police and Criminal Evidence Act 1984).

(c) If the application places the burden of proof on you (not always the case; see eg, s 76 of the 1984 Act), set out the allegations of fact that you rely on, relating each of them to the legal requirements on which you must satisfy the court. Do not deal with the relevant law unless you are applying it to the alleged facts.

(d) Allow your opponent to present any counter-arguments.

(e) Ask for an opportunity to reply, if you need one.

(f) The court announces its decision on the application.

(g) Carry on with the trial, at a point and in a manner consistent with the court's decision.

7.2.2 Clear and logical: opposing an application

Much of what concerns the advocate who is making an application is inapplicable to an advocate who must respond to that application. Typically, it will be unnecessary to introduce yourself when you first speak to the court as that should have been done by your opponent. Any relevant documentation should also be before the court by now and you can simply make use of it, without needing to introduce it.

Clarity here simply requires that each of your arguments is clearly differentiated. Do not conflate two separate points; keep your arguments as simple as they can be. Logic will often dictate that the order in which you raise issues and present your arguments on them is the same as the order adopted by your opponent. That may be unfortunate for two reasons. First, their order may differ from your preferred order for tactical reasons and, secondly, you may have to rearrange your running order at the last possible moment. Even so, that is probably the best course of action rather than sticking to your own intended order unless the order chosen by your opponent was, in your opinion, defective for some reason. In this situation you may want to indicate that you will not be following the order of points used by your opponent, and perhaps explain why. Then you should go on to explain what your order will be, to minimise any confusion for the court.

It is not of great assistance to work on a framework when you are opposing an application, for reasons just stated. But you should have an order for the arguments, in case you want to substitute your order for that used by your opponent. Thinking about the appropriate order for your arguments also requires you to think about which arguments are your strengths and which are your weaknesses. This is an extremely useful process when preparing for court and should never be overlooked. The judge may have already asked your opponent some questions. These questions could indicate matters which the judge is concerned about. You might then concentrate on those matters in your submission.

8 Delivering your application

8.1 Introduction

Once again, as with several of these chapters, you will wonder why on earth we need a chapter on such an ordinary topic—isn't speaking something that you do every day? Yes, like most of the skills that are used by a competent advocate, we all use our speaking skills every day. But now the circumstances are different; we are not speaking privately or personally, as we are used to doing, but we are to speak in public, on behalf of someone else and, in a sense, on the record. Our client is depending on our ability to speak well for him or her, and other people are judging us on our speaking ability, among other things. In short, we are now in the public eye and what we are engaged in is public speaking. You may have had a taste of this already, in a variety of situations as diverse as a debating society, a mooting competition or a wedding. If so, you will be familiar with the nerves that accompany your first efforts at speaking to an audience, with the strain you feel in trying to project your voice into a large room and with the problems you seem to be having with your breathing.

Speaking as an advocate imposes stress on the speaker and that stress manifests itself in several symptoms. These are most common in the novice and become more bearable (and thus less noticeable) with experience. However, it is much better to work on such matters before your first appearance as an advocate, so that your personal discomfort may be reduced and there is less danger of your client's interests suffering because of your inexperience.

Chapter 10 gives you some guidance on techniques to use for working on relaxation and breathing, as well as articulation and projection. We have tried to make this as 'law-relevant' as possible but some of the exercises may strike you as inappropriate. If so, please take the following steps. Get a video camera and set it to record yourself. Then spend a few minutes delivering a set speech (or reading from a favourite text) to the camera. Now play it back and observe yourself. See if there are any nervous mannerisms that you can spot: are you including lots of ums, ers and ehs? Are you pausing in the right places to give the appropriate emphasis to your words? Is it too fast? Or too slow? Have you got to turn the volume right up on the monitor to hear yourself? Now imagine that you are doing the same thing again, but this time in a courtroom with other people present. Do you think your performance will be better, or any more comfortable, now?

It is time to realise that, although not all advocates are frustrated actors, the competent advocate requires many of the techniques which are commonly used in drama. Actors on a stage do not get themselves heard at the back of the auditorium if they use the same voice that they use when talking to a friend on the telephone. If you want to be heard in court, you need to be able to utilise the same techniques that actors use to ensure that their voices are heard and their words are clear.

8.2 Speak clearly and fluently

Communication is the name of this game. If you don't speak clearly, then your words might just as well have never been uttered. Worse still, they may be misunderstood and convey a wrong impression to your listeners. For the advocate must be both the creator and the performer: you have to think of the words and you have to say them. The first part calls for good language skills, a broad vocabulary and a basic understanding of grammar. The second part requires you to articulate those words so that your listeners can:

- hear your words;
- comprehend your words; and
- attach the correct interpretation to them.

So do not mutter, do not use a 'small' voice, do not look at the floor, do not speak at a pace so fast that your listeners cannot keep up nor so slow that they lose interest or concentration. Do look at your listeners, take care over your pronunciation, speak at a reasonable pace, use appropriate variations in tone and use pauses, too.

Writing as someone who has spent several years listening to people taking their first steps in training as advocates, I have found the common faults of speaking to be concerned with the following.

8.2.1 The pace of speaking

This can be too fast or too slow but typically it is too fast. Why? It seems that the appearance in court is an ordeal that the speaker wants to get over as quickly as possible. It also seems to be believed that, by speaking fast and maintaining a steady stream of 'noise', there may be less opportunity for anyone else to intervene and do anything unsettling such as asking a question, or changing the subject.

The more competent performer will speak at a more normal pace, will pause for breath whenever necessary and, indeed, will make positive use of **pauses**. What do I mean by that? A pause may be used for various purposes: to get your breath; to mark a transition between one point and the next; to give emphasis to the previous point; and finally to allow the listener to make a note if that is what they are doing. A competent advocate should feel able to use pauses in all of these ways and not be frightened that someone may intervene or 'take the floor' from them. If that happens, you should be prepared for it and respond, for example by answering a question. When that happens, you impress the questioner that you are in control, of both yourself and this case; that is a persuasive plus for you.

8.2.2 The volume of your voice

It is important to remember that you will often be addressing your listener over a distance of several feet. You may be across a table from, say, a district judge in his or her room or you may be twenty feet away from a judge in a courtroom. Both must be able to hear you, and neither should think that you are speaking too loudly or too quietly. It is likely that you will find less of a problem in speaking at the right volume to someone across a table, than across a room. Generally, we are unaccustomed to speaking over such distances, other than in a classroom during schooldays. You must be able to turn up the volume, whenever the situation demands it. That does not mean that you should start shouting, though!

8.2.3 Fluency

When required to speak in public, it is often the case that one's mind goes blank and ideas have almost to be forced out. Your voice becomes more staccato, less natural and the number of ums, ers and ehs increases dramatically. Try to eliminate these 'fillers' if you can; they can become very distracting to the listener. All they really are is a subconscious way of trying to disguise the fact that you have nothing better to say at present. Worse, they may have become a habit which is present whenever you speak, on a par with 'like' or 'you know'. These phrases are meaningless and should always be avoided. Although to eradicate them from your speech may require some attention, and the initial attempts to do so will simply result in your becoming more aware of them and self-conscious, the longer that you consciously try to do without them when you speak, the easier it will be for your listener to follow the words that really matter.

8.3 Use appropriate language and manner

What is meant by the phrase 'appropriate language and manner'? Our aim, when talking, is to communicate with our listeners and we will do so most effectively when our vocabulary is a shared one and our listeners have no distractions.

When I say 'appropriate language', this does not include nor require anyone to use what critics sometime call 'legalese'. The competent advocate should always use a vocabulary which is suited to both the listener and the situation. So you should ask yourself, who am I talking to, who is listening to me? In many situations, the answers will be the same, but that is not so when dealing with a witness, for example.

8.3.1 Obscene language

As an advocate, you must show respect for the court; there should be no place for obscene language or swearwords of any kind from you certainly, and if they come from a witness, you should stop them immediately. There is one exception to this, though, and that is where the evidence relevant to the litigation contains swearwords itself. An example might be found in *R v M,* The Times, 23 April 1996, where evidence was produced in a murder trial that the appellant had described 'cutting' her victim because he was 'acting like a fucking hero'. Here, the obscenity is an integral part of the appellant's words and it would be appropriate to present the court with the unexpurgated version, both as part of the evidence and within a closing speech in the trial.

8.3.2 Vernacular language or slang

Again, this has to do with respect for the court; it also has to do with clarity. A single word may have a variety of different meanings and the way that words most quickly acquire new meanings is through the language of the streets. If we use (or allow others to use) words which have a slang sense and are being used thus, our listeners who do not share this vocabulary may lose the message that we are trying to convey.

Don't use vernacular words or phrases yourself unless, as before, they are a relevant piece of the evidence before the court. Even then, some explanation or clarification may be called for so that the correct interpretation can be put on the words by your listeners. Occasionally, you may find that your listeners needed no such explanation but it is better to err on the side of caution.

8.3.3 Jargon

Try to avoid this if you can. Perhaps, if you are appearing before a professional judge and another qualified advocate, you may use common spoken 'shorthand', as long as you are certain that there can be no misunderstanding by your listeners. Otherwise, there will be lay people present, your client, perhaps, or a witness, or even people in the public gallery in court and all of these people are entitled to understand and follow what you are saying. In those circumstances, while it may be tempting to abbreviate words or use Latin tags, for example, you would do much better to use plain English. Often, it is tempting to use jargon because you may think that it shows that you are on the inside, in the know, an experienced advocate. In fact, there are many other ways by which those who are experienced will judge whether you know what you are talking about; jargon alone will not convince them that you are experienced in your work if all of the other signs do not.

One particular situation which cries out for you to use jargon is when dealing with an expert witness. Now the temptation is to prove to others not that you are an experienced lawyer but that you are an expert in another field altogether. This is a tactic fraught with danger as the likelihood is that either you are not an expert and do not fully understand the expert's jargon, or the person deciding the facts in the case does not understand the jargon. In this latter situation, the fact-finder will feel, rightly, that he or she is being excluded from the dialogue between you and the witness. That may eventually result in some information not being communicated to the fact-finder successfully, at best, and in a feeling of hostility towards you (and maybe your client, too), at worst. The North Americans have a saying, 'Keep it simple, stupid' and this sums up (albeit rather brutally) what should be your guiding principle, both here and in other areas.

8.3.4 Labels for people

How should you refer to the other people in court? They fall into five basic categories:

(a) the tribunal itself;

(b) your fellow advocates;

(c) parties to the litigation;

(d) witnesses;

(e) everyone else.

8.3.4.1 The tribunal

Novice advocates are told how to address judges in various courts. A High Court judge is always 'My Lord/Lady' or 'Your Lordship/Ladyship'; these are not interchangeable. 'My Lord' is the equivalent of the judge's name (it represents the vocative case), while 'Your Lordship' is simply the equivalent of 'you' (the accusative case). While wishing to adhere to the earlier injunction against using jargon, one must bow to what is standard practice in every court.

Don't use 'you' when speaking to a High Court judge, although I don't think anything adverse would happen if you did say, 'Have you got the Particulars of Claim in front of you?'. This sort of innocuous question, incidentally, can cause problems for even the most conscientious novice. The question coalesces in their mind as it appears above. It strikes them as a reasonable question to ask, little danger of it backfiring, so they engage first gear and start to ask it. As they do so, they remember that a High Court judge should be addressed as Your Lordship and not 'you'. The question emerges as 'Has Your Lordship [well done!] got the Particulars of Claim in front of . . .' and then their voice fades as they begin to see where this is leading them. Avoid a surfeit of 'My Lords' and 'Your Lordships'; they are not necessary and can become extremely repetitive. The question would have been perfectly acceptable as 'Has Your Lordship got the Particulars of Claim?'. (For further help with addressing judges, see **Chapter 13**.)

Two other possible problem areas are juries and magistrates. Juries can be addressed as simply 'members of the jury' or, sometimes, 'ladies and gentlemen of the jury'. Statements to justices of the peace are usually addressed to the chairperson, who is referred to as 'Sir' or 'Madam'. For a reason obscure to me, it is quite common for police officers and solicitors to address magistrates as 'Your Worships', while barristers rarely if ever use the expression.

8.3.4.2 Fellow advocates

It is usual to refer to a barrister as 'my learned friend' and a solicitor as 'my friend' (in the vocative case), and to use 'him' or 'her', 'his' or 'hers' and 'you' wherever you would normally do so.

8.3.4.3 Parties to the litigation

The parties to the litigation are given titles, separate from their names. So the person who is suing in a civil claim becomes 'the claimant' while the person being sued becomes 'the defendant'. If many people are suing, they are 'the first claimant', 'the second claimant', etc. Typically, they are referred to by these titles, rather than as (say) 'Mrs Freda Barrett', when the advocate is addressing the court, but they are addressed as (say) 'Mrs Barrett' when appearing as a witness.

8.3.4.4 Witnesses

When talking to, or referring to, a witness, you should give them their full and correct title when first addressing them and usually do so thereafter. For example, a witness who, when asked to tell the court his name, replies, 'Eric Barrett', should be referred to subsequently as either 'Eric Barrett' or 'Mr Barrett'. To abbreviate this to 'Barrett' would imply a lack of respect for the witness; that in turn requires an exercise of judgement by you and that is never the function of an advocate.

8.3.4.5 Everyone else

What about everyone else? There aren't too many people left whom you might need to address but people associated with the court will usually be referred to by their job description, as in, for example, 'Usher, could you give this to the witness?'; 'I wonder if the stenographer could read the witness's previous answer to the jury?'; or 'I will hand this letter up to the clerk'.

8.3.5 Appropriate manner

It is sensible to remember that, as an advocate, you are appearing in a court of law and important issues are being decided in the litigation (at least as far as the parties to the matter are concerned). This is not the appropriate place to look in detail at non-verbal language but do note that you need to give the appearance of taking things seriously, and of giving due respect to the court. Furthermore, your ultimate aim as an advocate is to persuade the tribunal to decide in your client's favour; you must appear to have confidence in the merits of your arguments or evidence and you must do nothing that may interfere with your communications with the tribunal.

It follows that:

(a) you will stand up when saying anything in open court, unless it is the practice in that court not to do so;

(b) you will stand up when being spoken to;

(c) you will not put your hands behind your head and lean back in your seat as if to convey an air of innate superiority;

(d) you will not speak to anyone in court with your hands in your pockets;

(e) you will not do anything discourteous at all (such as pick your nose, clean out your fingernails);

(f) when not speaking in court, you should be taking a note of what is being said or done (that should help to occupy your hands);

(g) when speaking in court, you should try not to distract your listeners from your words with any gesture or movement of the hands, unless it has some relevance to your words (so, no fiddling with pens, scratching your nose/ears/neck, stroking your chin, playing with keys, pocket snooker, etc).

8.4 Refer to notes when necessary or desirable

It is a fact that there are some very experienced advocates around who use very detailed plans for their work in court. One example is Brian Leveson, QC who was noted by reporters to have used almost a script when appearing for the prosecution in the trial of Rosemary West for murder (in 1995). That is perhaps a good illustration of the truism that what works for one does not necessarily work for all. If you or I tried to work to a script, the effectiveness of our advocacy might well fall sharply. Let us consider the pros and cons.

8.4.1 Pros and cons of a script

First, the pros:

- you have all of your preparation to hand;
- there is little danger of you missing something out if you stick to your script;
- you will deal with topics in the order you intended;
- your delivery is quite likely to be clear and fluent.

What about the cons?

- you will be reading from your script so your delivery may be flat or monotonous;
- because you are reading, you are looking at your notes, not at the judge or jury or magistrates or witness;

- you cannot respond easily or swiftly to questions or other unexpected deviations from your plan because:
  - (a) although you may have the answer in your plan, you don't have it in your mind;
  - (b) your plan is so full, it is time-consuming to find specific pieces of information within it; and
  - (c) you may lose your place in your plan and lose your concentration;
- although you will deal with all of the points that you planned to, others may have arisen in the course of the trial or hearing which you hadn't planned for and those may now be overlooked.

On balance, I think that the evidence is strongly in favour of **not** using a script.

8.4.2 Why you should not use a script

It is quite understandable that, when you are first on your feet as an advocate, one of your main fears is 'drying up', when your mind goes blank and all your careful preparation evaporates into thin air. That has happened to all advocates at one time or another. Another big worry is that you will overlook something important; although you had planned to deal with *argument x,* in all of the cut and thrust somehow you forgot to say it. So people often use plans to guarantee fluency and ensure a thorough coverage of the issues. That is understandable but the disadvantages are so great that very few advocates can overcome them.

Imagine what it is like to be spoken to by someone who never looks at you, indeed who never looks at anything except the pages clutched in his or her hands? Does that person inspire confidence? Do they look as if they have a good understanding of the case, or even their own arguments? Do you believe them? It is true in some cultures that it is considered rude to maintain eye contact and that it is more polite to look down when addressing someone in a position of authority. Plainly, in a multi-cultural society you should be aware of that **but** that will not help you if you do not come from such a culture or, if you do, the people that you are addressing are not aware of your cultural background. As a general rule, in this country many people rely, at least in part, on assessing credibility by measuring eye contact. Expressions such as 'looking shifty' and 'he couldn't even look me in the eye' are indications of the importance that is often attached to eye contact. There is at least a danger that by using a script you will begin to lose some of your credibility.

Imagine someone talking to you about something of interest to both of you. You ask them a question but they don't answer it. You might be puzzled. If it happened again, you might be annoyed. If it keeps happening, and you are a judge, you just might stop listening to what that person has to say—they are not talking to you but at you. The advocate has to be someone who responds to those around him or her. If you have a very short note or plan, that will force you to concentrate on holding all of your arguments in your head. If you know what you want to say but only decide exactly how to say it seconds before you do so, then your words will have a more natural ring to them. If you are watching your judge and see that a certain argument (or even a phrase or word) has the judge nodding in agreement, then you might want to make more use of that argument (or phrase or word) than you had intended originally.

The final nail in the coffin for scripts, I hope, is this. Suppose that you are due to question a witness. It is almost impossible to predict how a witness is going to behave in the witness box—whether they will be garrulous or monosyllabic, nervous or relaxed, helpful or not—until you actually see them in that box. That is one reason why examination-in-chief is so much harder than cross-examination: you haven't had time to gauge the witness's demeanour and ability to answer questions. In those circumstances, it is really very difficult to plan an exact sequence of questions and stick to them. The planning is easy of course, but witnesses seldom turn out quite the way you planned they would. To use a detailed script here (a bit like the notes of a police interview but with the answers still to be filled in) would almost certainly result in a total loss of flexibility: you would be unable to respond to the witness's last answer by adapting the next question to suit. That must suggest that you are not listening to the witness's answers and, if you appear not to be, why should anyone else?

8.4.3 Why you don't need a script

Remember what I said your two big worries were as a novice advocate? (See **8.4.2.**) The first was drying up and the second was overlooking some topic or argument. It might not seem like it when you are starting out but these are both easily overcome. As for drying up, this is simply a product of your nerves and what you need to do is relax. Your first move is to pause; this is quite natural and no one will suddenly think that you are incompetent and don't deserve to be an advocate. Then take a deep breath or two and try not to think of anything for a second or two, if you can. If that doesn't work and you need longer, ask for it. 'If I might have a minute, Your Honour' is a phrase not unknown to Her Majesty's judiciary. The judge is unlikely to be unsympathetic; after all, it has probably happened to him or her more times than they care to remember.

Once you have relaxed a little, your mind is more likely to recollect what you wanted to say. Suppose that does not happen? Why not say, 'I should like to return to that point a little later, if I might' and move onto your next point? Your next point should not be hard to find, as it is in your plan. Now we come to the second big worry, overlooking something. You should not have a script but you should have some sort of plan; its function is really that of a prompt. It is not there as a substitute for your memory, nor as a comfort blanket whose thickness clearly shows the number of hours' preparation you have put into this case. Your plan needs to be short and the points expressed concisely. A bullet-point format is ideal. If you look down at your plan and see 'Negligence' or 'No serious issue to be tried', for example, that should act as a trigger for your memory and the relevant arguments (or questions) should come to mind. The bonus for you is that, as you carry on with the case, the point that you have dried up on, or forgotten, will often come back and you can deal with it a little later than planned. This is not usually fatal to your chances of success in the action. So be relaxed, have faith in your memory, use bullet points in your plan and you should have few hiccups; those that do afflict you will be less painful.

8.4.4 Using a skeleton argument

If you find that you are to make an application before a court and you are expected to prepare a skeleton argument, the points above may need some modification. First, the skeleton argument is written to support the application and the judge will normally receive and read it in advance of the application hearing. Typically, a copy will also have been supplied to your opponent. In this situation, it makes sense to acknowledge the existence of the skeleton in planning and making your application (or opposing one).

A skeleton is not a script and the last thing the judge will want is you simply reading out large excerpts from it (let alone all of it!). Use it sparingly, make occasional references to it and regard it as a resource which allows you to take points more shortly where appropriate to do so. For example:

> Your Honour, clearly I must persuade the court that there is a serious question to be tried. I have addressed that matter in my skeleton at paragraph 4 and, unless Your Honour has any questions, I do not propose to add anything to that.

9 Persuasion

9.1 Introduction

When we look at persuasion, we begin to explore what lies at the heart of 'advocacy'. Is it a skill, or a knack? Are great advocates born, not made, as some would assert? The *Concise Oxford English Dictionary* defines *persuade* as:

> to cause another to believe
>
> to convince
>
> to induce
>
> to lure, attract, entice, etc.

These may (or may not) have been put in descending order but, as advocates, we might try to identify with the first couple of definitions, while hoping to avoid accusations of the latter pair.

When we watch advocates in practice, we often come to a conclusion about an individual's persuasiveness. Perhaps we should try to define in more detail exactly what we mean, in order that we may try to emulate it.

9.2 How do we persuade?

It is beyond the scope of this manual to devote the amount of space to this topic that it deserves. There are other books which concentrate wholly on this topic and you are recommended to go and seek them out. There are a couple of points to use as starters, though.

First, the more that your message is one that the trier(s) of fact can identify with and the more your proposition strikes the listener as just 'common sense', the more likely you are to persuade your audience that what you say is correct (we don't need to start exploring notions of 'truth' or what 'really happened' as we don't really look for these in court).

Second, your message must be memorable. If your judge (or jury or magistrates) cannot recollect your message at the important time, ie, when coming to a decision, then you have lost the case. So your presentation of your case must be designed to give the maximum help to your audience to remember your points.

These basic points both refer to your 'message'. What we need to look at are your communication skills, a basic grasp of psychology (or understanding human nature, if you prefer) and a brilliant grasp of the facts of your case. The *Penguin Dictionary of Psychology* defines **persuasion** as 'a process of inducing a person to adopt a particular set of values, beliefs or attitudes'.

It goes on to say that a number of factors are likely to be used in this process, both rational and non-rational, for example, credibility and persuasive communication. Persuasive communication, the dictionary says, consists of both external aspects:

- the message itself;
- the arguments presented;
- the credibility of the source;
- the medium used;

and internal aspects:

- the person's original beliefs;
- the person's credulity.

As to communication skills, the ability to speak clearly and fluently is dealt with elsewhere (in **Chapter 8**) but it is understood that you must possess the ability to articulate at an appropriate pace, with suitable volume. If you are not heard (because you are too loud, too quiet or too fast), the message will not get through. But you need more than the ability to talk; you need a facility for language. Very often, what decides a case is the ability to choose the right phrase, or the best word, for the situation. There may be many ways to describe something or someone—an incident, a document, a witness—and part of being persuasive is the ability to select the description that 'fits' best. That means 'fits' for your listener, not for you. What is important here is getting your message across, communicating with the court. The choice of words or phrases is of great importance to success as an advocate.

What about understanding human nature? Well, that arises in various ways. For example, judges generally don't like to be lectured about the law. From time to time, you will have a case that requires argument on a point of law, but even then judges don't want a lecture on the history of the legal topic, what they want is help; whatever you say must be of direct and clear relevance to the dispute that the judge has to settle. Similarly, where someone has suffered some type of loss or damage (especially physical injury), any court is likely to have some sympathy for that person and the advocate representing the 'other side' must be sensitive to that. This doesn't mean that if, say, your case is that the 'victim' was in fact 100% contributorily negligent, you shouldn't say so; it does mean that you should appreciate that it may be a difficult message for the court to accept.

Last point, for now—having a brilliant grasp of the facts of your case. It does not matter if by 'facts' we mean the undisputed facts in the case, or a combination of what's not in dispute and your client's version of what is in dispute, you should have a clear understanding of both. Further, as far as it is possible to, you should have a clear understanding of your opponent's case, too. Lord Hewart CJ once said that the advocate must 'claw the facts' and indeed you should work very hard to have the fullest possible understanding of the detail in each case, from the microscopic (eg, what the likely answer will be to **this** question) through to the macroscopic (eg, which of the possible case theories is the best 'fit' here).

We should not leave this section without observing that you must have a good understanding of the law which is relevant to the case, too. Without it, all the other skills are useless. But gaining that understanding should be relatively straightforward for you; in many cases, you will already possess all the legal knowledge that you need before you receive the case papers. Legal knowledge is something that you can improve every day, with no reference to anything other than statutes, law reports and text books. You should of course try to keep abreast of legal developments. What is different about each case and every client is not the relevant law but the facts: the names, dates, places and people. Those are the things that must be learnt, forgotten and then learned afresh with every new case.

9.3 What's your message? Developing a case theory and themes

How do you prepare a case for a hearing in court? First, you sit down and read through the documents; there may be statements of case, statements from witnesses, a proof of evidence from your client and documentary exhibits. Then, you check that your legal knowledge is up to scratch. You consider what else you need to know, or to have available for court, and write an advice on evidence, calling for extra statements, other documents and so forth. You also have a conference with your client, there may be things you need to tell the client, almost certainly questions that you want to ask. Having prepared as thoroughly as you can, you begin to see where you are likely to be at the end of the trial or hearing, what evidence will be before the court, which issues need to be proved and the probable strengths and weaknesses of both your client's case and that of your opponent. What you need to do now is consider your theory of the case.

I say **your** theory, because you will have evolved it but we must be aware of ethical traps here. It is sometimes said that advocacy trainers are good on advocacy skills but worse on ethics. You must not put forward a theory of the case just because it seems to have a good chance of success. It must be supported by the evidence, it must further the objectives of your client and it must not mislead the court. You should always explain your proposed case theory to your client and get their agreement to use it. That is not to say that your case theory must be carved in stone, though. One important thing a novice advocate soon learns is that, when you get into court, things don't always turn out the way you expected them to. As each trial develops, so the way things are seen may change, witnesses become more (or less) credible, an anticipated strong point becomes a weakness; the advocate must respond to these shifts and so must your case theory.

An experienced practitioner at the Old Bailey used to say that he would start several hares running at the beginning of a trial and see which one the dogs chased. It is permissible to have more than one theory of the case, perhaps intended to meet a variety of possible outcomes. What the practitioner meant was that an advocate must retain adaptability until the end of the trial when, finally, any ambiguities must be resolved. He hoped that, when he advanced the case theory in its final form, he chose the one he felt confident would have the most appeal for the jury.

9.3.1 Themes

It is often said by prosecutors that the Crown does not need to show a motive, to explain why the accused committed the crime. There is no crime where the elements of the offence include greed, jealousy, revenge or anger. Nevertheless, when we are asked to determine whether a particular act was done, or a particular state of mind existed, then we automatically seek out clues that make such an act or state of mind more (or less) likely. If we can see a reason (ie, motive) for someone saying or doing a particular thing, then we are more likely to find that the person did say or do that thing. Offering a reason is not necessarily conclusive when we have to persuade others, but it certainly helps. Themes are often put forward to enable the trier(s) of fact to assess properly the witnesses they see and hear, the documents they read and the arguments of the advocates. A witness may be accused of lying in court, a proposition easier to believe if there is evidence to show jealousy, say, against the advocate's client.

Suppose you want to say that an apparently credible eyewitness to a road accident is not to be believed. You could just say so but that is not very persuasive. If your theme is that the witness was too far away to have a proper view and is doing her best to help the court (not the party calling her, because we'll run into problems of showing partiality) but is nevertheless wrong, your theme for that witness is that she is honest but mistaken.

Compare, for example, what prosecuting counsel, Timothy Langdale, QC, was reported to have told the jury in opening the Crown's case against Sandra Wignall, charged with the murder of her husband, some 17 months after their marriage. The only elements of the offence that the Crown had to prove were that Sandra Wignall was a party to the unlawful killing of her husband and had an intention either to kill or to cause grievous bodily harm to him. Counsel told the jury (see the Guardian, 27 October 1993) that:

> lust and greed were the driving forces behind the murder . . . Sandra Wignall was a woman to whom sex was all-important and although she might fall for a number of men, there was one man who was a special object of desire to her, one man who seemed to have a hold over her so she would do his bidding [one of her co-accused, and her alleged lover, B] . . .

Later on during the trial, the prosecution called a witness, described in reports as a friend and neighbour of the accused woman, who testified that:

> Once she [Sandra Wignall] told me he [B] blindfolded her and tied her to the bed and brought a man in to have sex with her with . . . [B] present.

It is clear that, subject only to some apparent latitude by the court as to the relevance of this information, the prosecution's theme for Sandra Wignall was that she was besotted by her lover and would do anything for him, including playing an intimate part in the murder of her husband. Subsidiary themes which supported the 'rightness' of this theme were that the deceased man had a life insurance policy which would pay Sandra Wignall £21,000 on his death, that B had heavy debts and that Sandra Wignall had previously discussed selling her house to raise money for him.

9.3.2 Case theory

This should be a short and simple statement which sums up how the issues in the case should be decided, based upon the evidence, and how that results in a verdict favourable to your client. To take the case of Sandra Wignall again, the prosecution's case theory was that the murdered man was taken for a night-time walk in local woods by his wife, that she 'in the hope of lulling him into a false sense of security . . . had gone so far as to perform oral sex upon him as the attackers came upon him' and that he was then set upon and stabbed three times with a knife, twice in the heart, dying before help could reach him. You can see there the essential allegations against Sandra Wignall:

(a) a man was killed (her husband);

(b) unlawfully (stabbed with a knife);

(c) with intention to kill (inferred from her role in the attack).

In a different case, the prosecution in 1994 of Gordon Foxley for corruption, Foxley had been a senior civil servant at the Ministry of Defence when he allegedly took 'backhanders' of some £1.5 million from three foreign companies. Prosecuting counsel, Victor Temple, QC, told the jury at Snaresbrook Crown Court that the trial, expected to last two weeks, was almost entirely concerned with documents. You may think that with that amount of documentary evidence, the jury needed a peg to hang the prosecution case on. Counsel gave it to them:

> The Crown say this defendant agreed to take a series of substantial backhanders, and in doing so took dishonest advantage of his position, breaching the trust bestowed upon him by his employers.

Again, the essential allegations are clear:

(a) this defendant (Foxley had already been identified as a senior official in the MOD: any person serving under the Crown would be covered by the relevant legislation);

(b) agreed to take (one can commit the offence of corruption by offering or receiving a bribe, in Foxley's case the latter);

(c) a series of substantial backhanders ('any gift or consideration' is what the law requires);

(d) took dishonest advantage of his position (the Crown did not need to show dishonesty, just that Foxley knew the payments were connected with the past or future performance of his duties, as reward or inducement but this is perhaps an example of a theme emerging within the case theory);

(e) breaching the trust bestowed . . . by his employers (again, directed towards showing that Foxley acted corruptly, that is, purposefully doing an act which the law forbids as tending to corrupt, accepting any improper or unauthorised gift).

9.4 Delivering the message

The advocate should present himself or herself and their arguments in such a way as to convince the court of their merits. Let's not delude ourselves, sometimes cases are won **despite** the best efforts of the 'winning' advocate, not because of them. But it cannot hurt your client's prospects of success if you appear to be confident and in control. If the court can feel that you are to be trusted, then your credibility is likely to increase. That may help your client. What is confidence? It includes acting naturally (and not sweating unduly, or looking shifty), speaking clearly and naturally (no unnaturally long pauses, no inappropriate language) with variations of tone and pace to maintain interest and emphasise certain points.

The advocate should be seen to have a clear idea of what they are arguing for and to have an understanding of the relative strengths of their possible arguments. Have they sorted the relevant from the irrelevant and then **re-sorted** to refine the available material down to what the court really wants to know about? The effective advocate is the one who does not throw in everything including the kitchen sink but who, having done all the preparatory legwork, is prepared to dump most of it and focus their energies on what lies at the heart of that specific case.

Having identified what the client wants from the proceedings, and compared that with what the court is likely to give, the persuasive advocate thinks about how to 'sell' their arguments to the court, how to make them share what your client wants. In his book on advocacy, *Advocacy in Court*, Keith Evans describes defence counsel in a jury trial as having to 'show the jury the way home', that is, how to arrive at the desired outcome by the least painful means. If you have a point that needs making but it is weak, then you should appreciate that and act upon it. Don't pretend it is not a weakness, you will be found out; better to acknowledge it as a weakness (again, you show you can be trusted and are acting practically), then produce supporting argument to bolster it. If you can do all of these things, then you have passed beyond the stage of novice advocate and are on the way to being really effective and persuasive in the courtroom.

9.5 Responding to the judge's interventions

As the use of skeleton arguments becomes more and more widespread in civil hearings, advocates are finding that judges enter the courtroom rather more well-informed about the case and the arguments than perhaps they were in the past. Also, with the emphasis given in the Civil Procedure Rules to a proactive judiciary, advocates are finding judges much more interventionist than has traditionally been the case. No longer are judges prepared to sit silently as the advocates present their carefully crafted arguments. Now, judges have read the evidence, they have read the arguments in the skeletons and they have questions to which they want the answers.

Some people might regard an interventionist judge with trepidation. Won't they ask all sorts of difficult questions? Well, yes, they will, and that should be welcomed with enthusiasm! An enquiring judge is not a problem for the advocate but is of potentially great assistance. No longer need you stand there, arguing away with no clues as to whether you are addressing the judge's concerns until he or she announces the decision. When a judge asks you a question, it usually indicates an issue which is troubling him or her. You now have the opportunity to target your arguments to maximum effect. No need to waste time talking about matters that are already sorted—instead spend your time helping the judge on those topics which are still to be determined. Of course, the potential pitfall for the advocate is that the interventionist judge makes greater demands on the advocate in terms of his or her grasp of the facts of the case and the relevant law. The judge's questions may be on a part of your submission that has not yet been reached—too bad, the judge wants an answer—now! The advocate really must be on top of the case, with excellent preparation skills. This should always have been the aspiration of the advocate, now it is a necessity.

The flexibility that this demands from the advocate is nothing new really. It is surely better to spend five minutes addressing a judge's real concerns than fifteen minutes addressing everything that you think might possibly be of concern to the judge. Tackling the real issues and showing how to resolve them in a way that should ensure the success of your application must be what persuasion is all about. The opportunity to engage the court in a dialogue should be seen as a tremendous asset for any advocate. It is only a threat for the uninformed and under-prepared, two things an advocate should never be.

Part III

Preparing for advocacy

10

You and your voice

10.1 Introduction

As advocacy is central to the working life of a barrister, it should go without saying that having a clear and effective voice is a vital professional tool. You will also need an adaptable voice to fill the largest courtroom or the smallest interview room. The more we use technology as our form of communication, the less our voices are being relied upon to articulate in a powerful way. This chapter provides suggestions and exercises for improving your voice. As with any instrument, you will need to practise regularly to reap the rewards. Do not dismiss these exercises on the basis that you did not choose the Bar to do exercises—you have chosen to be an advocate and you must do what it takes to become a good one. Actors, singers and professional speakers use these exercises. The good barrister needs the quality of voice these exercises can help to produce.

A 'good voice' is a basic requirement for ease of communication. This does not mean that you have to have the sonorous tones of one of our great actors or public figures in order to be a success in your chosen profession. However, an enlightened understanding of your own individual instrument and ways and means to achieve a balanced and tuneful voice can only enhance your work, particularly in court.

Good sound can work to your advantage and can be a positive vocal support to your argument. It builds a sense of trust, enabling your client to feel more relaxed and able to express him or herself. With a healthy attitude towards your vocal training much can be achieved in a relatively short space of time.

What follows is a basic explanation of the importance of good posture, relaxation and breathing, how the voice works and how speech is formed. This is followed by a series of exercises to help you with the development of these. The aim of the exercises is for you to use your voice effectively, without having to think about it. A good voice becomes part of you.

If you wish to learn to speak more effectively, and without strain, some voice training is essential. You will be well advised therefore to work on your voice by yourself, preferably every day, or to seek specialist help.

10.2 Posture and relaxation

The control of the breath is what makes an effective and strong voice. However, in order to find the breath you must first look to the main support for it within your body.

The way you function in everyday life, in both your work and social environments, will affect the way you use your body; and indeed the way you use your body will have a knock-on effect on the way you function. It becomes a catch-22 situation.

The primary focus is the central support for the spine, which is a central support for our skeleton. Acquiring a fluidity and elasticity in the spine will enable the rest of your framework to follow suit. Both a collapsed or 'C' shaped spine and an over rigid 'S' shaped spine will result in extremely bad posture, which in turn can lead, in later life, to rheumatic and/or arthritic conditions. Just carrying a heavy bag over one shoulder regularly for any length of time can lead to a minor curvature of the spine, which, unless corrected, will become set.

It is strongly recommended that some work with an Alexander specialist would be highly beneficial. Alexander, as a movement principle and technique, works best on a 1:1 teacher–student ratio. It teaches you to know the strengths and weaknesses of your own alignment and how to handle them efficiently. There is a book you can read about the Alexander technique called *The Alexander Principle: How to Use Your Body Without Stress* by Wilfred Barlow (Orion, 2002).

Using many of the skills for other activities that you may take part in, for example, martial arts, dancing, yoga, etc, will aid you in the correct use of breathing, stretching and centring.

10.3 Breathing

A detailed analysis of the breathing apparatus seems unnecessary when you can find simple and clear explanations in the books on voice listed at the end of this chapter. *The Right to Speak: Working with Your Voice* by Patsy Rodenburg (Routledge, 1993) would be a good starting point.

The following points are worth remembering. The action of breathing is a reflex action from the brain. We require oxygen and so we breathe. When breathing for public speaking, we learn to increase and strengthen and, indeed, control the movements already made when breathing involuntarily, as when relaxed or asleep. The books on voice explain how this happens, and you will find a detailed description of the muscles used in breathing in the exercise section.

10.4 Phonation

When breathing out, air passes from the lungs into the windpipe (trachea), and continues its journey towards the mouth by passing through the vocal folds (larynx). It is here that phonation—the production of vocal sounds—takes place.

The larynx comprises several bony cartilages and is very intricate in its structure. The front bony cartilage of the larynx is your Adam's apple and can be felt between the finger and thumb at the front of your neck. The Adam's apple (thyroid cartilage) protects your vocal folds. These are two muscular membranes (white in colour) lying across the glottis (throat) inside the larynx. By a series of complicated muscular movements, the various cartilages are made to open and close these vocal folds. When breath passes through them in a closed position, they oscillate with the pressure and vibrate, so producing *note* or *phonation*. The greater the frequency of vibration and the greater the tautness of the vocal folds, the higher the pitch of the voice. It is therefore very important that the breath supply passing into the larynx is relaxed and sufficiently supported by the musculature of the abdomen and chest so as not to cause vocal strain or damage.

10.5 Speech and accents

Strong regional accents do not always give clarity of understanding (and fashionable characteristics of speech, eg, overuse of the word 'like' or upward inflections on the end of sentences causing them to become questions, can have a similar effect). You need to produce sounds that will be generally understood without losing the originality of your speech. To the ears of other people we are how we speak. It helps them to place you. There is absolutely no necessity for a uniform pronunciation to emerge; merely a refining of the stronger characteristics of regional accents.

5 long pure vowels	/iː /	/triː /	tree
	/ : /	/b ɜː d/	bird
	/ : /	/h ɑː t/	heart
	/ : /	/w ɔː k/	walk (s.l.a.)
	/uː /	/f uː d/	food (s.l.a.)
7 short pure vowels	/ /	/pɪ g /	pig
	/e/	/hen/	hen
	/ /	/ ð ə /	the
	/ /	/k æ t/	cat
	/ /	/l ʌ n tʃ/	lunch
	/ /	/dɒ g/	dog (s.l.a.)
	/ /	/b ʊ k/	book (s.l.a.)
8 diphthongs	/ eɪ /	/ple ɪ s /	place
	/ aɪ /	/fa ɪ t/	fight
	/ ɔɪ /	/b ɔɪ /	boy (s.l.a.)
	/ əʊ /	/b əʊ t/	boat (s.l.a.)
	/aʊ /	/h a ʊ s/	house (s.l.a.)
	/ ɪə /	/h ɪə /	here
	/ εə /	/ ð εə /	there
	/ ʊə /	/p j ʊə /	pure (s.l.a.)
(s.l.a. = secondary lip articulation)			

10.6 Posture and relaxation exercises

10.6.1 Posture breakdown

Stand with your feet hip-width apart, weight on the balls of your feet. Allow the knees to relax and your arms to hang by your sides. Try to keep your jaw relaxed, by not clenching your teeth. Gently bounce from your knees, allowing every part of you to move freely, rather like a rag doll. Stop bouncing and allow your head to drop forward, so that your chin is almost resting on your chest and let the weight of your head gradually pull the upper part of your body towards the floor, so you end up hanging over from the waist, with your arms dangling towards the floor. Remain in this position and imagine you are trying to shake a large shawl from your shoulders, and shake it off onto the floor. Gently breathe in and out a few times, in through your nose and out through your mouth. Then slowly build back up to standing—as if your spine is a set of building bricks and you are carefully and evenly placing one on top of the other. Let your head be the last to come upright—to centre—checking that your head is neither jutting forward nor thrown back, but is lengthened through the spine with the chin to a level position.

Gently breathe in again through the nose and as you quickly release the breath allow your body to flop from the waist so you feel like a puppet whose strings have been cut in the upper part of your body. Gently, but firmly, build up again. Remember to keep your knees relaxed.

At this point, have a really good stretch right through to your fingers and toes and the top of your head. Let yourself yawn, too, if you feel like it. Use lots of sound! Then have a good shake, by imagining that you're shaking all your flesh off. Start with one leg, then the other, then the arms and then shake them all together, as wildly and crazily as possible and try to let your head go, too.

Stand again with your feet hip-width apart and imagine you have a heavy yoke across your shoulders, which is pulling your shoulders and neck forward and down. Really feel how uncomfortable it is and let your arms become part of the action, too, by stretching them out sideways, away from your body, with the palms facing downwards. Gradually get rid of the yoke by turning your palms to face the ceiling and rolling your shoulders up and out, so freeing your neck and head and feel your head floating to the ceiling, as if someone is pulling you gently by a string from the crown of your head. Finally, lower your arms to your sides and let the hands hang free. You should feel more open, without being rigid, across your chest. Then, keeping your arms down, slowly roll your shoulders in a full circle, first forward, up, back and down, and second, back, up, forward and down. Each time let the weight fall on the downward movement so it becomes quite rhythmical. Do this several times, keeping your arms and hands relaxed.

In a similar way, let your whole head complete a circular roll. Drop the head forward to begin with and slowly allow it to swing like a pendulum over to your left shoulder, keeping your eyes front. (If you find yourself looking over your left shoulder, you will have twisted your head, rather than rolled it. This is wrong, so start again. Your head pivots at the top of your spinal column; and twisting will only cause excess tension in your neck and shoulder muscles.) From your left shoulder, continue rolling your head, allowing the mouth to open and the jaw to relax, with the rest of your body still relaxed and central. Don't let the head drop right back. Imagine that your head is the big hand of a large clock. Remember to keep breathing! Complete the roll, by continuing over to your right shoulder and then letting your head drop forward again. Rest here a moment, always breathing, and then do a complete roll the other way, starting to the right shoulder and finishing over the left. It is important to work through this slowly, as we all store large areas of tension in our necks. At first, you may find it quite painful, especially when your head is dropped back. So do take your time and keep the movement fluid and continuous. Remember, this is not disco dancing! Once the head roll is complete, float your head back to the centre, so that your eyes are facing front again.

This is a fundamental posture workout and can gradually become more detailed, although only in the hands of a professional movement or voice teacher.

10.6.2 Relaxation

One way of relaxing (without involving a second party) is to lie on a soft floor on your back, knees bent and with your feet flat on the ground at hip-width apart. This is the most relaxed position for the body, as well as being the most beneficial for breathing. It allows the spine to flatten naturally, without tension. If you find your neck and head are uncomfortable in this position, support your head on a book, no more than an inch thick; this will allow your shoulders and head to be free. Let your arms rest by your sides, with your palms facing the ceiling, so letting your shoulders roll out and down. If you find your knees falling outwards, turn your toes in slightly. Remember to keep your jaw relaxed by not clenching your teeth or sticking your tongue to the roof of your mouth!

At this stage, it is difficult to separate the relaxation work from that of breathing, as they go hand in hand. However, if it is possible to put on some soothing music of your choice, close your eyes and listen for 20–30 minutes. You will most probably fall asleep. The breathing will keep a positive energy force passing through you.

10.7 Breathing exercises

Lie in the semi-supine position (see **10.6.2**).

10.7.1 Exercise 1

Allow yourself to yawn. Breathe in deeply and steadily through the nose until you feel like yawning, let your mouth open wide and fully, stretching your lip muscles in a circular fashion, rather like a lion, and let the air come flooding out. Don't worry if you make a lot of noise! Imagine you are slowly filling the room with your outward breath, so allow yourself to do this as many times as you like. Each time you do it, you should feel more relaxed and yet more energised.

Picture a really exotic flower and place it in front of you. Breathe slowly and deeply in, through the nose, smelling the exquisite perfume; this will help stir your senses and open both your nasal and throat passages. Then gently blow the air out again, through your mouth, pursing your lips, and imagine you are dispersing tiny pollen grains which have gathered on the petals of your flower. This must be a very sensitive process, so as not to ruin the flower's beauty. Do this three or four times.

10.7.2 Exercise 2

Imagine yourself lying on a beach. (If only!) You are very warm and relaxed. It is quite late in the day and you are quite close to the water's edge, so that you can hear the waves lapping gently on the smooth sand. Mirror the movement of the waves, ebbing and flowing, with your breathing in, silently, through an open, relaxed mouth, and as the waves flow, so you breathe out, again through your mouth. Only this time, use a continuous 'sshhing' sound on the outward breath, so it really sounds like the music of the sea. Where are you? The Mediterranean? Barbados? Thailand? Make sure you have a positive image. Remember, no two waves are ever the same, so really let your imagination have a free rein. Use your lips on the 'sshh' to focus the breath forward. If you choose to open your eyes, you can really see yourself sending the breath up and away from you, again steadily filling the room. You can do this for as long as your imagination lets you.

Floor work is by far the most beneficial for breathing, as you do not need to support yourself. You can achieve the best results this way, so make the best of it!

Now we get a little more technical. We need to make sure you are breathing from your diaphragm and lower ribs, and not taking the air into your upper chest. This is not easy, especially as old habits die hard, so persevere and don't try too hard to make it work. Remember breathing from your diaphragm is an involuntary action in repose and we need to extend this slowly for good voice production.

10.7.3 Exercise 3

Place your two hands palms down on your abdomen, just underneath the swell of your ribcage and with your lower fingers over your belly button. Hold yourself firmly, using the whole of your hands and keep your elbows spread and resting on the floor.

Allow yourself to cough gently and, indeed, laugh, and feel the movement of the muscles underneath your hands. The movement you will experience is the action of the abdominal muscles, the most inferior of these being the diaphragm (inferior meaning 'deepest'). You cannot actually feel your diaphragm moving, it is too deep within your body for that. What you will feel is the relaxation of the various abdominal muscles as you breathe in, so allowing room for the diaphragm to descend and the lungs to expand from top to bottom, and the contraction of these same muscles as you breathe out, so aiding the diaphragm to rise again to its former position, helping the lungs to deflate slowly, releasing air up through the trachea (windpipe) and out through the nose and mouth. Consequently, as you breathe in (inhalation or inspiration), your hands will rise gradually and smoothly towards the ceiling, so increasing your capacity and size. As you breathe out, the reverse will happen, your hands will drop slowly away from the ceiling, back to their former position. Try to be aware of your upper chest and ribcage moving as little as possible during this process, without forcibly holding them still. They are bound to rise more than necessary to begin with, but slowly, as you learn to breathe deeper, the movement should lessen. A slight swelling at the lower end of the sternum (breastbone) is quite all right, but an obvious heaving of the whole of the upper chest should be avoided at all costs. Indeed, should you find this happens, you will also discover an adverse movement underneath your hands. The abdominal muscles will suck in as you breathe in and harden slightly. Then, as you breathe out, they will relax and even push against your hands. This is completely wrong. If you find you are unable to stop this incorrect breathing pattern, with time (and patience!) it would be best to seek professional help from a voice teacher to put you right.

For all the following exercises, you need to get into a routine of breathing in through the nose and out through the mouth, imagining a free passageway, like a ship's funnel, from the movement of your hands to your open mouth. The wider the ship's funnel is, the freer the airflow through. The whole process of breathing which has been described above applies to every exercise described below. The more often you complete this sequence, the less you will have to think about it and the more spontaneous it will become.

10.7.4 Exercise 4

Breathe in to a mental count of 3 seconds (nose) and breathe out (mouth) to a mental count of 10 seconds. Really be strict with yourself over this. If you cannot manage 10 seconds, start with 6 and gradually build it up. Get a steady rhythm going and always make sure the inward breath is silent. On the outward breath, use 'sshh', very gently and freely.

10.7.5 Exercise 5

Breathe in for 2 seconds and out on a slightly voiced count. Start with 2 and build it by 1 count on each breath.

Breath IN 1, 2	Breath OUT 1, 2
1, 2	1, 2, 3
1, 2	1, 2, 3, 4
1, 2	1, 2, 3, 4, 5
1, 2	1, 2, 3, 4, 5, 6
	and so on to 10

Gradually add more voice—but never very loud. Imagine you are speaking to someone about 3 feet away from you.

You can swap the count for days of the week or months of the year; signs of the horoscope; a shopping list; 'This is the house that Jack built'; a legal definition or phrase!

Eventually you can take a speech you are preparing and break it into sensible breath phrases. Speak it quietly, allowing the meaning to carry the breath, and pausing at each phrase end to mentally breathe in for 3 seconds. Keep practising this discipline, until eventually you feel able just to allow the breath to drop in spontaneously without a mental count.

10.7.6 Exercise 6

All of these exercises can eventually be carried out sitting or standing. But you will soon discover that the moment you need to support your body again, the old habits will return. Remember, when sitting, to keep the bottom back in the chair and the spine supported. Keep both feet on the ground at least hip-width apart. This is a very positive way of sitting. Do **not** cross your legs; this throws your centre weight off balance. Place one hand on your diaphragm and the other on one front side of your **lower** ribcage. Encourage the movement to happen spontaneously and together, so that the lower ribs expand outwards as the abdominal muscles swell. This can take some time to occur satisfactorily. If any difficulties occur, consult a voice teacher. Remember you are looking for all-round expansion, so imagine, as you breathe in, that you are blowing up a rubber ring round your waist.

When standing, and before commencing, go through the posture breakdown and keep your feet firmly on the ground. Avoid shifting your weight from foot to foot, as this will throw you off balance and is an over-casual attitude anyway.

10.8 Articulation exercises

The aim here is to achieve clarity of diction. A good facial warm-up is the basis of a mastery of good diction. Have fun!

Sit down in front of a mirror.

Using your hands, massage your whole face, keeping jaw bone loose.
Screw your face up tight and then slowly stretch it fully. Widen your eyes as well.
Puff your face up with air and suck it in through the cheeks.
Slowly open your lips wide and then purse them in tightly to a small hole.
Smile slowly and hold it for 10 seconds.
Frown and try pulling your lip corners right down. Without your hands!
Blow air through your lips, loosely.
Place the tip of your tongue behind your bottom teeth and stretch your tongue out of your mouth, by raising the back of your tongue.
Point your tongue out of your mouth slowly. Try not to clench your tongue between your teeth or lips, but use only the muscles in the tongue. And then relax the tongue out of the mouth.
Repeat slowly several times. Then point your tongue in different directions. Up, down, left and right.
Repeat several times.

Release your tongue, by flapping it repeatedly against your top front teeth, keeping your jaw loose.
Roll your r's (don't worry if you can't).
Click your tongue against the roof or your mouth. Try to keep the jaw relaxed, but still.
You can help yourself by lightly placing your hand under your chin to steady it, with your palm towards the floor.
Chew slowly, as if eating a large sticky toffee.
Lift the back of your tongue slowly up to your soft palate, with the jaw open and relaxed, so making the sound 'ng' as in *sing* and continue the sound into an open 'AH' and back again to 'ng'.
Repeat and slowly build the pace. The air passage will move from nose to mouth.
Really focus on the sound and sing it: 'ng'—'AH'—'ng'—'AH'—'ng'—'AH'.
Lastly, gently shake the face out, keeping the jaw and tongue loose.

There is a page of tongue twisters at the end of this chapter for you to try. Remember to keep relaxed and use only minimal voice. Start slowly and build the pace as you get more skilful. Try to keep the rhythm and rhyme of each tongue twister. There are also some extremely good articulation pieces in Michael McCallion's *The Voice Book*. They are mainly stories, so use them as such and don't forget to breathe.

Remember that for all articulation work your tongue is your main organ of speech and like many muscles in your body, it requires exercise. Don't spend more than 15 minutes, daily, doing articulation work, otherwise you will tire your tongue out. Gradually you can extend the time limit to 30 minutes as you get more skilful. You need to have full control over your organs of speech; especially because, when nervous, you will have a tendency to speak too fast and fall over your words. So, the greater dexterity you have, the more you will be able to disguise your nerves.

10.9 Resonance exercises

These exercises will help to add 'colour' to your breathing and should only be added to your daily routine after your breathing has become established and centred. In other words, not before the end of your first year's practice. This may seem mad, but they will not work for you otherwise.

10.9.1 Exercise 1

When lying on the floor, imagine your voice mirroring the movement of a waterfall. Let the breath come in for the usual mental count of 3 seconds, imagine your yawn and indeed think of the flower, or your own favourite smell and gradually release the breath on a quietly voiced 'AH'—shaping the waterfall from its height to its depth. This way you allow your voice to fall naturally and easily through its range. Stretch your range a little each time, so that you may start with a range of eight notes (an octave on a piano) and increase it to 16 (two octaves). Allow the voice to slide, rather than step down the range. You can even try beating your chest with your hands while doing this and listening to the sound it produces. Don't beat your chest too hard, though! Then reverse the image, like running a film backwards, and take the range from bottom to top; this is far more difficult and requires a greater breath capacity. Don't end in a squeak! Eventually as you begin to feel quite skilful at this, you can move the voice freely all around your range, changing your tongue and lip positions and experimenting with different sounds. Use different vowels, several on one breath, AW, OO, EE, AY, or try humming. (Remember humming creates a vibration on the lips, as well as in the nose; keep the teeth unclenched and the tongue resting in the bottom of your mouth.) Humming 'mmm' will help to focus your voice to the front or 'mask' of your face. If you travel the hum through the range, feel the vibration travelling down and up the middle of your face. Alternating 'mmm' with 'AH' or, indeed, any vowel, will also focus the voice forward.

10.9.2 Exercise 2

Sit in a chair and paint a picture with your voice. Imagine your voice painting grey, flat clouds; yellow, tall sunflowers; red, fast cars. If you find this too childish, which we hope you won't, then paint a courtroom scene, and paint all the different types of people within it. This exercise can do wonders for moving the voice, so be as silly and mad as you can.

10.9.3 Exercise 3

Take your count of 1–10 and vocalise a staircase with it. Move up and down it freely, remembering to breathe. Try to let your voice do all the action and not your head. You will be surprised how easily your head can move and therefore distract the listener.

10.9.4 Exercise 4

Take a prepared speech and really exaggerate it. Over-dramatise it, lifting and dropping the voice, so it sounds totally artificial. Be really ingratiating; speak it as if telling a story badly to children—speak down and be really nauseous. Exaggerate all the nasal sounds, m, n, ng and lengthen all the l's. Roll your r's!

10.9.5 Exercise 5

Stand up now and hum a song you know—a nursery rhyme if nothing else comes to mind, the 1812 Overture if it so takes your fancy! Remember to breathe and phrase it correctly. Some great tunes for resonance work are:

Smoke Gets in Your Eyes
I Only Have Eyes for You
Blue Moon
Strangers in the Night
Summertime
Stormy Weather
Ferry Cross the Mersey
Michelle (Ma Belle)

And if you enjoy singing—well, sing them!

10.9.6 Exercise 6

Then take one of your speeches and sing it, too! Try different styles: grand opera; Gilbert and Sullivan; crooning; a lullaby; soul; rap. Imagine yourself slowly winning the jury over to your way of thinking and alter the style and tempo to suit. You may find you have three or four movements within one speech! Just remember to keep breathing.

10.10 Projection exercises

Achieving good projection, without risk of vocal damage, is a painstaking process. Again, it should really be an area which is left alone until the second year of voice training. It should be approached with caution and with a great awareness of relaxation and breath control.

Start any projection work by lying on the floor. If you lie on your front, this will both aid capacity in the back ribs and enable you still to feel the movement of the diaphragm against the floor. Lie, stretched out, with your forehead resting on your hands, palms down, with the elbows spread.

10.10.1 Exercise 1

Imagine yourself in a rowing boat, a team of eight, say, out for a practice on the river. Take time to establish the image of yourself, pummels (handles of the oars) at the ready. As you reach down to your feet, lifting the blades out of the water, you breathe in; as you smoothly pull the oars through the water by bringing the pummels up to your chest, you breathe out, initially using a 'ssshh'—lengthening the breath right through the movement. Start to get this working to a regular rhythm, allowing yourself to breathe in through the mouth. See yourself beginning to make progress down the river, gradually gathering momentum with each outward stroke and breath. When you get really skilful at this, the breath will drop in easily and quickly and you can put yourself into a racing situation, changing the 'ssshh' to a steady count of 1–10, which again gathers pace and intensity with each stroke. The important part of this exercise is not only learning to let the breath drop in, but also to 'ground' the voice, making sure you don't let the pitch rise with the speed and intensity. This means you're really allowing the breath to do the work and not letting constriction in the throat muscles take over.

10.10.2 Exercise 2

Another exercise is imagining yourself to be a dog! Get down on the floor again, place the body in an all-fours position, with the hand and knees shoulder- and hip-width apart, respectively. Your back should be flat and supported like a table top, with the head hanging free. But your 'undercarriage', your diaphragm and abdominal muscles, should be allowed to relax completely on the inward breath. This way the breath drops in, without any conscious effort. On the outward breath, imagine you are strongly blowing all the dust and muck off the floor. Do this several times, then gently collapse the whole body into a prostrate praying position. Let the bottom sit snugly on your feet and let the arms be extended, with the elbows resting on the ground. Your forehead should also be resting on the ground. Just gently breathe in and out in this position, to relax after quite a vigorous exercise.

Once you have rested a couple of minutes, start to use the 'building count' exercise described earlier. Only this time, don't only extend the count:

1,2

1,2,3
1, 2, 3, 4
1, 2, 3, 4, 5
and so on . . .

but also build the volume level, obviously starting very quietly. Try to let the muscles relax each time to let the breath come in quickly, but don't quicken the count. Keep this steadily contained in its place, so that you can really tap the breath supply.

10.10.3 Exercise 3

Another exercise, which you can do lying, sitting or standing, is to take a piece of poetry. Choose a lyrical poet like Tennyson or Swinburne and say the poem, or part of it, only shaping the vowel sounds ('The Lotus Eaters' by Tennyson is particularly good for this). Take away the consonants and make your tongue, and lips when necessary, really pass through the vowels, linking each one to give you the shape of the phrase. Make sure you are still conveying the meaning, even if it sounds rather odd. This will help give you a weight and length to your breath and voice. Go back to the top of the poem and speak normally.

10.10.4 Exercise 4

Lastly, take a particularly fiery political speech, or suchlike, and start by lying on your back, using only 'ssshh', throughout each breath phrase. You can emphasise the stresses this way, too. Work to make the breath return quickly. Eventually you can stand up and use the words, giving it the appropriate gusto and energy, but remembering where to breathe.

p Peter Piper picked a peck of pickled pepper, a peck of pickled pepper Peter Piper picked, if Peter Piper picked a peck of pickled pepper, where is the peck of pickled pepper Peter Piper picked.

b Bibby Bobby bought a bat, Bibby Bobby bought a ball, with that bat he banged the ball. Banged it bump against the wall, but so boldly Bobby banged, soon he burst the rubber ball. Boo sobbed Bobby, goodbye ball. Bad luck, Bobby, bad luck ball. Now to drown his many troubles, Bibby Bobby's blowing bubbles.

sts There were three ghosts, Sitting on posts, Eating buttered toasts, And licking their fists, Right up to their wrists, Weren't they beasts.

fr You can have fried fresh fish, fish fried fresh, fresh fried fish, fresh fish fried, or fish fresh fried.

s-sh Susan Schumann shot a solitary chamois and received a short sharp salutary shock from such shameless slaughter.

m She stood on the balcony inexplicably mimicking him hiccupping and welcoming him in.

h Heather was hoping to hop to Tahiti to hack a hibiscus to hang on her hat. Now Heather has hundreds of hats on her hat rack. So how will a hop to Tahiti help that?

b Betty Botter bought some butter, but she said this butter's bitter. If I mix it with my batter it will make my batter bitter. So she bought some better butter and she mixed it with her batter, and she made her batter better.

t A tutor who tooted the flute, Tried to tutor two tooters to toot, Said the two to the tutor, 'Is it easier to toot, Or to tutor two tooters to toot.'

th Theo Thistler, the thistle sifter, sifted a sieve of sifted thistles into a sieve of unsifted thistles, then sifted a sieve of unsifted thistles into a sieve of sifted thistles, for Theo Thistler was a thistle sifter.

s-sh To sit in solemn silence in a dull dark dock, in a pestilential prison with a lifelong lock, awaiting the sensation of a short, sharp shock. From a cheap and chippy chopper, on a big black block.

s, sh, z Sheila is selling her shop at the seashore,
For shops at the seashore are sure to lose,
At her shop on the seashore should Sheila sell shellfish?
Or should she sell sandpaper, sherry and shoes?

ng Sending a ring through the post was plain sailing,
Sending a ring through the mail was just fine,
Writing a note to his girl friend and hailing,
A taxi, to take it to Ealing on time.

w-ch If a woodchuck would chuck wood, the wood that a woodchuck would chuck is the wood that a woodchuck could chuck, if the woodchuck that could chuck wood would chuck.

10.11 Further reading

Rodenburg, P. *The Right to Speak: Working with the voice,* Routledge, 1993.

Rodenburg, P. *The Need for Words,* Methuen, 1994.

These are more practical for those who have not studied voice before:

Berry, C. *Your Voice and How to Use it,* Virgin, 2000 (an excellent book but quite technical).

Davies, P. *Your Total Image* (How to communicate success), Piatkus, 1990 (deals with body language as well as voice. Interesting reading!).

McCallion, M. *The Voice Book,* Faber & Faber, 1998 (this is particularly good for articulation).

11

Memory and recall

11.1 Introduction

In **Chapter 2** the point was made that the able barrister has a wide variety of skills, several of which may need to be deployed at any one time. Some of these can be honed to your advantage so that they become almost second nature. One example is the ability to take accurate notes swiftly. Another is the ability to remember in a trial what a witness said five minutes/hours/days before.

It is of vital importance that the barrister can recall what a witness actually said in his or her testimony. An accurate note will help but, sometimes, you may not have the time to find your note. Also, in a trial you may be faced with a question like: 'Isn't there an authority on this point? A recent decision of the Court of Appeal?' It will be to your advantage to show that you are knowledgeable on current law but you cannot carry around an entire library. You have to rely on your memory.

This chapter contains some ideas on how you might improve your memory and recall, while **Chapter 12** has some tips on note-taking and shorthand.

11.2 Memory and recall techniques

You need to remember what you hear so that you can ask further questions in examination-in-chief, ask the right questions in cross-examination and re-examination and, if you are making a closing speech, so you can emphasise those aspects of the oral evidence which support your theory of the case. Developing a good aural memory requires practice.

What can you do to help you remember what you hear? The following techniques can improve your ability to recall oral communications accurately.

Try to understand what you hear. Process the information you hear as you hear it. One of the problems which arises in processing the information as you hear it is that you may let your mind wander away from the speaker when the speaker is between words. This happens because you can think faster than anyone can speak and you will have processed the information as soon as, or even before, the last word is spoken. The pause in the speaker's communication to you then gives your mind time to dwell on other things which can interfere with the processing of the next piece of information. Try to keep your mind fully on the speaker even when the speaker pauses for thought. One way of maintaining your concentration is to predict what the speaker will say next and record mentally when you are correct and when you are wrong.

Trace the development of the ideas being communicated. Concentrate your attention and interest continuously on the speaker and what he or she is saying. Mentally repeat or summarise key ideas or statements, or associate related ideas as they are being communicated. Always remember that you can get the witness to summarise what he or she has said or to repeat what has been said. If possible, and a 'must' when you are cross-examining, take notes of the key ideas or facts. But do not take extensive notes as this will divert your attention away from what has been said. In the context of the cut and thrust of advocacy, you may not have time to refer to your notes of what the witness has said, before you need to retrieve the information to use in examining another witness or in your closing speech.

11.3 Memory and recall exercises

The following exercises contain a number of passages taken from *Total Recall: Successfully Boost Your Memory Power* by J. Minninger (Thorsens, 1987), pp 206–9. Ask a colleague to read one to you and then see if you can list accurately the main points of the passage.

11.3.1 Exercise 1

Your wife or husband says:

> We have a lot to do before the party tonight. I don't know if we have enough glasses. Could you call your brother, George, and ask him to bring ice when he comes if he's coming before 7.00. If he won't get here until later, ask Harriet to pick it up on her way home from work. The tablecloths are still in the dryer, and the folding chairs have to be brought up from the basement. I suppose George can do that if he comes early. I don't know if we have enough glasses. I better go get those tablecloths out of the dryer before they get wrinkled. Do you think your brother and Harriet will hit it off?

You have a lot of extraneous information. Your goals here are to decide what you were being asked to do and arrange them in proper sequence. Here's what you should have 'heard':

Call George and see if he is coming before 7.00 pm.

If yes: (a) Ask him to bring ice.

(b) Tell your wife he will be early, so he will bring the ice and can help carry the chairs up from the basement.

If no: (a) Call Harriet and ask her to buy ice on her way home from work.

(b) Tell your wife that Harriet is bringing the ice, and you will have to carry the chairs up from the basement.

Optional: Count the glasses.

11.3.2 Exercise 2

That was a typical family situation. Now try one that you may have run into in your business life. Your boss, Mr Fickle, also likes to 'think out loud'. Mr Fickle says:

> I need some cigarettes from the drugstore downstairs. Get me a pack of Camel Lights and charge it to my wife's account. Try to get Steve to take care of you because the older guy may give you a hard time. Before you go down, take this report to Mr Samson on the 13th floor in the annex and

give it to his secretary. If she's not there, get somebody to sign for it. Last month some jerk lost the report and I got my ear bent. Make two Xeroxes of it just to be safe. One of those copies has to go to headquarters today, so drop it off at shipping, but tell them to send it second class. Mr Samson says we're spending too much on postage, so if it takes longer to get there, that's his sweet problem. Do you think something's wrong in his department? He's been crabby as the devil lately.

This was a hard one, but typical of many busy offices. Most of what was said were instructions, spoken and implied, but they certainly were not in order. You might even have had to grab a pencil and write down what was wanted to be sure you got it all. Here's what you were being asked to do.

(a) Address an envelope to headquarters (implied).

(b) Make two photocopies of the report. Place one copy in the envelope you just addressed.

(c) Deliver the original report to Mr Samson's secretary on the 13th floor in the annex. If she is not there, leave the report with someone else and get a signed receipt.

(d) Deliver the 'headquarters' envelope containing the photocopied report to shipping and ask them to send it second class.

(e) Buy a pack of Camel Lights at the drugstore and charge them to Mrs Fickle's account. Try to be waited on by the younger assistant.

(f) File the second photocopy of the report as a backup, in case one of the other copies is lost (implied).

11.3.3 Exercise 3

Remember that the skills acquired in one context will serve you equally well in another. Getting instructions from a teacher, colleague or sales assistant can be tricky. See how much of the following you actually need to remember, and try to organise it into a sequence.

The paint store sales assistant says:

Put the stain on with a soft brush and really rub it in. If you try to put it on too thickly, the surface will dry while the underneath part is still wet. Then you'll get a rippled surface because the hard top skates over the wet bottom. Did I tell you that you have to mix it well before you start? Don't use your best screwdriver. The lighter colours really look good in this finish, but I think the dark colour you've chosen will be OK. You have to seal it afterwards with two or three coats of polyurethane varnish, otherwise the rain will soak in and warp the wood. Oh, but you're using it inside, so that's not a problem, but be sure you clean the wood first to free it of dust and dirt.

You had to discard some of the information you got here. If you put the remainder in a working sequence, it should come out like this:

(a) Clean the wood first.

(b) Stir the stain if necessary.

(c) Rub the stain into the wood thoroughly with a soft brush.

(d) The sales assistant doesn't like dark stains.

As the exercises illustrate, an excellent means of ensuring that you remember things is to start by analysing and reorganising the information you need to remember.

There are many books which describe such techniques, including: *Use Your Memory,* Tony Buzan, BBC Publications, 2006; *Total Recall: How to Maximize Your Memory Power,* Joan Minninger, MJF Books, 1997; *The Brain Book,* Peter Russell, E P Dutton, 1984.

11.4 Witnesses and the court

The exercises in **11.3** were designed to start you thinking about exactly how adequate your memory is and how you might set about improving it, as you almost certainly need to do. As advocates, though, we also rely on other people's memory skills.

11.4.1 Witnesses

If a witness cannot recall the events, words or documents that led to their being called as a witness, then it may be that some vital information is being lost to the court. While one might expect a witness who is being cross-examined to suffer a little from problems of memory, the same should not normally be said of a witness during their examination-in-chief. However, problems certainly do arise in-chief and one of the main causes is the requirement that you do not ask leading questions of your own witness. That is, you cannot ask the witness questions which suggest the desired answer to the witness. This frequently produces very open questions such as:

'What happened next?' or
'Did anything else happen?' or (just about the worst question you could ask)
'Is there anything else that you would like to say to the court?'

While the advocate who asks questions like these cannot be guilty of suggesting the desired answer to the witness, they are certainly not providing much help to them either. Let us suppose that a witness has already told us part of what they remember of an incident. You might ask a 'What happened next?' question but it does not specifically take the witness to that part of their story that you want them to talk about now. So, since the testimony of the witness might be compared to a spool of audio tape (or video film) gradually unwinding from their memory, you could offer some sort of marker to let them know where on the tape you want them to go. How about:

> You have told the court that the claimant's car swerved across the road and onto the opposite carriageway. What happened next?

Now the witness has an idea of where you want him or her to take up the story, although still you have not indicated a particular incident or topic to him or her. If the witness is still stuck for an answer, you might then try (assuming it is not in dispute):

> Were there any cars travelling along the road in the opposite direction from the claimant's car?

If you particularly want the witness to continue to talk about the claimant's car, you could ask:

> Once the claimant's car crossed to the opposite carriageway, could you still see it?

Let's assume the witness answers 'Yes'; she now should have in her mind's eye that car across on the wrong side of the road. So you might risk:

Q. Did you see what happened to the claimant's car then?
A. Oh yes, a white van drove into it and pushed it off the road completely.

Now the incident has come back to life for the witness and you should be able to get them talking more fluently. Witnesses' memories are like anyone else's, they sometimes need a bit of prodding to get them working and, like everyone else, they are more likely to respond to questions which give little bits of (non-contentious) information and start them visualising the incident at a particular point in what they saw or heard.

11.4.2 Judges, juries and magistrates

If the people who have to find the facts cannot recall your arguments or the important pieces of evidence when the time comes for their adjudication, you are in trouble (and so is your client). As with witnesses, the court will remember something best if they can visualise it. It is obviously more difficult for the court to do this than it was for the witness since the court may be unfamiliar with the scene, for example, and anyway the judge wasn't there when the incident happened and engraved itself on the witness's mind. This is an acid test of your skills as an advocate because you must bring the incidents to life for the court: not for nothing do we say that part of the function of an opening speech is to 'set the scene'. The better the court can get inside the head of the witnesses and almost see through their eyes, hear through their ears, the better your chance that the court will remember the evidence. Witnesses who are allowed the freedom to tell their own story are much more memorable than one who just has to answer 'Yes' or 'No' to a series of questions. Witnesses whose testimony is largely uninterrupted (or whose answers are not cut off by the advocate) are likely to be more clearly recollected later by the court, as well as probably seeming more credible. In your speeches or submissions to the court, try to concentrate on your strongest points: first, there won't be too many, which always makes things easier to remember; and second, you can get away with repeating yourself on a couple of points but not on a dozen. Repetition, whether of a word or phrase, or a verbal snapshot of a moment during an incident, always helps people to remember. If the court can remember your arguments, then you stand a chance of succeeding in the case; if it can't remember them, you have wasted your time and your client's money.

12

Note-taking

12.1 Note-taking in practice

Of course you can take notes. You did it at school, let alone at university. You don't need to learn about notes now.

Fair enough, but:

(a) How often have you taken a note that did not make sense when you reread it?

(b) How often have you taken a note that was not even legible later?

(c) How often have you not been able to find a particular point in your notes when you reread them later?

(d) How often have your notes missed out an important point?

This sort of problem is irritating, but in the past it has probably been no more than that. You felt slightly less secure because your notes were not very good. You may not have understood something properly because a note did not make sense, or you may have lost a few marks in an exam because your notes on a particular point were not very good.

However, as a professional barrister there is far more at stake for you than simply being irritated or not understanding a point very well. If your skills in taking notes are not good enough, the result may be that you fail to remember an important point that a client has told you, that you spend extra hours in a library because you cannot remember where you looked something up, or that you do not have a good enough basis on which to make a closing speech or a cross-examination.

From now on bad notes will cost time and money, and will have a real impact on how good a job you do for the client. In going into a profession where the accurate and efficient use of words is vital you can no longer afford to make do with inadequate notes.

Recall problems that you have had with notes you have taken in the past. Look back at notes you took as a student and examine them critically. Were they as good as they could be? Try to identify what the weaknesses were.

Taking good notes is not something that will magically happen when your first real client walks in the door. You will have to be ready in advance. So analyse now what the weaknesses in your note-taking are, and start working on them **now**!

Even if your existing note-taking techniques are not too bad, they could still be more polished. In any event, you will still need to adapt your note-taking abilities for practice. Taking notes as a student is not the same as taking notes as a professional lawyer. In the past you could always complain or miss out bits if the lecturer was going too fast, but you are not going to be able to do that when a judge is giving judgment—you have to get it all and you have to get it right first time!

The rest of this chapter on notes is for guidance. It provides suggestions on how you might develop your own skills. There are also some comments on how basic note-taking skills can and should be adapted for different purposes. As with so much in learning skills, the point is not simply whether you can understand the need for good notes, but whether you can produce them.

12.2 Essentials of good notes

The following checklist has some obvious ingredients, but it should still be useful for reviewing how good your note-taking is, and may suggest some points on which you could work. A good set of notes needs to have:

(a) *Reasonable legibility* It is not easy to improve bad handwriting, but there may be something you can do to improve or speed up the way you write.

(b) *Good organisation* You must be able to find something in a set of notes. Points should be dealt with in groups.

(c) *Clear layout* Subheadings, underlinings, indentations, etc for easy reference.

(d) *Comprehensive coverage* Every important point must be included. It is more important to get the sense and the understanding than to get every word down.

(e) *Selectivity* You cannot write down everything, you must get down what matters without wasting space on what does not. If the exact wording does matter, it must be recorded.

(f) *Abbreviation* To be able to get words down fast when necessary some form of coherent abbreviation, shorthand or speedwriting technique is essential. (See **12.9**.)

12.3 Research notes

You are probably already familiar with making notes of research. Anyone contemplating a career in the law needs to build a skill in taking notes from statutes and cases. In practice you will frequently need to identify the law in an area you are unfamiliar with, or the detailed and up-to-date law on a specific point. You are also likely to need to take notes from a variety of sources in order to build up a complete picture of the law, which adds to the complexity of the task.

Part of the skill of research is finding the best sources and knowing how to read them to extract the points that are most relevant, following a research trail. This is dealt with in the ***Case Preparation*** manual. However, keeping coherent and comprehensive notes of your research is also very important. When you are immersed in the research process it is easy to think that you only need to jot down a few key references and you will easily be able to find things again. In fact the moment you have finished the research you will move onto some other task, or go and do something completely different, and in very little time you are likely to find that you have forgotten quite a lot of what you found out, and that it is difficult to find the material again without spending almost as much time as you did doing the original research.

The reasons why good notes are an essential part of effective legal research and effective legal practice are:

- Legal research is often a task in itself, as you may be asked to do legal research for a pupil supervisor or an employer.
- It is very useful to keep a detailed note of your research with a brief for future reference so that no part of what you have already done needs to be repeated.
- You may need to do further research on a specific point in the light of further information from a client and it is useful to be able to go straight to the right source.
- You need a full list of sources for reference in an opinion or in advocacy.

Good legal research notes are not restricted to a list of sources, cases and statutory sections. You will only over time build the skill to write down exactly what is most useful, and what level of detail will best serve a purpose. While it is not essential, there is some merit in recording your notes in the form of a research trail rather than just noting what you have found. Research needs to follow a trail anyway as you look up key words and move to footnotes, cross-references and go from source to source. Briefly noting the trail can be very helpful in finding something again, in reminding you what sources you used, etc. There is more material on this in the ***Case Preparation*** manual.

12.3.1 Vital points in taking notes of research

(a) *Be systematic* Never retain a point you have researched in your head or put it on whatever paper is handy. Boring though it may be, all research should be properly and systematically recorded.

(b) *Always keep clear references* When researching an area of law in a textbook or in *Halsbury*, always make sure that you clearly note which book you are using and which page of the book the note comes from, or you may not be able to find it again. When researching a case, make sure you write the name of the case and the reference at the top of the note. It may be useful to quote references to the solicitor so that he or she can look the point up. If you are researching electronically, keep a precise note of the web page, not just the website.

(c) *Make full notes from each source* Make sure you note all cases, statutes, etc that are mentioned in one source that will need to be followed up in another. If part of a judgment is particularly important, make sure you note down which judge gave the judgment and the page number of any quotation. In researching a statute, make sure you note the section and subsection exactly, and note whether you have written down the exact words of the statute or just a summary.

(d) *Note all points, not just those in your favour* Although you are researching your client's case, always note points against you. Although you may not want to use them you must be prepared to meet them, and you must not mislead the court as to the effect of an authority.

(e) *Anticipate the future use of sources you research* Make a clear note of which authorities you may actually wish to refer to in court. In some cases, as in magistrates' courts, it may be necessary to have photocopies of an authority that you wish to refer to if it is not likely to be easily available at the court.

(f) *Make careful use of photocopies and printouts* Photocopying sources is a useful and time-saving way of gathering research material. If you take copies or a printout, ensure each is clearly labelled with the case to which it is relevant. Never assume that you have researched a topic simply because you have taken a photocopy of a relevant page and put it in the file—you must read it!

(g) *Make up clear and coherent summaries* Sometimes the original notes of research are clear, but in a complex case they may be confused and may need to be copied out more coherently for use. Again this may be boring, but if you don't do it you will sooner or later have a case where you wish you had!

(h) *Always keep notes of research* Never throw your research notes away. The case may come back or a similar case may come in. Using existing notes saves time, and it is pointless to have to start again with a point you have researched. Do not send the notes back to the solicitor with the brief or they may get lost.

One way of keeping notes efficiently is always to take notes of research in the same notebook, starting a new page for each case you research and heading it clearly. If these research notebooks are kept together it is then easy to refer back. If you do use separate pieces of paper for research in each case, make sure that you have an efficient filing system.

Your notes of research should be good enough to be worth keeping. Good research notes ultimately save time and can become not only a resource but also a source of confidence and strength in constructing a case.

12.4 Notes made in preparing a case

Methods of information management in the preparation and presentation of a case are fully dealt with in the appropriate chapter of the ***Case Preparation*** manual. Only a few points are emphasised here. Even more than with research, there is a tendency in preparing a case simply to make rough notes and throw them away as soon as they have been used. This shows a real lack of appreciation of how important a resource good notes can be to the practitioner, and what a sound basis they provide in the preparing of a case properly.

Having said this, the first notes made on reading a brief or on reading a document may well only be of temporary use—they are simply first impressions of what is relevant and first notes for full chronologies. There is no reason why these notes should not be on the back of an envelope! However, in all but the simplest case, much fuller notes about the case should follow. A full set of notes that are clearly written, clearly set out and properly filed so that they can easily be found, will be the best possible basis for preparing a case.

12.4.1 Vital points in taking notes in preparing a case

(a) *Prepare brief and clear notes on each aspect of the case* Each aspect of a case should be summarised for easy reference. For example, most cases would need the following: a full chronology, a list of dramatis personae, lists of events, lists of documents, lists of evidence available and evidence required, etc.

(b) *Take care with layout* A good layout will enable you to find a point quickly, and sooner or later you will appreciate how important that can be in court!

(c) *Appreciate the importance of good notes as a basis for a case* Clear notes are the basis of the good and confident presentation of a case, in terms of advocacy and of writing and drafting. You must have a case at your fingertips if you are to present it clearly and coherently, and clear concise summary notes will be the best basis for this.

(d) *Appreciate the extent to which good notes save time and money* Making good notes on all aspects of the case will make it much easier and quicker to look things up and will save having to duplicate work on a brief when points have been forgotten.

(e) *Appreciate the extent to which good notes clarify thinking* The more complex a case, the more difficult it is to get on top of it. Making good sets of notes about a case helps to bring it into focus.

(f) *Always keep a full set of notes* As with legal research, it is important to put one's notes on a case together in a coherent and legible form, and to keep them for future reference. Although it is quite tempting to throw notes away the moment a brief goes back to the solicitor, it is important to keep them as the case may come back again. Notes made in preparing to write an opinion can be invaluable in getting into a case quickly when the case comes back to be prepared for trial.

12.5 Notes made in preparation for writing

If you make good notes in the course of preparing a case, the thorough understanding gained will give you the soundest possible basis for clear writing. If you have good preparation notes, you do not need to rifle through the papers continually while you are writing an opinion or preparing a draft. If you have good notes of all the basic detail, there is much less chance that there will be errors in your writing.

You should have all the notes that you made in preparing the case to hand while you are writing an opinion or a draft, so that you can refer to them easily. In addition, it is good practice to make special outline notes for the opinion or draft prior to writing it.

12.5.1 Vital points in making notes prior to writing an opinion or draft

(a) *Appreciate the importance of notes in ensuring clarity and coherence* By making notes you can check that you have identified everything that should be included in the opinion or the draft.

(b) *Appreciate the importance of notes in providing a clear structure* Making notes can help to give the clarity of structure that is vital, and should avoid the waste of time that often occurs if you start writing and then suddenly realise that you have left something out or failed to deal with it in the right place. The notes should also give you a framework for order of paragraphs and the proposed contents of each.

(c) *Appreciate the importance of notes for accuracy* It is vital that an opinion or draft is completely accurate, or it will at least create a bad impression, and may weaken a case. Good notes should provide an easy source of reference to ensure accuracy.

12.6 Interview notes

There are particular difficulties in taking notes of an interview or conference, and yet such notes are important as they may be the only record of what was actually said. The requirements of note-taking during an interview are rather different from those of taking notes from research or for written documents, but people do not always remember this to start with, and often take inadequate notes as a result. In addition, it is important that note-taking supports the interview rather than making it more difficult, the problem being that you must concentrate primarily on the client rather than on the notes.

(a) Attention tends to centre on getting everything on paper rather than on making sure that everything is said.

(b) In making notes, you will look down quite often, losing eye contact with the client, and therefore possibly making the client feel less involved and less communicative.

(c) In making notes, you may miss visual signs of how the client is reacting.

(d) You cannot write down everything, and must make instantaneous decisions about what is important enough to write down.

(e) In writing down one point you may miss what is said next.

(f) Sometimes there will simply be physical difficulties in taking notes, for example, when you talk to the client outside court and there is not even anywhere to sit down, let alone a table to lean on. The difficult circumstances do not make the notes any less important!

(g) The points that need noting will not necessarily come out in the right order.

(h) The points that need noting will not necessarily come out with the right degree of emphasis.

(i) There is only one chance to take notes. Although you can to some extent go over notes to check that they are correct, there is only a limited extent to which this can be done without undermining the client's confidence.

Because of some of the difficulties of taking notes during interviews, there is a tendency to try to find alternatives, but the drawbacks of potential alternatives must be appreciated.

Using a tape recorder for an interview to avoid the need to take notes is not necessarily a good idea. You cannot refer back to points easily—it may be difficult to rewind to the right point and you cannot really do that during the interview. If you want the interview in a form in which you can more easily refer to it then the whole tape must be typed out, which takes time and will produce a long manuscript which will take some time to read, especially if the client is verbose or wandering. It is generally preferable to have written notes which can concentrate on the main issues without repetition and be easily referred back to.

You can get someone else to take the note. A barrister taking a conference will often ask a solicitor or a pupil to take a note. This may well be a good decision as it leaves the barrister free to deal with the client, but the main drawback is that it is often done in a rather offhand manner, and the resulting notes often fail to contain some items that the barrister needs. If someone else is to take the note, it must be made absolutely clear what points they should concentrate on, what form the notes should take, and so on.

12.6.1 Vital points in taking notes of an interview

(a) *Use a framework for the notes* It may well be possible to have a framework in mind for the interview before it starts if you know what it will be about. This can provide a basic framework for the notes. If you have not had the opportunity to get a framework in mind, form one as soon as possible.

(b) *Decide who will take the note* If a solicitor and a barrister are at a conference, they do not both need to take a full note. There may also be a pupil or a trainee solicitor present who could take the note. Whenever there is a choice, it must be made clear who will take the full note. The barrister taking the conference may well still wish to take a few notes of particular points personally.

(c) *Have proper materials ready for taking notes* This is easy enough in chambers, but may be more problematic if the interview is in a cell or a corridor. A proper notebook or paper with something to lean on should be carried, and notes taken fully and systematically however difficult the circumstances.

(d) *Keep a relationship with the client* Try to avoid taking notes at the very start of the interview. It is important to establish a relationship with the client before starting to take notes, and to maintain it while taking notes. Explain to the client what you are taking notes of and why, and ask the client to pause while you write something down. However important the notes are, the client is more important.

(e) *Make selective notes* You cannot write down everything the client says. You must be intelligently selective. When you do start taking notes, try to note the main issues briefly and clearly. Make notes on the main points with large gaps which you can then fill in later in the interview. However, beware the generalised summary where detail is required.

(f) *Note appropriate details* Do not try to write down too much. The details that matter, be it descriptions or figures, can often be recorded with few words. If the actual words said matter, do make sure you get them down.

(g) *Make notes at the right time* Try to judge when to write things down. It may not help if you take notes while a client is dealing with something he or she finds painful to deal with—knowing that everything is being taken down may discourage the client from speaking at all.

(h) *Check the notes before the interview ends* Check your notes with the client before the interview ends. This will not involve pedantically running through every point, but summarising issues and checking details to ensure the notes are accurate.

(i) *Check the notes after the interview* Try to reread your notes of the interview as soon as possible after it takes place to ensure that they are comprehensible and include all the relevant information. At that stage you may still remember enough of the interview to be able to make corrections—later you will not!

(j) *Keep a proper copy of the notes* Do not leave the notes of an interview on odd pieces of paper, unless the original notes are very clear. Make a copy of the notes with everything set out clearly and in a suitable order. When you are preparing for trial, a note of an early interview can help to recall the details of the case that might otherwise be forgotten. Also keep a note of advice given—you may need to refer back to it later.

12.7 Notes in court

Taking notes during a court case may sound strange—the barrister is in court to talk, not to write. But there are various aspects of the case that will need recording for different purposes, and good advocacy is based on proper preparation and good notes.

Although some barristers do make full notes for what they will say in court, it is generally better for good advocacy to make brief and clear notes to which you can refer quickly and easily just to remind yourself what comes next. You should know your case well enough for this to be sufficient, and the advocate who is always shuffling papers and who appears to be just reading out notes will rarely look or sound convincing. You can also miss a lot if you are looking at papers rather than at people in court. Only a framework and the most important questions should generally be noted in advance. (See, for example, **21.2.2**.)

12.7.1 Opening speech

An opening speech will often be based on notes. You need to make notes for the speech itself, separate from notes on the case. These should be summary notes. Writing the speech out in full is not advisable as you will tend to look as though you are reading an essay.

There are again some special techniques for taking these notes.

(a) An appropriate order is vital.

(b) Make the notes big and clear for easy use.

(c) Some form of highlighting must be used so that the notes can be glanced at quickly. You should know the case well enough for that glance to be sufficient.

(d) The points that must be made must be clearly emphasised so that none are forgotten.

(e) The notes should have some system for emphasising the changes of area and thought so you can use them to best advantage.

12.7.2 Dealing with witnesses

Examination-in-chief There are two basic approaches that tend to be taken by student barristers preparing an examination-in-chief of a witness. The first is to write out every question fully, and the second is simply to use the witness's witness statement without making notes. Both approaches have real weaknesses. If you write out every question, you will soon encounter the difficulty of not getting the answer you expect and not knowing how to proceed, or you will ask your next question rather than reacting properly to the witness's answer. The process is easier where a witness statement will stand as the evidence-in-chief.

So an examination-in-chief should be based on notes properly prepared expressly for the purpose:

(a) Identify the areas on which the witness should be questioned and put them in a suitable order. These may be areas only where there is additional information.

(b) Each of these areas and each change of issue should be emphasised in the notes to be easily followed.

(c) Identify the basic point of each question you consider asking and include that in the notes, but never write out whole questions unless there are particular points where the exact wording is vital.

(d) Annotate the notes with points about how to ask a question or what you are really trying to achieve by asking it.

(e) Always be ready to depart from your notes if reality requires it!

Cross-examination There are also two fairly common reactions to learning cross-examination. One is to write out long lists of hostile questions and the other is simply to panic! In fact for the vast majority of people a good cross-examination is again most likely to be based on good notes.

In preparing notes for a cross-examination:

(a) List all the points that you need to put to the witness, either because they undermine the witness's testimony or because they are part of your own case.

(b) Put these points into a suitable order.

(c) Note ideas for questions under each point.

(d) For cross-examination there may be some point in writing out whole questions, as there is more importance in the exact form of the question to make the point you want.

(e) Include in the notes some indication of how hard to push a point, depending on how important it is to your case.

(f) Review your notes in detail during the examination-in-chief, being ready to add to them, delete from them or reorder them to most effect.

(g) Make sure your notes are clear enough for easy reference. For effective cross-examination it is especially important that you do not constantly refer to your notes. To be effective your concentration must be on the witness, not on a piece of paper.

(h) It is particularly important to be prepared to depart from your notes when the reaction of a witness demands it, but beware of being lured into a departure that may do your case harm!

Taking notes of what witnesses say As well as making notes for questions to ask witnesses, it is also important to take notes of what a witness says. This point often does not occur to the student barrister—you just listen to what the witness says and hope it is what you want! You need to become adept at compressing a question and answer to note down what you need, and sometimes it is useful to note down verbatim what a witness says. In taking notes, however, never forget that watching the witness is important.

There are various purposes for which you may wish to take notes of what a witness says. First, while a witness is giving evidence-in-chief you may need to note a point for cross-examination, or for your closing speech, as appropriate. This might be needed where a witness says something that did not appear in any written statement, or where some point can be made about the exact words that a witness uses. Second, during a cross-examination you may need to note what the witness says for re-examination or for your closing speech. Remember that you may need to note what a witness says while you are questioning them, as well as asking questions and dealing with replies.

12.7.3 Closing speech

Basic notes for a closing speech will often be made while you are preparing the case for court—you can note what the main lines of argument and the main strengths of the case are, and organise a suitable order for dealing with them. Some notes must be made in advance as you will often have limited opportunity to work on your closing speech while the case is in progress, especially early in practice. In addition, these notes will need to be reviewed during the case, in the light of arguments made by the other side and the evidence that is produced.

Some people say that good advocacy stems from a good closing speech—you decide what you will say and everything else is then constructed to build up to it. This is probably only true for big criminal cases, but it does emphasise the importance of coherent and detailed case planning.

12.7.4 Summing-up

While it is not necessary to take full notes of the summing-up, you should be ready to take notes of important points, not least because you may wish to refer to what the judge said on an appeal. While it may be possible to get transcripts from court, this will take time, and it can be valuable to have your own note to work with. On drafting grounds of appeal based on a summing-up, see the ***Drafting*** manual.

12.7.5 Judgment

Judgments are written out in law reports, and in most courts are recorded, so why should a barrister ever need to write them down personally? You only need to know if you won or lost, how much, and what is to happen about costs.

This reaction is to some extent true. You do not need notes of a whole judgment. But you frequently need some notes from a judgment, for example:

(a) to explain the details of a judgment to the client,

(b) to decide whether to appeal,

(c) to decide on what basis to appeal, if some grounds turn on precisely what the judge said.

Even when transcripts of judgments are available they take time and cost money, so you may well need a sufficient note on which to give basic advice and take decisions. Notes may also be important for drafting grounds of appeal.

12.8 Note-taking in other contexts

The note-taking skills described in this chapter may be applied to other aspects of the lawyer's work. There is, for example, the need to take notes in carrying out a negotiation. It is important to make notes in advance of what your options are, what is the most and least you might achieve and so on. You also need to take notes during the negotiation, of anything that the other side reveals and of anything that is agreed.

There is also the need to take a proper note of a telephone conversation. It is increasingly common for barristers to give advice over the telephone, but all too often the barrister does not write anything down and has to be reminded of the whole case if the solicitor comes back for further advice. When advising by telephone, or simply using the telephone to get further information, taking a full and clear written note is important.

Finally, there are two particularly important possibilities for the young barrister. First, your pupil supervisor will almost certainly ask you to take notes during conferences, and a clear note that you can refer to quickly to check points or that you can hand over to be kept with the brief will impress. Second, in early practice one is often asked to do devilling work on a brief, which will frequently involve organising and making notes. Again, if this is done well it will impress.

12.9 Shorthand

The importance of an ability to take good notes in almost every skill the barrister uses has been outlined already. One central element of note-taking is a need to write quickly. You may already be able to write shorthand, or you may already have devised your own methods of abbreviation. However, many students will not be familiar with a speed-writing system, and others may well be able to improve their approach. This section gives guidance on speed-writing. It is adapted from *Self-Shorthand* by C. G. L. Du Cann (London: Council of Legal Education, 3rd edn, 1982).

12.9.1 Why create your own system of self-shorthand?

It will enable you to take notes much more rapidly than, and just as accurately as, longhand. It may enable you to dispense with the drudgery of learning an established shorthand system, and yet gain for yourself all the advantages you personally need of shorthand. It will lessen your labours and save your time for more important use than mere transcription.

12.9.2 Elements of a system of self-shorthand

12.9.2.1 Initials

You already know, and probably use, hundreds of nationally recognised initials. This is the foundation of your extended use of initials.

Read the list given in any good dictionary, once or twice if you wish.

In general, you will find that such as you need will 'stick'. Besides, most of them speak adequately for themselves and cannot be confused with anything else.

These accepted initials are permanencies. That is a great advantage. Another great advantage is that they are generally understood.

Use initials with discretion. So long as it is not going to mislead, confuse, puzzle or delay you, they are invaluable. Remember that context is everything. If the word 'government' occurs over and over again and no other word such as 'God', which might be confused with it in interpretation and transcription, the letter 'G' will stand very well for 'government' and save the writing of nine letters wherever it occurs. In one piece of writing, hundreds of letters may be saved.

12.9.2.2 Abbreviations: national and professional

Abbreviations are of the utmost importance. Some which are nationally recognised you know already and have probably more or less accepted before you ever thought of self-shorthand.

'Abbreviate the abbreviations wherever practicable' says self-shorthand. Very often it **is** practicable. For the nationally recognised abbreviations were not scientifically thought out to the best advantage; they grew like a wild plant.

Applying the important principle of 'abbreviating the abbreviations' to the weekdays, for example, we can get down to 'MWF' for 'Monday, Wednesday and Friday', but 'T' and 'S' would equally stand for 'Tuesday' and 'Thursday' and 'Saturday' and 'Sunday'. Clearly then, you cannot abbreviate down to initials in this instance.

But by the aid of another principle, the small-letter principle—to be explained below—we may overcome this difficulty. M^{y}, T^{y}, W^{y}, Th^{y}, F^{y}, St^{y}, S^{y} will do very well indeed. Make a habit of this abbreviated abbreviation and think of the time and labour saved in a lifetime.

Never use an abbreviation, however conventional and nationally recognised, where a briefer and equally intelligible abbreviation exists. Be on the lookout for abbreviations which can be abbreviated, and cut them ruthlessly.

The set of professional abbreviations of the greatest general importance to the ordinary person is that of the journalistic and printing occupations.

There is a well-recognised list of these in all publishing, journalistic and printing establishments. Most of these were agreed as long ago as the International Shorthand Congress of 1887.

List of abbreviations for longhand

A	a	.(a dot on the line)
	about	abt
	according	acc
	account	acct
	advertisement	ad
	affectionate	aff
	affectionately	affl^{y}
	afternoon	aft^{n}
	again	ag^{n}
	against	agst
	American	Amer
	among	am^{g}
	amount	am^{t}
	ance (suffix at end of words)	-ce
B	because	b^{ec}
	been	b^{n}
	between	b^{tn}
	brought	bro^{t}
C	caught	Ca^{t}
	chairman	ch^{m}
	circumstance	cir^{ce}
	committee	com^{e} (or cte)
	could	c^{d}
D	difference	dif^{ce}
	different	dif^{t}
	difficult	dif^{clt}
	difficulty	dif^{clty}
E	*-ence*	-ce
	England, English	Eng.

	especially	esp
	evening	ev^{g}
	ever	-r
	every	ev^{r}
	excellent	exc.
F	faithfully	ff^{y}
	for	f
	Friday	Fri
	from	f^{m}
	further	fur^{r}
G	general	gen
	generally	gen^{y}
	good	g^{d}
	government	gov^{t}
	great	g^{t}
H	had	h^{d}
	have	h
I	importance	imp^{ce}
	important	imp^{t}
	-ing	g
	-ion	n
L	large	lge
M	manuscript	Ms
	meeting	m^{tg}
	-ment	m^{t}
	Monday	Mon
	morning	m^{g}
N	notwithstanding	notw^{g}
O	objection	obj^{n}
	occasion	occ^{n}
	o'clock	o'c
	of	o
	opinion	op^{n}
	opportunity	pp^{y}
	other	o^{r}
	ought	o^{t}
P	page, pages	p. pp
	particular	part^{r}
	popular	pop
Q	query	q^{y}
	question	q^{n}
	quotation	quot
S	said	s^{d}
	Saturday	Sat
	several	sev^{l}
	shall	sh
	should	sh^{d}
	-sion	n

	specially	spec
	Sunday	Sun
T	that	t
	the	/(the first stroke of t)
	their, there	th^{r}
	though	tho
	through	thro
	Thursday	Thurs
	-tion	n
	together	tog^{r}
	truly	ty
	Tuesday	Tues
V	very	v or v^{y}
	very good	vg
W	Wednesday	Wed
	whether	wh^{r}
	which	wh
	with	w
	without	w^{t}
	would	w^{d}
Y	yesterday	yest^{y} or y'day
	you	y
	your	y^{r}
	yours	yrs

These handsomely repay learning by heart. Many of them are self-suggestive so they are easy to master. Many of them, as already pointed out—notably the days of the week—can be further abbreviated.

But they will not only repay learning. They repay being studied. Note the *principles* behind them. Our initial principle is here. So is small-size and positional writing. So is the use of symbols like the dot for an 'a' and 'an' and the simple downstroke for 'the'.

12.9.2.3 Conventional spelling

Like the Americans, take the needless 'u' out of words like 'labour' and 'honour' at all times. But, of course, such words as these you can abbreviate further, for lab' and hon' are intelligible beyond confusion or mistake. Cut suffixes like ette to 'et'. So write 'cigaret', 'suffraget' at the most, while you can at the least write 'cig' for 'cigar' and 'ci^{gt}' for 'cigarette'.

You will have noted the superfluous apostrophe in words like 'don't' and 'can't' and others. It reminds us—unnecessarily—that a letter has been eliminated. In rapid writing the reminder is inopportune and distracting. So cut out the apostrophe as a set policy. Write 'cant', 'dont', 'wont', 'shouldnt'.

12.9.2.4 Fast-writing habits

Practice is the chief secret of success. But some people's writing lends itself to rapidity. A cursive or running style of handwriting is best. If you have a slow, crabbed hand through wrong teaching or wrong imitation when young, it may be difficult to adopt a new hand.

So eliminate unnecessary loops, for instance, both top and bottom. Journalists, who are fast writers from professional necessity, have a habit of joining words. This helps speed. It is a habit worth adopting, as it obviates delay caused by lifting the pen from the paper.

12.9.2.5 Small and large-letter principles

In **12.9.2.2** you met the small-letter principle. It spoke for itself at once, and showed how useful and important it was.

The large-letter principle will cause you no difficulty.

For example, take the letter 'A':

Archbishop	Ab^{p}
Abridge	Ab^{r}
Absolutely	Abs^{ly}
Acceptance	A^{cc}
Acknowledgement	Ack^{t}
Affirmative	Afft^{ive}
Aeroplane	A^{pln}
Affidavit	Aff^{t}t
Agriculture	Ag^{ture}
Agent	Ag^{t}
Appendix	App^{x}
Archdeacon	Arch^{d}
Astronomy	Ast^{y}
Assistant	Ass^{t}
Average	Av^{ge}

Positional and small-size writing are useful in calling attention to abbreviated forms. You met with it in **12.9.2.2** at the ends of words like 'should' being written 'sh'. But it can be applied to beginnings as well as to ends of words, just as advantageously. Use it for prefixes as well as suffixes.

Thus the prefix 'con'—or 'com'—is frequent and can be indicated by a small 'c' positionally written, for example:

content may be written ctnt

compromise may be written cprme

And 'circum' can be equally well written by a small 'c'. If you feel you must distinguish it from the symbolic letter 'c' for 'con' or 'com' you can use 'cstroke' thus: 'c/'.

circumference—c/fmce

circumflex—c/flx

Other prefixes can be similarly reduced. Further examples are the very frequently occurring 'per' and 'pro'. Thus:

proposition—p/pstn

proposal—p/psl

while 'per' can take the small raised 'p' as in:

perspicuity—^{p}spct

thus clearly distinguishing it from:

prospect—p/spct

Prefixes and suffixes, in fact, are one of the most fertile fields for the ingenuity of the self-shorthand writer.

12.9.2.6 Eliminations

Often the words 'a', 'an' and 'the' can be omitted without loss. So can formal words like 'the member' or 'this ancient and honourable society', for the transcriber will recollect such formal adjectives.

Thus write 'hm' and 'hr' for 'him' and 'her', for such contractions cannot be mistaken for any other word.

Sometimes two or even more vowels can be dropped with real safety. Thus:

'plain' can be written 'pln'

'contentment' can be written 'ctmtt'.

12.9.2.7 Key words and recurrent expressions

This should remind the student that in self-shorthand one must always have regard to the context. It is the context which governs key words and recurrent expressions and how they are represented.

For example 'deft' is the recognised legal abbreviation for 'defendant', and a very useful abbreviation it is. But a note-taking judge, magistrate, barrister or non-phonographic reporter in court will not keep writing four letters when one will do all that is wanted. A capital 'D' is enough here—though on other occasions a capital 'D' might well mean something other than 'defendant'.

12.9.2.8 Arbitrary symbols

Do not be afraid of using arbitrary symbols, even if they are algebra to other people. Use them freely according to your convenience. But recollect that the more they spring naturally from the word or phrase they represent, the easier they are to decipher and to remember.

12.9.2.9 The commonest words

The self-shorthand writer needs, of course, to pay special attention to the commonest, that is to say, the most frequently occurring words in the English language. Obviously, to make and learn abbreviations for these is of special importance. The 12 commonest words are also 12 of the shortest. These 12 words, it is authoritatively stated, make up 25% of all normal English, whether written or spoken.

1. a or an	7. that
2. and	8. in
3. the	9. any
4. of	10. to
5. be	11. is
6. it	12. his

12.9.3 Warning

Never get so involved in taking notes of what is being said by a client or witness that you fail to listen and watch for the non-verbal clues which will help you understand what is being said and whether it can be believed.

13 Modes of address

13.1 Introduction

Whenever you appear as an advocate you should always know the correct way to address the person or people who are in court to decide the issues of law and fact. Using an incorrect title is a sign of possible disrespect or inexperience. Most judges and magistrates will not object strongly to being addressed by an incorrect title, so you may not realise until later, if then, that you had risked upsetting the court. Of course, some judges do mind and will soon let you know if they think that your choice of title is inappropriate. You may find that their chosen response is to say, rather obscurely, 'I can't hear you, Miss Jones.' Your response may be simply to talk louder, assuming that either you are speaking too quietly or the poor old judge is a little deaf! What they mean by this expression is not that they can't hear you but that they won't—you sometimes get a similar response if a judge thinks you are dressed inappropriately for their court. With luck, your opponent will realise what the judge's objection is about and help you out, if possible.

If you are unlucky, the judge won't tell you about your gaffe, but will simply sit there and smoulder! Your chances of persuading the judge to decide in your client's favour may be diminishing with every fresh example of the slight. As a novice advocate, you will get much of your early experience in the magistrates' court or County Court, so you will become used to addressing the court as 'Sir/Madam' or 'Your Honour'. Problems may then arise if you are sent to the High Court, and confusion may increase if your appearance there is before a circuit judge, sitting as a judge of the High Court!

A few years ago, a very junior barrister appeared at the Old Bailey in a hearing with several more experienced barristers. He was the last one to address the judge and his task should have been a simple one; sadly, although most of what he said made sense, he addressed the judge several times as 'Sir'. This was a considerable slight since any Crown Court judge is entitled to be called 'Your Honour' and, even worse, anyone sitting as a judge in the Old Bailey is entitled to be addressed as 'My Lord/Lady'. The judge said nothing but sat there and glowered fiercely at the young barrister. The barrister eventually realised that something was up but could not think what, until he noticed that counsel sitting by his side was muttering something. The young barrister's first reaction was to think, 'How rude'; his second was to listen to what his colleague was muttering. It was 'My Lord—**my Lord**'. Realising his error, the barrister apologised at once, the judge recovered his previous complexion and everything went as planned thereafter.

In order to avoid similar embarrassment yourself, read the rest of this chapter with care.

13.2 Using the correct form of address

13.2.1 Vocative/accusative

The way in which you address the court may vary depending upon whether you are using the vocative case (ie, calling upon the judge as if by name) or the accusative case (ie, in place of 'you').

(a) Where the correct form of address is 'Sir/Madam', 'Master' or 'Your Honour' there is no real distinction between addressing the court in the vocative or accusative cases.

Examples

Vocative:

'*Sir/Madam*, the defendant is content for the matter to be dealt with today.'
'In my submission, *Master*, the claimant has failed to show a total failure of consideration.'
'Your Honour, there are three affidavits in this case.'

Accusative:

'May it please you, *Sir/Madam.*'
'If you look at the document marked "A", *Master*, you will see that . . .'
'Does *Your Honour* have a copy of the defendant's antecedents?' (Note: you should avoid calling a Circuit Court judge 'you'.)

(b) There is, however, a marked difference between the appropriate use of 'My Lord/ My Lady' and 'Your Lordship/Your Ladyship'. Use 'My Lord/My Lady' whenever you are addressing the judge in the vocative sense. Use 'Your Lordship/Your Ladyship' in place of 'you'.

Examples

Vocative:

'*My Lord*, the third defendant has taken no part in these proceedings.' 'I am obliged, *my Lady.*'

Accusative:

'*Your Lordship* may be minded to . . .'
'I am happy to tell *Your Lordship* that the parties have reached terms in this matter.'
'Does *Your Ladyship* have the claimant's affidavit sworn on the 13th March 2006?'

(c) It is perfectly acceptable to combine both forms of address in one sentence.

Example

'*My Lady*, if I may deal with the points which *Your Ladyship* has raised . . .'

(d) Use 'His Lordship/Her Ladyship' and 'His Honour/Her Honour' in place of 'him' or 'her', ie, when referring to the judge in the third person.

Examples

'Describe the layout of the room to *His Lordship*.'
'Tell *Her Honour* what you saw when you entered the room.'

13.2.2 Hybrid situations

Figure 13.1 shows the way to address a person who is sitting as a deputy Circuit or High Court judge. Some confusion, however, arises where a Circuit judge is sitting also as a deputy judge of the High Court in order to hear a mixed list, ie, some County Court and some High Court cases. In these circumstances, it is the case itself which determines the mode of address. If your case is a County Court matter, address the judge as 'Your Honour'. If the case is a High Court matter, address the judge as 'My Lord/My Lady'. Note, however, that if a High Court judge hears a case which is listed as a County Court matter, he or she must still be addressed as 'My Lord/My Lady' and not demoted!

Another hybrid situation occurs when it is necessary to see the judge in his or her private room, eg, to seek an indication regarding sentence (for the limited circumstances in which this might be appropriate see *R v Turner* [1970] 2 QB 321). In this situation, address the judge as 'Judge'.

Youth Court and Magistrates' Court	District Judge (formerly Stipendiary Magistrate):	'Sir/Madam'
	Chairman of Lay Bench:	'Sir/Madam'
	Members of Lay Bench:	'Your colleagues'
Tribunals	Chairman:	'Sir/Madam'
	Other members:	'Your colleagues'
County Court	Circuit Judge:	'Your Honour'
	Recorder or any person sitting as a deputy Circuit Judge:	'Your Honour'
	District Judge:	'Sir/Madam'
Crown Court	High Court Judge:	'My Lord/My Lady'
	Circuit Judge:	'Your Honour'
	Recorder or any person sitting as a deputy Circuit Judge:	'Your Honour'
	Exceptions [see: PD [1982] 1 All ER 320]:	
	Central Criminal Court—any person sitting as a Judge:	'My Lord/My Lady'
	Recorder of Manchester/ Liverpool:	'My Lord/My Lady'
High Court	Judge:	'My Lord/My Lady'
	Any Circuit Judge sitting as a Judge of the High Court:	'My Lord/My Lady'
	District Judge:	'Sir/Madam'
	Master:	'Master'
Court of Appeal	Lord Justice:	'My Lord/My Lady'
House of Lords	Lord of Appeal in Ordinary:	'My Lord'

Figure 13.1 Modes of address

13.2.3 Referring to another judge

It is often necessary to refer the court to (the judgment of) another judge. In so doing, use his or her proper title.

Examples

Refer to 'Roper J' as 'Mr Justice Roper'.
Refer to 'Roper LJ' as 'Lord Justice Roper'.

13.2.4 Social occasions

Occasionally, you may meet a judge socially, for instance, on the train to court. The proper form of address in these circumstances is simply 'Judge'.

14

The advocate as a storyteller

14.1 Introduction

We can often remember quite easily the earliest stories we were told and, if we have children, we are quite confident that we can recall and tell those stories to them. It may be that we can remember those tales just because we were young and our memories were very absorbent; it may also be because the stories were clear and had a simple structure. Also, the storyteller seemed to be familiar with the story so that they were fluent, had a confident manner and perhaps were able to do other things at the same time as telling the story (for example, monitor the listener's attention—'Are you listening to me?').

We don't remember those stories because we can easily identify with their situations—mermaids and flying horses, talking animals and sentient toys—but the good storyteller will engage the listener's imagination. They are transported into a form of acceptance and we might call this a form of **persuasion**.

When telling a story, it is always a good idea to have a clear leitmotif (or recurrent theme associated with a particular person, idea or situation) and our childhood stories are full of those, even down to the names of the characters. What does the listener recall of the story later? All of it or just bits and pieces? If the 'story' is the evidence at a trial, then the advocate may want to ensure that the listener does indeed recall only bits and further that only those bits which favour the client are recalled. How might the advocate do this?

Perhaps the most important step is to decide whether the story is acceptable to the listener; does it 'fit' with the listener's idea of how the world and humankind work? Everyone who sits in court to adjudicate on competing versions of the 'facts' in a case brings with them some prior knowledge and beliefs about how things work, what makes people act in certain ways or what they mean when they say certain things. If your client's story fits better into that wealth of knowledge and beliefs than your opponent's story, you have the advantage in persuading your audience to find the facts as you allege them to be. Alternatively, since you are likely to have to present your client's story as it is, rather than as you might like it to be (an ethical requirement), you may need to think about strategies to adopt in order to alter the mindset of your listener, so that the story becomes more acceptable and so more credible.

Much has been written on the importance of storytelling as a part of the persuasive process. The rest of this chapter tries to put this into context for advocates.

14.2 Why should an advocate be able to tell a story?

It is important for an advocate to be able to tell a story well. You must, of course, obey the rules of professional conduct (eg, not to mislead the court) and you must always use information supplied by your instructing solicitors (usually from the lay client), rather than making it up for yourself (!). But the essence of proceedings in the courts of England and Wales is their oral nature. For a barrister, this is most obvious when you are called on to make a speech in a trial. This is your opportunity to present your story to the court. When you look at the chapters on speeches, bear this in mind.

The section on fact management in the ***Case Preparation*** manual **(11.6.2)** refers to the concept of **themes** as part of the preparation for trial. For example:

> The theme . . . may be defined as that part of the 'story' presented in court which the lawyer selects and presents because of its particularly persuasive effect in relation to the ultimate conclusion which the lawyer wants the tribunal of fact to draw.

Much of the story which is involved in a trial cannot be told, maybe because of:

(a) lack of witnesses at the time of trial; or

(b) rules of evidence (eg, rule against hearsay); or

(c) it is legally irrelevant to the issues in dispute at the trial.

A good example is the Bodkin Adams prosecution at the Old Bailey in the 1950s. Several books have since been written about the case and its defendant, Dr John Bodkin Adams. This, in itself, might suggest that the whole story did not emerge at the trial. In what is perhaps the most authoritative work on the topic, by the trial judge (then Devlin J), Lord Devlin devotes several pages to a consideration of the opening speech for the Crown by the Attorney-General. He then concludes:

> the whole story of Dr Adams was not told at the trial. The story emerges from his long years in practice at Eastbourne during which he acquired a curious reputation as a legacy hunter. It slips through the death of Mrs Morrell in 1950 which passed unnoticed at the time. It bursts into the news in August 1956 after an inquest has been held on the body of another wealthy patient, Mrs Hullett. After that the rumours spread to cover many other names, including that of Mrs Hullett's husband who had died six months before her.
>
> So it came as no surprise to the public to hear in December 1956 that Dr Adams had been arrested and charged with murder. What was a surprise was that he was charged with the murder, not of Mrs Hullett, but of Mrs Morrell who had died so long before [1950]. Then, when the preliminary proceedings in the Morrell case were begun before the Eastbourne magistrates in January 1957, the public learnt that the Crown would be calling evidence to show that Dr Adams, although not formally charged with the murder of either Mrs or Mr Hullett, had in fact murdered both of them. But when the trial began at the Old Bailey nothing at all was said about the Hulletts. The name was not mentioned until the last day after Dr Adams had been acquitted. Many people believe that, if the doctor had been tried for the murder of Mrs Hullett instead of Mrs Morrell, he would have been convicted.

Good advocates can make an implausible story sound credible; even a poor orator will benefit from having a good story to tell.

14.3 The story

Plausibility is often a good foundation in telling a story. Do all your facts fit together? What was the defendant's motive for committing the act? Is that how most people behave? Is it how the court might believe someone in your client's position might behave? This represents the contents of your story. You will need to consider these contents before starting a trial. In choosing your theory of the case before trial, you have to consider the cause of action; the issues that you must prove; and the admissible evidence at your disposal.

14.3.1 Example

Let us take an example. At the end of this manual, in the **Appendix**, there is a criminal case, *R v Heath*. Take 15 minutes to read it now.

Now consider the evidence which is available to both prosecution and defence. From the standpoint of prosecuting counsel, what is your story? An everyday story in these depressing times, of mindless violence out of all proportion to any provocation? Or is it an argument, started by an overreaction from the landlord and ending with an unreasonable piece of self-defence from the accused? Has this been a row simmering for months, since Heath was convicted and barred from the pub? Is Heath a simple lager lout or a more cunning thug with a preconceived plan? Was the glassing done on the spur of the moment? Or was this another episode in the continuing jealousy of Heath and John Bull in their rivalry for the affections of the barmaid, Tracey Croft?

To a large extent, these matters and the choices you make have nothing to do with what we are concerned with at the trial. That is determined by the counts on the indictment and the criminal law. But to be plausible, to be persuasive, the evidence that you use at trial must make sense in human as well as legal terms. It really is not enough to call witnesses to say they saw Kevin Heath push a beer mug into a publican's face—if at all possible, your story should explain why this happened.

To return to a trial mentioned earlier, *R v Bodkin Adams,* it may be that the indictment was too restrictive to allow a truly credible story to be told (see Lord Devlin's observations cited above). But you must work with whatever material you have to convince the triers of the facts that your story is the correct one. It matters not whether your trial is in the magistrates' court, in front of a jury or a High Court judge—your audience is always more likely to accept a story which fits in with their beliefs, knowledge, experiences and prejudices.

14.4 The telling

Our focus is shifting now, away from the story itself to the listeners. They will judge (quite literally) whether you have told a good story or not. In part they will be assessing the story but also they will be assessing you and the way in which you told the story.

Since storytelling can occur at the start of the trial (or your client's part of it) as an opening speech or at its conclusion, as a closing speech, you may find that the 'ideal' story you told at the start has had to be modified by the end because of the evidence that has emerged or the demeanour of certain witnesses in giving their evidence. What you can and should do is: repeat key words or phrases throughout the case, use them frequently so that they can be leitmotifs of characters, places or situations. Choose the elements of your story with care, eg, if you are relying on a particular interpretation of an incident, how likely is it that your audience will accept that interpretation as likely or credible? If a 13-year-old tells her headmaster that she was late for school because she was abducted by aliens from Alpha Centauri, she is unlikely to be believed. If she repeats the story to a meeting of the local UFO society, she may well be believed. Although the ability to adduce hard evidence to back up our stories always helps, the more the story fits in with the way our listeners see the world, the more likely they are to accept it. So, the point to remember is, know your audience.

Always use language that your listener will understand easily. Barristers in a trial often use only a few documents; information is communicated by word of mouth so your meaning must be readily comprehensible to your listener. If you want the audience to absorb your points, don't rush and don't become prolix. The most memorable points are often the shortest ones. Be fluent, making sure pauses are deliberate and have some purpose. Use short, simple sentences. Avoid subordinate clauses like the plague. They are very tempting, especially when while uttering one thought another occurs to you and you have a concern that unless you fit the idea within the sentence you are delivering you will forget it. Sometimes you can. Generally, however, you will lose the proper impact of both ideas. You may lose your main verb. You are likely to lose your subject and your object. By then you will have forgotten how you started the sentence and will not have the faintest idea how to finish it. Your aim must be to construct sentences which are grammatically correct. They are so much easier to listen to and consequently much more likely to persuade.

Be sparing with gestures. Arms flailing like the sails of a windmill do not add to the force of any argument and they are tiring to watch. Any gestures used should be deliberately chosen solely to add emphasis to the words you are using. Above all, stand still. Do not fiddle with papers or with the keys in your pocket or your buttons or anything. Such constant, restless, mindless movement distracts and will eventually irritate your audience.

14.5 Exercises

You may want to practise your storytelling abilities; after all, anyone can read a good story but it takes a lot of practice and hard work to be able to transport your listeners into your story—for example, to take the jury at Croydon Crown Court back to Christmas Eve 2008, in the bar of The Cutpurse pub in New Addington (see p 374 *R v Heath* in the **Appendix**); or to the homes of the rich and elderly in Eastbourne who were the (now deceased) patients of Dr Bodkin Adams.

It may be quite useful to start practising storytelling in a non-legal context. Choose a situation with which you are more familiar and which does not have the same restrictions as a legal trial. The following exercises are suggested.

14.5.1 Exercise 1

Using one of the following scenarios, devise a short story (no longer than five minutes). Try to commit it to memory so that, when you try to relate it to a colleague, your performance is fluent.

Consider the information that you want to convey, whether there are any key words or phrases that you could use. Perhaps most important, think about your audience—who are they, what sympathies might they have, what might their 'official' attitude be towards you or your story?

(a) You are a pupil at school who has missed 'gym' and are about to go before the headmaster to explain your absence (your third missed class this term).

(b) You are an employee of a large company. Yesterday you were late for work (fifth time this month) and you are now waiting to see the Supervisor, who has asked you to explain your latest absence and why it keeps happening.

(c) You have been charged with stealing property from a car on 3 September 2003. You are about to keep an appointment with your solicitor. You told her on the telephone that you are not guilty and have an alibi, with potential witnesses. She asked you to come and give her the details of the alibi.

(d) Your bicycle is in collision with a van on the road. The van driver does not seem injured; you have several cuts and grazes and a terrible pain in one of your arms. The police have been called and now an officer wants you to tell her what happened.

14.5.2 Exercise 2

Find a set of statements and instructions in a case that you can use (perhaps the *Heath* case set out in the **Appendix** to this manual, or from one of the other manuals or from a cooperative barrister). Study the papers for, say, an hour then report the case orally to a friend in 45 minutes. The following day, present your report in 25 minutes and, on the third day, tell it in 15 minutes to someone who knows nothing about the case. Each time, see if this 'stranger' has grasped the essential points of the case. This will help you to distil your stories to their essence; it should also ensure that your stories are ones that stay in the mind(s) of your audience. These times may be varied according to the size and complexity of the case.

14.6 Further reading

Armour, J. 'Stereotypes and Prejudice: Helping Legal Decision-makers Break the Prejudice Habit', *Calif Law Rev,* 1995, pp 733–72.

Baron, Jane B. 'Intention, Interpretation and Stories', *Duke Law Journal,* 1992, pp 630–78.

Bennett, W.L. and Feldman, M.S. *Re-Constructing Reality in the Courtroom,* Tavistock, 1981.

Devlin, P. *Easing the Passing; the trial of Dr John Bodkin Adams,* Faber & Faber, 1986.

Evans, K. *Advocacy in Court,* Blackstone Press (OUP), 2nd edn, 1995.

Lopez, 'Lay Lawyering', *UCLA Law Review,* Vol 32 (1984).

Ohlbaum, Edward D. 'Basic Instinct: Case Theory and Courtroom Performance', *Temple Law Rev,* 1993, pp 1–57 and appendices.

Sarmas, L. 'Storytelling and the Law: a Case Study of *Louth v Diprose*', *Melb U Law Rev,* 1994, pp 701–28.

Stone, M. *Cross-Examination in Criminal Trials,* Tottel Publishing, 2009.

Case Preparation manual (**Chapter 11**)

15 The course of a trial

15.1 Introduction

The most straightforward way to learn advocacy skills is through their performance, in a variety of tasks. Sometimes, however, to focus on the details of those tasks makes it harder to see the bigger picture and how each task fits into the overall pattern of the particular case. In this chapter, we have endeavoured to describe the usual running order of a trial, both in a criminal court and a civil court.

15.2 A criminal trial

The following numbered sequence charts the course of a trial on indictment involving two co-accused, D1 and D2 (named in the indictment in that order), and two offences, Offence X and Offence Y. D1 and D2 are jointly charged with Offence X. There is a separate count charging D2 alone with Offence Y.

The arraignment, as is now normally the case, took place at the Plea and Directions Hearing. The counts in the indictment were put to D1 and D2 to plead guilty or not guilty. In the case of D2, a plea was taken on each count separately. D1 and D2 pleaded not guilty to Offence X. D2 pleaded not guilty to Offence Y.

Square brackets indicate stages which may or may not be taken depending upon the precise facts and circumstances of the particular case.

15.3 Course of a criminal trial

(1) Jury empanelled by clerk calling at random 12 names from the panel summoned to attend.

(2) [Subject to challenges for cause, the prosecution exercising their 'right' of standby and the judge's power to exclude jurors] each juror takes the juror's oath/affirmation.

(3) Clerk asks the jurors if they are all sworn and puts D1 and D2 in their charge, ie, '. . . D2 also stands charged with the following . . . (Offence Y). To this charge he [or she] has also pleaded not guilty. It is your charge to say, having heard the evidence whether he [or she] is guilty or not guilty.'

(4) Prosecution opening speech (which should exclude any references to evidence which is either clearly inadmissible or to which counsel for the accused have indicated, or either of them has indicated, that D1 and/or D2 will object).

(5) Prosecution evidence including, as appropriate, real evidence, documentary hearsay and formal admissions.

(6) [Each prosecution witness may be cross-examined by D1 and D2, in that order, and may then be re-examined by the prosecution.] Prosecution declares that that is all of its evidence—ie, 'closes' its case.

(7) [Submission of no case to answer by D1 and/or D2. Note: the jury are asked to leave the court before any such submission is made. Defence counsel makes his or her/their submission(s) and prosecuting counsel is given an opportunity to reply. The judge announces his or her decision and the jury return to court. If the submission is upheld in relation to all counts on the indictment, the judge explains this to the jury and asks them to appoint a foreman, and the clerk takes from the foreman on each count a verdict of not guilty on the direction of the judge. If the judge decides that there is no case to answer on one count—eg, the count containing Offence Y—but that there is a case to answer on the other, the judge will direct the jury that (a) he or she will direct them, at the end of the trial, to return a verdict of not guilty on D2 in relation to Offence Y and (b) during the remainder of the trial they should ignore the count containing Offence Y. If the judge rejects the submission of no case on all counts, the jury are told nothing and the case continues.]

(8) Counsel for D1 (and D2) either (a) informs the court that D1 (D2) will give evidence or (b) does not so inform the court, or informs the court that D1 (D2) does not intend to give evidence. In the latter case, ie, (b), the judge should then inquire of counsel whether he or she has advised his or her client about the fact that the jury may draw inferences from a failure to testify. If counsel replies in the affirmative, the case proceeds. If counsel replies in the negative, then the judge must direct the representative to advise his or her client on the matter, and should adjourn briefly for this purpose. See Criminal Justice and Public Order Act 1994, s 35 and Practice Direction (Criminal Proceedings: Consolidation) [2002] 1 WLR 2870, para 44.

(9) D1 presents his or her case: co-accused must present their cases in the order in which their names appear in the indictment.

(10) [D1's opening speech.] Note: if the only defence evidence is to be given by D1 or by D1 and witnesses speaking only as to his or her good character, D1 has no right to an opening speech.

(11) [D1 called to give evidence.] Note: Police and Criminal Evidence Act 1984, s 79: if an accused (D) intends to call two or more witnesses to the facts of a case and those witnesses include D, D must be called before the other witness(es) unless the court in its discretion otherwise directs.

(12) [If D1 does testify, after examination-in-chief he or she can be cross-examined by counsel for D2. Then the prosecution may cross-examine and counsel for D1 may re-examine.]

(13) [D1's other evidence, including, as appropriate, real evidence, documentary hearsay and formal admissions. Witnesses called by D1 will be examined-in-chief and then may be cross-examined by counsel for D2, then by the prosecution and counsel for D1 may re-examine.]

(14) D2 presents his or her case: see (9)–(13) above, reversing 'Dl' and 'D2' throughout.

(15) [Prosecution closing speech.] Note: the prosecution have no right to a closing speech if an accused (a) is unrepresented and (b) had no right to an opening speech—see (10) above.

(16) D1's closing speech.

(17) D2's closing speech.

(18) Judge's summing-up: functions of judge and jury; burden and standard of proof; definition of offences charged; direction to treat D1 and D2 separately and to treat the separate counts separately; summary of evidence; directions on evidence as appropriate [eg, effect of character evidence, effect of silence, etc]; advise appointment of foreman and retirement with a view to reaching a unanimous verdict.

(19) [If the jury return to court or are sent for by the judge after 2 hours and 10 minutes or such longer period as the judge thinks reasonable, and the foreman, upon being asked whether they have reached a unanimous verdict, answers 'no', the judge may give a majority verdict direction: see Practice Direction (Criminal Proceedings: Consolidation) [2002] 1 WLR 2870, para 46 and the Juries Act 1974, s 17.]

(20) Jury's verdict on each count:

(a) guilty (unanimous); or

(b) guilty (majority); or

(c) not guilty (unanimous); or

(d) not guilty (majority); or

(e) failure to agree upon any verdict.

Concerning (b) and (d), the procedure, following a majority direction and on the jury's return to court, is to ask if at least 10 out of 12 are agreed; if yes, to ask whether guilty or not guilty; if guilty, to ask how many were in favour, how many against; if not guilty, simply to accept the verdict.

If the verdict is either (a) or (b), the court may adjourn for reports prior to sentence, in which event there is still a prima facie right to bail: see Bail Act 1976, s 4. If no reports are sought, there is usually no right to bail although an application for bail may be made pending appeal against conviction and/or sentence. The Crown Court judge will only be able to grant bail if he or she certifies the case is fit for appeal (rare).

If the verdict is either (c) or (d), the judge will direct the accused that he or she is free to leave the dock (provided, of course, he or she has not been found guilty on some other count and is not in custody on other matters).

Concerning (e), the judge may ask the jury to retire again [with or without a majority direction] or discharge the jury. Discharge of a jury in such circumstances is not an acquittal—there may be a retrial.

Mitigation should be prepared in advance: preparation during the jury's retirement may be interrupted by their early return to court!

15.4 A civil trial

The following numbered sequence charts the course of a civil trial involving two defendants, D1 and D2, who appear in the pleadings as First Defendant and Second Defendant. The material documents were collated into a trial bundle, with identical sets for everyone to use. If the case is proceeding in either the Queen's Bench Division or Chancery Division, there may also be a reading list, and there should be a case summary. This latter document is a short one, summarising the issues in the case and dealing with any relevant procedural matters. In a case proceeding in the High Court, counsel should provide the court with a list of any legal authorities, no later than 5 pm on the day before the hearing. Finally, the court should have skeleton arguments—these are compulsory in the High Court and optional but sensible for the County Court. For more detail on this sequence, refer to *Blackstone's Civil Practice,* Chapter 59.

15.5 Course of a civil trial

(1) The case may be tried by a District Judge (small claims, cases in the fast track and some in the multi-track) or by a circuit judge or Recorder in the County Court or a High Court judge (most multi-track cases).

(2) The hearing will be in public generally. In exceptional situations, the court may decide to exclude members of the public. An example would be if privacy was needed to protect the interests of a child involved in the litigation.

(3) A trial timetable may determine time limits for making speeches and questioning witnesses. This will usually have been decided at a pre-trial review, if one has taken place.

(4) The claimant usually begins the trial, unless the burden of proof is on the defendant(s). The starting point is an opening speech. This may be dispensed with, particularly in a case where the judge has had the chance to read the trial bundle. If a speech is made, counsel for the claimant will set out the nature of the claim and use either the statements of case, or the case summary, or both, to identify the issues for resolution in the trial.

(5) Claimant's evidence is then called. This can include, as appropriate, real evidence, documentary evidence and witness statements, as well as oral testimony. Remember that hearsay is not inadmissible in civil trials (see Civil Evidence Act 1995). So, depositions or affidavits or witness statements may be used as evidence; usually, a witness statement will serve as the evidence-in-chief of its maker.

(6) Further examination-in-chief may take place. For example, a witness may provide supplementary information, with the permission of the judge. Cross-examination can then be done, if necessary. Under the provisions of the Civil Evidence Act 1995, a witness statement may be relied upon as evidence even if its maker is not called as a witness or available for cross-examination. A witness's absence from the witness box will be a matter relevant to the weight of that evidence. If a witness is to be cross-examined then, if there is more than one defendant, the order of questioning will be determined by the order in which they appear on the court record, so—First Defendant, then Second Defendant. The witness may then be re-examined for the claimant. The claimant will finally declare that this is all of the evidence by 'closing the case for the Claimant'.

(7) Submission of no case to answer may be made now. This is less frequent than in criminal trials. It is usual for the judge to make a defendant choose between making a submission of no case or calling evidence in support of his case. In exceptional circumstances, this choice may not have to be made.

(8) In the absence of a submission of no case, the defence may present its evidence. If calling evidence, counsel may begin by making an opening speech for the defence. In practice, defence counsel often forgoes this opportunity.

(9) The defendant and any other witnesses may be called to give their evidence to the court. Each witness may undergo examination-in-chief, cross-examination and re-examination. A number of defendants, if separately represented, will present their evidence in the order in which they appear on the court record. Thus, the evidence for the First Defendant will be presented before that for the Second Defendant, and so on. Eventually, all defendants will have 'closed their case'.

(10) The Defence closing speech may now be made, if the defendant has called evidence. This is clearly an important stage of the trial—if pressed by a time limit (imposed via a trial timetable), counsel may rely upon their skeleton argument for a fuller treatment of the issues in the case. Where there is a number of defendants, their speeches will follow the usual pattern.

(11) Claimant's closing speech. The claimant usually has the last word before the judge determines the case.

(12) Judgment is given. This may happen immediately or later (in which case, it is described as a 'reserved' judgment).

(13) Costs are considered in light of the judgment. Arguments as to who should bear the costs should have been prepared in advance, to cover every likely outcome in the case. As to how much the costs should be, a statement of costs should have been served 24 hours before the hearing. There may be a summary (or on-the-spot) assessment of costs by the trial judge; if so, that will be based on the statement.

Part IV

Opening and closing a case

16

Opening speeches

16.1 Introduction

The opening speech is the first opportunity that advocates have to set out the case theory which, in their opinion, will persuade the court to determine the issues in favour of their client. Very often, these days, the court will be quite familiar with the likely evidence in the trial—for example, in many civil trials now, there will have been a mutual exchange of witness statements. The judge will have a trial bundle consisting of those and the statements of case in the case. Similarly, in the Crown Court the judge will have seen the indictment and the prosecution witness statements before the trial begins. The big difference is that the triers of fact in criminal trials are magistrates and juries. Crucially, they will have next to no knowledge about the case before the trial starts, apart from hearing the charge against the accused read out and hearing the plea of not guilty entered. Thus, for the triers of fact in criminal trials, the opening speech is the first real chance to become acquainted with the issues; whereas, in civil trials, the judge already has a good idea of what the case is all about before the advocate ever stands up. This may mean there are certain differences of emphasis when opening a case to a judge, rather than to magistrates or a jury. Nevertheless, there are some general factors which should be ever present in an opening speech.

16.2 The basic purpose of an opening speech

The opening speech serves as an introduction to your client's case. It should set out the essential facts on which your case is founded; it should fill in a little background so that the triers of fact begin to see the 'bigger picture'—otherwise there is a danger that the speech and the subsequent evidence will appear rather disconnected as if the witnesses were simply a group of people chosen almost at random; and, finally, the speech should introduce one (or more) possible case theories.

The opening speech comes at the very outset of the presentation of your client's case to the court. If you were writing a book, this speech would be an introduction or prologue to assist the reader and bring them up to speed with the plot and characters. If this were a restaurant and not a courtroom, the speech would be replaced by an enthusiastic maître d', talking the diners through the delights of the menu and offering an hors d'oeuvre or two to whet their appetite. Last analogy!—the triers of fact are about to board a bus, driven by you. It could turn out to be a mystery tour, where everyone finishes up at your intended destination (the end of the trial) but no one is quite sure how they got there or what they saw on the way. Indeed, some passengers may have seen different sights from the rest, some or all may have missed some very interesting sights along the way simply through ignorance. That's not what you want. Your opening speech must be like the very best guided tour—one where the travellers know from the off where they are going, how they are going to get there and what they are likely to experience along the way.

So, the speech is an outline and a guide. It is an introduction and it should introduce the circumstances that gave rise to the litigation, the parties who are involved in it, what your client seeks from the triers of fact and, most crucially, how the issues will be resolved in such a way as to make the outcome sought by your client the inevitable result of the trial. You should always take great care when preparing an opening speech, whatever the court, as what you say now will act as a template for the rest of the case. If you tell the court that a witness will say *x* in their evidence, and that witness fails to do so, your opponent is likely to draw the court's attention to that failure. It may not be a significant omission to you but the triers of fact may disagree. Also, if you advance a particular case theory in your opening speech and the evidence turns out not to support that but is fine for a different case theory which could also win the case for your client, you will have to work hard to persuade the court to let you walk away from your original theory.

This sounds like a recipe for caution, keeping things vague and talking in generalities. You can take this advice too much to heart but there is a great gap between what you **need** to say in an opening speech and what you **can** say by way of comment on the facts that you expect to prove. Too much caution is bad, but some caution is sensible; moderation is the rule. Never open a case 'higher' than you need to. It is a dangerous technique to be too bullish in your opening, bold assertions now that facts *x, y* and *z* will be proved may come back to haunt you later, what appear now as justified and confident predictions about the evidence may just turn out to be hostages to fortune. Take the example of prosecuting counsel in the obscenity trial concerning *Lady Chatterley's Lover* by DH Lawrence. Extracts from the speech to the jury show him saying:

> the heroine, Lady Chatterley, and the hero, the gamekeeper, are, you may think, little more than bodies, bodies which continuously have sexual intercourse with one another . . .
> . . . the story of the book . . . is little more than padding . . .
> . . . sex is dragged in at every conceivable opportunity . . .
> . . . the book puts promiscuous sex on a pedestal . . .

Each of the propositions was subsequently used by the defence as the basis for a question to the defence expert witnesses. They became ammunition for the defence to shoot back at the prosecution and no advocate can afford to supply his or her opponent with bullets. Of more concern, no client can afford to indulge an advocate who, through lack of foresight as to consequences (or maybe just lack of imagination), fails to see how what they perceive as strengths can swiftly become turned around into weaknesses. There is almost nothing your opponent will enjoy more than being given the chance to do this.

16.3 The elements of the speech

A competent opening speech consists of the following elements:

(a) introducing your role as advocate in the case, and that of your opponent(s), to the court;
(b) giving a clear summary of the facts of the case;
(c) giving a clear statement of the disputed issues between the parties;

(d) giving a brief outline of the evidence of witnesses, if the admissibility of that evidence is not challenged;

(e) addressing the court on the law, when appropriate;

(f) speaking clearly, using appropriate language;

(g) delivering the speech without reading from a prepared script;

(h) complying with the rules of professional conduct.

16.4 How to structure your opening speech

What follows are several suggestions on how to structure an opening speech in various contexts. They are not intended to be prescriptive and, when you become more experienced as an advocate, you will find that you prefer to do things in your own way. That is as it should be but you must always remember that the purpose of the opening speech is to put the essential facts of your client's case before the court and the basis for liability or its denial. Always try to keep your speech as concise as possible, appear to be decent and honest in your dealings with the court now. Remember the rules of professional conduct.

16.4.1 Civil trials

The structure of speeches in civil trials will be largely the same, whether taking place in the County Court or High Court (although in the latter forum, replace 'Your Honour' with 'My Lord/Lady'). The opening speech will usually be given by the advocate who represents the claimant but, occasionally, it may be the right of the defence to start the trial with a speech. It really depends upon who bears the burden of proof on the matters in issue in the trial.

It is quite usual in civil cases to have a skeleton argument prepared in advance of the trial. This document sets out, quite briefly, the issues which are in dispute between the parties (these may not be instantly clear from the individual statements of case and it requires an overview which can only be done after all statements of case are available). The skeleton argument should summarise the party's case on the issues and summarise the propositions of law which the party relies upon. Finally, it should contain cross-references to the statements of case, the court bundle (any documentary real evidence or witness statements), and the legal sources which support the propositions of law. The skeleton argument should underpin your opening speech; the written document is not intended to replace the oral speech. For more guidance on skeleton arguments, see **Chapter 25**.

In your opening speech, you should ensure that you do the following:

(a) **State the nature of the case**

For example, 'Your Honour, this is a claim for damages for personal injury arising out of a road traffic accident, caused by the defendant's negligence' or, 'Your Honour, this is a claim for damages based on an alleged breach of contract'.

(b) **State the issues in the case, ie, the areas of dispute between the parties**

For example, 'The issue between the parties is whether the car was of merchantable quality' or, 'The issue between the parties is whether the defendant fell below the standard of care expected of a reasonable prudent driver when he overtook the lorry on the roundabout' or, 'There are three issues in this case: first, has the respondent committed acts of violence against the petitioner and, if so, is there a danger that he will do so again? Finally, if there is such a danger, should the respondent be excluded from the matrimonial home?'

(c) **Summarise the facts which have been established or will be established during the trial**

Thus, any significant factual matters which are relevant but not in dispute should be identified, you will want to identify the circumstances that gave rise to the events which are the subject matter of the litigation, as well as its aftermath.

For example, in a claim for damages for personal injury, you would want to set the scene, describe what was happening immediately prior to the injury being suffered, how the injury was sustained, what happened immediately thereafter and what the longer-term consequences were.

(d) **Read out the statements of case and the relevant parts of any documents whose use has been agreed by the parties**

This may seem unnecessary to you. After all, the judge has the statements of case and your skeleton argument. You may be right: the judge will often indicate that he or she will read the statements of case for themselves now or has already read them. If so, you should still take the judge to the key points in the statements of case (for example, the allegations of negligence in a personal injuries case) as it remains important to ensure the judge has absorbed these important allegations.

(e) **Refer to any relevant legal principles contained in statute, regulation or case law**

Again, this may seem unnecessary. The judge will have considerable experience of handling cases like this and may be thoroughly familiar with the relevant law. Indeed, often the legal position will be agreed between the parties, and the court has to resolve only issues of fact. This may be where the skeleton argument comes into its own, particularly as no judge ever welcomes a lecture on the law! Unless the relevant law is quite esoteric, it is probably best to keep such references to a minimum.

(f) **Briefly state why, on the law and facts as you understand them, the claimant should succeed.**

16.4.2 Opening for the defence in a civil trial

It should be quite clear that much of what needs to be done in opening the case for the claimant need not be repeated by the defence. For example, the statements of case only need reading once. However, if the defence is calling evidence at the trial, it may be that an opening speech is desirable, in addition to any skeleton argument that the defence has prepared for the court. Remember that any opening speech for the defence will come after the evidence for the claimant has been presented to the court. Any defence opening should, therefore, concentrate on the matters which it is intended to establish through the evidence to be tendered on behalf of the defence, together with a summary of the case theory for the defence. This last point is important; up to this point in the trial, when defence counsel has cross-examined the claimant's witnesses, that has been done with two things in mind. The first is the statement of case entitled 'defence', which the judge has a copy of, the second is the defence theory of the case, which the judge does not have. A good judge can probably make a reasonably accurate guess as to the defence case theory, based upon the defence itself and the questions asked by defence counsel in cross-examination, but this is not the time to play guessing games with the judge. Use a short opening speech to clarify what your theory of the case is and why the defendant should succeed.

16.4.3 Criminal trials

A distinction must be drawn here between trials in the magistrates' court and trials in the Crown Court.

16.4.3.1 Magistrates' court

The basic rule here is that each side (prosecution and defence) is entitled to make just one speech to the magistrates. In certain circumstances, they may be allowed to make two speeches (in which case this must also be permitted to their opponent) but these situations are rarely encountered. The most typical scenario finds the prosecution advocate making an opening speech and the defence making a closing speech. So, we don't have to worry about a defence opening speech—there won't be one. What about the prosecution?

We have to remember that, although justices of the peace are not professionally qualified for their position, they do adjudicate on many cases every year. The upshot is that they acquire plenty of judicial experience and don't need long lectures on the law (or only rarely). Also, factually they may be familiar with most of the scenarios that are likely to be played out in a summary trial. So what does the prosecutor say in the opening speech? The answer is next to nothing. A typical opening might run thus:

> Sir (or Madam), in this case I appear on behalf of the Crown and my learned friend, Miss Smith, represents the accused. This is a simple case of driving without due care and attention, contrary to the Road Traffic Act. I will now call PC Jones.

You could expand this if you wanted to, perhaps to identify the witnesses and their part in the proceedings, but that will seldom be necessary. This advice—to err on the side of extreme brevity—should be redoubled if you find yourself prosecuting in front of a district judge. They **are** legally qualified as well as hearing perhaps in excess of a hundred summary trials each year; they really have heard it all and, as there is no statement of case to refer the court to (unlike a civil trial) except maybe a quite uninformative charge sheet, you might as well get on with calling the evidence.

16.4.3.2 Crown Court

The prosecution opening speech Here, the prosecution is entitled to open the case to the jury and should always do so in a full and proper way. What follows is intended only as a starting point. You should always assess in each case whether or not the suggested structure is appropriate and, if not, you must alter it to suit the circumstances of that case.

The jury will probably find it helpful if your opening speech starts by setting out, very shortly, the essential facts which are the prosecution case. You might want to refer to the indictment here and, if it is a complicated one (perhaps it contains alternative counts covering the same behaviour), you might want the jury to look at it while you explain the counts to them. You should have ensured there are sufficient copy indictments for all the jurors to have sight of one. In simple cases, the jury will have heard the count(s) read out to the accused and his plea(s), or they will have been told what the counts are by the clerk to the court, so you won't need to spend much time on this part of the speech.

Typically, the prosecutor will then go on to review the facts in more detail. Of course, at this stage there are no facts usually, only allegations. But what you try to do is to set the scene, establish some sort of context in which to place the bald facts of the crime itself. No offence occurs in a vacuum: crimes are committed by humans, acting on human impulses and emotions and with motives that other humans can understand. The jury need to be persuaded of the truth and, while the prosecutor is always there to see that justice is done rather than simply secure a conviction, the truth may become more identifiable if the jury are able to get a good feel for what was going on around the time of the offence. They may need to be given some understanding of the scene where the offence was committed, who was present and the relationship between them, and how the accused committed the offence. Into this (which is essentially a story-telling exercise), you could insert references to particular witnesses who will testify for the prosecution, as a prelude to their testimony. That is sensible and helpful but what you must avoid is overstating your case and in particular, appearing to rely too heavily on specific witnesses to establish particular points for your case. If you are only calling a single witness, then you may want to indicate in quite explicit terms what he or she will say on oath; after all, if they don't then your case will collapse anyway. But, where you are calling several witnesses, be wary of setting expectations too high for them. It is much better to leave yourself some flexibility since you can never be quite sure how the evidence is going to develop during the trial. This is one of the hardest things for a novice advocate to grasp, ie, that a trial is a dynamic, growing process of discovery. Of course, as the advocate you should have a better idea than most of exactly where you are all going and what is likely to happen by the end of the trial but you are mistaken if you believe that advocates are never taken by surprise by what witnesses say and never have to adapt their case to meet the situation as it confronts them. Your ability to respond is compromised if you have been too specific (and optimistic) in opening the case. There is also a risk that too much detail now will result in you losing the jury's attention; after all they are here to listen to the evidence and find the facts.

When you refer to specific evidence in your opening speech, you should always check first that your opponent does not challenge its admissibility. Now, you don't have to do that with every single piece of evidence but some items are almost certainly going to be challenged (eg, police evidence of an alleged confession by the accused). You should always check with defence counsel, preferably before going into court, whether there will be an objection. This may have been dealt with at a pre-trial hearing but you should double-check. If the answer is no, then you can mention the evidence in your speech. If the answer is yes, then you must omit any reference to that evidence from your opening speech. If the issue was not resolved at a pre-trial hearing, the judge will usually have to determine the question of admissibility later, in the absence of the jury, and if you mention the evidence now, that determination will be otiose. It may be that the confession is really all the evidence that you have against the accused; in that situation, you can ask the judge to take the admissibility point as a preliminary issue before your opening speech. If so, the jury will be excluded while the point is argued. If you win the argument, you open your case as intended and refer to the confession; if you lose, you will probably not make an opening speech but offer no evidence and halt the case instead.

On a similar note, it may be that the defence disputes the identity of the offender, saying that while a crime may have been committed, the defendant was not the offender. If identification is a live issue in the trial, then you should not say that the accused was seen at a particular time or place, you may only say that a man (or woman) was seen at that time and place and that your witnesses will say that the man (or woman) was the accused.

It may be that you can anticipate with some confidence what the likely defence case will be. For example, the accused may have offered an innocent explanation during an interview with police, such as self-defence or alibi. The defence statement may have shed more light. Now, the burden of proof for most defences in criminal trials rests with the prosecution. While it is for the defence to raise some evidence to suggest, say, self-defence, if they do so then it is for the prosecution to prove beyond reasonable doubt that the accused did not act in self-defence. In such circumstances, it might be thought sensible to mention any such defences in your opening speech, so that you can knock them down again. In practice, your confident guess as to the nature of the defence case could turn out to be just that—a guess. Most of the time it is not worth spelling out to the jury what you think the defence case is going to be. It is much better to keep your guess to yourself, while planning accordingly.

The advice on the legal content of a prosecutor's opening speech given in previous editions of this manual can be summarised thus:

> State what the elements of the offence(s) are and that the prosecution bears the burden of proof which it can only discharge if the jury is convinced beyond a reasonable doubt of the defendant's guilt.

Further guidance on the subject has now come from the Court of Appeal (Criminal Division). In *R v Lashley* [2005] EWCA Crim 2016, Judge LJ stated that prosecuting counsel did not need to discuss relevant law with the jury when opening the case for the Crown. The crime alleged in *Lashley* was theft and the Court of Appeal agreed with the trial judge that 'everyone knows in general terms what theft is'. Judge LJ went on:

> The presumption should be that an opening address by counsel for the Crown should not address the law, save in cases of real complication and difficulty . . .

This extended to the view that it was by no means in every case that a jury needed reminding of the burden and standard of proof. No further explanation was offered as to why such guidance would not be helpful to a jury.

Defence opening speech The defence is only entitled to make an opening speech if calling witnesses to testify on the facts (and the accused himself doesn't count for this purpose). So, you may not have the right to make an opening speech at all and, even if you do, you may decide that it is sensible not to. It may be better to leave your arguments to the closing speech. As a general rule, perhaps you should not make an opening speech if you are not confident of what your witnesses will say on oath; better to wait and see, then your speech can be based on what the witnesses actually said and so, more importantly, can your theory of the case. Conversely, the longer the time that defence witnesses will spend testifying, the greater the need for some guidance for the jury before the witnesses start their evidence.

If you are going to make an opening speech, you should indicate that you are entitled to do so by informing the judge, 'Your Honour, I shall be calling witnesses of fact in addition to the defendant'. Then proceed to knit together the following five strands:

(a) *Comments on the prosecution evidence* You may want to do this, especially because the prosecution could not. However, this is the sort of job that you will definitely want to do in your closing speech and the jury may wonder why you are just repeating yourself. It is usually best to keep your comments for your closing speech, then you can combine them with observations based on the evidence of the defence witnesses, too.

(b) *Outline the defence evidence* This is quite similar to the job that the prosecutor had. As then, you should be alert to the fact that witnesses sometimes fail to say what we expect them to (and some even say things we never expected them to!). It is best to paint your picture with a broad brush, that way you leave some room to adapt your case as the evidence is given, and you avoid giving too much advance information to your opponent.

(c) *Your theory of the case* Even applying a broad brush, you should still have a good idea of how the defence case is likely to unfurl in court. So you should have a case theory now (of course, you should have had a case theory before setting foot in the courtroom) and you may want to set it before the jury. A combination of the uncontested evidence in the case and your client's version of the matters in issue should enable you to present a theory of the case to the jury. You want to try to make the jury see that the only reasonable inference to be drawn from the evidence is that the defendant is not guilty and your case theory is the better/more appropriate/correct one. However, do this concisely and leaving some room for flexibility later, should the need arise. Of course, no one expects the defence case to collapse, as witnesses fail to deliver their expected testimony, but even if they all 'come up to proof', the jury won't want to hear you simply repeat your opening speech at the end of the trial.

(d) *Weaknesses in your case* It is a very moot point whether you should mention these now. After all, you may be fortunate and the witness you had the least faith in does superbly. But in some instances you know that, even if everything goes well, a certain issue or incident will still be a source of potential danger for your case. Your choice is to say nothing now and try to deal with it when it arises in testimony and in your closing speech, or to raise it now. The latter strategy has a disadvantage in that you alert your opponent to the weakness, but it has the advantage of honesty. In the eyes of the jury, you will be seen as frank and open: the fact that you are prepared to acknowledge the flaws in your case, yet still demonstrate how the defendant is not guilty, may be quite persuasive. Openness now also shows that you are not being taken by surprise when the weakness become manifest during testimony, it shows control and confidence. If you do decide to be frank, never describe a weakness in those terms; simply state the point that is the weakness and try to put it in the best light that you can.

(e) *Burden and standard of proof* You should take this opportunity, if making a speech, to remind the jury shortly that the prosecution brought the case and it is for them to prove it, beyond a reasonable doubt. The defendant does not have to prove his or her innocence, it is enough if they raise a question (or reasonable doubt) in the minds of the jury.

16.5 Dos and don'ts

16.5.1 Things to avoid doing in an opening speech

You should not:

(a) argue—now is not the time to discuss the pros and cons, nor is it the time to persuade—that will come later;

(b) state your personal opinions—either on the facts or the credibility of any witness—frankly, no one cares and it is not your job to waste time on this;

(c) overstate your client's case—the trier(s) of fact may remember what you say now, especially as they may be reminded of it by your opponent. Try to understate;

(d) read your speech from a prepared text—of course, you should have notes but if possible try not to look at them. If you are prepared properly, you should be able to make your speech with very little need to look at your notes; besides, there are other more important places to observe, eg, the jury box or the Bench.

16.5.2 Things you should consider doing in an opening speech

You should:

(a) consider the best way to enable the trier(s) of fact to empathise with your client—a typical example is by using your client's name, rather than his or her title in the proceedings (eg, 'Mr Smith' and not 'claimant', or 'accused');

(b) decide on the best way to minimise any empathy the court may have for the opposing party—for example, you may want to try to depersonalise them by using only a title when referring to them (eg, 'the claimant');

(c) try to look at the trier(s) of fact—eye contact is desirable, although you don't want to stare. If addressing justices of the peace or a jury, try to make individual eye contacts rather than simply staring at a point on the wall above their heads. It is sometimes said that, for a jury trial, it is a good idea to forecast who the chairman of the jury will be and concentrate your efforts on them. I would not recommend that as you may be wrong and the other jurors may feel slighted.

16.6 Telling a story

The opening speech is your first chance to acquaint the court with your theory of the case, and the themes which give depth and colour to the cold, two-dimensional allegations between the parties. First impressions are very important and this will be the time when the court has its first real impression of you. As an advocate, your job is **to persuade** and one of the best ways of doing this is to recreate the moments (or longer) leading up to the matters that gave rise to the litigation and assist the trier(s) of fact to 'see' what happened. Most cases are decided on their facts, not on nice questions of law, and the sooner you knit 'the facts' (that is, the uncontested facts and your client's version of those in dispute) into a single coherent story, the more likely it is to be remembered later. This 'storytelling' element of your speech is the best setting for your case theory to be introduced, but the story is more than just the theory. If your version makes sense as a story, it is likely to be persuasive. (See **Chapter 14**.)

16.7 Checklist for preparation

What should go into the introduction?

What are the main facts of the case? How will they be developed (that is, through the testimony of witnesses, or documentary evidence, or other exhibits)?

What are the issues in the case? Which 'facts' are in dispute? What are the legal principles on which you will rely to establish your client's case?

What are your main themes in the case?

What are your subsidiary themes in the case?

What is your theory of the case?

What weaknesses are there in your version of the case, in your client or in your witnesses?

16.8 Further reading

Bergman, P. *Trial Advocacy in a Nutshell,* West Wadsworth, 3rd edn, 1997.

Du Cann, R. *The Art of the Advocate,* Penguin, 1993, revised, pp 72–91.

Evans, K. *Advocacy in Court,* Blackstone Press (OUP), 2nd edn, 1995.

Hyam, M. *Advocacy Skills,* Blackstone Press (OUP), 4th edn, 1999.

Mauet, T. et al. *Trial Techniques,* Aspen, 2002.

Sonsteng, Haydock and Boyd *The Trial Book, A Total System for Preparation and Presentation of a Case,* West Publishing Co, 1984.

17 Closing speeches

17.1 Introduction

You will almost certainly have seen some great closing speeches without going anywhere near a courtroom. Many writers of stage plays, cinema films and television series have recognised the drama of the situation and the potential that it offers to stir the emotions with pleas for justice and the truth. Often these dramatic works are of American origin and involve jury trials. It cannot be denied that such scenes have tremendous appeal—they are exciting, moving and thrilling. How often is it like that at three o'clock on a hot June day in an airless courtroom in Acton? Not very often is the simple answer.

Although the closing speech does offer certain opportunities for counsel to indulge in an otherwise frustrated theatrical nature, it must be remembered that not every closing speech takes place in front of a jury (the vast majority will not), and that what may work in Hollywood won't be so effective in Cricklewood.

What you, as a barrister, must do is to consider your audience and what you are asking them to do. Closing speeches can be made in criminal trials and civil trials; they can be made to juries or to magistrates, to Crown Court judges or judges in the High Court or County Court; they can be made for the claimant or the prosecution or for the defendant. What you have to do and the ways in which you seek to do it will vary, according to all of these factors. Your manner is also likely to be affected by the topic of the litigation—a closing speech to a judge in a personal injury claim may be quite different from another speech to the same judge when hearing a fraud trial. So, how should you go about making a closing speech?

17.2 The purpose of a closing speech

17.2.1 Persuasion

The purpose, at heart, never varies. You seek to persuade the person or people who have to decide the facts to come down in your favour. You should have put your theory of the case already, shown the court your story and your themes. Now you are trying to knit all these strands together into a coherent whole—to show them the picture as you want them to see it. This may sound like an incitement to distortion or deceit but it is not.

No barrister should ever mislead a court (specifically, whoever is responsible for determining the facts). You must never tell your audience that a witness said A when he or she really said B. You may need to remind the court of the times when a witness said something which made the going tough for your client, in order to explain it away (your opponent may remind the court without the favourable explanation!). But having said that, you are entitled to reinforce your client's story in so far as you have the evidence to back it up.

17.2.2 Unfavourable evidence

So the main purpose of a closing speech is to persuade your audience of the merits of your case, by interweaving your story with the appropriate evidence. Another major purpose has been alluded to—the necessity of dealing with the evidence that undermines your story, that knocks holes in your theory. Usually, this will be the evidence of your opponent's witnesses, perhaps unshaken by cross-examination. Sometimes, it will be evidence from your own witnesses—some damning admission made in cross-examination or an unexpected answer which just slipped out. Whatever its origin, do not ignore it. To do so runs the risk of misleading the court and since your opponent and/or the judge is almost certain to refer to this evidence, you will appear at best careless and at worst dishonest in the eyes of the court. If the court forms this opinion of your veracity, the client will be 'sunk without trace'.

17.2.3 The law

Having dealt with themes, stories and the evidence, what is left? Usually the law. The length of time and the detail that you devote to the legal points raised in the case will obviously depend on the nature of the case. You should not duck making submissions on the law but you should remember a few important points.

First, in a jury trial the judge decides questions of law and will direct the jury accordingly. Anything you say to the jury about the law is subject to whatever the judge says. (If he gets it wrong, the place to correct it is in the appeal court—don't have a slanging match in front of the jury.) Second, in a trial where a professional lawyer is adjudicating, whilst you can make sophisticated legal points in your speech, remember that the audience is human—he or she will eventually cease listening to you; and he or she is legally trained—make your points on law succinct and keep to the point, the court does not want a lecture on the law of nuisance (for example). Third, if you must quote from decided cases or statutes, you should do your utmost to ensure that the court has sufficient copies of the report to follow your remarks. (Curiously, it is not common to do this when addressing a jury, even though they are the audience most likely to be ignorant of the law.)

17.3 The content of a closing speech

17.3.1 Keep it to the point

Keep things short and to the point. It is often unnecessary to reiterate a great deal of evidence from the trial. Take what you need to remind the court of your themes and theory—use the evidence to reinforce the validity of your arguments. Remind the court of those things that you said you would demonstrate in your opening speech (if you made one), then highlight the evidence which (you say) makes your points.

17.3.2 Setting out the theory of the case

If you did not make an opening speech, now is the time to set out your theory of the case, how the evidence knits together to substantiate your assertions. Distil your arguments to a minimum—concentrate the minds of your audience on those few essentials which, if decided favourably to your client, will mean that judgment goes in your favour. Never appear to express your personal opinion of the evidence or of a witness. You should preface any comment on the evidence with an objective phrase such as 'Members of the jury, you may think . . .'.

17.3.3 The law

Deal with the relevant law but not in great detail or at length. When addressing an audience of non-lawyers (lay magistrates, jurors), remember that they may need points explained in quite straightforward terms. Do not labour any points. Always reiterate the appropriate burden and standard of proof. In a criminal trial, the defence barrister, when confronted by apparently watertight prosecution evidence which is directly contradicted by the defence, will remind the jury (or magistrates) that a 'Not Guilty' verdict does not mean that the defendant has proved his or her contentions, simply that they have been left in doubt and must give the defendant the benefit of it.

17.3.4 Order of presentation in your speech

It is normal in a civil trial to deal first with the claimant's case and then with that of the defendant, regardless of whether you are making a closing speech for the claimant or defendant. Similarly, in criminal trials your speech will usually start by reviewing the case for the prosecution and then that for the defendant. So you follow the sequence in which the evidence was presented. This is because, generally, it is the claimant or prosecution who has the legal burden of proof—their case will be lost if the evidence in their favour is not up to the requisite standard. Because the claimant (or prosecution) started the litigation, it is usually they who have defined the issues in the case or 'chosen the battleground' and it is sensible to set out those issues within the context of their 'case'.

17.3.5 Preparation

If possible, do not make a closing speech without a chance to prepare it fully. This is so obvious that you may think it does not need saying. In a trial, it is not always possible to predict precisely when you will be called upon to make your closing speech. Often it will be straight after the last witness has finished his or her testimony and the defence has closed its case. If you have been occupied in examining witnesses, you may not have your closing speech in anything like its ideal state. It now becomes important to see who has 'the last word'.

17.4 Order of speeches

17.4.1 Civil trials

Closing speeches always occur in an established sequence. In a civil trial, the defendant's counsel goes first, followed by the claimant's barrister. So, the barrister appearing for the claimant gets more time to marshal his thoughts and the evidence, and to perfect a plan.

(If there is more than one claimant or defendant, speeches go according to numerical order: 1st defendant, 2nd, 3rd, etc.)

17.4.2 Criminal trials

In a criminal trial, the basic principle is that the defence closing speech goes last. After that, you must distinguish between trials with magistrates and with a jury.

17.4.2.1 Magistrates

Where magistrates are to decide guilt or innocence, the rule is that, normally, each side may make a single speech in the case. This usually works out so that the prosecution makes a short opening speech before any evidence is heard, then the defence makes a closing speech after all of the evidence is completed. If either barrister wishes to make a second speech (ie, to close as well as to open the case), this can be done but only with the court's permission and your opponent must be given the same opportunity, where it is still possible.

17.4.2.2 Trial by jury

If you are in a trial by jury, then usually both the prosecution and defence can make a closing speech, regardless of whether an opening speech was made. The prosecution barrister may forgo a closing speech if he or she made an opening speech and either there was no defence evidence or the only witness was the accused—counsel may feel that there is nothing to add to the opening. A defence barrister should never surrender the chance to make a closing speech. Often, the defence do not make an opening speech (either through choice or the rules) but, even if the defendant's case was opened with a speech, the chance to have the last word to the jury is generally seen as a vital asset.

17.4.2.3 More than one defendant

If there is more than one defendant in a criminal trial and each is represented separately, the closing speeches for them will take place in the order in which they are named on the indictment. The defendants have no say in determining this order: sometimes the least important defendant is last, sometimes the most important. Whoever's name appears last gets the plum position for their closing speech. (Note that in this situation, the prosecution makes a single speech, dealing with all the defendants.)

17.4.2.4 Value of the final speech

When making the final speech that the jury hear (subject to the judge's summing-up) before they consider the verdict, one can deal cogently with all the issues in the case, whether raised by the prosecution or any co-defendant. Those barristers who preceded your speech could only guess what you were going to say and how you would say it; you have the advantage of knowing what they said.

17.5 Planning your speech

It should be clear that you need to think about the content and structure of your closing speech (if one is to be made) before the trial starts. It can only be a rough plan but you should have it ready for the beginning of the trial. As the trial progresses and witnesses substantiate (or undermine) the points you want to make, keep a record of what they said (highlight it in your notes or put an asterisk by it) so that it can be found easily. Try to refine and fill in the detail of your plan after each witness, or during adjournments. Such 'free' time is often limited in a trial, especially those lasting a day or less, so make the most of every chance you get to polish your speech. Even if you do so, you will inevitably have to carry a lot of material in your head.

This is no bad thing. You should be able to recall the really important pieces of evidence quite clearly. It will help you to do this if you have chosen a few key words or phrases (or even mental pictures) taken from your theory of the case and its themes. This will help you when making the speech to get your message over—as key words stick in your mind, so they will with the jury, judge, etc. The fewer points you ask your audience to think about, the more likely they are to do so and with reasonable recollection of the relevant evidence.

17.6 Delivering your speech

'May it please you, Your Honour/Sir/Madam/members of the jury . . .'. This is the traditional, courteous way to start a closing speech. Some judges deprecate use of the phrase 'may it please you'. After that, the manner in which you present your speech is really a question of individual style. You will develop your own style with time but it is a good idea to watch more experienced barristers when you go into court during your pupillage. You may see good and bad examples of a closing speech—be discriminating. Think about the sequence of events used in the speech, about the tone used by the barrister and the pace of delivery. Then consider how effective it was.

Just as you watched the judge's pen while examining a witness, so you must observe your audience during your speech. Make sure that you don't go so fast that they lose track of your arguments; but don't go so slowly that their eyes start to glaze over! Remember to look the jurors (or whoever is deciding the facts) in the eye but don't stare at individuals. Don't look wildly around the room—you are talking to a specific group of people and it is legitimate to concentrate on them. The best advocates will establish such a rapport with their audience that, for both sides, there is no one else in the courtroom.

Some barristers like to use hand gestures, others don't. You will probably do whatever is natural to you; but remember, you want your listener(s) to recall your arguments and evidence, not the fact that you looked like a Punch and Judy man without the puppet! So if you are going to use gestures, do so sparingly and to emphasise your points. Judges generally prefer the more detached approach, with points made calmly and rationally, without appeal to the emotions. You will almost certainly 'lose' a judge if you indulge in too many gestures or any 'purple' prose. Remember that Horace Rumpole is a creature (of fiction and) of the Old Bailey—he works with juries, not in the Chancery Division of the High Court.

17.7 Further reading

Du Cann, R. *The Art of the Advocate,* Penguin, 1993, pp 189–218.

Evans, K. *Advocacy in Court,* Blackstone Press (OUP), 2nd edn, 1995, pp 66–7, 80–7.

Murphy, P. and Barnard, D. *Evidence and Advocacy,* Blackstone Press (OUP), 5th edn, 1998, pp 210–11, 226–7.
See also Stone, M. *Cross-examination in Criminal Trials,* Tottel Publishing, 2009.

17.8 Checklist for a closing speech

(a) Prepare a plan before the trial. (Once you know where you want to be at the end of the case, it will help you to concentrate on how you are going to get there.)

(b) Use key words or phrases to encapsulate the important points of your case. (Both you and your audience are more likely to remember a few simple phrases.)

(c) Remind the court (especially non-lawyers) of the appropriate burden and standard of proof on the contentious issues in the case.

(d) Make any concessions that seem appropriate in the light of the evidence given in the case. (It helps to focus attention on the real issues and may make you seem quite a reasonable person.)

(e) Using your key words, review the important points in a sensible order. Refer to the evidence which supports or undermines your case.

(f) If there is evidence which damages your case, deal with it. You might be able to offer an explanation for it which is consistent with your case; you might suggest that the witness is mistaken or lying; you might argue that, even if the evidence is accepted by the court, it does not prove what your opponent says it does.

(g) Watch your audience. Try to keep their attention. Think about how they might see the evidence and arguments, then try to present your speech in a manner that makes your points comprehensible to them.

(h) Decide before you begin what your closing words will be. If need be, write them down. Nothing reduces the impact of a speech more than the sight and hearing of an advocate who runs down at the end of a speech simply because he does not know how to end it. It saps the life out of everything that precedes it. It gives an unmistakable appearance of a lack of confidence in the advocate in the case he is presenting. It is easily avoided.

(i) Don't go on for too long.

17.9 Epilogue

'My poor client's fate now depends on your votes.'
Here the speaker sat down in his place,
And directed the judge to refer to his notes
And briefly to sum up the case.
But the judge said he never had summed up before;
So the Snark undertook it instead,
And summed it so well that it came to far more
Than the witnesses ever had said!

(From 'The Barrister's Dream' in Lewis Carroll's *The Hunting of the Snark.*)

Note: the Snark should not be used as a role model!

Part V

Witnesses

18

The task ahead

The following five chapters (**Chapters 19** to **23**) look at how advocates deal with witnesses. The chapters concentrate on the practical issues of technique and objectives. Please read them all carefully and use case studies as the raw material to practise them on (see, for example, *R v Heath* in the **Appendix** to this manual). Try working with your friends and colleagues, taking turns to play the role of the witness.

At The City Law School, we have devised a set of advocacy training criteria by which we can measure the competence of an individual advocate when questioning a witness. These criteria are set out in full in **Chapter 19.** You will get a better understanding of the following chapters if you read **Chapter 19** first. Whenever you practise questioning a witness, try to apply those criteria to your work and consider the results. Equally valuable will be the comments of your friends and colleagues if they can base their feedback to you on those criteria. Of course, you can also apply them to any example of questioning a witness that you see, for example while visiting a court or watching a training video. The best advocates reflect upon their work frequently and think about ways in which they might improve.

One of the criteria that you should pay particular attention to is that which deals with questioning technique. For an advocate to abide by professional rules and the rules of evidence, the questions that he or she asks should appear in an appropriate form. An example of this is that, when you question your own witness, you should not 'lead' them. This means that the witness should be enabled to tell their own story in their own words. **Chapters 20** and **21** explain more about that and other questioning techniques which are appropriate for examination-in-chief. Conversely, when you question an opponent's witness, you should aim to exert considerable control over the witness. In cross-examination, you should not give the witness an opportunity to repeat the damage they have just inflicted on your case when they were questioned by their advocate; nor should your questions allow the witness to elaborate or give more details in ways that simply strengthen the case against your client. Competent cross-examination demands that you put your case to the witness, in an affirmative fashion, and that you exert control over the witness by asking plenty of closed, 'leading', questions. These questions should restrict the witness's freedom by severely limiting the range of answers that he or she can possibly give. **Chapter 22** tells you more about the techniques of cross-examination, and its aims and objectives. **Chapter 23** looks at the important, and often overlooked, skill of re-examination. This aspect of questioning is becoming even more important in civil cases as the opportunities to examine-in-chief are restricted. Re-examination often becomes the only significant chance which the advocate gets to question their witnesses at all, in court. We mentioned earlier the need for any advocate to abide by professional rules when questioning witnesses. This includes the need to comply with relevant rules of professional conduct, of course. It also includes the need to behave properly and sensitively towards witnesses. **Chapter 3** drew your attention to these important matters, since to proceed in ignorance of them may affect not just your own professional obligations but also your client's prospects of success in the instant case. If necessary, reread **Chapter 3** before continuing.

19

Basic components for witness handling

19.1 Introduction

You have already encountered some of our basic components in this manual. In **Chapter 4**, we introduced the criteria which can be used to gauge the effectiveness of advocacy in the context of applications and submissions. These were then considered in more detail in the rest of **Part 2**. It is now time to introduce the criteria which we use at The City Law School when advocacy involves questioning a witness. For our purposes, this consists of two contexts—examination-in-chief and cross-examination. Although there is a third context for questioning—re-examination—this does not really raise any different skills or techniques (see further **Chapter 23** on the topic of re-examination).

The next point to bear in mind is that we are not starting from scratch. Many aspects of the criteria that were relevant to advocacy in applications and submissions are just as relevant now, when questioning witnesses. There is still the need for thorough preparation, for a clear and logical structure and for the advocate to communicate clearly in the courtroom. However, examination-in-chief and cross-examination both introduce new criteria which are of great importance if witnesses are to be questioned properly and effectively. Let's start by setting out the criteria.

19.2 Advocacy training criteria for examination-in-chief

In order to question your witness satisfactorily, you must show your ability in these areas:

(1) **Law and analysis**

- (a) **Prepare** the case effectively, understanding:
  - (i) the case that has to be proved;
  - (ii) the issues in the trial;
  - (iii) the issues on which this witness can give evidence;
  - (iv) the rules of evidence and procedure;
  - (v) the principles of examination-in-chief.
- (b) **Questioning content:** ask questions which:
  - (i) seek to elicit only admissible evidence;
  - (ii) seek to elicit only relevant evidence whether to an issue or to credit;

(iii) enable the witness to establish all of the evidence he or she can give (including the production of exhibits).

(2) **Structure** the questions in a way which:

(i) is clear and logical to the witness and the tribunal;

(ii) is responsive to the witness's answers;

(iii) takes into account the relevance of this witness to the case as a whole and the client's interests.

(3) **Delivery**—speak clearly and fluently, at an appropriate pace, using appropriate language and manner, referring to notes when necessary or desirable.

(4) **Questioning technique**—control the witness and elicit evidence using appropriate questioning techniques which:

(i) enable the witness to give his or her evidence in as coherent and persuasive a way as possible;

(ii) respond as appropriate to the witness's answers.

Remember that the rules of professional conduct should always be observed.

19.3 Advocacy training criteria for cross-examination

In order to question an opponent's witness satisfactorily you must show your ability in the following areas:

(1) **Law and analysis**

(a) **Prepare** the case effectively, understanding:

(i) the case that has to be proved;

(ii) the issues in the trial;

(iii) the issues on which this witness can give evidence, in particular those on which this witness is helpful, damaging or neutral to your client's case;

(iv) the rules of evidence and procedure;

(v) the principles of cross-examination.

(b) **Questioning content:** ask questions which:

(i) seek only admissible evidence;

(ii) seek only relevant evidence (whether to an issue or to credit);

(iii) cover all relevant evidence of the witness including that relating to exhibits;

(iv) enable the witness to assist your client's case insofar as he or she is able to do so;

(v) in so far as it is necessary to do so:

- put your client's case to the witness;
- undermine the testimony of the witness;
- undermine the credibility of the witness;

(vi) make appropriate use of contradictory material.

(2) **Structure** the questions in a way which:

(i) is clear and logical to the tribunal;

(ii) is responsive to the witness's answers;

(iii) takes into account the relevance of this witness to the case as a whole and your client's interests.

(3) **Delivery**—speak clearly and fluently, at an appropriate pace, using appropriate language and manner, referring to notes when necessary or desirable.

(4) **Questioning technique**—control the witness and elicit evidence using appropriate questioning techniques which:

(i) confine the witness's testimony appropriately to the evidence you seek to adduce;

(ii) respond as appropriate to the witness's answers.

Remember that the rules of professional conduct should always be observed.

19.4 Planning to work with witnesses

In this section, we examine the matters that the advocate should consider before going into court for a trial, or other hearing which involves calling witnesses.

19.4.1 Thinking about the evidence

As with any appearance in court, you must identify several matters:

- What are the appropriate legal tests that will be applied?
- What are the facts in issue in the case? (In a civil case these should be clear from the statements of case; in a criminal case, a plea of not guilty requires proof of all the elements of the offence and one should then consider the possible/probable defence case as disclosed by the defence statement.)
- What evidence do you intend to adduce to ensure each issue is resolved in favour of your client?
- How do you intend to adduce that evidence?

This final point lies at the nub of how we start to prepare for calling witnesses. Will the evidence be in the form of answers given by a witness to questions asked by the advocate? Will the evidence emerge from a document, such as an affidavit, or from examination of an exhibit, such as a sketch plan or the alleged weapon, stolen property, etc? If so, who will produce the exhibit in court? Might the admissibility of the evidence be challenged?

What you need to do is to plan how the evidence needed to prove each material issue can be put before the court. Look at your papers critically to determine each place where a material fact can be proved with the use of a witness and/or an exhibit. You can set out your conclusions in tabular form, using a column to identify each fact in issue, then another to show that there is evidence to prove that fact (maybe just a tick would do), then a third to identify the source(s) of that evidence. There could be more than one source—for example, several eyewitnesses to an accident who can each speak about what they saw happen. If one source is open to challenge—for example, a confession in a criminal trial might be excluded—that point should be recorded and alternative sources to supply the same evidence should be shown. That way, you can identify in advance all the possible ways to prove your case (or attack the opponent's case), consider the arguments for and against issues of admissibility, and think about your best response if your preferred source of evidence on an issue fails to do the job that you wanted.

In the courtroom, when questioning witnesses, try to be as flexible and responsive as you can be. We have just considered one way to do this—by plotting different routes by which you can reach the same conclusion. Another way to resist inflexibility is to avoid using a detailed list of questions. By all means, have a concise note of those facts that you want the witness to tell the court about, and an idea of how you want to present this witness to the court (if it is your witness, they should appear to be reliable, truthful and accurate).

You should have a structure when working with witnesses. You need to think about the order for calling the witnesses, if you have more than one, and you always have to think about the structure of each witness's testimony.

19.4.2 Preparing the evidence in your case

There are some conventions that are used in deciding the order in which several witnesses may be called into court to give their evidence. In criminal cases, it is usual to call the victim first. In cases of violence, they will usually establish that the assault took place, what injuries were suffered and perhaps identify the assailant. In cases of dishonesty, where property has been taken, the victim can assert that they did not give permission for their property to be dealt with in that fashion. In cases involving illicit drugs, the prosecution will need to prove the nature of the substance, requiring expert evidence of the testing of a sample recovered from the accused. They will also need to prove that the sample of substance tested by the expert was the one taken from the accused—this requires the prosecution to show a chain of possession, with the substance being taken into lawful custody, put into a sealed container, labelled and initialled and then transported through various pairs of hands until it reached the expert. The prosecution should be ready to call every person who provides a link in this chain, if it becomes necessary to do so.

The order of witnesses for the defence in a criminal trial is not wholly a matter of choice for the advocate and the client. The Police and Criminal Evidence Act 1984, s 79, prescribes that if the defendant is to testify at trial, they must be the first witness to be called for the defence. This is subject to the court's discretion to allow another defence witness to be called into the witness box before the accused testifies; the discretion is only likely to be used where the other witness will talk about non-contentious facts and there is some good reason for taking their evidence out of the usual order. Generally, witnesses in criminal cases are kept out of court until the time comes for them to testify. The objective that lies behind s 79 is that, as this rule cannot be applied to the accused, there is a risk that the accused may modify his or her testimony to 'fit' what evidence has already been given. This risk (which arises because the accused can see and hear all of the testimony in the case, up until he or she testifies) can be kept to a minimum if he or she is the first defence witness. Defence witnesses who will talk only about the character of the accused should always be called after the accused has testified.

Within these limitations, the advocate must still consider the best running order for the presentation of the evidence which he or she will rely upon. One excellent rule of thumb is to put yourself into the position of the trier(s) of fact—what would best enable the tribunal of fact to understand your client's case? Will the court be able to see how each witness contributes to your case? Will the significance of their testimony be clear? How do you want the story to unfold? These are all important questions but perhaps the most practical one is—who is available? Witnesses sometimes fail to turn up at court when they should. This may be due to nerves, illness or even forgetfulness. Unless you are granted an adjournment by the court to secure the witness's attendance, you will have to do the best you can with what you have. That is one reason why you should have identified already the various alternative sources of evidence which you could use to establish each contentious issue in the case. Now you are able to stay calm and use your flexibility to your advantage—your advance planning is already paying dividends!

19.4.3 Planning the testimony of individual witnesses

Having determined the (probable) sequence for calling the witnesses, we must now look at each witness individually. The order in which you explore topics with a witness will depend in large measure upon whether they are called to support your client's case or that of the opponent.

19.4.3.1 Planning for examination-in-chief

For examination-in-chief of 'your' witness, you will be concerned to see that:

(a) the witness is encouraged to recall the events;

(b) he or she can express their recollection clearly;

(c) the witness can talk about matters in the required degree of detail; and

(d) the court can follow and recall the evidence easily.

You can usually achieve these aims by helping the witness to go through the material events in a chronological order. After all, that is the sequence in which the events occurred so it should seem quite natural to the witness and the court to talk about them in that order. It may be that you do not get the necessary amount of detail about a particular matter from the witness when they talk about it for the first time. That can happen because you must not 'lead' your witness but use open questions which prompt them to tell the story in their own words. This will mean that, from time to time, you will need to interrupt their narrative in order to go back and cover a topic in more detail. For example, 'You have told the court that you arrived at the bus stop at about 10.30 am. Can you recall what the weather was like then?' and then, 'After you arrived there, how many people were at the bus stop?' If the witness is the first to be called for your client, you may want to get their story out quite swiftly, so that the court can see what happened, in broad terms. Having established the backdrop, as it were, you can then backtrack and enable the witness to fill in more of the detail.

Sometimes, you will decide that the court will have a better understanding of events (or perhaps be more sympathetic to your client) if they learn first what happened to bring the parties to court at all, and then find out what events led up to that conclusion. Having settled the witness with the usual questions, such as, 'Please tell the court your full name' or 'What do you do for a living?', you might then ask the witness, 'Do you know why you are in court today?' When the witness replies affirmatively, you can then ask, 'Please tell the court what happened'. The witness is likely to start talking about the conclusion of a sequence of events, for example, 'My car was stolen' or 'I was hit over the head and had to go to hospital' or 'This man came up to me in the club and said I'd been talking to his girl'. You can then concentrate on those events with the witness, before turning to more preliminary matters.

Finally, we should also consider the use made of witness statements in civil cases. In both civil and criminal cases, witnesses usually provide statements to the parties calling them, in advance of the hearing. Generally, these statements will be exchanged between the parties before the trial, so that there are no surprises at the hearing itself (one significant exception to this is with defence witnesses in a criminal trial). In criminal cases, such statements will usually be disclosed only to the parties and their lawyers, and the judge in Crown Court trials; the witness's evidence at trial will be what they say in the witness box rather than what they said in the previous statement. In civil cases, the witness's previous statement will often be ordered to serve as their evidence-in-chief (see eg, Civil Procedure Rules, r 32.5). This has consequences for any examination-in-chief by the advocate.

The start of the (civil) examination-in-chief will look something like this:

Having asked the witness to identify themselves, the advocate will have the court usher show the witness 'a document'.

Advocate:	'Do you see a signature on the document?'
Witness:	'Yes.'
Advocate:	'Whose signature is it?'
Witness:	'Mine.'
Advocate:	'When did you make that statement?'
Witness:	[replies]
Advocate:	'Were its contents true when you made it?'
Witness:	'Yes.'

At this point you (as the advocate) may sit down, leaving your witness to be cross-examined. However, you may wish to ask the witness to augment the evidence that is in their statement. You will need to ask the judge for leave to do so. The judge may refuse and suggest that you can pick up any points during your re-examination of the witness, after cross-examination. If you are given permission, then you may build on the witness's earlier statement. For example, 'Mr Smith, in paragraph 3 of your statement, you say that, "Because the weather was so hot, I took the safety guard off the machine that I was operating." What did you do with the safety guard?'

Because, in effect, you are combining the written statement with the oral testimony, you can be more selective with the topics that you ask the witness to deal with in the witness box. Concentrate on those topics which are central to your case, and which will help the court to form a view of the witness's reliability and recollection. It is probably helpful to work through those topics in the order in which they appear in the written statement. As you will often use the statement as the 'springboard' for a question, the witness should understand clearly what you want them to talk about. Another reason to question your witness in court is where their statement is now out of date. Here, strictly speaking, you do not need to get leave from the court before asking questions but you should tell the judge what you are proposing to do. The judge may be concerned that a second, up-to-date statement should have been taken from the witness and served on your opponent before the trial. Since your aim now is to bring out new information, rather than looking at known events in greater detail, you should probably follow a chronological sequence, as we saw earlier.

19.4.3.2 Preparing for cross-examination

Your aims are rather different when you question the witnesses that have been called by your opponent. For one thing, you do not expect that they will support your client's case (although they may do in some topics). It is usual for a cross-examiner to want to undermine either the testimony of the witness (or the credibility of the witness) or to show its irrelevance to the issues in the trial. Further, as the witness's recollection of events is likely to be significantly different from the one that you seek to establish, you want to make their recollection more obscure than clear. You are also under a duty to question the witness on issues where your client's case differs from their recollection (known as 'putting your case to the witness'). In cross-examination, you are allowed to ask questions which suggest things, or put propositions, to the witness. So, you might say, 'But the man in the green jacket never had a knife in his hand, did he?' or 'You never saw his hand.' or 'The man in the green jacket had left by then.' In other words, you have a different story to tell and you do not want to give the witness a second chance to repeat their evidence-in-chief.

In cross-examination, then, your order of topics should be clear to the **court.** You want the tribunal of fact to understand why you are asking the questions that you use: you want the court to appreciate the discrepancies between the competing versions of events. But you do not always want the **witness** to see where you are going or what you are trying to do. The order of topics needs careful consideration, as does the order of questions on a particular topic.

You may wish to try to bait a trap for the witness, rather than immediately confront them with the proposition that you would like them to accept. So, for example, you may want to cast doubt on a witness's earlier testimony that when they saw the man in the green jacket, he was holding a knife in his hand. If you simply say to the witness, 'The man in the green jacket never had a knife in his hand, did he?', the likely answer you will get is, 'He did'; blatant confrontation seldom produces agreement. If you begin by exploring the circumstances in which the observation took place, you may find either that the witness accepts that your proposition is reasonable or the court may well decide it is reasonable and not accept the witness's testimony on the matter. So, you might suggest (if to do so is consistent with your instructions) that the venue was dark, or busy, or the witness's attention was distracted, or something of that sort which might lead onto the witness acknowledging at least the possibility that they might be mistaken, in all the circumstances.

19.5 Asking questions—the purposes of questioning witnesses

This is the equivalent of 'content', the second criterion for applications to the court. However, it is a more complex topic in relation to witnesses than it is for applications. You might want to turn to **19.2.2** and **19.2.3** and reread the advocacy training criteria on examination-in-chief and cross-examination with specific reference to item (1) (b) in both lists.

19.5.1 Your witness

What you ask a witness will be governed by several considerations. First, you must not ask your witness leading questions on matters in dispute (see **Chapter 21**). If you do, then although the subject matter of the question may be 'relevant' and based on a sound understanding of the law and allegations, it may not be 'appropriate'. Thus, you should use appropriate questioning techniques.

In any hearing where witnesses are called to testify, you should have identified what evidence they can give which will help to establish your client's case. This will decide the relevance of your questions and their answers. If you don't ask questions to make the optimum use of the witness and get all of the relevant evidence that they could give, you probably have not conducted an examination-in-chief which is wholly appropriate to the circumstances of that case. Further, you should not ask a question which requires the witness to speak about inadmissible matters; such questions may be logically relevant but are not legally relevant (see for example *R v Blastland* [1986] AC 41). Finally, you should try to insulate your witness from attack by your opponent in cross-examination. That may mean getting the witness to talk about topics relevant to your opponent's case as well as your client's case. Such topics may not be of direct legal relevance to your client's case but it could certainly be appropriate to canvass them at this point.

19.5.2 Your opponent's witness

As before, what is required here will be fact-specific to the individual case, as determined by the issues between the parties and what evidence the witness can give. You should use appropriate questioning techniques here, too, but what is appropriate has changed (see **Chapter 22**). In general terms, examination-in-chief is about **trust**, the advocate allowing the witness the freedom to tell their story in their own words, but cross-examination is about **control.** The cross-examiner doesn't want the witness to tell their story in their own words; instead, the cross-examiner asks leading questions designed to convey the story of the cross-examiner's client in words chosen by the cross-examiner. In one sense, it does not matter what answers most witnesses give in cross-examination because the cross-examiner never expected the witness to agree with the proposition in the question anyway. One of the functions of cross-examination is to put your client's case to the witness (see **Chapter 22**) and such 'questions' are unlikely to produce much agreement between the advocate and the witness. The degree of control exerted on witnesses in cross-examination can often be seen if you keep a note of the questions and answers; typically, the questions contain the detail while the answers are just 'Yes' or 'No'. Questions asked during examination-in-chief are generally not so detailed but can produce quite lengthy and complex responses from the witness.

Other aims of cross-examination, which make certain questions appropriate, are the need to use the witness to assist your client's case and the possibility of undermining the witness and/or their evidence. On the former point, it is not always the position that a witness called by the opposing party will be 100% damaging to your client's case, more often than not the witness may be a source of assistance on at least some topics. If you can see a way in which your opponent's witness could supply answers which help your client, it is appropriate to ask the questions which produce those answers; evidence given by opposing witnesses which supports your case always seems to be more persuasive. On the latter point, undermining, you might ask questions which attack the credibility of the witness themselves (for example, to show they are biased) or of their version of events (for example, comparing it with other evidence given in the cases which is inconsistent with their version).

19.6 The structure of questions to a witness

19.6.1 Your witness

During examination-in-chief, you should be using each witness to tell the court what they know of the story of the case. In each trial there are one or more issues which the parties dispute and which the court must resolve; sometimes these are disputes of law but much more often they are disputes of fact. You should structure your sequence of questions to a witness with a primary objective of getting the witness to speak clearly and logically about the 'facts'. Your questions should assist the witness to achieve a good communication with the trier(s) of fact. That means that you go through topics in a sensible order, that the witness is enabled to give all of the evidence that they could give (and which is useful to your client's case) and they do so by telling their story in their own words, as much as possible. Studies of witness credibility have shown that juries are likely to find a witness much more credible (and persuasive) if they demonstrate a good understanding of what they are testifying about and appear confident in what they are saying. It also helps, apparently, if the advocate does not interrupt very often.

What you need to do to start the examination-in-chief is to settle the witness. They need to get used to their surroundings, to being the focus of attention, and to the sound of their own voice projected across the courtroom. So you start them with easy, short questions to which they know the answers and which allow them to talk a little. For example, in a case where the witness's job or workplace is relevant:

- Please tell the court your name?
- What is your occupation?
- Where do you work?
- How long have you worked there?

Such questions pose no major test for a witness and so they help to take the pressure off. Once the witness has relaxed, you can move onto the substance of their evidence. What sequence might you adopt there?

You will usually find that, as the witness is telling a story, they will recollect it best (and the trier(s) of fact will remember it better) if you enable the witness to work through their story in a chronological order. As this is your witness, you should not ask leading questions, even if you wanted to (see **Chapter 21**). Open questions which allow the witness some freedom to tell their story are the ones that should be in the majority at the beginning of the examination-in-chief. Obviously, the lack of direct control that you have when using open-type questions means that sometimes the witness says something ambiguous or obscure and further explanation is required. Then you have a choice; either you interrupt the 'flow' of the witness's narrative, as in:

> Stop there, please, Sergeant. You just said that Mr Jones was drunk. What led you to that conclusion?

and immediately seek further clarification from the witness. Or you can let the witness continue to answer open questions until they have concluded their narrative, and then return to topics raised by the witness earlier, getting the detail through more specific questions. The former tactic is acceptable (it is sometimes called the 'funnel' technique; and see **20.8**) but you must be careful not to go into so much detail now, through overuse of closed questions, that the court cannot see the wood for all the trees.

As well as using your witnesses to establish your client's case, you may also want to use them to cast doubt on your opponent's case and you may want to protect your witness from a damaging attack in cross-examination. Both objectives are likely to result in you asking questions which are not an obvious part of your client's theory of the case. In order to minimise any confusion that may arise in these circumstances, it is usually better to leave these topics to later in the witness's evidence, after they have done their best to establish the evidence favourable to your client.

The other consideration is that you should be responsive to a witness's answers. You cannot simply plough on, appearing to others to pay no regard to the answers the witness is giving. The sequence of questions and answers should flow in a clear and logical fashion. When breaks occur, and there is a change of subject, that should be clear from the first question on the new topic, as in, 'I want to turn now to the moment when the ambulance arrived. What did . . .?'.

So you see that, when thinking about the sequence of your questions for examination-in-chief, you should have a clear idea of the basic running order of topics through which to take the witness. The sequence in which specific questions are asked may be better left until you are actually on your feet questioning the witness, otherwise you risk being too tied to a plan and not responding appropriately to the witness's answers.

19.6.2 Your opponent's witness

When cross-examining a witness, your aims are a little different. Now you are likely to be less concerned with assisting the witness and allowing them to tell their story. In fact, you probably don't want them to tell their story (again). You won't be able to finalise your running order for the topics you need to cross-examine on until the moment that your opponent concludes the examination-in-chief. That doesn't give you a lot of time! Obviously you need a list of all the topics you might need to question the witness about, and you should think about a sensible order in which to raise those topics. But suppose the witness never gave an anticipated and crucial piece of evidence? A large part of your intended cross-examination may just have become redundant. You must be able to respond to the evidence actually given by the witness in-chief. If they haven't hurt your case, don't cross-examine them, leave them well alone.

You need to analyse each opposing witness to see on each issue in the case:

(a) do they have evidence relevant to this issue;

(b) if so, does it hurt my client's case; or

(c) does it help my client's case; or

(d) is the witness effectively neutral?

Once you have done that, you will have an overall picture of the witness as potentially harmful, helpful, neutral or a mixture of these depending on the particular topic. In turn, that will help you to decide on your likely running order for the topics. If you think the witness can help you on a particular topic, it might be best to deal with that at or near the start of your cross-examination, especially if you think you may have to attack them on other topics. They may be less willing to agree with your questions towards the end of your cross-examination if you have given them a tough time earlier on.

Finally, as with the examination-in-chief, listen to the witness's answers and respond to them. Your response will probably be different since the answer may be a damaging one, but you should constantly be reassessing what questions you need to ask this witness. One difference between the sequence of questions in examination-in-chief and in cross-examination is this: in examination-in-chief, you want to help the witness and so you raise topics in a clear and logical order (typically chronological). In cross-examination, you want your questions to be structured in a way that makes them clear and logical to the trier(s) of fact but maybe not so clear to the witness—at least until it is too late for them to do anything about it! The key here may be to have a gentle and patient build-up, through a series of relatively innocuous questions, until you have painted the witness into a corner. Then you ask the key question (probably putting some part of your client's case to the witness), saying something like, '. . . That must be right, mustn't it, Miss Smith?'. If you have built up the previous questions and answers sensibly and patiently, the court is likely to agree with your proposition even if the witness does not.

19.7 Speaking and delivery

You should refer to **Chapter 8** which dealt extensively with the subject of communication and that has not altered in this context. However, you will need to bear in mind that, as well as having to communicate with one or two sets of listeners in the courtroom—judge, magistrates, jury—there is now an additional recipient of your communications—the witness in the witness box. When you question a witness, he or she must hear and be able to understand your question. Equally, the judge and any other fact-finders must be able to hear your question, usually in order to make sense of the answer from the witness. This places an added burden on you to speak clearly and at the appropriate pace and volume. You must also assist the witness to communicate clearly with the judge or magistrates and jury (if there is one). For example, remind your witness that his or her answers should be directed towards the judge (or magistrates or jury) and not towards you. Tell them to speak at a comfortable pace and suggest perhaps that they watch the judge as he or she takes a note of their evidence, to ensure the pace is comfortable for the court, too. You will still need to monitor the pace of the witness's answers—don't leave it up to the witness to judge! You will also need to consider the pace of the exchanges between yourself and the witness. Is it too fast/too slow? If you are asking a lot of closed questions, say in cross-examination, and the witness is just responding with yes or no, the exchanges can get quite fast. In that situation, you may need to build in an occasional pause.

19.8 Controlling the witness and using appropriate questioning techniques

Control is essential whether dealing with your own witness or one called by an opponent. A witness is not in the witness box to say just what they want, how they want. They are there for a purpose. The party calling the witness wants to use them as a source of credible and helpful evidence which is relevant to the facts in issue. The party who has not called the witness often wants to limit the damage done to their case by this witness. The cross-examiner may want to exert quite overt control over the witness, typically by the use of leading, closed, questions. The examiner-in-chief will exert control more subtly, usually, through selection of topics, interventions when a witness strays into inadmissible or irrelevant evidence, and courteously stopping an answer when too much information is being given for the court to absorb. **Chapters 21** and **22** contain very helpful guidance on the aims and techniques of examination-in-chief and cross-examination, which are unnecessary to duplicate here. In summary, though, examination-in-chief avoids the use of leading questions, whilst these are quite acceptable in cross-examination. Open questions, which allow the witness to give relevant evidence in their own words, are the main staple for examination-in-chief.

20 Basic questioning skills

20.1 Introduction

This chapter provides a brief introduction to the different types of questioning techniques that you will need to grasp and be able to apply when conducting the examination of witnesses.

20.2 The open-ended question

This is a question that does not limit the scope of the answer. The witness will usually give a narrative answer.

Examples

Q: 'What happened after he struck you?'
Q: 'Why did you telephone her?'
Q: 'Where did you go after you left the police station?'
Q: 'How did you cope at work with one arm in plaster?'

This type of question is particularly useful when you want the witness to tell the story or part of it in his or her own words. It helps to move the story along. It can, however, allow the witness too much scope for 'rambling' off the point and overuse of open questions risks a loss of control.

20.3 The closed question

This is a question which limits the scope of the answer. It is particularly useful when you are seeking to elicit a particular piece of information or detail from a witness. It allows much greater control of the witness than an open question.

Examples

Q: 'What time was it?'
Q: 'How far away were you at that point?'
Q: 'In which hand was he holding the gun?'

20.4 The transition

Transitions are a means of moving the witness from one piece of evidence or topic to another. They communicate a change of topic or place to the witness and also to the court. They may take the form of a statement such as 'I want to turn now to the moment when the ambulance arrived', or a question (either open or closed) such as 'After that day, when did you next see the defendant?' Transitions are a useful way of structuring the testimony, controlling the witness and moving from irrelevant to relevant information.

Suppose, for example, you wish to elicit two pieces of evidence from the witness:

(a) that she was present in the doctor's surgery on the day in question; and

(b) approximately 20 minutes after her arrival, she heard the defendant threaten the doctor.

After establishing the witness's presence in the waiting room at the doctor's surgery, you might ask:

Q: 'What, if anything, happened then?'

A: 'Well, I picked up a magazine from the table, you know one of those fancy ones, I think it was *Country Life*. As I was reading it, they have such beautiful pictures in it you know, Mrs Reid from down my road came in with her Sandra who had this awful chest cold. Mrs Reid was telling me about the arthritis in her hands and the pain she was in. Then we heard this commotion and all of a sudden, Brian Peters came storming out of the doctor's room shouting that he'd be back and that next time he'd make sure the doctor never practised again. . .'.

Although you got there in the end, it would have been much more effective if you had used a transitional question instead, for example:

Q: 'Did there come a time when something unusual/unexpected happened while you were sitting in the waiting room?'

A: 'Oh yes. I was sitting chatting to Mrs Reid about her arthritis' (there is a limit to the extent you can control some witnesses!) 'when we heard this terrible commotion. All of a sudden, Brian Peters came storming out. . .'.

20.5 The point of reference (or 'piggy-back' question)

This is the method of including in your question a fact or facts which have already been elicited from the witness. It provides a context for the question and is a useful technique for emphasising an important fact, clarifying the evidence, obtaining greater detail from the witness, controlling the witness and/or providing a transition.

Examples

Q: 'What happened directly after you heard Miss Jones scream?'—emphasis and detail.

Q: 'When you said he left, to whom were you referring?'—clarification.

Q: 'Describe the knife you saw in the defendant's hand'—emphasis and detail.

Q: 'Did you see Mr Green again after he left your office that afternoon?'—transition and control.

Note that a point of reference can be included in either an open or closed question and form part of a transitional question.

20.6 Leading questions

A leading question is one that suggests or tends to suggest its own answer. It usually calls for a 'yes' or 'no' response. It often assumes a fact that has not yet been established.

Examples

'Were you in Manchester on 5 May 2006?'

'Did you see the knife in his hand?'

'Was she standing three feet away from you?'

A non-leading question in the same circumstances would have been:

'Where were you on 5 May 2006?' (date not in dispute).

'What did you see?'

'How far away was she?'

A leading question undermines the witness's credibility. It leaves the impression that you are afraid to let the witness open his or her mouth. It allows you to give the evidence yourself—that is not your function! It is for the witness to tell his or her account to the court. As a general rule, it is therefore not permitted to elicit evidence in **examination-in-chief** by the use of leading questions. There are two exceptions to this general rule.

20.6.1 Circumstances in which a leading question may be asked during examination-in-chief

20.6.1.1 A leading question may be asked when the subject matter is not in dispute

Example

There is no dispute that the parties met at the claimant's office on the evening of 10 March 2006.

Q: 'Did you meet the defendant at your office on the evening of 10 March 2006?'

Sometimes one piece of information is agreed while another is not.

Example

There is no dispute that the parties met on the evening of 10 March 2006. The time of the meeting is in dispute.

Q: 'Did you meet the defendant on the evening of 10 March 2006.'

A: 'Yes.'

Q: 'What time did you meet?'

Example

There is no dispute that the parties met one evening at the claimant's office. The date is in dispute.

Q: 'Do you recall an evening when you met the defendant at your office?'

A: 'Yes.'

Q: 'When was that?'

Counsel often use a leading question when the subject matter is unlikely to be contentious. For instance, where there is unlikely to be any dispute that a conversation took place, counsel might ask 'Did you have a conversation with the defendant?'. It is important to differentiate between the fact of a conversation taking place and what was said during that conversation. One may be in dispute while the other is not. If in doubt, check with your opponent.

20.6.1.2 A leading question is permitted when you are seeking to elicit a denial from your own witness as to his or her own alleged conduct or actions

Example

Q: 'Did you tell Mr Smith on 4 January 2006 that he was "dead meat"?'

A: 'No.'

What is in reality a leading question may appear to be non-leading by the simple device of offering the witness limited choices. As a matter of common sense, the answer must be one or the other.

Example

Q: 'Were you in this country or abroad on 6 February last?'

In this example, the answer is suggested in the question, in the sense that the witness will select one or other option. This type of question, although leading in its strictest sense, is rarely objectionable. It has the advantage of enabling you to guide the witness where you want him or her to go. Note that the non-leading version is to ask 'Where were you on 6 February last?'.

20.7 Non-leading questions

How then do you formulate your questions so as to avoid asking your witness a leading question? There are two basic methods you can use:

(a) Start your questions neutrally with one of the following interrogatives:

Who. . .?
What. . .?
Why. . .?
When. . .?

Where. . .?
How. . .?
Or with a neutral invitation:

Tell	Describe
Explain	Demonstrate

These will enable you to elicit the answer from the witness. Generally avoid asking questions which start with the words 'Did you. . . ?', 'Were you. . . ?', or 'Was it . . . ?'—these will normally contain suggestion(s) and tend to lead!

(b) Another basic way is to think of the answer you wish your witness to give and then omit any reference to the answer when framing the question. The question should come quite naturally.

Example

Answer required: 'Sunday'.
Q: 'What day was it?'
NOT: 'Was it a Sunday?' (a leading question)

Answer required: 'Blue jeans and a white t-shirt'
Q: 'Describe what he was wearing.'
NOT: 'Was he wearing blue jeans and a white t-shirt?'

Answer required: '(He left) three weeks ago.'
Q: 'When did he leave?'
NOT: 'Did he leave three weeks ago?'

The above illustrations show the advantage of preparing by using short headings or points. You should see the benefit of a simple form of 'bullet point' preparation such as: 'Setting the scene—Sun/8 pm/wet?'.

20.8 Combining questioning techniques

If you use too many open-ended questions you run the risk of losing control of the witness and too much irrelevance clouding his or her testimony. If you use too many closed questions, you will leave the court with the impression that the witness is a robot whom you have pre-programmed. Instead, achieve a balance by combining these techniques for the maximum effect:

(a) ask open questions to allow the witness to tell his or her story;
(b) ask closed questions to elicit details from the witness or emphasise part of the story;
(c) ask open questions to enable the witness to continue with the next part of the story;
(d) ask closed questions to elicit details, and so on.

This is sometimes referred to as the funnel technique.

20.9 In summary

Leading questions	*Non-leading questions*
(Avoid in examination-in-chief; use in cross-examination)	(Use in examination-in-chief; avoid in cross-examination)
You said. . .?	Who?
You saw. . .?	What?
You did. . .?	Why?
You were. . .?	When?
It was. . .?	Where?
Did you?	How?
Didn't you?	Tell/Describe
Were you?	Explain/Demonstrate
Weren't you?	
Was it?	
Wasn't it?	

21 Examination-in-chief

21.1 Introduction

Examination-in-chief is the process of eliciting evidence from your own witness and is the first opportunity the court has to assess the witness. A strong impression made at that stage will outlast many an attack in cross-examination.

21.1.1 The aims of examination-in-chief

The aims of conducting any examination-in-chief should therefore be threefold:

(a) to establish your case or part of it through the evidence elicited from the witness;

(b) to present the evidence so that it is clear, memorable and persuasive;

(c) to insulate the evidence, in so far as possible, from anticipated attack in cross-examination.

Before turning to look at how these aims can be achieved, let us first consider some preliminary matters.

21.2 Preparation and planning

21.2.1 Establishing an order

While preparing your case (see ***Case Preparation*** Manual), you will have already identified what you need to prove or disprove at the trial and have determined the facts and legal principles which are relevant to establishing your case. You will have also selected the theory of your case and the key elements of the evidence that support it.

You are now ready for the next step in your preparation. This involves:

(a) selecting the order of the witnesses;

(b) selecting the order of the evidence to be elicited from each witness.

21.2.1.1 Selecting the order of the witnesses

(a) It is preferable to start and finish your case with a witness who makes a strong impression. Avoid calling as your first witness one whose evidence is particularly vulnerable to cross-examination (for example, because it contains many inconsistencies or the witness's recollection is poor).

(b) In a large proportion of cases, it is usual to start with the witness whose evidence is first in time. This may, however, create difficulties where a number of your witnesses deal with matters which are relevant to the whole of your case. It may then be preferable to call as your first witness the one who gives the greatest overview of your case. This is likely to be your client, although not necessarily so.

(c) As a general rule, you do not have to call your client as your first witness. The one exception to this is provided by the Police and Criminal Evidence Act 1984, s 79. As defence counsel in a criminal trial, you must call the accused (if he or she is giving evidence) before any other witness of fact unless the court directs otherwise.

(d) Avoid calling your client in the middle of your witnesses. It makes a stronger impression if you call him or her either first or last. If you call your client as your final witness it may give him or her an opportunity to settle down and familiarise himself or herself with the atmosphere of the court.

(e) Corroborative witnesses should be called as close as possible to the evidence they are corroborating in order to support and insulate that evidence.

(f) Beware of calling too many cumulative witnesses or of seeking to overprove your case. This may backfire (you may even be penalised in costs on detailed assessment). Calling six witnesses who claim to have seen the same incident may give your opponent the opportunity of highlighting inconsistencies between their various accounts. If you must call a number of cumulative witnesses, particularly where you are prosecuting in a criminal trial, simply tender some of them for cross-examination.

(g) Expert witnesses called at the end of your case will enable you to finish on a strong note and may provide you with an opportunity to recap and/or emphasise the evidence you have already elicited from your previous witnesses. While there is no hard-and-fast rule, it is preferable to call your expert either first or last and not in the middle of your witnesses. Note, however, that the availability of your expert witness might determine when you call him or her.

21.2.1.2 Selecting the order of the evidence to be elicited from each witness

Your aim should be to organise the key elements of the witness's testimony in a logical order so that the judge, jury or tribunal can understand how each part fits into the overall theory of your case. This will normally result in a strict chronological presentation of the evidence, particularly in the case of a witness to a specific incident. For example, in a claim for damages for personal injuries sustained at work, the claimant might give evidence in this order:

(a) his or her background;

(b) his or her training and experience;

(c) safety instruction in the job;

(d) description of site where the accident occurred or of the machinery being used at the time;

(e) what occurred just before the accident;

(f) how the accident actually occurred;

(g) what happened immediately after the accident;

(h) initial treatment, pain and suffering;

(i) continued treatment, pain, suffering, loss of amenity;

(j) present disabilities: physical, mental, emotional;

(k) financial losses to date.

Not every case, however, lends itself to a strict chronological presentation of the witness's evidence. Nor is it always the best way of presenting the evidence. In this situation you should structure the evidence so as to emphasise the key elements which establish or support your case rather than simply eliciting the details in chronological order. For example, imagine you are representing a father seeking a residence order of his child. Your aim is to elicit evidence from the family's au pair regarding the mother's financial irresponsibility, alcoholism and physical abuse of the child. You could deal with everything the witness has to say, in a strict chronological order, from the moment she entered the household; but it will be more effective if you elicit the evidence by topic. This does not prevent you from dealing with the subject matter of each topic in a chronological order. However, by eliciting the evidence by topic you will leave the trier of fact with a much stronger cumulative picture of each aspect of the behaviour.

21.2.2 Written preparation

Many novices prepare for examination-in-chief by writing out in longhand all the questions they propose to ask each witness. This is usually done as a confidence booster in case they forget to ask the relevant questions or are unable to form their questions spontaneously in an appropriate manner. Some advocates also favour this practice and consider it an essential part of their preparation. Most advocates, however, favour a more selective use of this practice, writing out in full/memorising only those questions which they anticipate will be difficult to formulate 'off the top of their heads' and/or those which involve some complex factual concept/situation, eg, when dealing with expert testimony. In simple cases, they prefer to examine without using a fully prepared script.

If you have your face in a notebook, you will probably pay scant regard to the witness's answer in your anxiety to find and read the next question. You may lose the vital opportunity of watching the witness, his or her reaction to the question, the manner in which he or she responds and the impression he or she makes upon the court. You may miss what your opponent has seen, the telling gesture, the judge's expression, the jury members' looks of incredulity. You may convey an impression of disinterest in your witness's account. Most important of all, if your preparation is too rigid, you will find it difficult to adapt your questions to suit the witness's answer(s), to cope with an unexpected answer (witnesses do change their stories!) or a piece of evidence which has emerged during the trial.

Therefore, while recognising that the practice varies at the Bar, you will be encouraged, during the vocational training course, not to rely upon a prepared script of written questions. If you need to write out some of your questions as a confidence booster, you will be encouraged to restrict these to a couple at the start of the witness's evidence and/or to the most important issues in the case. It is normal practice to use the witness's proof of evidence/statement (containing what the witness ought to say) as the basis of examining him or her in-chief.

This does not mean that you should not prepare for examination-in-chief; preparation and planning are vital. Rather than writing down a string of questions, you will be encouraged to write down a note of the topics you want to deal with, broken down into subheadings or points, where appropriate. Preparing your case in this way, using 'trigger notes' or 'bullet points', will enable you to concentrate on the issues, the key elements of the evidence and allow you greater flexibility. You can then see at a glance where you wish to guide the witness.

21.3 Presenting the evidence

21.3.1 Calling the witness

It is time to call your first witness! You normally do so as follows:

> 'Sir/Madam, I (now) call Mrs Mary Brown';

or, as a matter of courtesy, just after you have finished your opening speech/statement:

> 'With your leave Sir/Madam' or 'With your Honour/Your Lordship's leave, I call Mrs Mary Brown'.

While the witness is taking the oath, you must stay both silent and still. Do not shuffle papers!

21.3.2 Getting started

What you need to do to start the examination-in-chief is to settle the witness. Help the witness to get used to their surroundings, to being the focus of attention, and to the sound of their own voice projected across the courtroom. So you start with one or two easy, short questions to which they know the answers and which allow them to talk a little. For example:

Q: 'What is your full name, please?'
Q: 'What do you do for a living?'/'Where do you work?'
Q: 'What is your position in that company?'
Q: 'What are your responsibilities?'

The circumstances of the case will dictate the extent to which it is necessary to elicit personal background information from the witness. Once the witness has relaxed, you can move onto the substance of their evidence.

21.3.3 The initial hurdles

You must now guide the witness to the starting point of his or her evidence. This will normally establish his or her connection with the case. Much now depends upon the extent to which the facts are in dispute as this will dictate the extent to which you may or may not lead at this stage. It may be clear from the statements of case/affidavits/witness statements that a matter is non-contentious. If it is not apparent, check with your opponent. You must frame your question(s) so as not to lead on disputed matters.

21.3.3.1 Where there is no dispute

Q: 'Did you let a room at your home to the defendant in July 2005?'
Q: 'Did you examine the claimant in your surgery on 15 May 2006?'

Q: 'Did you meet the defendant in the "Horse and Hounds" public house in Ealing during the evening of 6 October last?'

Q: 'Were you employed by the claimant, Mrs Gray, as a housekeeper during the period from October 1998 to June 2006?'

Q: 'Did you attend at the security office in Harrods store during the afternoon of 3 August 2006?'

21.3.3.2 Where a matter is only partially in dispute

Q: 'Where were you during the morning of 4 September 2006?' (date and time not in dispute)

Q: 'Did you let a room at your premises to the defendant?' (date in dispute)

Q: 'In what capacity were you employed in October 2005?' (job role in dispute)

Q: 'Did you meet the defendant during the evening of 6 October last?' (place in dispute)

21.3.3.3 Where there is a disputed matter

There are some occasions, however, when it is clear that a matter is entirely in dispute or when your opponent asks you not to lead on a particular point. The way in which you deal with this varies in every case. As a general rule look for some common ground or begin with an uncontentious matter (this may be apparent from the statements of case/witness statements). It may be necessary to generalise or ask the witness about an event which occurred at an earlier time.

Example 1

Q: 'Where do you work?' (working not in dispute)

A: 'At Lloyds Bank, Charing Cross Road.'

Q: 'How long have you worked there?'

A: 'About two years.'

Q: 'How do you get to work in the mornings?'

A: 'I catch the tube to Charing Cross and then walk down the road to the bank.'

Q: 'During the last two years, has anything exceptional happened in that vicinity on your way to work?'

A: 'Yes. I once saw a car crash.'

Q: 'Where precisely was that?'

Example 2

Q: 'Do you know Mr Jones?'

A: 'Yes.'

Q: 'When did you first meet him?'

A: 'We met at an office party about a year ago. He came with one of the girls I work with.'

Q: 'How long was your meeting?'

A: 'We were introduced and chatted for about 10 minutes at the party. He and his girlfriend then gave me a lift home.'

Q: 'Did you ever see Mr Jones again?'

A: 'Yes.'

Q: 'When was that?'

A: 'It was 11 June 2006, the night I was burgled.'

Example 3

Q: 'Do you recall an occasion when you spent a weekend in Manchester?'

A: 'Yes.'

Q: 'When was that?'

A: 'The beginning of May last year.'

Q: 'On what date did you return home?'

A: 'I came back on Tuesday 5 May.'

Q: 'Did you notice anything in particular on your return?'

A: 'As soon as I got to the house, I noticed that the front door had been kicked in and was hanging off its hinges . . .'

21.3.4 Setting the scene

Having guided the witness to the start of his or her evidence, it will probably be necessary to 'set the scene' further by eliciting details of the surrounding or background circumstances. This is particularly so in the case of a witness to an incident.

Examples:

Q: 'Describe the weather/traffic/road surface conditions.'

Q: 'Where were you standing?'

Q: 'Who else was present at the meeting?'

Q: 'When did you first meet the defendant?'

The nature of the case will determine the extent to which you need to develop a picture of the surrounding/background detail.

21.3.5 Witness statements

The preparation and exchange of full witness statements, directed to stand as the witness's evidence-in-chief, has increasingly replaced the need for examination-in-chief in civil cases. In such a case, it is unnecessary for the witness to repeat the content of his or her statement. The start of the (civil) examination-in-chief will look something like the following.

Having asked the witness to identify himself or herself, the advocate will ask the witness to turn to his/her witness statement in the trial bundle and ask:

Q: 'Do you see a signature on the document?'

A: 'Yes.'

Q: 'Whose signature is it?'

Inviting the witness to then confirm the making and truth of the statement will usually be sufficient for examination-in-chief. The witness is then asked to remain in the witness box for cross-examination.

Note that the judge retains a discretion to override a direction that the witness statement stands as the evidence-in-chief. The judge will therefore indicate if there are matters on which he or she would like to hear oral testimony despite the fact that they are dealt with in the witness's statement.

You may only adduce evidence of additional matters in-chief, the substance of which was not contained in the witness's statement if (i) the other party consents, or (ii) such additional evidence relates to new matters which have arisen in the course of the trial, and (iii) you obtain permission of the court.

21.3.6 The heart of the testimony: achieving the aims of examination-in-chief

We considered briefly at the start of this chapter the three aims of examination-in-chief:

(a) establishing your case;

(b) making the evidence clear, memorable and persuasive;

(c) insulating the evidence, in so far as possible, from anticipated attack in cross-examination.

How can these aims be achieved? Unfortunately, there is no single 'magic' answer to this question but if you observe the following basic principles, you should begin to master the skill of conducting a successful examination-in-chief.

21.3.7 Twenty basic principles

21.3.7.1 Know your objective

Concentrate on the key elements of the witness's testimony and keep them to the forefront of your mind. You should be asking yourself questions such as: What am I seeking to show through this witness's evidence? What part of my case does this witness (help to) establish/support? What is it that I want him/her to deal with? In what order do I want to cover these matters?

21.3.7.2 Do not rush

The trier(s) of fact will be listening to the evidence for the first time. It takes longer to absorb new information when hearing it rather than reading it. The main points can be submerged if drowned in too much peripheral detail.

21.3.7.3 Do not lead on a fact that is disputed (or that may be disputed)

Avoid questions that suggest or tend to suggest the answer to the witness where the subject matter is in dispute. Do not assume facts are in evidence before they have been elicited from the witness. Where a fact is clearly not disputed, you may adduce evidence of it by using a leading question.

21.3.7.4 Know the answer before asking the question

In general, you should avoid asking questions to which you do not know the answer. There is always a danger that the answers to such questions may damage your case. There is no rule that you cannot ask such questions. You can, and often must, ask them *but* only where the (unknown) answer will not, or cannot, damage your case *and* it will assist the judge/jury to understand the case.

21.3.7.5 Scene first, then action

Before the trier(s) of fact can understand what happened, they will need the background or context against which to understand the action. Set the scene first.

21.3.7.6 Keep it clear

Break the evidence down into intelligible pieces. Ask one question at a time. Avoid jargon or legalese. Keep your questions short and simple: seven to eight words per question is a good length. Plant a firm question mark at the end of each question and allow the witness time to answer. Cut out unnecessary preamble, eg, 'Could you please tell the court what the registration number of the car read?'. Ask instead 'What was the car's registration number?'. Use plain English, eg, 'see' rather than 'perceive', 'car' rather than 'vehicle'.

21.3.7.7 Organise the key elements of the testimony

A logical progression or structure to the order in which the information is introduced will make it easier to follow. You will usually find that, as the witness is telling a story, they will recollect it best (and the trier(s) of fact will remember it better) if you enable the witness to work through their story in a chronological order. The aim here is to enable the trier(s) of fact to understand how each part fits into the overall theory of your case. Do not hop backwards and forwards from one subject to another. Structure the testimony rather than merely presenting it in a haphazard fashion.

It may be that you do not get the necessary amount of detail about a particular matter from the witness when they talk about it for the first time. That can happen because you must not 'lead' your witness but use questions which prompt them to tell the story in their own words. This will mean that, from time to time, you will need to interrupt their narrative in order to go back and cover a topic in more detail. For example, 'You told the court that you arrived at the party at about 10.30 pm—how did you get there? Who did you see when you first arrived? What was he doing at that time?' and so on.

Sometimes, you will decide that the court will have a better understanding of events (or perhaps be more sympathetic to your client) if they learn first what happened to bring the parties to court and then find out what events led up to that conclusion. Having settled the witness with the usual questions, such as, 'Please tell the court your full name' and 'What do you do for a living?', you might then ask the witness, 'Do you know why you are in court today?'. When the witness replies affirmatively, you can then ask, 'Please tell the court what happened'. The witness is likely to start talking about the conclusion of a sequence of events, for example, 'My car was stolen' or 'I was hit over the head and had to go to hospital' or 'I fell over a broken paving stone and cut my leg'. You can then concentrate on those events with the witness, before turning to more preliminary matters.

21.3.7.8 Get the witness to tell the story

Allow the witness to tell the story in his or her own words. The witness was there—they saw, heard or perceived what happened. It is much more effective and memorable if they relate their experiences to the trier(s) of fact than if they simply answer a series of questions in monosyllables.

21.3.7.9 Let the testimony flow

Try to avoid constant interruption of the witness. A fractured account may leave little impression on the trier(s) of fact. Allowing the witness to tell their story 'in paragraphs' rather than 'sentences' can help to build a picture of the events in the mind of the trier(s) of fact. As indicated below, detail can always be picked up afterwards.

21.3.7.10 Listen to the answers and respond accordingly

Do not give the impression that you are not listening to the answers the witness is giving. Look at the witness and listen to their reply. You may need to ask a follow-up question to ensure the testimony is clear and complete or that a technical word needs explaining. Or you may need to stop the witness answering your question if, for example, he or she begins to introduce inadmissible material.

21.3.7.11 Exercise control, keep it relevant

Control the witness by using transitions, a point of reference or by asking a closed question to cut out irrelevant information. If the witness is talking too fast or is dealing with irrelevant matters, interrupt the flow in a firm but polite manner, eg, 'I'm afraid, Mr Smith, that you are going too fast for His Honour to take a full note of what you are saying. Try and watch His Honour's pen. . .' or 'pausing there for a moment, Mr Smith, I would like to deal with. . .'. Then follow this up with closed questions, keeping them as short as possible.

21.3.7.12 Combine questioning techniques

Vary the types of questions you ask, combining the questioning techniques you have learned, open and closed questions, transitions and points of reference—this should lead to clarity of presentation and enable you to exercise control when required.

Example:

Q: 'Did you see Mr Green again after he left your office that afternoon?' (not in dispute)

A: 'Yes, I saw him two days later.'

Q: 'Where was that?'

A: 'He called at my home.'

Q: 'Were you expecting him?'

A: 'No, I was not.'

Q: 'At what time did he call?'

A: 'About 10.30 pm.'

Q: 'Was he with anyone else?'

A: 'No, he was alone.'

Q: 'Who else was at home?'

A: 'No one. My wife was out visiting her mother.'

Q: 'What happened when Mr Green arrived?'

A: 'As I opened the front door to let him in he pushed past me, knocking me against the wall. He started shouting that he was going to teach me a lesson. Then he pulled a gun out of his coat pocket and threatened me with it.'

Q: 'Pausing there, how would you describe Mr Green's demeanour when he arrived?'

A: 'He was angry, almost mad.'

Q: 'Please describe the gun.'

A: 'Yes, it was a small black pistol.'

Q: 'Where were you when he pulled out this small black pistol?'

A: 'I was still against the wall where he had pushed me.'

Q: 'Approximately, how far away was Mr Green at that time?'

A: 'At first, he was about two feet away but then he came closer.'

Q: 'What happened as he came closer?'

21.3.7.13 Use pace to keep the story vivid

Use pace as an effective means of emphasising important evidence or conveying the speed with which something happened. You and not the witness choose the pace at which the evidence flows from the witness. Keep an eye on your audience—you need them to understand and follow the witness's account.

Example:

Q: 'What happened as he came closer?'

A: 'He came right up to me, mouthing obscenities, pinning me against the wall. He spat on my face. Then he stepped back and whipped me in the face with the pistol. I could feel blood on my cheek.'

Q: 'How did you react?'

A: 'I tried to push him away but he kept coming at me, trying to whip me again with the pistol. I was screaming for him to stop, trying to get the pistol away from him, he was fighting like a maniac. . .'

In the above series of questions, the questioner has let the evidence flow, allowing the witness to tell the important part of the story with little interruption. He or she could have interrupted, for example, to obtain greater detail of the 'obscenities' or 'of how Mr Green had pinned the witness against the wall' but it would have spoilt the effect, 'fractured' the witness's own account of what happened and slowed down the pace. Such detail can be elicited at a later stage, for example:

Q: 'You stated that Mr Green was mouthing obscenities. Do you recall the words he used?'

21.3.7.14 Use frequency for emphasis

A number of specific questions on the same subject emphasises its importance and builds a picture of the event in the mind(s) of the trier(s) of fact.

Example:

A: 'Then the defendant hit me.'

Q: 'With what did he hit you?'

A: 'His fist.'

Q: 'Which fist did he use?'

A: 'His right fist.'

Q: 'Can you show the court how he held his hand?'

A: 'It was with a closed fist, like this [demonstration].'

Q: 'Where did he hit you with this closed fist?'

A: 'In my face.'

Q: 'Whereabouts in the face?'

A: 'My right cheek.'

Q: 'How many times did he hit your cheek?'

A: 'Just the once.'

21.3.7.15 Make the connections

Tie the evidence up. Do not leave loose ends. Do not leave it to your closing speech to make or show the connections between one fact and another or a series of facts and the conclusion they support. Develop the specific facts and then the conclusion which rests upon them or elicit the conclusion and then fill in the supporting facts.

Example 1

(Supporting facts first; conclusion second.)

A: 'The defendant tried to get out of the car.'

Q: 'How?'

A: 'He opened the car door and put one leg out. He couldn't get any further without my assistance. He could hardly stand up on his own.'

Q: 'Did you have any conversation with the defendant?'

A: 'Well I tried to but he kept slurring his words. He stank of alcohol.'

Q: 'Officer, did you form any opinion as to the defendant's condition?'

A: 'Yes, I did. He was drunk.'

Example 2:

(Conclusion first; supporting facts second.)

A: 'The defendant tried to get out of the car.'

Q: 'Officer, did you form any opinion as to the defendant's condition at that time?'

A: 'Yes, I did. He was drunk.'

Q: 'Upon what did you base that opinion?'

A: 'He stank of alcohol and kept slurring his words. He couldn't get out of the car without my assistance. He put one leg out but could hardly stand up on his own.'

The first example makes a lasting impression. It is persuasive. The second example probably makes less impact although it has the advantage of conveying at an early stage the thrust of the witness's testimony.

21.3.7.16 Fill in the gaps

Do not leave holes in the witness's evidence. Think about what you might ask if you were in your opponent's shoes. For example, in the case of an identification witness, establish (in respect of each occasion he or she has seen the subject) such details as the lighting conditions, distance, angle, length and quality of observation. In this way, you may insulate the evidence from attack in cross-examination to the effect that the witness only got 'a fleeting glance'.

21.3.7.17 Be realistic

For instance, do not expect a witness to repeat verbatim a conversation which took place a long time before or one which is lengthy. The risk with asking 'What did he say to you?' is that you may get an 'I don't remember' response. If this is likely to happen, avoid it in this way:

Q: 'Do you remember exactly what the defendant said?'
A: 'No, it's too long ago.'
Q: 'Do you remember the substance (or gist) of what he said?'
A: 'Oh yes. He said something to the effect that . . .'

21.3.7.18 Illustrate the evidence

Use illustrative aids where they will assist the trier of fact to follow the evidence, for instance, a sketch plan of the scene of the accident, a floor plan of the store, a schedule of figures. See **21.3.8** for the introduction of exhibits.

21.3.7.19 Avoid bad habits

Do not comment on the evidence or give your opinions on the witness's response to your question. Avoid irritating habits such as thanking the witness or stating 'I see' or 'Yes, I see' after every answer. It is equally irritating to keep repeating everything the witness has just said. Do not make a lot of noise or shuffle papers while the witness is giving his or her evidence. It is distracting. It creates an impression of disinterest in the witness's answer or of lack of preparation or both.

21.3.7.20 Establish as much of your case as the witness can testify to

Before you sit down, check that you have elicited from the witness all the relevant evidence that he or she can give to help you establish your case or part of it.

21.3.8 Introducing real evidence

'Real evidence' is evidence in a tangible form such as a weapon, an article of clothing, a document (letter, contract, diagram, lease) or a photograph. There are several matters to consider before introducing such evidence during the examination of a witness.

(a) Location of the exhibit—it may be contained in one party's bundle of documents or exhibits, in an agreed bundle of documents or exhibits, it may be in the possession of a witness or you may have the original in your possession.

(b) Disclosure—ensure that the item/document has been properly disclosed to your opponent and/or that your opponent has had the opportunity to inspect it.

(c) Admissibility—ensure that the item/document is admissible and can be introduced by the witness in question. It may be necessary to lay a proper foundation before it can be admitted in evidence, eg, by satisfying the requirements of the Civil Evidence Act 1995, s 9 in respect of business records.

(d) Continuity—ensure that, if necessary, you can show continuity of possession, eg, in a drugs case, unless the defence concedes the issue, you will need to prove that the substance analysed in the laboratory was the same substance as that found in the defendant's possession. You can do this by eliciting evidence as to the taking of the drugs from the defendant; the packaging of the drugs in a sealed bag and the recording of the seal number; the transmission of the sealed bag to the forensic laboratory; and the analysis of the substance by seal number. (In most drugs cases, however, continuity is admitted. The issue normally relates to whether or not the defendant was 'in possession' of the drugs.)

21.3.8.1 Marking the exhibit

Where the item is not already in an identifiable bundle, it is usual to ask the judge for the exhibit to be marked with an identifying number—this will identify the person or party producing it and enable the exhibit to be distinguished during the trial, eg, 'Your Honour, may that be marked D.1.' (D for defendant.)

21.3.8.2 Introducing the evidence: no dispute

There are several ways of introducing the evidence. Where there is no dispute, you may lead the exhibit, for example:

Example 1

A: 'I saw the defendant with a gun in his hand.'

Q: 'Please look at this gun—is that the gun?'

A: 'Yes.'

Q: 'Your Honour, may that be marked P.1?' (Prosecution exhibit 1.)

Example 2

Q: 'Please look at page 3 of the bundle of documents—did you write that letter?'

A: 'Yes.'

Example 3

Q: 'Did you send the defendant a notice to quit the premises?'

A: 'Yes.'

Q: 'Is that a copy of the notice you sent?'

A: 'Yes.'

Q: 'Your Honour, may that be marked C.2?' (Claimant's exhibit 2.)

21.3.8.3 Introducing the evidence: dispute

Where the item is in dispute, do not lead the exhibit. It may be necessary to lay a proper foundation for its admissibility or establish continuity.

Example 1

A: 'I saw the defendant with a gun in his hand.'

Q: 'Please look at this' (handed to the witness) 'What can you tell us about it?'/'How does that compare with the item you saw in the defendant's hand?'

Example 2

A: 'I found two jumpers hidden in the defendant's bag, both still bearing the store's labels and price tags.'

Q: 'Describe the jumpers you found.'

A: 'One was a size 14 ladies' jumper in plain blue; the other was a blue and white striped ladies' jumper, size 12.'

Q: 'What is the normal practice in the store when items are purchased?'

A: 'The sales assistant tears off the price tag, which is retained for stock purposes, then places the item with a till receipt in a store carrier bag.'

Q: 'What happened to the jumpers after you found them?'

A: 'I took them to the security office and placed them in a plastic bag which I marked with my initials. I then placed them in the security office safe.'

Q: 'Did you see them again?'

A: 'Yes, this morning—I retrieved the bag from the safe.'

Q: 'Will you produce the items to the court?'

A: 'Yes.'

Q: 'Your Honour, may they be marked P.3?'

21.3.9 The final question

When you come to your final question, try to make it an important one. Let the witness finish on a strong note. It can be useful to let the court know you are about to finish by starting your last question with the words, 'Finally, Mrs Brown . . .'.

At the end of the witness's answer, a simple 'Thank you, Mrs Brown' will suffice although it is perfectly acceptable to add such words as 'Just wait there, would you?'/ 'Please wait there'/'You will now be asked some questions by the defendant's counsel.'

21.4 Special aspects of examination-in-chief

21.4.1 Affidavit evidence

There are occasions where the witness has already sworn an affidavit dealing with the relevant issues. If you call the witness to give evidence, it is rarely necessary to examine the witness fully on the contents of his or her affidavit. Unless the judge requests it, he or she will not normally wish to hear a repeat of the matters already set out in the affidavit. It is, however, usual to give the witness the opportunity to explain any change in his or her circumstances since the affidavit was sworn, expand upon any matter which is not comprehensively covered, clarify any ambiguity and/or deal with any matters which have arisen since the affidavit was sworn.

Examples:

Q: 'Did you swear an affidavit in these proceedings on 6 September 2006 (you may add "dealing with. . . eg, your financial means/your involvement with the defendant company"). . .?'

Q: 'Has there been any change in your income/position since you swore that affidavit?'

Q: 'In paragraph 4 of your affidavit you refer to a Miss Styles. Who is she?'

Q: 'You deal in paragraph 8 with an incident in which the defendant threatened you. Was anyone else present at the time?'

Q: 'Have you had any further contact with the defendant since you swore your affidavit?'

Two further points about affidavit evidence. The court may have already directed that the affidavit is to stand as the witness's evidence-in-chief. If not, and you are unsure whether or not to take the witness through matters already dealt with in the affidavit, seek an indication from the judge, for example, 'Unless your Lordship/Your Honour considers it would assist, I do not propose to deal (at any length) with the matters already covered in the applicant's affidavit'. The judge will normally give you the required indication.

You may hear counsel at some stage inviting a witness to verify the contents of his or her affidavit, for example:

Q: 'Did you swear an affidavit in these proceedings on 6 September 2006?'

Q: 'At the time you swore it, were the contents of that affidavit true to the best of your knowledge, information and belief?'

The second question is unnecessary. The witness has already taken an oath to that effect at the time of swearing the affidavit. It is a bad habit to invite a witness to verify the contents of his or her affidavit—it is best to avoid it.

21.4.2 Memory-refreshing documents

The witness, particularly if it is a police officer, may need to refer to their notebook or statement in order to refresh their memory of the events or part of them. This is allowed if the statement records the witness's recollection at the time he made it and his recollection was likely to be better than it is now. Often police officers pool their recollections of the events and then only one police officer writes out the notes. The others may be permitted to refresh their memories from the same notebook provided they read and checked the notes at the time and were satisfied that the notes contained an accurate record of what they also saw or heard at the time.

Example

Q: 'Please give the court your full name and rank.'

A: 'Police Constable 239X Nigel Smith attached to Paddington Green police station.'

Q: 'Did you attend the scene of a car accident in Charing Cross Road on 4 February 2006?'

A: 'Yes.'

Q: 'What time did you arrive there?'

A: 'I can't recall exactly. May I refer to my notes?'

Q: 'When did you make your notes?'

A: 'About 50 minutes after the incident.'

Q: 'Where did you make the notes?'

A: 'In the canteen at Paddington Green police station.'

Q: 'Did you make your notes on your own or with anyone else?'

A: 'With Officer Bloggs.'

Q: 'How did you make the notes?'

A: 'We discussed what had happened and then I wrote the notes. Officer Bloggs then read them over.'

Q: 'Were the events/was the incident still fresh in your mind/memory at that time?'

A: 'Yes.'

Q: 'Your Honour/Sir, may the witness refresh his memory by referring to his notes?' (Note: the judge/district judge will usually enquire whether your opponent has any objections to this.)

The witness's notes/statement may contain inadmissible evidence. Warn the witness in advance to omit any reference to the offending part. When the witness comes to that part of the evidence, help him or her over it and onto the next admissible part by intervening with a question such as 'Did you then/subsequently. . .?'.

Note that when referring to a memory-refreshing document, the witness should use it merely to refresh memory. Some witnesses, particularly police officers, use it as an opportunity to read out their evidence; this is objectionable and the witness should be reminded not to do so, for example:

> 'Officer, refreshing your memory, if necessary, from your notes, what happened upon your arrival at. . .?'

There are other occasions when you may wish the witness to refresh his or her memory from a statement made at the time.

Example

Q: 'Can you recall exactly what the other driver said?'
A: 'No. It was too long ago.'
Q: 'Do you recall making a statement to the police after the accident?'
A: 'Yes.'
Q: 'How soon after the accident did you make it?'
A: 'About an hour later down at the police station.'
Q: 'Was the accident still fresh in your mind at that time?'
A: 'Yes.'
Q: 'Were the details of the conversation you had with the other driver fresh in your mind at that time?'
A: 'Yes.'
Q: 'Did you record them in your statement?'
A: 'Yes.'
Q: 'Your Honour, may the witness refresh his or her memory by referring to his or her statement?'

21.4.3 Alibi evidence

It is particularly important in the case of an alibi witness not to lead on the date or time. Do not ask an alibi witness 'Where were you on the evening of 9 March 2006?'. Elicit the date from the witness.

Example

Q: 'Did there come a time when you heard that the defendant had been arrested and charged?'
A: 'Yes.'
Q: 'When was that?'
A: 'The day of his arrest. His brother telephoned and told me.'
Q: 'Do you recall the exact date?'
A: 'Yes. It was a Friday, 10 March 2006.'
Q: 'What did you understand was the nature of the charge?'
A: 'He was supposed to have burgled a house the evening before.'
Q: 'Where were you during that evening?'
A: 'I was at a party with the defendant and two other friends . . .'

21.4.4 Expert reports

Where there has been a direction for the disclosure of expert reports, the expert witness's evidence will already be contained in the report. If the report is not agreed, it will be necessary to call the expert as a witness at the trial and for him or her to adopt the evidence contained in the report. The fact of prior disclosure is not sufficient for this purpose. It is necessary to elicit details of the expert's qualifications and experience at the outset (in order to satisfy the court that the witness is an expert) and then proceed in this way:

Example

Q: 'Did you examine the claimant at your surgery on 14 July 2006?'
A: 'I did.'

Q: 'Are your findings/are the results of that examination/is your evidence of the claimant's medical condition/contained in your report dated 17 July 2006?'

A: 'Yes, they are/it is.'

In civil cases, do not invite the expert witness to repeat what is contained in his or her report save for the purpose of clarification, expansion or updating his evidence. It is then usual to turn to the other expert's report and/or the joint statement produced by the experts (which identifies the areas they disagree on) to deal with disputed matters.

Example

Q: 'Have you read the report prepared by Dr Smith on 14 October 2006?'

A: 'I have.'

Q: 'Dr Smith's measurements of the degree of mobility in the claimant's left ankle are greater than yours. Can you account for that?'

A: 'Yes.' (Note: make sure you know the answer before asking this type of question!)

In criminal cases where the expert report (or part of it) is agreed, it (or the agreed parts) will be admitted. An admission (CJA 1967, s 10) will be read to the jury, setting out the agreed parts. Where there are disputed matters, the evidence of these must be adduced in the normal way in examination-in-chief.

21.4.5 Previous convictions

If, in a criminal trial, you decide to refer to the defendant's previous convictions in order to take the 'sting' out of the anticipated cross-examination, it is usually preferable to do this at an early stage in your examination-in-chief. Elicit the details of the defendant's past record in a business-like fashion, emphasising any favourable aspects such as the fact that the defendant pleaded guilty on each previous occasion.

21.4.6 Tendering for cross-examination

If the witness is a cumulative witness in the sense that he or she is giving the same evidence as has already been elicited from the previous witness(es), it is preferable to tender him or her for cross-examination. This often arises where, for example, you are calling several police officers to deal with the same incident. Establish who the witness is and his or her presence at the scene, for example:

Q: 'Officer, please give the court your full name and rank.'

A: 'Police Sergeant Richard Smith attached to Marylebone police station.'

Q: 'Were you on duty at the police station during the evening of 12 January 2006?'

A: 'Yes.'

Q: 'Were you present when the defendant was charged?' (no dispute)

A: 'Yes, I was.'

Q: 'Wait there, the defence may have some questions for you.'

22

Cross-examination

22.1 Introduction

Cross-examination is the name given to the process of examining the witness(es) called by your opponent or by another party in the case (eg, a co-defendant in either civil or criminal proceedings). It is the most challenging and, for the new advocate, the most intimidating of the tasks he or she has to perform. If successful, it provides an advocate with one of the most satisfying moments of his or her work.

First of all, forget what you have seen in films—the witness is not likely to break down in the witness box and confess all! You must accept that not all your cross-examinations are going to be successful. Cultivate a poker face. This is not easy but it can be learned. Show what you want to be seen by your audience and not what you feel.

Second, contrary to popular belief, cross-examination is not, nor should it be, 'cross' in the sense of angry, confrontational or controversial. Apart from applying the cardinal rule set out at **22.3**, cross-examination should be viewed as a constructive art and not necessarily a destructive one. There is no need to shout or adopt an unpleasant, sneering manner in cross-examination. Nor is it necessary to harangue a witness in order to be effective. This will probably only serve to antagonise the jury or the judge. While you must exercise control over the witness, the most effective way is to adopt a polite, courteous approach, use a combination of closed and leading questions and deliver them in the spirit of an inquiry. Appear business-like and quietly confident.

Consider, by way of example, the case of Lizzie Borden:

> Lizzie Borden took an axe,
> Gave her father forty thwacks.
> When she saw what she had done
> She gave her mother forty-one.

The murders occurred when she was alone in the locked house with her parents. Much blood must have been spilt when the axe was used and would have splattered the assailant. The prosecution case was that Lizzie must have taken her clothes off (this was the 1890s) while committing the murders and then washed and dressed again afterwards for there was no blood found on her clothing. Lizzie claimed to have been ironing and to have seen or heard nothing of the crimes until after they were committed. A neighbour was called and cross-examined:

Q: 'We have been told you were the first neighbour into the house.'

A: 'I have been told so.'

Q: 'Did you go into the room where Miss Borden was ironing?'

A: 'I did.'

Q: 'Was there an ironing-board in place?'

A: 'There was.'

Q: 'And an iron on the board?'

A: 'Stood on edge.' (This was the age of the flat-iron.)

Q: 'And was the ironing completed?'

A: 'There was a small pile of handkerchiefs which from so nearly as I could see had been ironed.'

Q: 'And ironing yet to do?'

A: 'There was a basket of handkerchiefs ready dampened.'

Q: 'Did you feel the iron?'

A: 'I did. It was warm.'

Note:

(a) the lack of hostility;

(b) the directness;

(c) the simplicity;

(d) the lack of comment;

(e) the preparation for the closing speech: a woman halfway through ironing, the most domestic of tasks, breaking off to murder her parents?

The objectives for this cross-examination were clearly identified before it began, pursued throughout the cross-examination and achieved. It was conducted in the spirit of a courteous enquiry into the facts rather than in a confrontational manner.

22.2 The aims of cross-examination

22.2.1 Aim 1: To advance your own case

This means asking questions which seek to establish facts fitting in with or corroborating your case. For this your manner will not appear hostile. You will, at least in the first instance, be seeking the cooperation of the witness. If the witness proves intransigent or difficult you may eventually need to apply pressure, but don't begin by doing so.

22.2.2 Aim 2: To undermine your opponent's case

Of course, these two aims overlap, at least in the sense that anything which advances your case at the same time undermines your opponent's. However, while preparing for cross-examination you should keep the two aims distinct. Your approach to the witness may depend on your aims and this may change during your cross-examination.

Remember too there is a substantial difference between seeking to undermine the witness's evidence and seeking to undermine the witness. In the former case you will probably need to go about your work without letting the witness know what you are about; in which case your manner will be bland. In the latter case it may or may not be so. The choice is yours alone. You will set, maintain or choose to adapt the tone of the cross-examination.

22.3 The cardinal rule of cross-examination

You must put your case. You must challenge all material parts of the evidence given by witnesses called by your opponent which your client (or his or her witnesses) does not accept. If the witness says that your client 'orally agreed to pay him £4,000' and your client denies both the agreement and the fact that the conversation ever took place, you must put these points to the witness. If you fail to do this, the judge will refuse to allow you to challenge your opponent's version in your final speech. He or she will tell you that your failure to challenge that version is the equivalent of accepting it. This can inflict fatal damage to your case.

Also, if you do not challenge the disputed parts, or put your client's version of the events to the witness, and then call evidence which contradicts your opponent's evidence in material particulars, you may find that your client and/or his or her witnesses are accused of inventing their evidence—on the basis that if their version of events was known before the trial began it would be known to you and you would have been obliged to cross-examine and 'put the case'. You did not cross-examine, therefore the version now given is a late invention. This is sometimes correct. In which case you can only sit and squirm. If, however, it is your fault because you have failed to comply with the rule, you must immediately stand up and say so—and apologise to the court!

The rule is one which admits of no exceptions. Our adversarial system of trial requires that witnesses be given the opportunity while in the box to answer the case presented contrary to their account of the facts. This does not mean that you have to challenge every unessential detail but you must cross-examine on material particulars.

22.4 Questioning technique

Cross-examination should not be a rerun of the examination-in-chief. You must avoid giving the witness the opportunity simply to repeat unfavourable testimony which he or she has already given in-chief. (The one exception to this may be where you suspect that the witness has memorised his or her testimony or has planned with another witness to tell an identical story. In that case, you may be able to highlight the fact that the witness is using identical phrases or repeating his or her or another witness's words verbatim.) Your twofold aim is to use the witness to advance your case and undermine your opponent's. The focus should therefore be on your case rather than allowing the witness the freedom to rehash theirs.

In the chapter on questioning techniques, **Chapter 20**, we saw that open-ended questions with neutral starts (who, what, how, which, when, where, why, tell and describe) give the witness a chance to give a narrative account, to tell the story in their own words. This is not what you want your opponent's witness to do when you are cross-examining—you want the focus to be on your questions and to retain control over the answers.

In cross-examination, there are therefore two golden rules:

(1) Tell: don't ask! Include the answer you want in the question.
(2) Lead, lead, lead—avoid open-ended questions wherever and whenever possible.

Of course, these rules do allow for exceptions and the more experienced the advocate, the more one might risk an open-ended question. But, at this stage, it is best not to do so unless the matter is peripheral or you are clear that the answer is unlikely to damage your case.

A combination of leading and closed questions will best enable you to control the witness. For example, imagine you represent the wife in a disputed maintenance case. Your aim is to show that her estranged husband is extravagant with money that ought to be spent on household bills:

Q: 'You go to the pub after work sometimes, don't you?'
A: 'Yes.'
Q: 'Usually with your work colleagues?'
A: 'Yes.'
Q: 'On average, two to three times a week?'
A: 'Yes.'
Q: 'And when there, you drink beer?'
A: 'Yes, usually bitter.'
Q: 'About 6 or 7 pints each time?'
A: 'Well, sometimes but not always.'
Q: 'You normally stay until closing time?'
A: 'Yes.'
Q: 'From about 6.00 pm?'
A: 'Yes.'
Q: 'So it would not be unusual to drink 6 or 7 pints during the 5 or so hours you are there?'
A: 'I suppose not.'
Q: 'A pint of beer costs about £2?'
A: 'Yes.'
Q: 'You sometimes grab a bite to eat too while in the pub?'
A: 'Yes although I usually have my main meal at lunchtime.'
Q: 'So, it would not be unusual for you to spend £20 during a full evening at the pub?'

During cross-examination, transitions and points of reference can also be used to good effect in moving from one topic to another or referring to the witness's evidence in-chief. (Note that if you are co-defending, although you may use leading questions when cross-examining the co-defendant, it may be wise not to do so where you are using the same defence. A series of leading questions in this situation will give the impression that you do not trust the witness to give favourable evidence without your careful prompting.)

22.5 Achieving the aims of cross-examination

22.5.1 Advancing your case

There are two basic ways of advancing your own case in cross-examination.

22.5.1.1 Eliciting favourable testimony

Frequently you will find that part of a witness's evidence is in fact helpful or potentially helpful to your case. Not everything a witness says is necessarily damaging. For example, a witness to an alleged shoplifting offence may agree that the store was very crowded; a witness to a road traffic accident may agree that the road surface was wet or that the other driver was driving fast; a witness in a child care case may agree that on the occasions when she saw your client and the children together, the children appeared happy and content or that it was usually your client who took the children to their doctor's appointments.

It is therefore important to approach each witness's testimony in the first place with an open mind—avoid dealing with the damaging part(s) of the evidence until you have considered the potentially helpful parts. Ask yourself: Is there any area of consensus between the witness's observation/recollection and my client's? Can the witness say anything which will assist/support my theory of the case? Does the witness say anything that can be expanded upon to assist my case? Is the witness silent on a matter which would have been mentioned if it was detrimental to my case? What must the witness admit if he or she was present at the time of the alleged incident? If having considered the evidence in this way there are positive aspects to the witness's testimony, these are the parts that you want to emphasise.

Generally it is accepted that it is tactically better to elicit any favourable testimony that the witness can provide before attempting to discredit the witness's evidence. This will enable you, at the very least, to obtain some positive help from the witness before he or she reacts in a negative or antagonistic way to the rest of your questions.

22.5.1.2 Developing your case

Both when 'putting your case' (cardinal rule, see **22.3**) and pursuing one or other or both of the aims (see **22.2**) you have the chance to develop your case in the sense that you can begin to show your audience the way you want them to look at all the facts. It is usually better to let the facts speak for themselves depending, obviously, on the nature and quality of the audience. It is very tempting to adopt the styles of advocates seen in films or TV who add plenty of running commentary to their questions but you should avoid this.

In putting your case, it is not necessary to use the words 'I put it to you that . . .'. Although you may hear counsel using this expression on occasions, many consider it unnecessarily formal. It can also alert the witness that you are about to challenge their evidence. If you say to a witness 'I put it to you that you have come here to tell the court a pack of lies', the answer will invariably be 'No, I haven't'. How far has that got you? It is equally unimpressive to argue with a witness along childish lines such as 'You did'—'I didn't'—'Yes, you did'—'No, I didn't'.

Be subtler when putting your case. Although in most cases, the witness will not agree with your client's version of events, at the very least you will introduce and develop your theory of the case and prepare the way for your witnesses to give evidence in support of it. Aim to do this without labouring your points or making them in a heavy-handed way. Consider this example:

Q: 'Since Mrs Smith left home, have you taken any steps to encourage the children to keep in contact with her?'
A: 'Well, I tried to but they refused.'
Q: 'Is it right that Mrs Smith used to telephone the household twice a week?'
A: 'Yes'.
Q: 'And on each occasion you put the telephone down on her?'
A: 'I had nothing to say to her and the children wouldn't come to the telephone.'
Q: 'Was that the reason why you changed your telephone number in May?'
A: 'I wanted to stop her bothering me.'
Q: 'Bothering you or the children?'
A: 'Just me.'
Q: 'Was that why you also changed the locks on the front door of the house?'

A: 'Yes. She'd left—she had no right to come back when it suited her.'
Q: 'Not even to see the children?'
A: 'I told you, the children didn't want to see her.'
Q: 'Mrs Smith sent the children several letters and cards, didn't she?'
A: 'A few.'
Q: 'And you returned them unopened?'
A: 'Yes. The children asked me to.'
Q: 'Do you always do everything the children ask you to?'
A: 'No, not always.'
Q: 'Did you consider that it was very rude to return mail unopened without the courtesy of a response?'
A: 'Not really.'
Q: 'Did you consider contacting Mrs Smith and explaining to her that the children were upset by her correspondence?'
A: 'No. It wasn't necessary.'
Q: 'It's right, isn't it, that you told Mrs Smith when she left you would ensure she never saw the children again?'
A: 'No, I didn't. I told her if she left, I wouldn't have her back.'
Q: 'And, in fact, since she left, despite her attempts, you have ensured she has not seen, spoken to or heard from the children?'
A: 'That was of her own making, not mine.'

Certain types of witness, for example police officers, may give identical, or similar evidence on one or more aspects of the case. It is not usually necessary to put the same challenges to every witness unless:

(a) you consider that in doing so you are likely to achieve a different or inconsistent response; or

(b) you consider that by putting your case more than once it will leave a greater impression upon the mind(s) of the trier(s) of fact.

If you do not wish merely to repeat the same challenges, indicate to the judge that you have already put your case to the previous witness(es) and that you do not propose to put the same challenges again to this witness unless the judge considers it necessary.

22.5.2 Undermining your opponent's case

This is the second aim of cross-examination. In order to undermine your opponent's case, you must successfully meet the unfavourable testimony given by his or her witness(es). This can be achieved in one or more of the following ways.

22.5.2.1 Limiting the testimony

Witnesses frequently observe only part of an incident or overlook the fact that their evidence leaves many unexplained or inconsistent gaps. Try to meet the unfavourable testimony by showing its limitations. Consider such evidence in the wider context of the case. Stress what the witness did not see; highlight the absence of matters that you would ordinarily have expected the witness to see/hear if he or she had witnessed the whole event or those matters that you would have expected to find if the situation was as the witness suggests/believes. For example:

(a) In the case of an alleged assault, a witness gives evidence that he or she saw your client strike the victim. If your case is that the blow was struck in self-defence, you may be able to get the witness to agree that he or she was not present prior to that moment or that his or her view was momentarily obstructed and that he or she was therefore not in a position to see a blow struck first by the alleged victim.

(b) In the case of an alleged burglary, a police officer gives evidence that he or she arrested your client outside the burgled premises. You may be able to limit his or her evidence by establishing that your client's fingerprints were not found at the scene of the crime, yet no gloves/socks were found in the vicinity of the premises or in the defendant's possession at the time of his or her arrest.

(c) In the case of an alleged identification witness, you may limit the evidence by stressing the dissimilarities between the defendant and the description originally given by the witness to the police.

(d) In the case of a contact dispute, the mother gives evidence of the child's apparent distress after Sunday visits to the father. You may undermine her evidence by establishing that there have been no reported problems from the school as to any change in the child's behaviour particularly on Mondays.

22.5.2.2 Discrediting the testimony

The assumption that in every case at least one person is lying to the court is a false one. In many cases, the truth lies somewhere between the witnesses' accounts and/or is obscured by misconception, mistaken/selective recall or simply a different interpretation of the facts. Your purpose in discrediting the evidence is to show or suggest that it is probably less true/reliable than appeared at the end of the examination-in-chief; the emphasis here is not upon seeking to destroy the witness.

Challenging the reliability of the testimony is the most common form of cross-examination. Blatant confrontation seldom produces agreement.

The following are the basic methods for exposing the weaknesses in the evidence:

(a) *Testing the limits of the witness's perception,* ie, the witness's ability and opportunity to observe the matter in question. It is quite common for a witness to 'fill in' the gaps in his or her observation/memory so as to present a complete picture of events. If a witness hears a car crash and then sees the angle of the cars, he or she may jump to a fairly quick assumption/conclusion as to what in fact happened. He or she replaces the missing gaps in his or her knowledge with what he or she believes to be the best explanation of what must have occurred. He or she then convinces himself or herself that this is what he or she actually witnessed and the more he or she repeats it, the more he or she believes it. It is not a deliberate attempt to lie or mislead the court. Most of the time this is done subconsciously.

To test the witness's perception, probe what the witness actually perceived or heard, eg, his or her angle of observation, distance from the events, any factor that may have interrupted, obstructed or distorted his or her view/hearing/powers of observation (eg, presence of other persons, bad weather conditions, fear, anger); the length and nature of his or her involvement/observation; consider what the witness ought to have seen/heard if he or she had witnessed the whole of the incident; elicit whether there has been any discussion with others since the event occurred which may have influenced the witness's perception.

(b) *Testing the witness's memory,* ie, the witness's ability to remember the details and his or her efforts to record them. Probe the witness's memory of peripheral matters, those facts which the witness ought to remember if he or she had seen the whole incident or was involved to the extent that he or she suggests. Concentrate on the time lapse since the event, the lack of record of the events, the absence of reference to a particular fact in the record of the events, the number of similar incidents which the witness has experienced that may affect his or her ability to remember (eg, the number of invoices which a secretary has typed/sent since the one in issue; the number of arrests which a police officer has made since the event in question), the fact of any conversation with others that may have influenced the witness's recollection.

(c) *Testing the witness's powers of communication/appreciation,* ie, the witness's ability to articulate what he or she observed or heard, and the witness's interpretation of what he or she perceived. Probe the witness's ability to record/assess information especially of a technical nature, to estimate distance, time, etc.

22.5.2.3 Discrediting the witness

On occasion, it may be possible to discredit the witness. The emphasis of this type of cross-examination lies upon destroying the witness's credibility, demonstrating that he or she is unreliable or unworthy of belief. There are three ways to discredit the witness:

(a) *Discrediting the witness's conduct:* Some witnesses give their evidence in a reasonable and persuasive manner which belies the inconsistency of their conduct or behaviour at the time of or after the events in question. For example, a woman seeking an injunction to restrain her husband from using violence against her gives evidence of an assault she suffered two weeks beforehand and her fear of her husband since that occasion. She fails to mention the fact that she went out for dinner with him the following week. Or a driver, who denies that his negligent driving was the cause of a collision, fails to mention that he left the scene of the accident in a hurry, refusing to call the police. Look for inconsistencies between the evidence and either the acts or omissions of the witness. Consider what you would have done in the witness's position, how you (and the trier(s) of fact) would have expected the witness to behave as a matter of common sense. You should, however, be prepared for the witness to offer an explanation—either in response to your questions or during re-examination.

(b) *Showing the inconsistencies in the testimony:* The witness's account may contain a fact which is inconsistent with a previous statement of the witness, contradicts other facts, is an exaggeration or is inconsistent with the evidence of another witness.

Many novices approach a prior inconsistent statement like a 'bull in a china shop'. In their anxiety to show that they have caught the witness out they fail to appreciate that the manner in which they show this may well spoil the effect; it may give the witness time to realise his or her error and either correct or explain it away.

The best technique for exposing a previous inconsistent statement is to structure your approach and execute it simply and swiftly. First, commit the witness to the fact that he or she asserts or asserted during examination-in-chief. Second, close the door on any possible explanation—consider how you might try to explain it away if you were the witness. Finally, contrast his or her answer with the previous inconsistent statement. For example:

Q: 'Miss White, you say that the man you saw was well over 6 foot tall?'
A: 'Yes.'
Q: 'How tall are you, Miss White?'
A: 'I'm 5 foot 5 inches.'

Q: 'Do you normally wear high-heeled shoes?'

A: 'Most of the time, yes.'

Q: 'Were you wearing them on that evening?'

A: 'Yes.'

Q: 'Approximately how high were the heels?'

A: 'About two inches.'

Q: 'That would have made you about 5 foot 7 inches—wasn't the man you saw about that height?'

A: 'No, he was much taller.'

Q: 'Didn't you tell Detective Constable Myles that the man you saw was about your height?'

A: 'I don't remember saying that.'

Q: 'You remember making a statement to the police a few hours after the incident?'

A: 'Yes.'

Q: 'Is that the statement you made?' (copy handed to witness)

A: 'Yes.'

Q: 'You made it shortly after the incident while everything was fresh in your mind?'

A: 'Yes.'

Q: 'Look at paragraph 2, third line: "the man was about my height . . . " That is what you told the officer at the time?'

A: 'Yes.'

You may also show inconsistencies in the evidence by exposing embellishments/exaggerations in the witness's account, by highlighting any self-serving conclusions or explanations and/or by uncovering differences between the various witnesses' accounts.

(c) *Impeaching the witness:* In some cases, you may be able to show that the witness himself or herself is unworthy of belief or that little weight should be attached to his/her evidence. The ways of limiting/discrediting the evidence in this manner are to establish:

(i) bias;

(ii) interest in the outcome of the proceedings;

(iii) motive for testifying in a particular manner;

(iv) previous convictions or bad acts.

This must be done carefully. For example, the fact that a witness is related to a party does not automatically mean that he or she has deliberately come to court to tell lies. Approach it gently. Feel your way in. For example, do not begin a cross-examination of a parent giving alibi evidence for a son by baldly accusing him or her of coming to court to tell lies on behalf of their child. Instead, develop the possible bias of a parent in favour of the child so as to show or at least to give the foundation to suggest that the parent is incapable of being impartial.

Q: 'Mr Reynolds, your son was living with you at the time he was arrested for assaulting Miss Clancy?'

A: 'Yes.'

Q: 'You enjoy a good relationship with your son?'

A: 'Yes.'

Q: 'You were surprised when he was arrested?'

A: 'Yes, I was.'

Q: 'As far as you are concerned, this must all be a dreadful mistake?'
A: 'Yes.'
Q: 'You've discussed it with your son?'
A: 'Yes.'
Q: 'On more than one occasion?'
A 'Yes.'

Three points emerge from this examination:

(i) the closeness of the relationship between father and son;
(ii) the father's inability to believe anything bad of his son; and
(iii) the fact that the father and son have discussed the matter in issue and may have influenced each other.

These points can then be emphasised in your closing speech. But remember that if it is your case that the witness could not be mistaken about the alibi evidence that he has given, and so must be telling lies, it is your duty to put that to him in cross-examination. The same questions also lay a good foundation for examining the details of the alibi to see how reliable it is. Remembering the cardinal rule (**22.3**) and applying it to a short and simple example like this, it will be necessary before finishing the cross-examination to decide whether you are suggesting simple unreliability in the parent or unvarnished untruthfulness. If the former, you could finish:

Q: Are you sure you are right about the date/time/place?

If the latter, you could finish:

Q: Are you more concerned to help your child escape the charge than help the jury with the truth?

22.6 Preparation for cross-examination

Provided your questions are relevant and you do not seek to elicit inadmissible evidence, you are generally free to ask whatever questions you consider appropriate. The only restrictions upon your conduct of the cross-examination are the limitations imposed by the Code of Conduct, for example, you must not ask questions which are 'merely scandalous or intended or calculated only to vilify, insult or annoy either a witness or some other person'.

Now that you appreciate the aims of cross-examination and the basic ways of achieving those objectives, you are ready to prepare for cross-examination.

The first step is to ensure that you have the issues clear in your mind. What must you prove or rebut? What is your theory of the case? What are the key elements of the evidence that will support or undermine your case? Make a note of these and keep them to the forefront of your mind at all times.

The next step is to decide whether it is necessary to cross-examine the witness at all. Never cross-examine just because you think the client expects you to or in order to justify your fee or because you think that is what your job as an advocate is all about.

You may already have a good idea of the evidence the witness is likely to give either from the witness statements, reports and/or documents disclosed pre-trial. This is your starting point.

(a) Look at the potential evidence with a critical eye. Can the witness assist your case in any way? Can he or she give evidence which may undermine/harm your case? Which of the essential elements of your case does the witness support/dispute/contradict? It may help to make a note of this.

(b) If the witness neither assists nor harms your case (ie, is neutral), will that be apparent to the trier of fact? Particularly in the case of a jury trial, will the jury appreciate, without a brief cross-examination, that the witness does not take the case against your client any further, eg, that the witness was not present at the time of an alleged conversation? Does this need emphasising?

(c) Consider whether you can elicit the favourable testimony or limit/meet the harmful part of the testimony more effectively in any other way, eg, through another witness/documentary evidence.

(d) Now apply the test: what is your purpose in cross-examining this witness? What do you hope to achieve? There must be a purpose to your cross-examination, even if it is only to 'put your case' to the witness. If you have no reason to cross-examine, no clear objective or identified purpose, then stay glued to your seat.

(e) Remember that this is the preparation stage. It will be necessary to reassess the situation, by running through this sequence again, after the witness has given evidence. This is to guard against any unexpected turn in the case or in the witness's testimony. What if, for example, the witness never gave an anticipated and crucial piece of evidence? A large part of your intended cross-examination may just have become redundant. You must be able to respond to the evidence actually given by the witness in-chief. If they haven't hurt your case, and there is no other reason to cross-examine them, leave them well alone.

22.6.1 Written preparation

Try to get used to jotting down bullet or 'trigger' points for cross-examination rather than the whole questions themselves. Although there are times when it may be necessary to write out (some of) your questions in full, for example, when dealing with an expert witness or a particularly difficult or important matter, it is preferable not to cross-examine from a prepared set of questions. To do otherwise may well impair your ability to watch the witness and adapt your questions to suit the manner of the witness's response. If you are restricted by a rigid set of questions, you will probably find it difficult to engage in the 'parry and thrust' of cross-examination.

This does not mean that you should not prepare for your cross-examination. On the contrary, preparation and planning are vital. You should map out the purpose of your cross-examination, the points you wish to deal with and the order in which you propose to deal with them.

22.6.2 Structure of cross-examination

You are not restricted to following the order in which your opponent examined the witness in-chief. Nor are you limited to asking questions which arise out of the examination-in-chief. In cross-examination, you want your questions to be structured in a way that makes them clear and logical to the trier(s) of fact but maybe not so clear to the witness—at least until it is too late for them to do anything about it! The key here may be to have a gentle and patient build-up, through a series of relatively innocuous questions, until you have painted the witness into a corner. Then you ask the key question, probably putting some part of your client's case to the witness. As a general rule, elicit the favourable testimony before dealing with the unfavourable. Aim to finish on a strong note.

22.6.3 Useful tips

Here are some general hints for conducting your cross-examination:

(a) Formulate your questions so that they contain one fact at a time. Use short questions. Do not recite facts at length and then ask the witness 'Is that right?'. Be clear and concise.

(b) Do not misquote the witness's evidence in-chief.

(c) Avoid getting bogged down in too much minute detail unless it is really necessary.

(d) Know the probable answers to your questions; if you must risk a question to which you do not know the answer, frame it in a closed manner.

(e) Ensure you listen to the answer before asking the next question.

(f) Keep it relevant—limit the areas of your cross-examination to the aspects of the witness's evidence which concern the key elements of your case. Do not pursue pointless cross-examination or get sidetracked by irrelevancies.

(g) Constantly reassess what questions you need to ask the witness.

(h) Keep a structure. Do not jump backwards and forwards from one topic to another. You may succeed in unbalancing the witness in this way but you will also confuse yourself and the trier of fact at the same time!

(i) Lay the foundations first before putting the conclusion to the witness. If you put it to the witness that he was drunk, he may deny it. If you build a picture, step by step, through your questions, showing that the witness had spent all afternoon in the pub, and had drunk several beers and whiskies, had not eaten anything and had been unable to drive home, the witness may still deny the conclusion you put to him (ie, that he was drunk) but the court will have formed its own view!

(j) Be a good actor, keep a poker face if the witness's evidence harms you and try not to show your reaction by your face, manner or voice.

(k) Know when to finish and avoid the temptation to ask one question too many. When you have elicited the evidence, leave the concluding argument to your final submission.

22.7 Special types of witness

22.7.1 The expert witness

The cross-examination of an expert witness is often the key to the whole case. Some expert witnesses are extremely difficult to deal with and, on occasions, you may find that you make little headway in cross-examination. All the more reason to ensure that you are fully prepared and have consulted your own expert on the possible weaknesses of your opponent's expert and/or in his or her opinion/reasoning/methods.

In addition to the cross-examination techniques we have already looked at, there are several other techniques which may be used effectively when cross-examining an expert witness. The aim is to cast doubt upon the expert's experience, methods or opinion. This may be achieved by:

(a) limiting the witness's apparent expertise. Narrow the extent of his or her expertise/experience by showing that it is not directly applicable to the case in question or, perhaps, by contrasting it to the experience of your expert;

(b) showing that the witness has had less involvement/contact with the case than your expert, eg, has only examined a party once; or viewed the machinery long after the accident;

(c) showing your knowledge of the expert's subject. By showing knowledge of the technical terms involved or the way in which any tests were carried out, the expert will be less inclined to dodge your questions;

(d) inviting the witness to define technical terms and use common language. Some find this difficult;

(e) challenging his or her methods, eg, showing that there were other tests which the expert could/should have carried out that might have produced a different result;

(f) inviting the witness to agree with the propositions that form the basis of your expert's opinion—he or she is unlikely to disagree with everything your expert says and you should know from your own expert those areas which are in dispute. Remember to 'put your case' to the expert by inviting him or her to deal with your expert's methods/opinion/conclusions;

(g) inviting the witness to agree that, in his or her field, legitimate differences of opinion frequently occur between qualified experts. This shows that the witness is not infallible and that his or her evidence is 'opinion' only;

(h) using hypothetical facts to test the strength of the expert's opinion. Testing whether a different interpretation of the same facts or a slight change in those facts would affect the expert's opinion.

22.7.2 The evasive witness

You may well find that some witnesses, who gave straightforward responses during examination-in-chief, become evasive during cross-examination. Such evasion can take many forms, for example, the witness may avoid answering the question directly, respond to an entirely different question, ask you to keep repeating your questions, or continually respond with 'I don't know/remember', 'I might', 'I could', 'I would/would not'.

You may deal with this in a number of ways. You can try to pin the witness down by repeating the question. If really necessary, invite the judge to direct the witness to answer the question. Or you can enquire whether the witness is having difficulty understanding or hearing your questions. Or let the witness 'hang himself or herself' by making a terrible impression upon the trier(s) of fact. You can then follow this with a reference to the witness's demeanour in your closing speech, eg, 'Members of the jury, you may think that Mr Smith was rather evasive . . .'.

22.7.3 The belligerent/argumentative witness

Some witnesses try to 'have their say' at length and either ignore the question or cover matters which you did not ask them; or they answer your question with another question; or become abusive or accuse you of not knowing what you are talking about.

Control the witness by using closed, leading questions. If a witness insists on talking, try to cut him or her off by interrupting the flow with your next question. Make each question short. This will contrast with the witness's response and show the trier of fact what the witness is doing. If the witness asks you a question, eg, 'What would you know about it?' or is abusive, simply sidestep the remarks and/or just repeat your question. You will usually find that the judge admonishes the witness. Never get involved in an argument with the witness.

22.8 A famous cross-examination considered

22.8.1 The cross-examination of Dr Crippen

The following is an edited version of the cross-examination of Dr Crippen, who was charged with the murder of his wife, Cora Crippen (also known as Belle Elmore). This extract is taken from *Notable Cross-Examinations* by E. W. Fordham. It illustrates many of the points which we have looked at in this chapter.

22.8.2 The background

First, the background. Mrs Crippen disappeared from the matrimonial home at 39 Hilldrop Crescent at the end of January 1910. In the course of that month, Dr Crippen had bought (for his practice) five grains of hyoscin hydrobromide, a drug used only in minute proportions by the medical profession. He alleged that his wife had gone to America. Shortly after his wife's disappearance, he pawned jewellery of hers for £195. He gave some of her jewellery to Ethel Le Neve, a girlfriend who came to live with him in March 1910. Shortly afterwards, he announced that he had received a cable informing him of his wife's death.

Suspicion was aroused and Dr Crippen was interviewed by the police. He admitted that he had not, in fact, received any news of his wife's death and had not seen her since February 1910. A description of Mrs Crippen was circulated describing her as 'missing'. Two days later, Dr Crippen and Miss Le Neve sailed for Montreal under the disguise of a father and son named 'Robinson'. A warrant was issued for Dr Crippen's arrest which was effected on board the ship.

Number 39 Hilldrop Crescent was thoroughly searched and human remains were found under the floor of the cellar. Death had resulted from hyoscin poisoning. A scar on part of the remains was one such as would have been caused by an operation which Mrs Crippen had undergone.

Two issues concerned the jury: were the remains those of Mrs Crippen? If so, was she murdered by her husband?

22.8.3 The cross-examination

In reading the cross-examination of Dr Crippen by R. D. Muir, you will see that he followed a distinct plan, progressing logically from one subject to another. The underlying purpose of his cross-examination was to show that Dr Crippen knew his wife was dead. He therefore directed his questions to exposing (a) the implausibility of Dr Crippen's assertion that his wife was still alive and (b) the inconsistencies between Dr Crippen's account and his conduct at the time of and subsequent to both his wife's disappearance and his arrest. Note Mr Muir's courteous manner and his use of short questions, each containing only one fact at a time. Note also Dr Crippen's tendency to give evasive answers.

Q: 'On the early morning of the 1st February you were left alone in your house with your wife?'

A: 'Yes.'

Q: 'She was alive?'

A: 'She was.'

Q: 'And well?'

A: 'She was.'

Q: 'Do you know of any person in the world who has seen her alive since?'

A: 'I do not.'

Q: 'Do you know of any person in the world who has ever had a letter from her since?'

A: 'I do not.'

Q: 'Do you know of any person in the world who can prove any fact showing that she ever left that house alive?' (*Note: This is central to the prosecution case.*)

A: 'Absolutely not; I have told Mr Dew exactly all the facts.' (*Mr Dew was the Police Inspector who arrested Dr Crippen.*)

Q: 'At what hour did you last see her on February 1st?'

A: 'I think it would be about between two and three some time that we retired; that would be the last time I saw her.'

Q: 'Did you breakfast at home?'

A: 'I did.'

Q: 'Who prepared your breakfast?'

A: 'I prepared my own breakfast; I nearly always did.'

. . . .

Q: 'We have heard that you were a kind and attentive husband?'

A: 'I was.'

Q: 'Preparing the breakfast in the morning, did you usually take her a cup of tea?'

A: 'Not often; once in a great while I took her a cup of coffee, but very seldom.' (*Note: Line of enquiry unfruitful—Not pursued.*)

. . . .

Q: 'What time did you come home on that night when you say you did not find your wife there?'

A: 'The nearest I should say is, it would be my usual time, about 7.30.'

Q: 'Do you not recollect on that momentous night what time it was you came home?'

A: 'I would not like to say. It was somewhere near 7.30, it might have been 7.25, it might have been 7.35, but it was close to 7.30.'

Q: 'Did you tell Inspector Dew that you got home between 5 and 6?' (*Note: Previous inconsistent statement being put to the witness.*)

A: 'I do not remember telling him that hour.'

Q: 'Listen: "I came back to business the next morning, and when I went home between 5 and 6 pm I found she had gone." Is that right?'

A: 'If I said that to him, that was probably right. I cannot trace it back.'

Q: 'That was a Tuesday?'

A: 'A Tuesday, yes.'

Q: 'The 1st February?'

A: 'Yes.'

Q: 'Where did you think your wife had gone?'

A: 'I supposed, as she had always been talking about Bruce Miller to me, that she had gone there. That was the only thing I could make out.' (*Dr Crippen alleged that his wife had been friendly with this man who, at the time of her disappearance, had returned to America.*)

Q: 'That is to America?'

A: 'To America.'

Q: 'Have you made enquiries?'

A: 'No.'

Q: 'As to what steamers were going to America on or about that date?'

A: 'No, I have not.'

Q: 'At no time?'

A: 'At no time.'

Q: 'Not since your arrest?' (*Note: Counsel showing the inconsistency between Dr Crippen's assertion that his wife was alive and his behaviour, ie, his lack of effort to substantiate it.*)

A: 'Not at all.'

Q: 'What?'

A: 'Not at any time.'

Q: 'Not to find out whether there was some steamer sailing for America in which there was a woman answering the description of your wife?'

A: 'I have not.'

Q: 'Nobody has made those enquiries?'

A: 'No.'

. . . .

Q: 'Going to America on the 1st February, did your wife take any of her furs with her?' (Note *the use of a point of reference to make a transition to another topic.*)

A: 'That I could not say. She had any quantity of furs—any quantity of dresses.'

Q: 'Did she take any of her boxes with her?'

A: 'I believe there is one missing. There were a lot of trunks and boxes in the house; I do not know how many, because she bought several lately—well, not lately, but early last fall. I believe she bought two or three boxes.'

Lord Chief Justice:

'You must kindly listen to the question; it is a very important one. You are not asked whether she bought them. Are you able to say whether she took any boxes with her?' (*Note: Judge admonishing the witness for an evasive answer.*)

A: 'I am not able to say definitely.'

Q: 'Is there a cabstand near your house?'

A: 'There is one round the corner somewhere—round in York Road there is a cabstand.'

. . . .

Q: 'Did you go to the cabstand to enquire whether any cabman had come to take away a box for your wife?' (*Note: Counsel asks a series of questions designed to highlight Dr Crippen's failure to seek proof that his wife was alive.*)

A: 'I did not.'

Q: 'At any time?'

A: 'At no time.'

Q: 'Not since your arrest?'

A: 'No.'

Q: 'Had you any neighbours at 39 Hilldrop Crescent on either side?'

A: 'Yes, we had neighbours on either side.'

Q: 'Have enquiries been made of the neighbours to know whether a cab or box was seen to leave your house on the 1st February?'

A: 'I have made none.'

Q: 'And, as far as you know none have been made?'

A: 'Not as far as I know.'

Q: 'You do not suggest that your wife, on a voyage to America in February, would walk away from the house?'

A: 'I am sure I do not know what she would do. She was a very impulsive woman.'

Q: 'But you have made no enquiries?'

A: 'I have made no enquiries.'

. . . .

Q: 'Have you enquired of the milkman whether he saw your wife alive after you had left the house on that morning of the 1st February?'

A: 'I have already said that I made no enquiries.'

. . . .

Q: 'It would be most important for your defence in this case on the charge of murder if any person could be found who saw your wife alive after the Martinettis saw her alive; you realise that?' (*The Martinettis dined with the Crippens on the evening of 31 January.*) (*Note: This is central to the theme of the prosecution case.*)

A: 'I do.'

Q: 'And you have made no enquiries at all?'

A: 'I have not conducted my own defence.'

Q: 'Of tradesmen, or neighbours, or cabmen? You say you have not conducted your own defence?' (*Note: Counsel picking up upon the witness's answer.*)

A: 'I have not.'

Q: 'You have been consulted about it, I suppose.'

A: 'Certainly.'

Q: 'Did you suggest enquiries of that kind?'

A: 'I did not.'

. . . .

(*Note: The following series of questions, designed to show that Dr Crippen knew his wife was dead.*)

Q: 'Have you made any suggestion to Mr Newton or anyone as to enquiries being made anywhere?' (*Mr Newton was Dr Crippen's solicitor.*)

A: 'That is a point that did not occur to me, so I have not made any such suggestions.'

Q: 'Did you know that any such enquiry would be fruitless?' (*Note: Counsel 'putting his case' in a very subtle manner.*)

A: 'I know nothing of the kind.'

Q: 'Supposing that your wife had written for her furs and jewels, what would have happened?'

A: 'I would have kept them. I paid for them, and I should not have given them up—after (her) leaving me.'

Q: 'Did you know that she would not write for them?' (*Note: Again, Counsel 'putting his case'.*)

A: 'I did not.'

. . . .

Q: 'Where do you suppose your wife was going to get the money to pay her passage to America?'

A: 'She always had plenty of money, apparently.'

Q: 'Did you give her any?'

A: 'I did not give her any, no; I asked her if she was provided with money, if she wished any, and she said, "No, she wanted nothing off me".'

Q: 'You asked her if she wanted any money?'

A: 'Yes.'

Q: 'When did you ask her that?'

A: 'I asked her at the time she said she was going to leave me.'

Q: 'How many times had she said she was going to leave you?'

A: 'Numerous times.'

Q: 'Did you always on those occasions ask her if she wanted money to go away with?'

A: 'I never paid any attention because she had never carried it out to such an extent.' (*Note the evasive answer.*)

Q: 'She said she did not want money from you?'

A: 'Yes.'

Q: 'Were you in want of money?' (*Note: Counsel prepares to expose an inconsistency in the witness's conduct.*)

A: 'I was not.'

Q: 'What did you do with the money that you got from pawning your wife's jewels?'

A: 'I used it for advertising a new scheme I was starting—a new preparation I was putting on the market.'

Lord Chief Justice:

'Do you mean the whole £200—the £80 and the £115?'

A: 'Yes, probably I used most of it.'

Lord Chief Justice:

'You are not asked "probably"; you were asked what you used the money for.' (*Note: Judge again admonishing the witness for an evasive answer.*)

A: 'For paying for the advertising.'

Q: 'Anything else?'

A: 'Well, I also bought some new dental instruments with it.'

. . . .

Q: 'Why were you in such a hurry to pawn your wife's earrings and marquise rings?'

A: 'Because when I contracted for the advertising I would have to pay cash.'

. . . .

Q: 'On the 2nd February you began to raise money (for this scheme) on your wife's jewels.'

A: 'Quite so.'

Q: 'Had you never pawned jewellery of your wife's before?'

A: 'I never pawned my wife's jewellery before.'

Lord Chief Justice:

'Had you ever pawned jewellery before?'

A: 'I had pawned jewellery before, yes.'

Q: 'Of your wife's?'

A: 'No, of my own.'

Q: 'Were February the 2nd and 9th of this year the only two occasions on which you ever pawned jewellery of your wife's?'

A: 'I refuse to accept the idea that it was my wife's.'

. . . .

Q: 'Did you say this to Inspector Dew, "I have never pawned or sold anything belonging to her before or after she left"?' (*Note: Previous inconsistent statement.*)

A: 'I did, but I did not consider it was her property. I considered myself justified in answering in that way.'

Q: 'You told the truth (to Inspector Dew) according to your view about the property?'

A: 'Yes.'

Q: 'Did you account for your wife's jewellery by producing those exhibits which you showed to Inspector Dew at the house?'

A: 'I showed him some she had left.'

Q: 'That she had left behind?'

A: 'Yes.'

Q: 'And did you tell the Inspector that she had other jewellery, and must have taken that with her?'

A: 'She did have some, as I have already said; she had some rings and a watch that belonged to her before she was married.'

Q: 'Did you intend the Inspector to believe that you were accounting for the whole of your wife's jewellery?'

A: 'Certainly.'

. . . .

Q: 'When you found your wife had gone you say you sat down to think how you could cover up the scandal?'

A: 'Yes.'

Q: 'You did your best to cover up the scandal?'

A: 'I did.'

Q: 'Is that your letter written on March 20th at 39 Hilldrop Crescent?' (*Letter handed to Crippen.*)

A: 'It is.'

Q: 'At that time was Ethel Le Neve living with you at that address?'

A: 'I would not be sure whether she came permanently to live with me at that time or not, but she had been on and off there.'

Lord Chief Justice:

'When do you say Miss Le Neve came to live at 39 Hilldrop Crescent?'

A: 'The first time she came there was 2nd February, the Wednesday night. From that time on she was with me probably two or three nights or perhaps more out of the week, but when she came permanently I would not like to say, except that it was shortly before Easter.'

Q: 'On the night of February 2nd did Ethel Le Neve sleep at Hilldrop Crescent?'

A: 'She did.'

(*Counsel now read out Crippen's letter to Mr and Mrs Martinetti of the 20th March*: 'Dear Clara and Paul, Please forgive me for not running in during the week, but I have been so upset by very bad news from Belle that I did not feel equal to talking with anyone. And now I have just had a cable saying she is so dangerously ill with double pleuro-pneumonia that I am considering if I had better not go at once. I don't want to worry you with my troubles, but I felt I must explain why I had not been to see you . . .')

Q: 'Had you, when you wrote that letter, arranged to go to Dieppe with Ethel Le Neve for Easter?'

A: 'Yes, I believe I had.'

Q: 'And did you want to wipe your wife off the slate before you went?'

A: 'It was not a question of that kind. It was that I felt something was necessary to stop all the worry I was having with the enquiries.'

Q: 'Did you want to announce your wife's death before you started for your holiday with Ethel Le Neve on the following Thursday?'

A: 'I do not think that follows a logical sequence.' (*Note the evasive answer.*)

Q: 'That is what you intended to do at the time you wrote that letter?'

A: 'I do not know whether I had at that time fixed the time when I would say that the other cable had arrived or not.'

Q: 'You prepared an advertisement of your wife's death for the Era?'

A: 'Yes.'

Q: 'When did you do that?'

A: 'I cannot tell you.'

Q: 'On the 24th March you sent a telegram to Mrs Martinetti saying that you had had a cable that your wife had died the previous night.'

A: 'Yes.'

Q: 'You sent that from Victoria Station on the eve of your departure with Ethel Le Neve?'

A: 'Yes.'

Q: 'Then you went off and took your holiday with her?'

A: 'Yes.'

Q: 'And you came back?'

A: 'Yes.'

Q: 'And you had to play the role of the bereaved husband?'

A: 'Yes.'

Q: 'Did you do it well?'

A: 'I am sure I could not tell you that.'

(A letter from Crippen to a friend on black-edged paper is put to the witness, recording his sorrow for his wife's death.)

Q: 'Sheer hypocrisy?'

A: 'I am not denying any of this.'

Q: 'Do you ask the jury to believe that, not knowing that your wife might write to those people, you told them she was dead?' (*Note: Counsel showing the implausibility of Dr Crippen's position.*)

A: 'Yes.'

Q: 'Where did you think she was?'

A: 'I thought she had gone to Chicago where Bruce Miller lived.'

Q: 'If she were alive she might call at any moment on her sisters?'

A: 'I did not think she would. If she went off with some other man I did not think she would have the face to go there.'

. . . .

Q: 'You had been a tenant of 39 Hilldrop Crescent for five and a half years?'

A: 'Yes.'

Q: 'Had the floor of the cellar of that house been disturbed during the whole of that time?'

A: 'Not to my knowledge.'

Q: 'You were familiar with the cellar; you knew where the place was?'

A: 'I have not said that I was not.'

Q: 'You know, of course, that those remains were found in the cellar?'

A: 'I was told when I returned to England by my solicitor.'

Q: 'So far as you know, they could not have been put there while you were tenants?'

A: 'Not that I know of; of course . . . I would not say it was impossible, because there were times when we were away.'

. . . .

Q: 'When did you make up your mind to go away from London?'

A: 'The morning after Inspector Dew was there—the 8th or 9th.'

Q: 'Had you the day before been contemplating the possibility of your going away?'

A: 'I would not like to say that I had made up my mind. When Inspector Dew came to me and laid out all the facts that he told me, I might have thought, well, if there is all this suspicion, and I am likely to have to stay in jail for months and months, perhaps until this woman is found, I had better be out of it.'

Q: 'What crime did you understand you might be kept in jail upon suspicion of?'

A: 'I do not understand the law well enough to say. From what I have read it seems to me I have heard of people being arrested on suspicion of being concerned in the disappearance of other people.' (*Note the evasive answer.*)

Q: 'You thought you were in danger of arrest?' (*Note now the effective use of short, leading, concise questions to highlight Dr Crippen's conduct and its consistency with guilty knowledge.*)

A: 'Yes.'

Q: 'And so you fled the country.'

A: 'Yes.'

Q: 'Under a false name?'

A: 'Yes.'

Q: 'Shaved off your moustache?'

A: 'Yes.'

Q: 'Left off wearing your glasses in public?'

A: 'Yes.'

Q: 'Took Le Neve with you?'

A: 'Yes.'

Q: 'Under a false name?'

A: 'Yes.'

Q: 'Posing as your son?'

A: 'Yes.'

Q: 'Went to Antwerp?'

A: 'Yes.'

Q: 'Stayed in a hotel there?'

A: 'Yes.'

Q: 'Stayed indoors all day?'

A: 'Oh no . . . we went to the Zoological Gardens and walked all over the place.'

Q: 'Enjoying yourselves?'

A: 'Certainly.'

Lord Chief Justice:

'What name did you give at the Hotel?'

Q: 'If I gave any name anywhere it would be Robinson.'

Q: 'The second description (in the hotel register) is that of Miss Le Neve?'

A: 'Yes.'

Q: 'Disguised as a boy?'

A: 'Yes.'

Q: 'Passing as your son?'

A: 'Yes.'

. . . .

Q: 'When you got to Quebec on board the steamer, or near Quebec, Inspector Dew came on board?'

A: 'Yes.'

Q: 'You were much surprised to see him?'

A: 'I did not expect to see Inspector Dew.'

Q: 'Did you recognise him at once?'

A: 'Yes . . . but not until he came into the cabin.'

Q: 'Did the Inspector say "Good morning, Dr Crippen, I am Inspector Dew"?'

A: 'Yes.'

Q: 'And did you say, "Good morning, Mr Dew"?'

A: 'Good morning, Mr Dew.'

Q: 'Did the Inspector then say, "You will be arrested for the murder and mutilation of your wife, Cora Crippen, in London, on or about February 2nd last"?'

A: 'I would not say that I took that in, because I was so very much surprised and confused that I did not quite have my right senses.'

Q: 'Did a Canadian officer, Mr McCarthy, caution you?'

A: 'He did.'

Q: 'And you realised you were being charged?'

A: 'Yes.'

Q: 'With what?'

A: 'I realised I was being charged.'

Q: 'With what?' (*Note: Counsel repeats the question which the witness has evaded.*)

A: 'Well, I realised that I was being arrested for murder; I remember hearing that.'

Q: 'The murder of your wife?'

A: 'Yes.'

Q: 'Up to that time did you believe she was alive?'

A: 'I did.'

Q: 'Did you put any question to Inspector Dew as to whether she had been found?' (*Note: Counsel showing the inconsistency in Dr Crippen's behaviour.*)

A: 'I did not put any question at all.'

Q: 'As to how he knew she was dead?'

A: 'No.'

. . . .

Q: 'As you left the cabin did you say to the Inspector, "I am not sorry, the anxiety has been too much"?' (Note: Counsel 'putting his case'.)

A: 'Yes.'

Q: 'Anxiety for what?'

A: 'Anxiety thinking I might be pursued from London.'

Q: 'For what?'

A: 'For the same reason that I ran away.'

. . . .

Q: 'Of course you understand that if your wife is alive there is no foundation for this charge at all?' (*Note: Counsel reinforcing his previous examination to show that Dr Crippen knew his wife was dead.*)

A: 'Decidedly not.'

Q: 'And that if she could be found you would at once be acquitted of it?'

A: 'Oh, rather.'

Q: 'What steps have been taken by you to find your wife?'

A: 'I have not taken any steps.'

. . . .

(*Note: Change of subject—Counsel showing that Dr Crippen had the means to kill his wife.*)

Q: 'When did you first think of prescribing hyoscin for your patients?'

A: 'The first I knew of it was in 1885.'

Q: 'Here in London?'

A: 'Yes, it was early in January this year I first prescribed it for patients.'

Q: 'You can give the names and addresses of the persons to whom you sent your remedies?'

A: 'If I went and looked them up.'

Q: 'Were you prescribing hyoscin for any of those patients?'

A: 'Yes.'

Q: 'As a medicine?'

A: 'Yes.'

Q: 'To be administered through the mouth?'

A: 'Decidedly.'

Q: 'For what disease?'

A: 'Nervous disease—coughs of a septic character and asthmatic complaints.'

Lord Chief Justice:

'If there is any book in which hyoscin is prescribed for use in this way, you had better produce the book.' (No such book was ever produced.)

. . . .

Q: 'Will you answer this question, have you got anywhere left any homeopathic preparation into which you put this hyoscin?'

A: 'They were all sent out as they were made.'

Q: 'You have none left?'

A: 'I have none left.'

Q: 'Have you got any patient to whom you sent such homeopathic preparations?'

A: 'Mr Newton has been looking the matter up; I do not know.'

The skill of Mr Muir's cross-examination was such that he made it appear easy! It is no surprise that the jury found Dr Crippen 'guilty'.

23 Re-examination

23.1 Purpose

As soon as the cross-examination of your witness has been completed, you have the opportunity to re-examine the witness. Re-examination does not mean 'repeat examination'. It is not an opportunity to repeat the evidence given during examination-in-chief. The purpose of re-examination is to clarify, explain or develop matters arising out of cross-examination so as to limit, where possible, any damage to your case.

23.2 The cardinal rules

The cardinal rules of re-examination are:

(a) You have the right to re-examine only on matters that arise out of cross-examination. Re-examination is therefore not an examination-in-chief all over again, nor is it an opportunity to ask questions on some matter which you forgot to ask about in-chief and on which your opponent has not asked questions. If you realise during the cross-examination that you omitted to ask in-chief about some point which could be important and you want to repair your own self-inflicted damage, then you must ask the judge for leave to do so. This will, of course, give your opponent the right to further cross-examination, so you ought to do this before you begin your re-examination. Remember to apologise. It is your mistake, not your client's.

(b) Never re-examine just for the sake of it. Never re-examine unless you are clear about what you can achieve by doing so. Ask yourself 'does the evidence need clarifying or explaining?'; 'can I achieve that by my question(s)?'; 'can the matter be developed further so as to shed a different light upon it?'; 'can I meet the attack on the witness's credit?'. Unless you are satisfied that the answer to one or more of these questions is 'yes', leave well alone.

(c) Never use leading questions to elicit evidence from your own witness in re-examination (see the exceptions in **20.6.1**).

(d) Never ask a question in re-examination to which you do not know the answer. This is a dangerous practice at any time: it could destroy your case at this late stage.

23.3 Is it necessary to re-examine?

The most common situations where it may be necessary to re-examine arise where:

(a) the cross-examiner has elicited only that part of a conversation or an occurrence which is favourable to his or her case; **or**

(b) he or she has attacked the witness's conduct/character; **or**

(c) he or she has highlighted an inconsistency in the witness's evidence or has impeached the witness with a prior inconsistent statement; **or**

(d) where the witness has become muddled or confused or you think the audience has become muddled or confused. In either event, order and clarity need to be restored.

23.4 Examples of re-examination

If you must re-examine, make it short and businesslike. Beware of the 'just one more question' syndrome.

Example 1

A mother, who is opposed to contact between her children and their father, is cross-examined to the effect that she stopped the visits only after the father reduced the maintenance he was paying her. She denies that the money had anything to do with her decision to stop contact between the children and their father.

Re-examination

Q: 'How much is your weekly income?'

A: '£102.'

Q: 'How is that figure made up?'

A: 'I get £27 in child benefit and £50 a week now from my ex-husband. The rest is made up from Income Support.'

Q: 'How much was your ex-husband paying you before he reduced it?'

A: '£75 a week.'

Q: 'What was your total income at that time?'

A: 'With the child benefit, it was the same, £102 per week.'

Example 2

The defendant is charged with taking and driving away a motor vehicle without the owner's consent. The owner is cross-examined to the effect that he had loaned his car to the defendant, his neighbour, on a previous occasion and had told the defendant he could take it at any time. The owner admits the former but not the latter allegation.

Re-examination

Q: 'You told the court, in answer to my friend, that you had let the defendant borrow your car on a previous occasion.'

A: 'Yes.'

Q: 'When was that?'

A: 'About six months beforehand.'

Q: 'What were the circumstances?'

A: 'It was the day of the tube strike. He asked me if he could borrow the car or he'd miss an important job interview. He brought it back a few hours later.'

Q: 'What happened to your car keys on that occasion?'

A: 'He returned them to me.'

Q: 'Did you give him your car keys at any other time?'

A: 'No.'

Q: 'Did you give him permission to borrow your car on any other occasion?'

A: 'No, I did not. It was a once-off.'

Example 3

The cross-examination of an assault victim has emphasised the fact that she originally told the police she did not know her attacker. It was only two weeks later that she 'pointed the finger' at the accused.

Re-examination

Q: 'Why did you tell the police initially that you did not know your attacker?'

A: 'I was frightened. He told me he knew where I lived and he would come and get me.'

Q: 'Why did you subsequently change your mind.'

A: 'I managed to find another place to live. I felt safer.'

23.5 In conclusion

If you decide not to re-examine, you can simply say 'I have no further questions (of this witness) Your Honour/Sir/Madam'.

Whether you decide to re-examine or not, it is proper to give the judge or magistrate the opportunity of asking the witness any question he or she deems necessary.

'Unless your Lordship/Your Honour has any questions?'/'Have you any questions, Sir/Madam?'

If the judge or magistrate does question the witness, he or she must give both you and your opponent the opportunity of asking further questions **arising out of** what he or she has asked.

23.6 Releasing the witness

Unless the witness is a party to the proceedings or the defendant in a criminal trial, you must ask the court to release the witness from continued attendance at court.

'My Lord/Your Honour/Sir/Madam, may this witness be released?'

The judge or magistrate will ask your opponent whether he or she objects to the witness being released. The answer is usually 'No'. The judge or magistrate will then indicate that the witness is free to go.

It is time to call your next witness or to inform the court: 'That is the case for the prosecution/claimant/defendant'.

Part VI

How-to-do-it guides

24

Using this Part of the manual

The chapters in this Part are all about making your life easier. They are a set of how-to-do-it guides which cover some of the most common types of applications that you may face as an advocate at the start of your career. Usually they are written by practising barristers with considerable practical experience of the matters they are writing about. The matters range from the sort of hearing where your application is the sole purpose for the hearing (for example, an application for summary judgment) to those applications which have to be made as and when the need arises, in the context of other proceedings in the case (for example, applying for bail when a criminal case is remanded). Some of these guides are necessarily more extensive than others.

As we have already noted in the manual, in practice different barristers may well have different styles which they use, different structures or techniques which they find work well for them. The aim of these guides is to give you an insight into how a particular application or hearing might work and what needs to be covered in it. As we said earlier, in the context of observing barristers in court—never slavishly follow what you see and hear, always think critically about it. Did that work? Why? Could I do that? Could I improve on that? The same advice should be borne in mind when reading any of these guides—they are simply one starting point for you.

The aim of these chapters is not to render you competent to make such an application overnight. You should read them in conjunction with the other BVC manuals and relevant practitioner works, as appropriate for the application. The aim is to give you some advance notice of what happens in court when a particular application is made: who starts, what documents are needed, how many copies must be provided and so forth.

After reading this material, you should have a basic idea of how to plan for a particular application, rather than making your first one in a state of '**un**blissful' ignorance! Never neglect the other resources at your disposal, though. You should always feel able to ask other, more experienced barristers for advice or hints when you are in chambers. If possible, try to get to court early so that you can watch how similar applications are being made; note the judge's likes and dislikes.

The chapters start with a general guide to the preparation of skeleton arguments, which may be used in civil and criminal cases. Next, you will find some guides for work in the civil courts and tribunals. It is hoped that these are of particular assistance as civil interlocutory matters so often take place in private, with only the parties and their advocates present, so there is limited opportunity simply to observe them. These are followed by some guides to work in the criminal courts.

25 Skeleton arguments

25.1 General

25.1.1 The importance of skeleton arguments

The ability to draft a strong, persuasive and yet precise skeleton argument in support of the case you are putting forward is now a fundamental skill required of an advocate. Owing to the importance increasingly placed by judges on skeleton arguments, the skill of preparing them should be seen by the junior barrister as one which is every bit as important as the skill involved in undertaking other forms of written work, such as drafting the statements of case at the start of the claim, or advising in writing during the lifetime of the claim.

A skeleton argument is designed to assist the court with a written outline of the main points to be put forward by a party at a subsequent oral hearing. It is produced by that party's advocate, and given to the judge, before the oral hearing. At the hearing, the judge will expect the advocate to follow it. The use of the word 'skeleton' is significant and its meaning in this context should be understood at the outset and never forgotten. The purpose of a written skeleton argument is to provide you with a structured framework on which you can hang your oral submissions to the court. It is, quite literally, the bones upon which you later build the flesh of your argument. It follows that all of the main issues which you will seek to deal with at the hearing should be covered.

It is now common practice for advocates to draft skeleton arguments, whether for use at interim applications or to form the basis of final submissions at trial after the evidence has been heard. The strict timetables imposed by the CPR have led to the ever more widespread use of written argument.

In criminal proceedings skeleton arguments are frequently used to form the basis of pre-trial argument, such as applications to exclude evidence or to sever an indictment. They are also used at the conclusion of the prosecution case if a submission of no case is to be made.

From time to time in practice advocates are asked to provide the judge with written submissions. These should be distinguished from skeleton arguments. A written submission is intended to be an *alternative* to oral argument (see *Sleeman v Highway Care Ltd* The Times, 3 November 1999). A skeleton argument is an *aid* to oral argument.

25.1.2 Practice Directions and guidelines

On 24 January 1995, Lord Chief Justice Taylor issued a *Practice Direction (Civil Litigation: Case Management)* [1995] 1 All ER 385, which applied to all lists in the Queen's Bench and Chancery Divisions, except where other directions specifically applied. The purpose of the *Practice Direction* was to improve case management, and to reduce the costs and delay of civil litigation. It required, not less than three clear days before the hearing of a claim or application, each party to lodge with the court (with copies being provided to the other parties) a skeleton argument concisely summarising that party's submissions in relation to each of the issues, and citing the main authorities relied upon, which may be attached.

Now that judicial case management takes place under the CPR, you will find in practice that for all multi-track cases in which a case management conference takes place, the court will give detailed directions for the steps to be taken up to the trial and for the trial itself. Those directions will inevitably include a provision requiring the parties to file skeleton arguments a certain number of days prior to trial or before any application of substance to a judge.

In addition, under PD 28 (the fast track) and PD 29 (the multi-track), the parties will be required to file a case summary prior to trial in the fast track and prior to a case management conference in the multi-track.

Skeleton arguments are also required when filing a notice of appeal (PD 52, para 5.9).

There is guidance on the drafting of skeleton arguments in Appendix 7 to the *Chancery Guide*, paragraph 7.11.12 of the *Queen's Bench Guide*, Appendix 9 to the *Admiralty and Commercial Courts Guide*, and PD 52, paras 5.10–5.11. No matter what court you are appearing in, and for whatever type of hearing you are preparing your skeleton argument, it would be wise to follow the requirements of PD 52 para 5.10, which reads as follows:

> (1) *A skeleton argument must contain a numbered list of the points which the party wishes to make. These should both define and confine the areas of controversy. Each point should be stated as concisely as the nature of the case allows.*
>
> (2) *A numbered point must be followed by a reference to any document on which the party wishes to rely.*
>
> (3) *A skeleton argument must state, in respect of each authority cited—*
>
> (a) *the proposition of law that the authority demonstrates; and*
>
> (b) *the parts of the authority (identified by page or paragraph references) that support the proposition.*
>
> (4) *If more than one authority is cited in support of a given proposition, the skeleton argument must briefly state the reason for taking that course.*
>
> (5) *The statement referred to in sub-paragraph (4) should not materially add to the length of the skeleton argument but should be sufficient to demonstrate, in the context of the argument—*
>
> (a) *the relevance of the authority or authorities to that argument; and*
>
> (b) *that the citation is necessary for a proper presentation of that argument.*
>
> (6) *The cost of preparing a skeleton argument which—*
>
> (a) *does not comply with the requirements set out in this paragraph; or*
>
> (b) *was not filed within the time limits provided by this Practice Direction (or any further time granted by the court),*
>
> *will not be allowed on assessment except to the extent that the court otherwise directs.*

But follow also the guidance in the Chancery Guide:
Appendix 7 Guidelines on Skeleton Arguments and Chronologies

> 1. *A skeleton argument is intended to identify both for the parties and the court those points which are, and those that are not, in issue, and the nature of the argument in relation to those points which are in issue. It is not a substitute for oral argument.*

2. *Every skeleton argument should therefore:*

   (1) identify concisely

   (a) the nature of the case generally, and the background facts insofar as they are relevant to the matter before the court;

   (b) the propositions of law relied on with references to the relevant authorities;

   (c) the submissions of fact to be made with reference to the evidence;

   (2) be as brief as the nature of the issues allows—it should not normally exceed 20 pages of double-spaced A4 paper and in many cases it should be much shorter than this;

   (3) be in numbered paragraphs and state the name (and contact details) of the advocate(s) who prepared it;

   (4) avoid arguing the case at length;

   (5) avoid formality and make use of abbreviations, eg C for Claimant, A/345 for bundle A page 345, 1.1.95 for 1st January 1995 etc.

Take heed also of the Queen's Bench Guide, which says:

7.11.12 A skeleton argument should:

(1) concisely summarise the party's submissions in relation to each of the issues,
(2) cite the main authorities relied on, which may be attached,
(3) contain a reading list and an estimate of the time it will take the Judge to read,
(4) be as brief as the issues allow and not normally be longer than 20 pages of double-spaced A4 paper,
(5) be divided into numbered paragraphs and paged consecutively,
(6) avoid formality and use understandable abbreviations, and
(7) identify any core documents which it would be helpful to read beforehand.

25.1.3 The length of a skeleton argument

As the *Practice Direction* makes clear, the purpose of a skeleton argument is solely to identify and summarise the points at issue. It is an aide-memoire for convenience of reference before and during the hearing. A skeleton argument should therefore be as succinct as possible. It is not the function of a skeleton argument to argue the case on paper. The guidance set out above suggests a normal maximum of 20 pages of double-spaced A4 paper, but in many cases skeleton arguments can and should be much shorter than this. It is wrong to assume that longer cases justify proportionately longer skeleton arguments. In the case of interim and shorter final appeals in the Court of Appeal, it should normally be possible to do justice to the relevant points in a skeleton argument of considerably less than ten pages. For short hearings before the district judge in the county court, of the type often undertaken by junior counsel in the early years of practice, and which might, for example, involve applications on disclosure issues, or seeking permission to call a particular expert witness, it is suggested that the skeleton argument should rarely exceed five pages.

In the case of *Tombstone Ltd v Raja* [2008] EWCA Civ 1444, [2008] All ER (D) 180 (Dec), the Court of Appeal was scathing about the length and quality of Tombstone's skeleton argument. In an appeal from a relatively short judgment, it ran to 110 pages plus 64 pages of appendices. Mummery LJ said (paras [124] and following):

> The length of Tombstone's skeleton did not assist the court. In fact, it tended to detract from Tombstone's case ...
>
> Practitioners who ignore practice directions on skeleton arguments ... are well advised to note the risk of the court's negative reaction to unnecessarily long written submissions ...

> We remind practitioners that skeleton arguments should not be prepared as verbatim scripts to be read out in public or as footnoted theses to be read in private. Good skeleton arguments are tools with practical uses: an agenda for the hearing, a summary of the main points, propositions and arguments to be developed orally, a useful way of noting citations and references, a convenient place for making cross-references, a time-saving means of avoiding unnecessary dictation to the court and laborious and pointless note-taking by the court.
>
> Skeleton arguments are aids to oral advocacy ... Too many practitioners, at increased cost to their clients and diminishing assistance to the court, burden their opponents and the court with written briefs. They are anything but brief. The result is that there is no real saving of legal costs, or of precious hearing, reading and writing time ...

This criticism by Mummery LJ should be remembered by all advocates when determining the amount of detail to be advanced in a skeleton argument. Accordingly, the first and foremost rule for the preparation of any skeleton argument must be to 'keep it concise'.

25.1.4 The content and structure of a skeleton argument

There is no strict formula, but a good skeleton argument will usually:

(a) Set out the nature of the application/submission.

(b) State briefly what the case is about (if necessary).

(c) Summarise the issues between the parties (if necessary).

(d) Set out the argument in the form of a series of legal propositions and submissions supported by authority and by evidence (with page/paragraph references as necessary).

(e) Assist the court to assimilate your argument with ease.

(f) Assist you to persuade the court to grant the order you seek.

(g) Identify precisely what the court is being asked to do.

The content of the skeleton argument will inevitably vary according to the complexity of the issues and the stage in the proceedings at which the submissions are made. You should bear in mind that your skeleton argument will be read in advance by the judge and your opponent. It is therefore your first opportunity to influence the outcome of the hearing. The structure should be logical with clear paragraph numbers and sub-headings. Although your skeleton argument should be informative, it should also be concise and easily absorbed. Above all a *skeleton* argument should be just that: the argument should not be fully fleshed out. It is for the advocate to develop the submissions orally. Finally, it is good practice, particularly in civil proceedings, to assist the court by handing up a chronology in a separate document.

In the same way as you develop a style for drafting statements of case, similarly you will develop a style for the preparation of skeleton arguments. The precise form for a skeleton argument will be very much a question of personal choice, which you will develop in your own good time. Nevertheless, one can provide some very basic 'dos' and 'don'ts', which must always be adhered to.

In the case of points of law, there should be a list of the propositions of law which are going to be advanced. The skeleton argument should clearly state the point being contended for and cite the principal authority or authorities in support, with reference to the particular page(s) where the principle concerned is enunciated.

Thus in a medical negligence claim, for instance, one might see early on in the skeleton argument the proposition: 'a doctor cannot be guilty of negligence if he acts in accordance with a responsible body of medical opinion (see *Bolam v Friern Hospital Management Committee* [1957] 1 WLR 582 at 587)'.

Imagine you are acting for a claimant in a trial involving an epidural injection of anaesthetic into the client's spine which it was alleged by the claimant (and supporting medical expert opinion evidence) had been negligently administered by a young and inexperienced doctor, in the wrong place, and not by a senior consultant as contended for by the defendant health authority. The local anaesthetic has escaped into surrounding tissues where it should not have been allowed to go, causing severe long-term injury.

In dealing with breach of duty, a skeleton argument might well have a sub-heading 'Breach of Duty' and then choose to list the central factual issues to be determined by the judge at trial as follows:

(1) Who performed the injection?
(2) Where was the needle sited?
(3) Where was the anaesthetic's intended target?
(4) Was the needle site appropriate?
(5) Was the local anaesthetic released at the target site in the spine?
(6) If the answer to question (5) is 'Yes', how did the local anaesthetic escape to the site of injury?
(7) If the answer to question (5) is 'No', where was the local anaesthetic released?

If such a list of questions were to feature in a skeleton argument being handed in at the start of the trial in this imaginary claim, clearly it would be of immense assistance to the judge when it came to understanding the case in opening, and also when deciding the case later on. If a skeleton is being prepared for a trial at first instance, obviously there would be no transcripts of evidence to be referred to. Reference would, however, have to be made within the skeleton argument to the evidence within the trial bundle (both lay witness statements and reports from the medical experts), which would assist the trial judge in answering the questions you have posed.

25.1.5 Citing authorities in a skeleton argument

There are some important requirements set out in a *Practice Note* [2001] 2 All ER 510:

Methods of citation

8.1. *Advocates will in future be required to state, in respect of each authority that they wish to cite, the proposition of law that the authority demonstrates, and the parts of the judgment that support that proposition. If it is sought to cite more than one authority in support of a given proposition, advocates must state the reason for taking that course.*

8.2. *The demonstration referred to in para 8.1 will be required to be contained in any skeleton argument and in any appellant's or respondent's notice in respect of each authority referred to in that skeleton or notice.*

8.3. *Any bundle or list of authorities prepared for the use of any court must in future bear a certification by the advocate responsible for arguing the case that the requirements of this paragraph have been complied with in respect of each authority included.*

8.4. *The statements referred to in para 8.1 should not materially add to the length of submissions or of skeleton arguments, but should be sufficient to demonstrate, in the context of the advocate's argument, the relevance of the authority or authorities to that argument and that the citation is necessary for a proper presentation of that argument.*

25.1.6 Other requirements

The Court of Appeal's *Practice Direction* specifically states that in the case of an appeal on a question(s) of fact, the skeleton argument should state briefly the basis on which it is contended that the Court of Appeal can interfere with the finding of fact concerned, with cross-references to the passages in the transcript or notes of evidence which bear on the point.

In the Court of Appeal, it is mandatory for the appellant's advocate's skeleton argument to be accompanied by a written chronology of events relevant to the appeal, cross-referenced to the core bundle or appeal bundle. Chronologies are also strongly recommended by the *Queen's Bench Guide* and *Chancery Guide*. The point to note here particularly is that the chronology is a separate document, and is not to be found within the skeleton argument. It is important that the chronology is kept as a separate document from the skeleton argument, in order that it may easily be consulted in conjunction with other papers.

25.2 Skeleton argument for use at a civil trial

25.2.1 Introduction

Given the very nature and purpose of a skeleton argument, in that it seeks to present an overview of a whole claim and the party's fundamental case to be presented, it is very difficult, if not impossible, within the space available here, to provide any really useful 'model' skeleton argument.

However, there is an example of a skeleton argument provided below. It involves an imaginary case in which a hospital cleaner is alleging she fractured her wrist whilst at work following a fall down some stairs. The defendant NHS Trust's case is that there was no accident suffered at work at all! There is no real issue as to the law and the trial will turn on the resolution of the factual dispute. You should note the basic structure of the skeleton argument, namely an introduction, a list of the issues contended for, how the defendant puts its case with regard to the accident, and also what the defendant says about the injury sustained.

25.2.2 Skeleton argument

IN THE HIGH COURT OF JUSTICE
QUEEN'S BENCH DIVISION

Claim No 2006 HC 6312

BETWEEN

SANDRA LOCKWOOD — Claimant

and

HARLEY NHS TRUST — Defendant

DEFENDANT'S SKELETON ARGUMENT

INTRODUCTION

1. The Claimant claims damages arising out of an accidental fall at work with the Defendant on 5th October 2004 ('the Material Accident') when she allegedly suffered a fracture of the scaphoid of the left wrist. The Claimant was working as a cleaner at the time of the alleged accident. Her case is that she fell down some stairs having tripped up on a defect at the top of the staircase.
2. A default judgment for damages to be assessed has been entered and, accordingly, the hearing on 26th June 2009 is an assessment of damages. The question is what damages, that is for personal injuries and consequential financial losses, can the Claimant prove she has suffered, if any, as a result of the material accident.

THE ISSUES

3. The Defendant contends that the principal issues are as follows:

    (1) Did the Claimant in fact suffer a fracture to her left scaphoid or indeed any injury to her left wrist in the Material Accident on 5th October 2004?
    (2) If the Claimant injured her left wrist in the Material Accident, what was the nature of the injury, did she have a pre-existing degenerative condition of the wrist and, if so, did the injury merely bring to light and/or exacerbate a condition that would in any event have caused the Claimant the troubles complained of and, if so, to what extent?
    (3) Which absences from work (if any) have been attributable to the Material Accident and was the Claimant's medical retirement from the Defendant's employment in July 2006 (on the grounds of 'scaphoid bone cyst') attributable to the Material Accident and, if so, to what extent has the Claimant's employability thereafter been restricted as a result of matters properly attributable to the Material Accident?

THE ACCIDENT

4. The Defendant's case is that in the Material Accident the Claimant suffered no injury to her left wrist (which is the *only* injury in respect of which she claims: see Particulars of Claim, para 7, Particulars of Injury, at Trial Bundle, page 8, 'TB 8').
5. Trial Bundle, pages 191 to 199 ('TB 191–199') to which reference is made below are annexed to this Skeleton.
6. On the day of the Material Accident, Tuesday 5th October 2004, at 14.00 hours first aid was given to the Claimant when she was found to be suffering from a 'badly bruised right upper arm and back of shoulder resulting from an accident at rear staircase'. The Claimant returned to duty at 14.15 hours. See First Aid Report at TB 191.
7. On Friday 8th October 2004, the Claimant herself completed an Accident on Duty Report recording that on 5th October 2004 at 14.00 hours on the rear staircase 'I slipped on top stair' and described her injury as 'bruised right upper shoulder': see TB 192.
8. The same day, 8th October 2004, a supervising officer's Accident on Duty Report and an entry in the Accident Book were completed (see TB 193–194 and TB 195 Entry No 935 respectively). The contemporaneous description of the Claimant's injury in both cases was 'bruised right shoulder'. The words 'plus wrist fracture' at paragraph 10 of the supervising officer's Accident on Duty Report, TB 193, were

added at a later date, after, the Defendant will contend, the Claimant had attended hospital on 18th and 19th October 2004. The same contention is made in relation to the words 'fractured left wrist' which were added to and then deleted from the Accident Book entry at TB 195.

9. The Claimant did not cease work until 18th October 2004: see her computerised sick absence record at TB 199.

10. The Claimant did not attend her general practitioner in respect of the Material Accident or any injury to her left wrist: see the clinical record cards at TB 125.

11. The Claimant attended the Accident and Emergency Department of the Burton General Hospital on Monday 18th October 2004 when she complained of 'Injury left wrist fell down stairs at work on Friday. Painful ever since'. (Friday would have been 15th October 2004.) She gave the history 'Friday: fell down stairs at work and hurt left wrist? mech (mechanism) of injury unable to recall how landed'. See the Casualty Officer's contemporaneous A & E Department records at TB 66–67.

12. The following day, Tuesday 19th October 2004, the Claimant returned to the Burton General Hospital as an out-patient where she gave the history 'Had a fall 4/7 (ie 4 days ago) landed on left outstretched hand. Seen at A/E Department 1/7 (ie 1 day ago). On clinical and radiological examination, she was found to have a left scaphoid fracture. Scaphoid type POP (plaster of paris) was applied. Today POP is satisfactory circulation is okay x-ray cyst in left scaphoid (fracture) through it.': see the clinical notes at TB 68.

13. The Claimant has never reported or complained to the Defendant of an accident at work on Friday 15th October 2004: see the Accident Book at TB 195 which records accidents up to 18th November 2004.

14. In the circumstances, the Defendant will contend that the Claimant suffered no injury to her left wrist in the Material Accident on 5th October 2004 and, therefore, her claim fails in its entirety, as the whole of her claim for both general and special damages is based upon an alleged injury to her left wrist.

15. In the event of this Court finding that she did injure her left wrist in the Material Accident, the Defendant's alternative arguments are outlined below.

THE NATURE OF THE INJURY

16. The contemporaneous clinical notes at the Burton General Hospital quoted above record that when x-rays were first taken they showed a cyst in the left scaphoid with a possible fracture running through it (TB 67 foot and TB 68). A further entry on 4th December 2004 noted, *inter alia,* 'X-ray no definite (fracture)': TB 69.

17. In the circumstances, if there was in fact a fracture to the left scaphoid the most it can be blamed for is bringing to light and exacerbating an existing degenerative condition in the wrist which would, in any event, have caused such problems in due course.

18. The Claimant was off work initially from 18th October 2004 to 4th December 2004 and then from 22nd December 2004 to 1st May 2005 with problems related to her left wrist injury. Thereafter, she returned to work and had no further absences attributable to her left wrist for nearly 9 months until 29th January 2006: see the computerised sick absence record at TB 199. During those 9 months her only substantial absences were in August and November 2005, 34 days with back pain, and January 2006, a total of 19 days absence, again related to back pain.

19. When in 2006 the Claimant again complained of problems relating to her left wrist these were said to have arisen from an injury to her wrist in February 2006 when she was 'pulling a bucket': see the memorandum from Dr Sheridan, the Defendant's Area Medical Adviser, dated 25th April 2006 at TB 108, the middle of the page. In the circumstances, the Defendant will contend that the Claimant's eventual medical retirement in July 2006 on grounds of 'scaphoid bone cyst' (see the Medical Retirement Certificate at TB 116) and her subsequent restricted working ability is not attributable to the Material Accident but to the pre-existing degenerative condition and/or a further accident, in February 2006.
20. If necessary, the Defendant will contend that in the light of the Claimant's full sick absence record (TB 196–199), irrespective of the material accident, the Claimant's employment with the Defendant would not have continued beyond her actual retirement date in July 2006 in any event.
21. In so far as may be necessary, in relation to the calculation of damages claimed the Defendant will rely upon its Counter Schedule dated 3rd June 2009 (TB 175–181).

22nd June 2009
4 Gray's Inn Place — BESS TOFFER

25.2.3 Commentary

The above skeleton argument, when set out in the conventional way, double-spaced on A4 paper, with generous margins, is seven pages long. This is well within the guidelines on length.

It is not easy to read and understand quickly, since you cannot follow up the references to the trial bundle, and the chronology needs to be clear in your mind. But read it again carefully in conjunction with this commentary and you will find it has a compelling clarity and logic. It is a good skeleton argument.

Note above all that it does not attempt to duplicate any other documents: it is not in any way setting out what would be found in the statements of case, the witness statements, the exhibits, the medical reports or the schedules of loss, but it draws on all of these to construct the argument.

It is fully headed, and the title of the document identifies whose skeleton argument it is ('Defendant's').

Introduction. Paragraph 1 is a very brief statement of what the case is about, setting the facts out far more briefly than they would be in the particulars of claim. The chief function of this paragraph is to identify and define the material accident, which is an essential point of departure for the argument that follows. Paragraph 2 simply states the broad issue before the court.

Issues. It is essential to summarise the issues at the outset, so that the judge can know what point the argument is addressing. It is more accurate to say 'the Defendant contends that the issues are' than 'the issues are', since the claimant may well have a different set of issues in her argument. Paragraph 3 then subdivides into the three main issues. Issue (1) is the most important and comes first: it is very clear. Issue (2) is arguably several sub-issues rolled into one, but it becomes clear when they are argued (in paragraphs 16 and 17) that they are inseparable. Issue (3) also raises several subissues, but they are closely connected and interdependent, so they can be identified as one.

The structure of the remainder of the skeleton argument is based on these three issues. Paragraphs 4–14 contain the argument on issue (1); paragraphs 16 and 17 contain the argument on issue (2); and paragraphs 18 to 21 contain the argument on issue (3).

Paragraphs 4 to 14. The argument on issue (1). This section begins by making a clear statement (in paragraph 4) of the proposition the argument is intended to prove, namely that there is no causal link between the accident complained of and the injury complained of. Paragraph 5 is then a formal statement of the pages annexed for the judge's convenience.

From paragraph 6 onwards the argument is built up step by step in a logical way. Note how every step in the argument is supported by evidence. The defendant is not saying what it would like to prove, but what it contends it actually can prove. Obviously the argument is based on evidence that has not yet been accepted by the court or tested by cross-examination, and it may be that when it comes to oral argument counsel for the defendant will need to make adjustments and recognise different strengths and weaknesses. But at this stage, the skeleton argument can only be based on the evidence that will go in as evidence-in-chief, and so it is.

In essence the argument is that:

(1) The accident on 5 October 2004 did not cause any injury to the claimant's left wrist. Evidence in support of this:

- (a) first aid report says right shoulder (paragraph 6);
- (b) claimant's accident on duty report says right shoulder (paragraph 7);
- (c) supervisor's accident on duty report says right shoulder (left wrist added later) (paragraph 8);
- (d) accident book says right shoulder (left wrist added and then deleted later) (paragraph 8);
- (e) claimant did not cease work after accident (paragraph 9);
- (f) claimant did not consult GP regarding accident (paragraph 10).

(2) If her left wrist was injured at all, it was injured in a separate accident on 15 October 2004. Evidence in support of this:

- (a) casualty notes from hospital including claimant's own complaint (paragraph 11);
- (b) further casualty notes including same complaint by C (paragraph 12).

(3) Any accident on 15 October is not alleged to be the fault of the defendant. Evidence—no entry in accident book (paragraph 13).

Paragraph 14. Sums up the argument by repeating the defendant's contention and stating the consequence that flows from it, namely that the claimant's claim fails in its entirety.

Paragraph 15. Acknowledges the fact that if the defendant succeeds on issue (1), issues (2) and (3) will not need to be argued or decided.

Paragraphs 16 to 17. The argument on issue (2). The argument here will depend on favourable medical opinion, but if the medical opinion is favourable, the argument is straightforward. The X-ray results showed a cyst (see paragraph 12) and no definite fracture (paragraph 16), so even if there was a fracture to the left wrist, and even if it was caused by the material accident, it only produced a condition which the claimant would have suffered from in due course in any event.

Paragraphs 18 to 21. The argument on issue (3). This argument addresses the quantum of damages for lost earnings and seeks to show that even if the wrist was injured in the material accident, and even if the defendant is liable for that injury, most losses of earnings claimed stem from other causes. The only concession, made at the start of paragraph 18, is that two periods of loss were due to the wrist injury. Thereafter she had periods off work due to back pain (paragraph 18), which the defendants will contend are irrelevant (it is not clear whether the claimant has claimed in respect of this loss anyway).

The main loss of earnings results from the claimant's retirement from work which the defendant contends was due either to the pre-existing condition or to yet another accident (paragraph 19). As a last resort the defendant says the claimant's sickness record taken as a whole was such that she would probably have retired when she did in any event for one reason or another (paragraph 20). The figures which flow from these contentions are to be found in the counter-schedule of loss (paragraph 21).

The skeleton argument should be signed by counsel.

25.3 Skeleton argument in support of interim application

The following is an example of a skeleton argument which might be used in an application to set aside judgment in default. The particulars of claim in this case and the witness statement in support of the application can be found in the ***Drafting*** manual at **9.5** and **20.8**, respectively.

25.3.1 Skeleton argument

IN THE HIGH COURT OF JUSTICE
QUEEN'S BENCH DIVISION
MANCHESTER DISTRICT REGISTRY

Claim No 2009 HC 98744

BETWEEN

SHILTON MACHINE TOOLS LIMITED Claimant

and

BANKS PLASTIC MOULDINGS LIMITED Defendant

SKELETON ARGUMENT OF THE DEFENDANT

Introduction

1. This is an application on behalf of the Defendant for judgment entered in default, under **CPR Part 12**, to be set aside under **CPR r 13.3** and for transfer of the proceedings to Leeds County Court.

Evidence

2. In support of the application the Defendant will refer to the witness statement of Brian Parkes (**'WS/BP'**), dated 15th November 2009, together with the following exhibits:

Exhibit BP1: Contractual documentation with United Plastic Containers Plc;

Exhibit BP2: Correspondence between the Claimant and the Defendant;

Exhibit BP3: Draft defence and counterclaim.

Background

3. The claim is for the sum of £69,000, being the price of moulding machines sold and delivered by the Claimant to the Defendant. The Defendant contends that the machines were defective.
4. Claim form/particulars of claim issued: 22.09.09

Date of Service: 3.10.09;

Expiry of time for filing acknowledgement of service/defence: 17.10.09,

Judgment in default entered: 07.11.09.

APPLICATION TO SET ASIDE DEFAULT JUDGMENT

The court's discretion

5. The court has a discretion to set aside judgment entered in default of a defence 'if the defendant has a real prospect of successfully defending the claim': CPR r 13.3(1)(a) or 'if it appears to the court that there is some other good reason why judgment should be set aside': r 13.3(b)(i) or 'the defendant should be allowed to defend the claim': r 13.3(b)(ii).
6. The four machines delivered to the Defendant by the Claimant were defective in that they were the subject of frequent breakdowns. A consulting engineer has advised the Defendant that two of the machines are so badly designed that they are incapable of meeting industry standards and cannot be repaired. Consequently, the Defendant has lost a lucrative supply contract with United Plastic Containers Plc. WS/BP, paras 2 and 3; exhibits BP1 and BP3. It is submitted that the defence has a real prospect of success.
7. It is submitted that the following are matters which the court **may** take into account in the exercise of its discretion and that they amount to good reasons why the judgment should be set aside or the Defendant should be allowed to defend the claim:
   (a) The Claimant's engineers had notice of the defects in the machines after delivery: WS/BP para 2
   (b) The Defendant sought the opinion of an expert in respect of the defects: **WS/BP,** *para 2*
   (c) The Defendant responded promptly upon receipt of the Particulars of Claim: **WS/BP, Para 3; exhibit BP2.**

Matters to which the court must have regard

8. In considering whether to set aside or vary judgment entered under **CPR Part 12** the matters to which the court must have regard include whether the application to set aside is made promptly: **CPR r 13.3(2):**

Judgment entered: 07.11.09

Application dated: 15.11.09

It is submitted that the Defendant has acted promptly in making this application. And that in the interests of justice judgment should be set aside.

APPLICATION TO TRANSFER

9. The power to transfer from High Court to County Court: **s 40(2) County Courts Act 1984**

Matters to which the court must have regard

10. These are set out in **CPR r 30.3(2)**

The Defendant relies upon the following factors:

(a) the financial value of the claim;

(b) whether it would be more convenient or fair for hearings (including trial) to be held in some other court; and

(c) whether the facts, legal issues, remedies or procedures involved are simple or complex.

11. Although the value of the claim exceeds the usual jurisdiction of the County Court of £50,000, the facts, legal issues, remedies and procedures involved are not complex. The machines which are the subject of the dispute between the parties are located on site at the Defendant's address in Leeds. The Defendant's expert is based in Leeds.

12. It is submitted therefore that, if the court is minded to grant the Defendant's application to set aside judgment, the case should be transferred from the Manchester District Registry to the Defendant's local court, namely Leeds County Court.

15th November 2009
4 Gray's Inn Place BESS TOFFER

25.3.2 Commentary

This is shorter than the previous example (not surprisingly, since this is for an interim application, whereas that one was for a trial). It is much more the sort of thing that students on a Bar Vocational Course will need to draft.

Introduction. As previously suggested, the skeleton begins by stating what the application is for. There are two applications to be made, and they need to be identified and in due course dealt with separately. Paragraph 2 draws the judge's attention to the relevant evidence to be looked at in conjunction with the skeleton argument.

Background. Paragraph 3 states the nature of the case and gives a brief chronology. The chronology is too short to be worth setting out in a separate document.

Paragraphs 5–8. Set out the argument in support of the first application. Since the order sought is a discretionary one, regulated by the CPR, Part 13, the argument must be based on the powers of the court and the circumstances in which the court may exercise its discretion in the defendant's favour. There are only two such circumstances, set out in r 13.3(1). The skeleton argument seeks to show that each of these circumstances exists. The precise sub-rule is identified in each case.

First, the skeleton argument tries to show (in paragraph 6) that the defendant has a real prospect of successfully defending the claim. This contention must of course be justified by the evidence, so the argument refers in outline to the relevant evidence and cites the sources of it. It concludes by stating the inference that the court will be invited to draw.

Secondly, the skeleton argument tries to show (in paragraph 7) that there is some other good reason why judgment should be set aside or the defendant should be allowed to defend the claim. It refers to the evidence upon which the argument will rely, picking out three specific points which the defendant contends are good reasons. It submits that in the light of these three points the 'good reasons' requirement is satisfied.

But as well as showing that the court has power to set aside judgment, the argument must also show why it should do so, and this is dealt with in paragraph 8. There are two submissions. One matter that the court *must* have regard to is stipulated by r 13.3(2), so the argument must address this issue. The fact that the application was made promptly can be shown simply by referring to the relevant dates, so these are stated, followed by the obvious submission. The second submission (the interests of justice) is not separately argued, but will obviously be supported by the matters set out in paragraphs 6 and 7.

Paragraphs 9–11. Sets out the argument in support of the second application. It must of course begin by identifying the court's power to make the order sought (paragraph 9). Then it needs to address the criteria to which the court *must* have regard (paragraph 10). Rule 30.3(2) sets out seven such matters, of which the defendant relies on three. If an argument is to be based on rules, it is clearly essential to refer to the rules first.

The defendant then puts forward three arguments in favour of transfer, relying on the factors already stated (paragraph 11). The precise relationship between the facts and the rules will doubtless be elaborated on orally, but for the purposes of the skeleton there is enough apparent connection for the judge to understand the outline submission.

Finally, the skeleton restates the conclusion that the court is to be invited to reach (paragraph 12).

25.4 Skeleton argument in a criminal case

25.4.1 Introduction

The following is an example of a skeleton argument which might be used in a criminal case. It forms the basis of an application to exclude evidence of pre-arrest questions and answers and of two police-station tape-recorded interviews. The defendant, Julia Smith, was charged with robbery jointly with Jason Barnes and Brian Lewis. The prosecution case was that on 30 April 2009 the three defendants met at an address and agreed that Smith would telephone a friend of hers, Rose Dean. The two females then arranged to meet at Dean's address. The three defendants then took a taxi to the address. Barnes remained in the car and the other two went to the front door. Smith rang the bell, spoke to Dean via the entryphone and when the door latch was released Lewis burst in with Smith, who then pretended to be a victim. Lewis then terrorised Dean, threatening her with a handgun and stole about £100 in cash from her. He then ran off and escaped with Barnes in the taxi, leaving both the females behind. Smith surrendered voluntarily to the police on 1 May 2009.

DC Jones gave evidence of the following:

(a) A conversation with Smith preceding her arrest on 1 May 2009 in which she denied all knowledge of Lewis and stated that she went to Dean's address by bus.

(b) An interview with Smith on 1 May 2009 in which Smith admitted knowledge of the plan to commit a robbery, that she assisted Lewis to gain entry and that she was present throughout. She stated that she knew Lewis and that she went along with the plan because she was frightened.

(c) A second interview on 3 June 2009 in which Smith still maintained she was frightened but made a number of inconsistent and incriminating remarks.

25.4.2 Skeleton argument

IN THE CROWN COURT AT WOOLWICH Indictment No T091234

THE QUEEN

V

JULIA SMITH

DEFENDANT'S SKELETON ARGUMENT

APPLICATION TO EXCLUDE EVIDENCE UNDER s 78 POLICE AND CRIMINAL EVIDENCE ACT 1984 [BLACKSTONE F2.21]

Submissions

1. Failure to caution

Conversation preceding arrest/caution 1st May 2009

Statement of DC Jones [Statement Bundle p 65]

Smith: It was terrible, as I got to her flat a masked man put a gun to my head and pushed me into Rose's flat.

DC Jones: Do you know this man?

Smith: No, I have never seen him before.

DC Jones: How did you get to Rose's?

Smith: The 35 bus.

DC Jones then went on to say that he had grounds to believe that Smith was involved in the offence and arrested and cautioned her.
It is conceded that the 1st remark made by the defendant is an unsolicited comment. It is submitted, however, that the subsequent questions and answers (underlined) should be excluded because DC Jones failed to caution the defendant before putting the questions.

Code of Practice C: 10.1 [Blackstone Appendix 2; D1.55]

R v Sparks [1991] Crim LR 128 CA

R v Pall [1992] Crim LR 126 CA

[Blackstone F2.30]

2. Failure to caution after break in questioning

Interview 1st May 2009—2nd tape

(Interview bundle p 44)

DC Jones: I must remind you that you are still under caution. Do you understand?

Smith: Mm

It is submitted that, after the break in the interview, DC Jones should have cautioned the defendant in full and should have ensured that she was aware that she remained under caution.

Code C: 10.1, 10.8 [Blackstone Appendix 2; D1.55]

3. Failure to explain the caution Interview 3rd June 2009

DC Jones: [*Caution given in full*] Do you understand the caution?

Smith: Yes.

DC Jones: Can you give me a brief explanation of what you understand by the caution, say how it affects you.

Smith: Well, if I don't say nothing now and I need to say something when I get to court I won't be able to say it because I should have said it now.

DC Jones: Right.

It is submitted that:

(a) The defendant did not understand the caution;

(b) DC Jones did not explain it in his own words; and

(c) DC Jones allowed the defendant to continue to misunderstand the caution, thereby appearing to endorse her understanding of it.

Code C: 10D Blackstone Appendix 2; D1.55]

4. Sufficient evidence for prosecution to succeed before interview 3rd June 2008.

(a) Interview 1st May 2009: defendant admitted knowledge of plan to commit robbery, that she assisted Lewis to gain entry and that she was present throughout.

(b) Statement of Rose Dean (victim) 1st May 2009: stated that it was a 'set up' (p 3).

(c) Statement of Mel Stokes (taxi-driver) 18th May 2009: stated that all 3 passengers were relaxed and happy (p 12); female not unhappy or afraid (p 13); she had plenty of opportunities to escape or alert him (p 13).

It is submitted that by 18th May 2009 there was sufficient evidence for this prosecution to succeed and therefore on 3rd June 2009 there should have been no further questioning of the defendant.

Code C: 11.6; C16.1 [Blackstone Appendix 2; D1.59]

1st February 2010

4 Gray's Inn Place ELIZABETH BLAKE

25.4.3 Commentary

You have now seen three different ways of laying out skeleton arguments. Do not assume that there is only one right way, or even that a barrister will always adopt the same format in every case. Choose a format that suits the structure of your argument.

As always the skeleton argument begins by stating clearly what submission is being made.

You must identify for the judge the power under which you are inviting him to act, so there follows a reference to the paragraph in *Blackstone's Criminal Practice* where s 78 of the Police and Criminal Evidence Act 1984 is printed. You will have noticed there are numerous such references in this skeleton argument. *Blackstone* is in wide use in criminal courts, and whatever you may say the judge will want to look it up, so be helpful by giving the references. You could alternatively give references to *Archbold.*

There are then four numbered submissions, each of which, you will argue, should lead the judge to the conclusion that some part of the evidence should be excluded.

Submission 1. The headline tells the judge the nature of the submission—failure to caution. The argument must of course be based on the evidence, so the skeleton sets out the relevant part of the evidence (after identifying where it comes from). There is no easy way to refer to the precise words in question other than by copying them out, so it is helpful to do so. This is followed by the submission itself and the authorities that will be cited in argument. PACE Code C, para 10.1 says that 'A person whom there are grounds to suspect of an offence . . . must be cautioned before any questions about an offence . . . are put to them, if either the suspect's answers or silence . . . may be given in evidence . . .'. The cases of *R v Sparks* and *R v Pall* hold that a failure to caution should be regarded as a 'significant and substantial breach' of the Code.

Submission 2. The structure of this submission is exactly the same as that of the first. There is a headline, reference to the source of the evidence, quotation from the evidence, the submission itself and legal citation. Code C, para 10.8 contains the main point: 'After any break in questioning under caution, the person being questioned must be made aware that they remain under caution. If there is any doubt, the relevant caution should be given again in full when the interview resumes.' This is not perhaps your strongest point.

Submission 3. This is the first of two submissions to the effect that the whole of the interview of 3 June should be excluded. The exchange between the officer and defendant is again quoted and it is self-evident that the defendant did not correctly understand the caution, and that the officer endorsed her misunderstanding. This not surprisingly justifies the first and third submissions. The second submission is based on Code C, note 10D: 'If it appears a person does not understand the caution, the person giving it should explain it in their own words.'

Submission 4. The interview of 3 June is also challenged on the basis that the police had sufficient evidence to charge the defendant before the interview took place and so should not have proceeded with it. The argument begins by identifying the evidence available to the police after 18 May (together with its sources) and then states the conclusion to be drawn and the relevant legal sources. Code C, para 11.6 says 'The interview . . . of a person about an offence with which that person has not been charged . . . must cease when the officer . . . (c) . . . reasonably believes there is sufficient evidence to provide a realistic prospect of conviction for that offence . . .'. By Code C, para 16.1, when similar conditions are satisfied, the defendant should be brought before the custody officer with a view to his being charged.

26

Default judgments

26.1 Setting aside default judgments—an introduction

A common type of interim application is that made to set aside a judgment which has been entered in default. A default judgment is simply a judgment obtained by one party as an administrative act (ie, by presenting the necessary forms to the court staff, ordinarily with no consideration of the application by a judge, Master, or district judge) because the other party has not taken some step required by the rules. Most default judgments are obtained by a claimant in ordinary Part 7 claims, because a defendant has not filed an acknowledgment of service or defence. However, default judgments are also regularly obtained on a CPR, r 20 counterclaim, because a claimant has not filed a defence to that counterclaim.

There is no requirement on the party entitled to enter the default judgment to do so quickly. The only time limit to bear in mind is CPR, r 15.11. If a default judgment has not been entered, it used to be thought that all the party in default had to do was take the necessary step late, and judgment could not be entered. However, in *Coll v Tattum* (2001) The Times, 3 December 2001 the court had to consider whether an extension of time was required for the party in default to file the document late. The court concluded that an extension of time was required, so a defaulting party could not simply file the document late as of right. The court observed that in most cases the extension would be granted, but it was a matter for the discretion of the court applying the overriding objective.

The label 'default judgment' is sometimes applied to a judgment obtained as a result of breach of a peremptory order of the court. A peremptory order is a specific order addressed to one or more parties specifying that in default of taking a certain step in the action within a specified time, judgment may be entered against that party. Peremptory orders are commonly referred to as 'unless' orders. Applications to set aside a judgment in default of an 'unless' order are considered separately at **26.6**.

The test for setting aside a true default judgment is to be found in CPR, r 13. The test for setting aside judgment entered for breach of a final or unless order is to be found in CPR, r 3.9. Although the tests are not the same, the key factor in both cases is whether there is a defence to the claim. A default judgment entered in proceedings that a defendant actually knows nothing about (for example because he has never seen the proceedings which are merely deemed served under CPR) will not be set aside if there is no defence: *Akram v Adam* [2004] EWCA Civ 1601. Similarly, where there is a clear failure to comply with an unless order, relief from sanctions will depend upon there being a defence: *CPL Industrial Services Holdings Ltd v R & L Freeman & Sons* [2005] EWCA Civ 539.

The effect of a decision on an application to set aside a default judgment was clarified by the Court of Appeal in *Mullen v Conoco Ltd* [1997] 3 WLR 1032, which held that a decision on an application to set aside a default judgment would give rise to a final determination (subject to any appeal) on whether a judgment was regular or not, but it would not be a final decision on any discretionary element. A discretionary refusal to set aside a default judgment because the proposed defence of set-off of a counterclaim was thought too weak did not give rise to a plea of *res judicata* or issue estoppel. A fresh action based on the proposed counterclaim was not an abuse of the process of the court and could not be struck out on that ground. This decision is one which ought to be followed despite the introduction of the Civil Procedure Rules.

26.2 Civil Procedure Rules

The distinction between irregular and regular judgments is maintained by the CPR. Irregular judgments are now known as wrongly entered judgments. Wrongly entered judgments are those falling within CPR, r 13.2, and the court must set them aside. In all other cases the Court has discretion whether to set aside or vary the default judgment (CPR, r 13.3(1)). The wording of the discretion mirrors the existing approach *(Alpine Bulk Transport Co Inc v Saudi Eagle Shipping Co Inc* [1986] 2 Lloyd's Rep 221). The defence must have a prospect of success which is better than merely arguable *(International Finance Corporation v Utexafrica nrl* [2001] CLC 1361). Delay remains relevant to the exercise of the discretion (CPR, r 13.3(2)). The court can still attach conditions to an order setting aside a default judgment (CPR, r 3.1(3)). Historically the most common condition was requiring the defendant to pay some or all of the money into court. That is likely to remain the most common condition.

26.3 Making the application

You should familiarise yourself with the requirements of CPR, Part 23 for all interim applications, for evidence and for selecting the court in which the application should be made. These are set out in your ***Civil Procedure*** manual.

If the judgment was for a specified sum of money then the application to set aside will be transferred to the defendant's home court, unless the case was commenced in a specialist list: CPR, r 13.4.

26.4 Documents required to set aside a default judgment

The documents required to set aside a default judgment are:

(a) an application (complying with CPR, Part 23) which should as a matter of good practice state the irregularity where it is alleged that the judgment was wrongly entered;

(b) evidence in support of the application, unless the application to set aside is only based on the judgment being wrongly entered.

26.5 The hearing of the application

At the hearing of the application it is for the party applying to set aside judgment to open the application. In the Queen's Bench Division the Master will probably not have seen any of the papers in advance of the hearing, so the party applying must hand in to the Master the original application notice and evidence in support and take the Master through the evidence in support. The party opposing the application should then take the Master through any evidence in answer. If the party applying has further evidence, the Master should be taken through that additional evidence. When the evidence stage is completed it is for the party applying to make submissions (if required to do so), then for the party opposing to make submissions (if required to do so) and finally for the party applying to respond (if required to do so).

In the Chancery Division and in the County Court there will be a court file which should contain the application notice and the evidence (provided it has been filed by the parties). Where there is a court file it is appropriate to ask the Master or district judge whether he or she has had an opportunity of reading any of the papers, before the parties go through the stages set out in the preceding paragraph.

It is sometimes convenient to deal with any question of wrongly entered judgment before considering any alternative application to set aside as a matter of discretion. This is particularly useful where the argument that the judgment is wrongly entered is strong. If the hearing is divided in this way it may save court time as, if the judgment is set aside as being wrongly entered, it is not normally necessary to consider the merits at all. If the judgment is set aside, the party applying should seek its costs and directions. If the judgment is not set aside as being wrongly entered, the Master will have to dismiss that application and go on to consider any alternative application on the merits.

A chronology is often required to show the court the sequence of events and any period of delay in making the application to set aside the default judgment. The only delay which is relevant is delay after issue of proceedings *(Thorn plc v MacDonald* [1999] CPLR 660). Usually some evidence explaining the delay is required but if the period of delay is short, the absence of an explanation is not now fatal to the exercise of the discretion to set aside. At the end of the submissions the Master or district judge should give a reasoned judgment. After judgment, if the application to set aside is dismissed, the only issues are likely to be the costs (which should follow the event), and any application by the party applying for a stay of execution pending any appeal. Permission to appeal will also be required.

If the application is successful and the judgment is set aside, there may be discussion about the directions to be given (eg, when the defence is to be filed by and other directions); about the conditions (eg, how long should be given for any money to be brought into court as a condition of the judgment being set aside); and costs. If the judgment was irregular, the party applying will be awarded his or her costs unless there is an exceptional feature such as substantial delay. If the judgment was regular, the party applying will normally have to pay all the costs of the entry of judgment, or any execution, and of the application and will usually be ordered to pay those summarily assessed costs forthwith rather than in any event.

Where there is a discretion to set aside the default judgment, the most common condition imposed (apart from requiring the costs thrown away to be paid by the party in default) is that some or all of the money claimed be paid into court as a condition of permission to defend the claim. The order will then provide that the judgment is only set aside if that condition is fulfilled within a specified time. If the money is paid into court by the defendant, it is not a CPR Part 36 payment (although it can be converted into one).

If the court decides that the default judgment ought to be set aside, it should not impose a condition that cannot be complied with: see *Yorke Motors v Edwards* [1982] 1 WLR 444 and, post-CPR, *Training in Compliance plc v Dewse* [2000] (unreported, Court of Appeal, 10 July 2000). The test is one of impossibility and not mere difficulty raising the money. The party applying for the default judgment to be set aside faces a choice: should evidence be filed that establishes that it could not pay any of the money into court or not? Without clear evidence of impecuniosity (and the burden is on the party alleging this), there must be a risk that the court could impose a condition that cannot be complied with. If evidence of impecuniosity is filed, it can create the impression that the application is merely a delaying tactic in relation to a judgment that cannot be paid. In most cases, the court will not adjourn the hearing of the application to allow further evidence to be filed on this point.

26.6 Peremptory or 'unless' orders

A judgment entered upon a failure to comply with a peremptory order is sometimes referred to as a default judgment. The judgment can consist of a dismissal of the whole or any part of the claim, judgment for a specified sum, judgment for damages to be assessed or some other judgment.

Judgment obtained for breach of an 'unless' order is quite different from other types of default judgment. Although the actual entry of the judgment is an administrative act, it almost always flows from consideration of the case by the court when the 'unless' order was made (the main exception being where a party consents to the order being made). Since the order is a specific one directed at a party, any failure to comply with the order is extremely serious.

Immediately prior to the CPR there were an ever increasing number of reported cases in which a party tried to avoid the consequences of an 'unless' order. Some of those cases are not easy to reconcile. For example, there is authority for the proposition that where a party's solicitor was solely at fault non-compliance should be excused *(Pereira v Beanlands* [1996] 3 All ER 528) and there is also authority for the proposition that a party is bound by the default of his lawyers *(Hytec Ltd v Coventry City Council* [1997] 1 WLR 1666). This is one area in which it is to be hoped that the approach in most of the old cases will be abandoned.

26.6.1 Making the 'unless' order

In the past it was not normal practice to make an 'unless' order for a first default. That approach is likely to end, particularly with fast-track cases where the timetable is tight. As the court exercises greater case management control, 'unless' orders may become more common.

One old rule which may survive the introduction of the CPR is that a party consenting to an 'unless' order cannot thereafter challenge the validity or extent of the order *(Fearis v Davies* [1989] 1FSR 555).

The 'unless' order should be absolutely clear in describing the action required to be taken by the party, the date and time by which it is to be taken and the sanction to be imposed if that order is not complied with. The sanction should be proportionate to the potential default and can consist of striking out part or all of the claim or defence (CPR, r 3.5, PD 40B para 8.2).

26.6.2 Challenging the 'unless' order

Once the 'unless' order has been made it should be treated in the same way as any other interim direction of the court: it should be complied with or appealed. It is unlikely that the courts will now, save in exceptional cases, allow a party to ignore an 'unless' order or escape the sanction merely because the order is not in proper form. The parties cannot agree to extension of time (CPR, r 3.8(3)).

26.6.3 Non-compliance with the order

Subject to the right to seek an extension of time for compliance (either before or after the deadline), the sanction set out in the order will take effect (CPR, r 3.8).

26.6.4 Extension of time for compliance

The court has power to extend time. Application should be made on notice supported by evidence. The court will then have regard to all the circumstances and the factors set out in CPR, r 3.9.

26.6.5 The hearing of an application for an extension of time

The evidence from the defaulting party should explain the default (where that is possible) and address the factors set out in CPR, r 3.9, and the overriding objectives. There may be evidence in reply which should address those same issues. It is the stated intention of the courts to take a far more stringent approach to default than hitherto.

At this type of hearing a carefully prepared chronology is probably the most useful weapon. If you are applying for the extension of time a chronology which shows that there have been delays by the other party, or 'unless' orders against the other party, may assist as part of the background before turning to the reasons for your particular application for extra time. If you are resisting an application for an extension, particularly if the delays have been largely or exclusively on the part of the party applying for the extension, or there have been previous 'unless' orders against that party, a chronology can be a devastating weapon in resisting a further extension of time or limiting the extent of the extension.

The party seeking the extension of time will almost always have to pay all the costs of the application, which will usually be assessed immediately.

26.6.6 Disputed non-compliance

Where an 'unless' order has been made and the time for compliance has expired, it will usually be obvious whether there has been compliance or not. If, for example, an order is made that unless the claimant file a List of Documents by 4.00 pm on 1 March the claim be struck out—either a List will have been filed by that date or it will not. If a List is filed then, on the face of it, the order is complied with. If the List is not filed then the claim is struck out without any further order being made.

However, there can be cases of purported compliance—for example, filing a List of Documents that contains only the pleadings and party and party correspondence and no other documents. In that situation, the case has not been automatically struck out, because there is a List. The court would have to determine whether there was sufficient compliance or not, or whether to make any further order or to impose any other sanction. Application should then be made under CPR, Part 23, or on notice at the next Case Management Conference for this issue to be determined.

26.7 Checklist for default judgment

What you should have:

- Copy of relevant practitioner work (here, *Blackstone's Civil Practice* or the White Book);
- Relevant paperwork (here, application notice compliant with CPR, Part 23 and supporting evidence or evidence to counter the application);
- Possibly a chronology, to show the court the sequence of events, including the time between the default judgment and the initiation of this application to set aside.

Your court will be:

- A Queen's Bench Division Master (addressed as 'Master'); or
- A district judge in a High Court District Registry or the County Court (addressed as 'Sir' or 'Madam').

Before the application:

- Tell the court staff that you are present and who you represent;
- Identify your opponent and introduce yourself to him or her;
- If it is your application, make sure that you know your opponent's name so that you can introduce him or her to the court.

What should happen in the application:

- If it is your application, you start;
- Introductions—for example, 'Master, I am Miss Jones and this is my application to set aside. Mr Smith appears for the Respondent/Greenways Ltd.';
- Hand in the application notice and evidence in support. *

* If the application is made in the County Court or in the Chancery Division, the application notice and the evidence should all be contained in a court file. If so, ask the judge if she has had the chance to read any of this paperwork before embarking on your exposition of the evidence as it may be unnecessary or you may be able to abbreviate it.

- Take the judge through your evidence;
- Sit down/stop so that your opponent can take the judge through their evidence;
- After the evidence has been presented to the judge, you may make submissions in support of the application (if required), either:
  - Set aside because judgment wrongly entered; or
  - Set aside by exercise of discretion ('on the merits').

- Answer any questions the judge asks. Indicate clearly when you have finished, usually by saying something like 'That is my application, Sir' or 'Those are my submissions, Master'. Your opponent may then be called upon to put their arguments;
- If you feel that a response to your opponent's arguments is needed, you may ask for permission to address the judge once more, saying something like 'If I might reply briefly on the issue of . . .';
- The judge will give a reasoned judgment;
- If the application succeeds, the applicant's advocate should ask for an order that the respondent pay the costs of the application and seek further directions (these may need to be discussed by the judge and both advocates);
- If the application fails, the respondent's advocate will ask for their costs. The applicant's advocate may ask for a stay of execution pending an appeal.

27

Summary judgments

27.1 Introduction

The Civil Procedure Rules 1998, Part 24, sets out a procedure whereby the court may decide a claim or a particular issue without a trial. The purpose is to deal summarily with issues which do not need full investigation or trial. Applications can be made by a claimant or by a defendant or of the court's own motion.

27.2 Before attending court

Check that the procedural requirements have been complied with, for example:

(a) when acting for a claimant ensure that the defendant has filed an acknowledgement of service or a defence; in cases against the Crown a claimant cannot apply for summary judgment until after expiry of the period for filing a defence;

(b) when acting for a claimant ensure the claim is one to which summary judgment is available, ie, not proceedings for possession of residential premises against a tenant, a mortgagor, or person holding over after the end of his tenancy, not proceedings for an admiralty claim *in rem*; small claims *are* open to summary judgment;

(c) has the respondent been given at least 14 days' notice of the date fixed for hearing and of the issues which it is proposed that the court will decide at the hearing?

(d) The contents of the application notice:

  (i) the application notice must include a statement that it is an application for summary judgment made under Part 24 of the Civil Procedure Rules 1998;

  (ii) it must state what order the applicant is seeking and why the applicant is seeking the order;

  (iii) it must identify the written evidence on which the applicant relies unless no evidence is relied on or the application notice itself contains all the evidence relied on;

  (iv) it must draw the respondent's attention to the time limit for filing and serving its own written evidence (at least seven days before the summary judgment hearing).

(e) Written evidence:

  (i) an applicant may rely on written evidence set out in his claim form, statement of case, application notice, or in a witness statement. Each item of written evidence relied on must contain a statement of truth. Affidavit evidence is also permissible but is subject to cost implications;

(ii) the applicant's written evidence must be served at the same time as the application notice;

(iii) the respondent must file and serve his written evidence at least seven days before the summary judgment hearing;

(iv) if the applicant wishes to rely on written evidence in reply, this must be filed and served at least three days before the summary judgment hearing;

(v) the application notice or the supporting evidence must identify concisely any point of law or provision in a document on which the applicant relies and/or state that it is made because the applicant believes that on the evidence the respondent has no real prospect of succeeding on the claim or issue or of successfully defending the claim or issue to which the application relates, and in either case state that the applicant knows of no other reason why the disposal of the claim or issue should await trial.

(f) Check that any directions given by the Master or district judge in relation to the hearing have been complied with.

Note: if a procedural requirement has not been complied with, consider whether the defect could be cured, eg, by an application to the court under CPR, r 3.10 for an order to remedy the error.

Familiarise yourself with the contents of the statements of case and the written evidence in support so that you are able to refer the court to specific passages and points quickly and smoothly even though this may not follow the set order you planned for your submissions. It is unlikely that the court will allow you to develop all your submissions without interruption—the court will strive to get to the heart of the issues as quickly as possible.

Take with you spare copies of the statement of case, the application notice and the written evidence. Although these should have all been filed, occasionally documents go missing from court files.

27.3 At court

The hearing will be either before a Master in the High Court at the Royal Courts of Justice or before a district judge, if in a High Court District Registry or in the County Court. If, however, a summary judgment application includes a claim for an injunction, the hearing should take place before a High Court or a County Court judge as Masters and district judges have limited jurisdiction in relation to injunctions. The hearings are likely to be in public but no robes are required.

27.3.1 Before a Master

Fill in a case slip outside court to enable the Master to have a note of the advocates' names. Don't forget to introduce yourself and your opponent to the court notwithstanding having completed a slip. Address the Master simply as 'Master'.

If you have a short appointment you are likely to have to address the Master from a standing position. Stand close to the Master's desk and use the shelf or ledge for your papers. Longer appointments are taken with the advocates sitting. As a rule of thumb, if there are no chairs in position facing the Master's desk, be prepared to make your submissions standing. The Master will indicate that you can bring chairs forward from the back of the room if she or he is minded to permit counsel to be seated.

27.3.2 Before a district judge

A member of the court staff is likely to be on hand to take your name and/or to ask you to fill out an advocate's name slip. Address the district judge as 'Sir' or 'Madam' as appropriate. The advocates will make their submissions seated however long or short the application is.

27.3.3 The hearing

Unless or until the court invites argument on a specific point or issues, the claimant's counsel should be prepared to give a brief outline of the application by referring to the particulars of claim and the terms of the application notice. She or he should ask whether the Master or district judge has had the opportunity to read the written evidence and if not whether the court would like them read now. Usually a Master or district judge will prefer to read such material themselves but it is courteous to enquire whether they wish to do this or to have the written evidence read aloud. If the written evidence is to be read aloud, the respondent's counsel should read the respondent's written evidence. Once the written evidence has been read the claimant's counsel will make his or her submission. In reply the respondent's counsel will make his or her submissions and the claimant's counsel will usually be given an opportunity to make further submissions after that. Do not be surprised if the court selects only certain points from your submissions or if the Master or district judge departs from the usual order of submissions. Do not be afraid to emphasise or reiterate what you consider to be your best point (or points) if the court seems to have ignored it or misunderstood it. When preparing your submissions or indeed making them remember how difficult it will be for a Master or district judge to pick up the issues in all the cases listed before him or her each day if advocates are overelaborate or verbose. Clear, succinct submissions will be welcomed.

27.3.4 The Court's approach

Where a claimant applies for judgment on his claim the court may give that judgment if:

(a) the defendant has no real prospect of successfully defending the claim or issue; and

(b) there is no other compelling reason why the claim should be dealt with at trial.

Where a defendant applies for judgment in his or her favour on the claimant's claim, the court will give the judgment if it considers that:

(a) the claimant has no real prospect of succeeding on the claim or issue; and

(b) there is no other compelling reason why the claim should be dealt with at trial.

Where it appears to the court possible that a claim or defence may succeed but improbable that it will do so, the court may make a conditional order.

27.3.5 The order

The court will give judgment orally, setting out reasons for the order and declaring the terms of the order. Make a verbatim note of both aspects. The court may order:

(a) judgment on the claim or on any issue therein;

(b) the striking out or dismissal of the claim or of an issue therein;

(c) the dismissal of the application;

(d) a conditional order which requires a party to pay a sum of money into court or to take a specified step in relation to his or her claim or defence and provides that the party's claim will be dismissed or his or her statement of case struck out if he or she does not comply;

(e) an order relating to costs.

After judgment is given the question of costs has to be decided. Costs are very important. Be prepared to make submissions on the appropriate order as to what the costs should be and why.

The court is empowered to give further directions about the management of the case when it determines a summary judgment application (CPR, r 24.6; PD 24, para 10). Be prepared.

27.4 Appeals

In order to appeal a summary judgment order it is necessary to obtain permission to appeal either from the court which made the order or the court to which the appeal is to be made. You need either to apply at the summary judgment hearing or make an application for permission in an appeal notice within 21 days from the initial hearing.

The appeal notice must be filed at the appeal court within such period as directed by the lower court or, in the absence of a direction, within 21 days of the date of the decision to be appealed. Copies have to be served on the respondents to the appeal not later than seven days after the appeal notice is filed. If you do wish to appeal, consider whether you need a stay pending appeal.

Note that permission is granted only where:

(a) the court considers that the appeal would have a real prospect of success; or

(b) there is some other compelling reason why the appeal should be heard.

See generally CPR, Part 52.

27.5 Checklist for hearing

Materials essential or useful at the hearing:

- Your brief;
- Counsel's notebook containing a skeleton or plan of your intended submissions;
- At least three pens;
- Spare copies of the application notice, the written evidence in support such as witness statements, and the statements of case (in case papers have gone missing from the court file);
- Copy of relevant practitioner work (*Blackstone's Civil Practice* or the White Book would be sensible but, whatever you take, it must contain a full copy of the Civil Procedure Rules in case you have to argue about associated matters such as the appropriate track, directions or costs);

- Three copies of any authorities you seek to rely on;
- A fully charged mobile phone with a reasonable amount of credit and a note of the telephone number of your instructing solicitors (in case they send no representative and you need to seek instructions or impart information quickly);
- Reading glasses, if you use them;
- A working calculator.

Additional materials essential or useful in order to attend the hearing:

- An adequate amount of cash and/or debit card and/or credit card for transport costs and emergencies;
- A note of the telephone number of the court (in case you are delayed and need to inform the court or chambers);
- A train timetable if you are travelling by train;
- A map extract indicating the precise location of the court you are seeking to attend if you are unfamiliar with the area.

Your court will be:

- A High Court Master (addressed as 'Master'); or
- A district judge in a High Court District Registry or the County Court (addressed as 'Sir' or 'Madam');
- If an injunction is being sought, the application will go before a High Court or County Court judge (addressed as 'My Lord/Your Lordship' or 'Your Honour' respectively); robes are not required.

Before the application:

- Tell the court staff that you are present and who you represent (this may mean that the usher writes your name on their list and/or that you fill in your details on a slip of paper and hand that back);
- Identify your opponent and introduce yourself to him or her;
- If it is your application, make sure that you know your opponent's name so that you can introduce him or her to the court.

What should happen in the application:

- If it is your application, you start;
- Introductions—for example, 'Madam, I am Miss Jones and this is my application for summary judgment. Mr Smith appears for the Respondent/Greenways Ltd.';
- Hand in the application notice, the statement of case and any evidence in support;
- Briefly outline the application, referring to your statement of case and the application notice;
- Ask whether the judge has already read the written evidence—'Have you had the chance to read the evidence in support, Madam?', for example. If the answer is 'No', offer to take the judge through your evidence;
- The judge will often say that she would prefer to read it while you continue with the application; alternatively, she may say that you can take her though it, which you will then do by reading it aloud;

- Sit down/stop so that your opponent can take the judge through their evidence;
- After the evidence has been presented to the judge, you may make submissions* in support of the application:
  - That the claimant/defendant has no real prospect of successfully pursuing/defending the claim or issue; and
  - There is no other compelling reason why the claim should be dealt with at trial.

* The judge may indicate that she wants to hear you address only a specific point or points, in which case that is what you will do.

- Answer any questions the judge asks. Indicate clearly when you have finished, usually by saying something like 'That is my application, Madam' or 'Those are my submissions, Master'. Your opponent may then be called upon to put their arguments;
- If you feel that a response to your opponent's arguments is needed, you may ask for permission to address the judge once more, saying something like 'If I might reply briefly on the issue of . . .';
- The judge will give a reasoned judgment (which you should make a note of, both as to the order itself and the reasons);
- If the application succeeds on the whole claim, the applicant's advocate should ask for an order that the respondent pay the costs of the matter;
- If the application succeeds on an issue, the applicant's advocate should ask for an order that the respondent pay the costs of the application and seek further directions (these may need to be discussed by the judge and both advocates);
- If the application fails, the respondent's advocate should ask for an order that the applicant pay the respondent's costs for the application;
- If summary judgment is ordered, the respondent's advocate may ask for permission to appeal there and then (or it can be sought from the court to which the appeal will be made, within 21 days).

28 Interim payments

28.1 Introduction

An order for interim payment is one of a number of interim remedies that a court may grant; CPR, r 25(1)(k). In the course of litigation it may be apparent that one party will receive an award of a sum of money from his or her opponent at the conclusion of the trial, but that the amount is hotly disputed. The courts have established an interim payment remedy to prevent a party from being kept out of the entirety of his money for too long. Thus an interim payment application seeks a payment on account of any damages, debt or other sum (excluding costs) which the respondent may be held liable to pay to or for the benefit of the applicant.

An order for interim payment can be obtained in all proceedings where the claim includes a claim for some form of money save for cases proceeding on the small claims track (CPR, r 27.2(1)(a)).

28.2 Procedural requirements

(a) An application must be made by filing and serving an application notice at any time after the time limit to acknowledge service has expired.

(b) A copy of the application notice must be served at least 14 days before the hearing of the application and must be supported by evidence; CPR, r 25.6(3). The evidence should usually be by witness statement; CPR, r 32.6(1).

(c) The written evidence must deal with the following:

- (i) the sum of money sought by way of interim payment;
- (ii) the items or matters in respect of which the interim payment is sought;
- (iii) the sum of money for which final judgment is likely to be given;
- (iv) the reasons for believing that the conditions set out in CPR, r 25.7, have been satisfied;
- (v) any other relevant matters;
- (vi) exhibit any documentary evidence relied on in support of the application, including in personal injuries claims the medical reports.

(d) In a Fatal Accidents Act 1976 claim the written evidence must give details of the persons on whose behalf the claim is made and the nature of the claim.

28.3 The basis of the application

28.3.1 Liability

The court may make an order for interim payment only if:

(a) the defendant against whom the order is sought has admitted liability to pay damages or some other sum of money to the claimant; or

(b) the claimant has obtained judgment against that defendant for damages to be assessed or for a sum of money (other than costs) to be assessed; or

(c) the court is satisfied that if the claim went to trial the claimant would obtain judgment for a substantial amount of money (other than costs) against the defendant from whom he is seeking an order for interim payment; or

(d) in a claim for possession of land, the court is satisfied that if the case went to trial the defendant would be held liable (even if the claim for possession fails) to pay the claimant a sum of money for the defendant's occupation and use of the land while the claim for possession was pending.

28.3.2 Claims for personal injuries

It is no longer a condition for the grant of an interim payment in a personal injuries claim that the defendant be insured or that it be a public body. However, in all types of claim where there are two or more defendants and the court is satisfied that if the claim went to trial the claimant would obtain judgment for substantial damages against at least one of the defendants (even if the court has not determined which of them is liable), the following additional condition applies. The court may only make an order for an interim payment if:

(a) the defendant is insured in respect of the claim; or

(b) the defendant's liability will be met by an insurer under section 151 of the Road Traffic Act 1988, or an insurer acting under the Motor Insurers' Bureau Agreement or the Motor Insurers' Bureau where it is acting for itself; or

(c) the defendant is a public body.

28.3.3 Quantum

Once satisfied regarding liability, the court has a discretion whether to make an interim payment and if so of what amount:

- CPR, r 25.1(1)(k): 'The court may grant an order for an interim payment . . .'
- CPR, r 25.7(4): 'The court must not order an interim payment of more than a reasonable proportion of the likely amount of the final judgment.'
- CPR, r 25.7(5): 'The court must take into account (a) contributory negligence; and (b) any relevant set-off or counterclaim.'

28.4 The hearing

In the High Court the appointment will be before a Master but prima facie in public. Address the Master simply as 'Master'. No robes will be required in whatever court the application is proceeding.

Outside London if the action is proceeding in the High Court the interim payment application will be directed to a district judge sitting in the District Registry of the High Court. The hearing will prima facie be in public. A district judge will be addressed as 'Sir' or 'Madam'.

In the County Court the application will be made to a district judge sitting prima facie in public who should be referred to as 'Sir' or 'Madam' as appropriate. It is possible for the hearing of an interim payment application to be conducted by telephone but the principles that apply are the same.

Your basic tools in an interim payment application will be the statement of case and the witness statements or other written evidence in support. Any evidence that is not included in the filed and served written evidence will be inadmissible and will require an adjournment, if you can get it, so that a supplemental statement can be provided.

The first step, if it is your application, is to introduce yourself and your opponent to the court. Then introduce the case by declaring what the application is for and briefly mentioning the claim in the main action and how it arises. The next step is to place the evidence before the court. Enquire whether the Master or district judge has had an opportunity to read the written evidence. The likelihood is that he or she will have read such material in advance. If not, direct him or her to the passages that he or she should read. Usually the Master or district judge will find it easier to read to himself or herself, but if in doubt, ask.

Prepare your submissions by dealing with liability first. In some cases this will require only a sentence or two if interim judgment has already been obtained or there is a clear admission in the statement of case. However, in other cases, liability will be a much greater problem. The standard of proof required is to the civil standard, but compare 'would succeed' with 'would be likely to succeed' (*British & Commonwealth Holdings plc v Quadrex Holdings Inc* [1989] QB 842; *Andrews v Schooling* [1991] 3 All ER 723). It is often useful when dealing with quantum to outline the overall size of the claimant's claim and then to deal with any heads of damage where the claimant is either bound to succeed or where the possibility of failure is remote. In personal injury actions the court may be assisted by a valuation of the damages for pain, suffering and loss of amenities. Take the *Judicial Studies Board Guidelines* or *Kemp & Kemp on Quantum of Damages etc* to court plus photocopies of what is relevant.

It is a requirement that the written evidence sets out the amount you are asking for. You will need to justify the sum as a fraction or percentage of the overall claim. The courts are sometimes wary of giving an interim payment when no specific need for the money has been dealt with in the written evidence or when the interim payment may be a payment on account of general damages in a personal injury action.

There was clear authority that there was nothing under the old Rules requiring the claimant to show a specific need (*Stringman v McArdle* [1994] 1 WLR 1653). You may need to be prepared to argue this not so much as a requirement but as an aspect that the court can take into account when considering its discretion. Also bear in mind that, with the expected improved speed of getting cases to trial, you may have to argue why the claimant should be awarded some money now rather than have matters disposed of in one go at trial.

It is easier if you can justify your interim payment against special damages, but there is no reason why a payment in respect of general damages cannot be obtained. Remember, the court is primarily concerned to see that there is no risk of overpayment at the interim stage, since return of the money if the claimant has spent it can often be problematic.

28.4.1 The interim payment order

The court will give judgment orally setting out reasons for the order and declaring the terms of the order. Make a verbatim note of both aspects.

In a personal injury case where there are repayments to be made to the Compensation Recovery unit, the order should set out the amount of the relevant deduction. Payment of the net amount only will be made to the claimant.

As the fact of an interim payment should be kept from the trial judge if another application is made at the same time which results in an order, there should be two separate orders drawn up, not one. Don't forget that you will have to deal with costs at the end of the application.

28.5 Appeals

In order to appeal an interim payment order it is necessary to obtain permission to appeal from the court which made the order or the court to which the appeal is to be made. You need either to apply at the interim payment hearing or make an application for permission in an appeal notice within 21 days from the initial hearing.

The appeal notice must be filed at the appeal court within such period as directed by the lower court or, in the absence of a direction, within 21 days of the date of the decision to be appealed. Copies have to be served on the respondents to the appeal not later than seven days after the appeal notice is filed. If you do wish to appeal, consider whether you need a stay pending appeal.

Note that permission is granted only where:

(a) the court considers that the appeal would have a real prospect of success; or

(b) there is some other compelling reason why the appeal should be heard.

See generally CPR, Part 52.

It is therefore usually easier to obtain the order you seek on the first hearing than it is to correct it on appeal.

28.6 Checklist for the hearing

Materials essential or useful at the hearing:

- Your brief;
- Counsel's notebook containing a skeleton or plan of your intended submissions;
- At least three pens;
- Spare copies of the application notice, the written evidence in support such as witness statements, and the statements of case (in case papers have gone missing from the court file);

- Copy of relevant practitioner work (*Blackstone's Civil Practice* or the White Book would be sensible but, whatever you take, it must contain a full copy of the Civil Procedure Rules in case you have to argue about associated matters such as directions or costs);
- Three copies of any authorities you seek to rely on, such as from *Kemp & Kemp* or the *Judicial Studies Board Guidelines* on quantum (currently in its 8th edition);
- A fully charged mobile phone with a reasonable amount of credit and a note of the telephone number of your instructing solicitors (in case they send no representative and you need to seek instructions or impart information quickly);
- Reading glasses, if you use them;
- A working calculator.

Additional materials essential or useful in order to attend the hearing:

- An adequate amount of cash and/or debit card and/or credit card for transport costs and emergencies;
- A note of the telephone number of the court (in case you are delayed and need to inform the court or chambers);
- A train timetable if you are travelling by train;
- A map extract indicating the precise location of the court you are seeking to attend if you are unfamiliar with the area.

29 Applying for an injunction

29.1 Introduction

This chapter considers the procedure at the hearing of an application for an interim injunction in civil proceedings (other than matrimonial proceedings).

Whether you are in practice or merely a regular visitor to a County Court you will soon notice that a very large number of applications for injunctions are made in matrimonial cases. While interim injunctions are less common in other civil litigation, they are by no means rare. It is important to be familiar with the basic procedure for applying for an interim injunction in non-matrimonial cases as injunctions are, by their very nature, often required quickly, and in the case of without notice (formerly *ex parte*) applications extremely quickly.

29.2 Some expressions explained

A number of expressions are used in connection with injunction applications with which you ought to be familiar. The main expressions are:

ancillary orders	refers to any order which is connected with the main injunction or injunctions (eg, an order to disclose the whereabouts of an object or asset);
Angel Bell	an order within a freezing injunction permitting the payment of certain (usually specified) business debts or commitments or living expenses. The order is named after *Iraqi Ministry of Defence v Arcepey Shipping Company SA* (*The 'Angel Bell'*) [1981] QB 65;
Anton Piller	the old name for a search order (see below);
freezing injunction	the new name for a *Mareva* injunction which freezes the use of some or all of the assets of a person, firm or company;
interim	a temporary injunction or order granted for a specified period of time 'until the . . . day of . . .' or 'until trial or further order'. Formerly known as an interlocutory injunction;
Mareva injunction	the old name for a freezing injunction (see above);
ne exeat regno	an ancient prerogative writ which prevents a debtor leaving the realm which fell into disuse in 1893, was applied for (unsuccessfully) in August 1968 and has been used on only a handful of occasions since then;
ouster order	common expression for an order removing (ousting) a person from property (usually a home), most commonly made in matrimonial proceedings but can also be obtained in other disputes;

quia timet	'because he apprehends' an expression used in relation to a threatened wrong which has not yet taken place;
radius order	an order prohibiting someone from entering a specified area near a building or home, commonly used in matrimonial proceedings but can be obtained in other proceedings, see *Burris v Azadani* at **29.3**;
return date	the date fixed for further consideration of the injunction (usually the with notice hearing fixed after a without notice injunction has been granted);
search order	the new name of an *Anton Piller* order, an order which requires the giving of access to premises and of immediate delivery up of documents or property. Order originally named after *Anton Piller KG v Manufacturing Processes Limited* [1976] Ch 55;
short service	an order obtained (usually without notice which permits an application to be considered when the other party has not been given the full notice required by the Rules);
penal notice	a notice on the court order which warns the person injuncted of the consequences of a breach of the order.

29.3 The nature of the order

An injunction is an order of the court requiring a person or company to do a specific act or acts (a mandatory injunction) or to refrain from doing some act or acts (a prohibitory injunction). The distinction between a mandatory injunction and a prohibitory injunction depends not upon the wording of the order but upon its substance. Do not waste time trying to make a mandatory order look as if it is prohibitory merely because the latter are more likely to be granted at an interim stage. Individual injunctions will be either mandatory or prohibitory (although both may appear in the same order).

Quite separately, injunctions can also be divided into final and interim (historically known as interlocutory injunctions). This distinction is often based upon when they are obtained in the proceedings. An interim injunction is usually obtained before any trial and a final injunction is obtained at the end of the case (usually, but not always at a trial). The statutory power for the High Court to grant an injunction is contained in s 37, Supreme Court Act 1981 and gives the power 'in all cases in which it appears to the court to be just and convenient to do so'. In the County Court the statutory power is now to be found in s 38, County Courts Act 1984 which gives the County Court power to make any order which the High Court could have made.

The traditional view is that injunctions are not a cause of action in themselves but a relief granted in support of an existing legal or equitable right (*The Siskina* [1979] AC 210).

In many cases the 'right' to be enforced by a proposed injunction will be obvious. However, the courts seem prepared to extend the concept of 'rights' where necessary. The House of Lords has qualified the strict approach to be found in *The Siskina* on more than one occasion. More recently the House of Lords has doubted whether the strict approach to 'rights' in *The Siskina* is correct; see, for example, the speech of Lord Browne-Wilkinson (with whom Lords Keith and Goff agreed on this point) in *Channel Tunnel Group Limited v Balfour Beatty Construction Limited* [1993] AC 334. To make matters more complex the Privy Council refused to uphold a wholesale challenge to *The Siskina* in *Mercedes-Benz AG v Leiduck* [1995] 3 WLR 718. However, it seems that the approach in *The Siskina* may now be limited to cases involving private law rights, and not the wider interests of the public, in cases such as those brought between a trustee in bankruptcy and the bankrupt (*Morris v Murjani* [1996] 2 All ER 384).

Thus, while *The Siskina* may be a good starting point, take care to consider the statutory power to grant an injunction 'in all cases in which it appears to the court to be just and convenient to do so' before deciding that there is no power in the court to make the particular order sought.

In the light of attacks being made on the traditional view in *The Siskina* it is becoming more and more difficult to decide the exact circumstances in which the court may grant an injunction. Seven recent examples may assist in demonstrating the way in which the traditional view of 'rights' has been extended by the courts.

Re Oriental Credit Limited [1988] 2 WLR 172 In this case the court granted an injunction restraining a former director of a company from leaving the jurisdiction until after completion of his examination under orders made pursuant to s 561, Companies Act 1985. The court held that power existed to make the order even though it was not to enforce a legal or equitable right as it was an order in aid of the existing Companies Act order.

TSB Private Bank International SA v Chabra [1992] 1 WLR 23 In this case the court granted a *Mareva* (now freezing) injunction in a claim under a guarantee which covered, *inter alia,* assets being sold by a UK company of which the defendant was the majority shareholder. The court, of its own motion, joined the company in the action as a necessary party under RSC O. 15, r 6(2)(b)(ii). The court then held that where a claimant has a right against one defendant, it had power to grant an injunction against a co-defendant against whom no cause of action lay.

Aiglon Limited v Gau Shan Co Limited [1993] BCLC 132 In this case the court found that the claimant's evidence disclosed a strong prima facie case under s 423, Insolvency Act 1986 which gave the claimant a direct cause of action under s 425(1)(d) of that Act, but also held that the court had jurisdiction under s 238 of that Act to grant the worldwide *Mareva* (now freezing) injunction even though that section gave no direct cause of action or claim.

Khorasandjian v Bush [1993] QB 727 In this case the majority of the Court of Appeal granted a *quia timet* injunction restraining persistent unwanted telephone calls as the inconvenience to the recipient constituted an actionable interference with the ordinary and reasonable use of property which could be restrained without proof of damage.

The Mercantile Group (Europe) AG v Aiyela [1994] 3 WLR 1116 In this case the Court of Appeal continued a *Mareva* (now freezing) injunction against a person who was not a judgment debtor, and against whom the claimant had no surviving cause of action, as the order was ancillary to the order against the judgment debtor and was properly made in the interests of justice.

Burris v Azadani [1995] 1 WLR 1372 In this case the Court of Appeal upheld the making of an injunction restraining the defendant from approaching within 250 yards of the claimant's home distinguishing (on grounds which are somewhat tenuous) the well-known earlier decision of the Court of Appeal in *Patel v Patel* [1988] 2 FLR 202.

Morris v Murjani [1996] 2 All ER 384 In this case the Court of Appeal limited the requirement that there be an existing cause of action as the basis for granting an interlocutory (now interim) injunction, to cases involving a violation of private rights. Thus an injunction restraining a bankrupt from leaving the country before the hearing of an application for his committal for breach of s 333, Insolvency Act 1986 could properly be made.

The courts seem prepared to extend the concepts of 'rights'. The exact limits of the concept of 'rights' is unclear and may now be different for cases involving private rights from those involving public duties. It should be noted that this extension does not mean that the court will simply grant any order which is sought, as two further examples will illustrate.

Law Debenture Trust Corporation v Ural Caspian Oil Corporation Limited [1993] 1 WLR 138 In this case the Court of Appeal accepted that a purchaser of property who acquired it in the knowledge of some contractual covenant binding the vendor might be restrained by negative injunction from breaching that covenant, but refused to extend that approach so as to grant a mandatory injunction against the purchaser to perform the covenant.

Zucker & others v Tyndall Holdings plc [1992] 1 WLR 1127 In this case the Court of Appeal refused to grant a *Mareva* (now freezing) injunction when there was only the threat of breach of a term of a contract which was itself not presently enforceable or performable.

Frequently, an injunction will be sought to prevent repetition of a wrong which has already taken place, or the undoing of the wrong (eg, removal of a trespass or obstruction). However, it is not necessary to wait until the proposed defendant has committed the wrong before applying to the court. A *quia timet* injunction can be obtained if a wrong is merely threatened; see, for example, *Redland Bricks Limited v Morris* [1970] AC 652. Two criteria normally have to be satisfied: first, that there is a threatened wrong; second, that the wrong infringes some right which the claimant already has (although this second criterion may now have to be reconsidered in cases involving some public duty).

It must be remembered that an injunction remains a discretionary remedy of the court to which equitable principles are still applied. Even if a clear right has been infringed, an injunction will not necessarily be granted at trial or at the interim stage. An injunction (like the remedy of specific performance) will be refused where it serves no useful purpose, but the mere fear that the defendant will not obey is not sufficient to justify the refusal to grant an injunction (*Castanho v Brown and Root (UK) Limited* [1981] AC 552). An injunction may be refused: where there is only a trivial infringement or threatened infringement of a right; where there would be undue hardship to the party being restrained; where the party seeking the injunction has been guilty of some equitable fraud or has unclean hands; or where there has been undue delay or acquiescence on the part of the person seeking the injunction.

The Civil Procedure Rules have not changed the discretionary nature of the injunction remedy. The general criteria for the grant of an interim remedy is now that it will give effect to the overriding object (CPR, r 1.2). Detailed provisions appear in CPR, Part 25 and PD 25 (Interim Injunctions).

29.4 Enforcement of the order

As an injunction is an order of the court, breach of its terms constitutes a contempt of court punishable by imprisonment, sequestration of assets or a fine. It is beyond the scope of this chapter to set out the detailed procedure for applying to commit a person for breach of an injunction. However, it should be noted that as the defendant's liberty may be in jeopardy, a technical approach is always adopted by the court both on the procedural aspects of the application and in interpreting the wording of the order. Although most injunctions are complied with, without any applications to commit being made, it is extremely important that the wording of the order is crystal clear and that the order which is served has a 'penal notice' included (see **29.11**). Finally, in some cases it is essential that the order has been properly served upon the defendant.

29.5 Jurisdiction

When applying for any interim injunction, it is important to consider both the jurisdiction of the court in which you intend to make the application and the jurisdiction of the person hearing the application to grant the order.

29.6 The undertaking as to damages

If a party wishes to obtain an interim injunction, it is normally necessary to give an undertaking in damages. The undertaking is a promise to the court to pay damages to the party restrained by the order if the court subsequently finds that (a) they have suffered any damage by reason of the order and that (b) the party obtaining the order ought to pay for that damage.

The courts do not require such an undertaking in every case. The main exceptions are:

(a) matrimonial injunctions involving conduct rather than money or property (such as those restraining assaults);

(b) applications by public bodies charged with enforcement of some area of law (*Kirklees Metropolitan Borough Council v Wickes Buildings Supplies Limited* [1993] AC 227).

In most cases the undertaking is only invoked by an inquiry as to damages either upon discharge of the order shortly after it is granted (eg, on discharge of an order without notice) or at the trial of the action when the parties' true rights are established. Upon discharge of an injunction prior to the trial the court will have to decide whether to order an immediate inquiry or leave the decision until the conclusion of the case. The practice to be followed has been considered by the Court of Appeal in *Cheltenham & Gloucester Building Society v Ricketts* [1993] 1 WLR 1545.

Five practical points need to be noted:

(a) Although it may not be absolutely essential that the court be given information about the financial status of the party seeking the injunction, it is good practice to do so in the evidence in support of the application.

(b) If you are aware of any factor which makes the undertaking in damages of doubtful value or worthless, that fact should be made known to the court. In *Schmitten v Faulkes* [1893] WN 64, a solicitor who failed to disclose to the court that the undertaking was worthless because he had commenced bankruptcy proceedings against his own client was ordered to pay the costs and damages personally.

(c) The fact that the undertaking is of limited value is not an absolute bar to obtaining an injunction; see the unusual case of *Allen v Jambo Holdings Limited* [1980] 1 WLR 1252 in which the Court of Appeal reinstated a *Mareva* (now freezing) injunction although the undertaking in damages was virtually worthless.

(d) In some cases the court may require an undertaking to be fortified by a guarantee or deposit of money or by an undertaking from someone else (eg, a parent company of a newly formed or impecunious subsidiary). Obviously you should ensure that you have actual authority to give an undertaking from someone else before doing so. In *Udall v Capri Lighting Limited (In Liquidation)* [1988] QB 907, the Court of Appeal ordered an inquiry into the conduct of the solicitor for the defendant and any losses occasioned by that conduct. The solicitor had given an undertaking that the defendant's directors would provide security for its liabilities towards the claimant by creating second charges in the claimant's favour on their personal properties but, when the judge subsequently ordered the solicitor to carry out his undertaking, the evidence showed that the directors were unable to fulfil the commitment. If the solicitor's failure to implement the undertaking was inexcusable and merited reproof, the judge could make a compensatory order of a disciplinary nature. A requirement for security may be imposed either at the without notice stage or at any later stage prior to discharge of the order as a condition of continuing the order. When a deposit or security is sought by the party restrained, the court would require evidence in support of the application to show that there is a risk of substantial loss being caused by the order and some sound basis for the belief that the undertaking given may be insufficient (*Bhimji v Chatwani* [1992] 1 WLR 1158).

(e) Although there is no question of a party buying an injunction merely by being wealthy enough to give a valuable undertaking in damages, if the person or company applying for the injunction has assets it will not harm them to say so. In the case of a company, filed accounts can be exhibited. In the case of an individual, some estimate or statement of net worth can be made.

If undertakings are given to the court and accepted in lieu of an injunction, take care that you note the difference in practice over the undertaking as to damages between (i) the Chancery Division and (ii) the Queen's Bench Division and the County Court set out at **29.12**. It is vital that it is clearly understood whether an undertaking as to damages has been given or not.

29.7 A without notice application

A without notice application can only be made in cases of urgency, for example where there is some imminent danger which the court is being asked to prevent. This element of urgency should be clearly set out in the evidence in support of the application, which should also state when the facts which are the foundation of the application became known to the party applying or to his or her advisers. (It is particularly important to state when those facts became known if they occurred some time before or if you cannot state exactly when they occurred.)

There is a duty of full and frank disclosure in applications made without notice and failure to make proper disclosure may lead to any order being set aside without consideration of the merits of the case. The duty extends to factors affecting the value of the undertaking in damages (see **29.6**). In *Intergraph Corporation & another v Solid Systems CAD Services Limited* [1993] FSR 617, the court stressed that merely exhibiting a large number of documents to the evidence does not constitute disclosure. Unless the judge reads the document on a without notice application it has not been disclosed.

29.7.1 Arranging the hearing

Your solicitor or your clerk may make the arrangements for the hearing of an application without notice. However, you should be familiar with the procedure, particularly for out-of-hours applications.

In cases of the utmost urgency it is possible to arrange for application to be made to the duty judge at any time outside court hours by telephoning the officer on duty at the Royal Courts of Justice on (020) 7936 6260. There is always a duty judge who will hear the application. The practice in the Queen's Bench Division is to be found in the *Queen's Bench Guide,* which explains the requirements for listing an interim application. The specific requirements of the Chancery Division appear in the *Chancery Guide* and for the Commercial Court in the *Admiralty and Commercial Courts Guide.* In all divisions a hearing can be arranged at the High Court, at the judge's home or in extreme cases application can be made by telephone; see, for example, *Allen v Jambo Holdings Limited* [1980] 1 WLR 1252. If you seek a prohibitory injunction, it is effective and binding on the person restrained as soon as he or she is notified of it (even before personal service of the order).

In cases which do not require an application to be made outside normal court hours, the hearing is arranged by contacting security at the Royal Courts of Justice and leaving details for a return call from the judge's clerk.

In the County Court the papers should be lodged prior to the hearing. If time permits, they can be lodged the day before the without notice application, but more commonly they will be lodged only when the Court Office opens on the day of the application. Take care if you are told that your application will be heard by the judge at 10.00 am as most County Court Offices do not open until that time and it will be difficult to lodge the papers at the Court Office and be heard by the judge at the same time (particularly if the judge is not sitting in the same building as the Court Office). Obviously appearing before the judge is likely to be more important than issuing the proceedings, as an undertaking to issue forthwith can be given to the judge if an injunction is granted. Whichever court you are making the application in, the standard documents required will be the application notice, claim form (issued or in draft), any particulars of claim or other statements of case, the evidence in support of the application and the draft order.

29.7.2 Procedure at the hearing

In the Chancery Division the hearing will normally be in open court and the procedure will be the same as for other applications (see **Chapter 31**). The applications judge may go through the applications in the order in the Daily List for that day to ascertain which are 'effective' (ie, agreement has not been reached between the parties on all the matters in dispute) and which are 'ineffective', and in each case the time estimate for the application. The judge is likely to indicate the order in which he or she will dispose of the applications when he or she has gone through the list that first time.

In the Queen's Bench Division and the Commercial Court the hearing will be in private with counsel not wearing their robes. The judge will normally allow you to address him or her seated if the application is heard in a room, but not if heard in court.

In the County Court applications are usually heard in private but the practice varies from court to court so you should ensure that you have your robes with you in case they are needed.

You should open your application by briefly describing the injunction you seek such as, 'My Lord [or 'My Lady'], this is an application for an injunction without notice restraining a trespass to the claimant's land . . .'. The judge should be taken to:

(a) the statements of case or draft statements of case to show the cause of action;

(b) to the evidence or draft evidence in support of the application and to any exhibits; and

(c) to the draft order which is sought indicating, if necessary, that only certain parts of the order are being sought at the without notice stage. The formal parts (eg, any undertaking to issue and the undertaking as to damages) can usually be dealt with very briefly.

If the judge has read the papers in advance (do not be afraid to ask whether that is the situation) you may not be required to go through the statement of case or evidence.

It should not be necessary to explain to the judge the test to be applied if you are relying upon *American Cynamid v Ethicon* [1975] AC 396. You should be familiar with the decision of *Series 5 Software Limited v Philip Clarke & others* [1996] FSR 273, which reconsiders or explains the factors to be taken into account in granting an injunction. If your case falls within an exception to the test in those cases, you may have to explain why it is exceptional and the test which is then to be applied.

You should end your submissions by asking the judge to make an order in the terms of the draft. There is almost always discussion about the draft order before the judge announces what order, if any, he or she is prepared to make. If you are seeking several different orders you should be able to link each part of the order sought to the evidence justifying the part of the order. For example, if you are seeking a freezing injunction and want an order that evidence be sworn setting out the defendant's assets, you may have to explain why the order requires that a particular officer of the company is to swear the evidence.

There will often be discussion about the duration of the without notice order. Liberty to apply to the court on specified notice to your solicitors to vary or discharge the order is almost always given. You should remember to put the name, address, telephone and facsimile numbers of your solicitors in the draft order when dealing with liberty to apply (in a freezing injunction or search order an out of hours contact number is frequently required to be given). Even where liberty to apply is given, the court may still wish to fix a date for further consideration of the order which will then appear in the order itself (a return date). In the Chancery Division and in the County Court it is still common practice to fix a date for further consideration of the order. In the Queen's Bench Division and in the Commercial Court it is less common to fix a date for further consideration, the liberty to apply provision being thought adequate for most cases.

The judge will then announce the terms of the order which he or she is making. It is rare for anything approaching a formal judgment to be given for a without notice application. The judge will normally merely state that an order is being made in the terms of the draft order, as amended in some stated respects.

If you are refused any form of without notice relief, you can still properly ask for permission to serve an application on short notice. If such an order is given, the judge will normally specify that there be a with notice hearing on a particular day provided that you serve the defendant quickly, often by a stated time later that day.

If you obtain any injunction or an order for short service, you must deal with costs. Normally at this stage costs should be reserved to the return date (if any) or to the trial. If you are refused both the injunction and permission to serve on short notice, there will be little point seeking any with notice costs order.

Your solicitors will have to arrange for the order to be drawn up and sealed by the court (except in the Chancery Division and County Court, where the orders are drawn up by the court itself). In every case your solicitors will have to arrange for service of the order, normally personal service of an order endorsed with a penal notice.

29.7.3 Procedure at the hearing for freezing injunctions and search orders

Freezing injunctions and search orders are, by their very nature, orders which are almost invariably required without giving any notice to the defendant. The procedure when applying for a freezing injunction and/or search order will be similar to that for any other without notice injunctions.

The procedure has been made much more straightforward as a result of the adoption of standard form orders for both types of injunction (CPR, PD 25 (Interim Injunctions)). The following additional points should be noted:

(a) if a defendant is outside the jurisdiction, you will have to satisfy the requirements of Council Regulation (EC) No 44/2001, so that service outside the jurisdiction can be effected without permission or you must obtain permission when you obtain the injunction;

(b) great care should be taken in giving full and frank disclosure as most of the applications to discharge for breach of this duty arise in freezing injunction and search order cases and the court seems to take an even more stringent view of the duty than it does with less draconian orders;

(c) there is normally a requirement to inform third parties of a freezing injunction order which affects them and to pay any costs of the third party in complying (such as the costs of a bank inquiring whether the defendant holds any accounts and whether those accounts are in credit);

(d) a freezing injunction order should normally have a maximum sum to which the injunction applies (calculated by reference to the proper value of the claimant's claim);

(e) a freezing injunction order should allow the defendant to draw reasonable living expenses and legal costs up to a stated sum, often with a proviso that the sum can be increased by written agreement between the parties' solicitors to save the time and expense of applying to the court for every variation of that amount;

(f) in both freezing injunction and search order cases the variety of ancillary orders is extremely wide and needs to be considered with great care particularly if a writ *ne exeat regno* is sought (see **29.7.4**).

Although the adoption of standard form orders has made the task of preparing the draft order simpler, the standard wording may not always be appropriate. It seems that the judges of the Queen's Bench Division are more prepared to vary the standard wording than other judges and some commonly accepted variations can be found in the editorial notes in the White Book. In error the standard forms make no provision for costs.

29.7.4 Procedure at the hearing for a writ *ne exeat regno*

The prerogative writ *ne exeat regno* is not strictly available merely as an ancillary order to another injunction such as a freezing injunction. It is for this reason that the court has used the general s 37 power in cases such as *Re Oriental Credit* (see **29.3**). The requirements for the writ are:

(a) that the defendant would have been liable to arrest prior to the Debtors Act 1869;

(b) that a good cause of action exists for at least £50;

(c) that there is probable cause for believing that the defendant is about to leave England and Wales unless arrested; and, crucially,

(d) that the defendant's absence will materially prejudice the claimant in the prosecution of his action.

Now that an established freezing jurisdiction exists which can, in appropriate cases, be extended worldwide, it will be exceptionally difficult to establish that each of the four criteria is established. The final criterion has been interpreted as restricting the use of the writ to the period before any judgment as thereafter it is judgment and not the action which is being prosecuted.

The application is made without notice and, if the above criteria are fulfilled, the writ will be issued addressed to the Tipstaff of the High Court requiring him or her to bring the defendant before the court as soon as possible so that any appropriate further order can then be made by the court.

29.8 The opposed without notice application

As it is now possible to send documents considerable distances very quickly by facsimile or email there is an increasing tendency (particularly in the Chancery Division) to notify a defendant or proposed defendant that application is being made for an order without notice. This practice is not used where giving the defendant prior notice of the order will enable him or her to defeat it (eg, in most freezing injunction and search order cases).

At an opposed without notice application the role of the defendant will be either to sit silently and take no active part in the proceedings, or to treat the hearing as a hearing with notice even if there has been no time in which to prepare evidence in answer. A defendant given notice of a hearing faces a considerable dilemma. If the defendant takes an active part in the hearing, he or she may encourage the court to make an order at that stage by, for example, being wholly unable to offer any explanation for some apparently obvious wrongful or unlawful act. If the defendant fails to attend or takes no part, it may appear to the court that the defendant has little interest in the outcome of the application. Finally, by attending, there may be additional pressure on the defendant to offer some undertakings rather than face the prospect of an injunction being granted.

The main disadvantage to the claimant in giving notice is that, if the application is dismissed, the claimant is likely to be ordered to pay the defendant's costs whereas, if the application were made without giving notice, the claimant would only be responsible for his or her own costs.

29.9 Applications to vary or discharge

An order may be made (whether with or without notice) giving liberty to the defendant and to third parties to apply to vary or discharge the order. If there is to be a hearing with notice shortly after the without notice hearing, you are less likely to find an express power to apply to discharge.

In some circumstances application may be made without notice to vary or discharge an injunction but the power will only be used in cases which are exceptionally urgent.

If there is an application to vary or discharge the injunction or some parts of the order, it should be supported by evidence setting out the reasons for the variation or discharge. The application can be made simply by giving notice but the usual course is to issue an application. The other documents required will be those used at the initial hearing, save that the draft order will be an actual order of the court. If time permits, there may be further evidence from the claimant. There are three main reasons for seeking an early variation or discharge:

(a) that there has been some non-disclosure by the claimant which entitles the defendant to have the order set aside;
(b) that the injunction should be varied or discharged because of some facts not known to the court or the claimant at the time of the grant of the order; and
(c) that the defendant wishes the court to impose conditions upon the continuation of the injunction (such as security for the undertaking as to damages).

Applications for discharge are sometimes made at a much later stage (eg, if the claimant having obtained the injunction does not proceed diligently with the action or because of a change in circumstances).

At the hearing of the application to vary, the defendant should have the right to open and close his application. The judge may be prepared to treat the hearing as if it were any return date already set and then dispense with a further with notice hearing making the injunction (whether or not varied) continue to trial or further order. The judge will consider all the evidence and determine whether the injunction should be set aside or varied using the same approach as on any return date.

29.10 Applications with notice

The procedure will differ according to whether there is an order without notice in place and whether the same judge deals with the with the notice hearing. If there was an order without notice and it is the same judge hearing the with notice application, it may be possible to introduce the evidence leading to the grant of the order without notice very briefly leaving it to the defendant to explain why the order should not be continued until trial or further order. If you have a different judge, or if there was no without notice hearing or order, it will be necessary for the claimant to deal with the case more fully.

The hearing of the with notice application will have been fixed when the application was issued.

Once counsel for the claimant has introduced counsel for the other parties, the nature of the application should be explained briefly. The statements of case should be explained to show the causes of action relied upon. Unless the judge indicates that it is unnecessary, the next stage is to explain the evidence before the court. Counsel for the claimant should take the judge through the evidence in support without comment (which may mean reading it out to the judge), the evidence in opposition should be gone through by counsel for the defendant(s) without comment, and finally any evidence in reply should be gone through by counsel for the claimant. When the evidence stage has been completed counsel should make their submissions. Counsel for the claimant should address the court in support of the orders sought, going through the proposed order in detail. Counsel for the defendant(s) will then answer (if called upon to do so). Finally (if called upon to do so), counsel for the claimant can reply. The reply should not be merely a repetition of the opening submission but should address the points made by counsel for the defendant(s).

It may be possible for counsel to agree before the hearing what test should be applied by the court. It should not be necessary to explain to the judge the test to be applied if you are relying upon *American Cynamid v Ethicon* [1975] AC 396. You should be familiar with the decision of *Series 5 Software Limited v Philip Clarke & others* [1996] FSR 273, which reconsiders or explains the factors to be taken into account in granting an injunction. If your case falls within an exception to the test in those cases, you may have to explain why it is exceptional and the test which is then to be applied.

In many cases there will be discussion between counsel over the possibility of the application being disposed of by the parties giving undertakings (see **29.12**). If undertakings are offered in lieu of an injunction it should be made clear whether the offer is an open one (ie, one which can be mentioned to the judge) or is made 'without prejudice' (ie, may only be used on any questions of costs).

In many cases that strict sequence of events for a with notice hearing will be varied at the request of the judge who will have particular questions or issues which he or she wishes counsel to deal with as they arise. The result may be that the evidence stage becomes muddled with the submissions stage. If the judge announces that he or she is going to grant an injunction, there may be further discussion about the wording at that stage, even though it may already have been dealt with in submissions. In a complex case counsel may be asked to prepare a form of wording which reflects what the judge ordered.

Finally, the judge will need to deal with the costs of the injunction. See **Chapter 35.** If costs were reserved to this hearing, it is important that they are mentioned to the court.

29.11 The order

It is extremely important that the order is clearly worded so that the defendant will know exactly what he or she can or cannot do. In the County Court the wording of orders has been changed after the experimental work carried out on the North Eastern Circuit. The word 'forbidden' is now used instead of 'restrained' and 'servants or agents' has disappeared when the defendant is an individual rather than a firm or company.

The order should also contain a penal notice. The penal notice is the warning which tells the defendant that he or she must obey the order or be guilty of contempt of court for which he or she may be sent to prison. In the County Court the wording now appears in bold immediately after the name and address of the defendant to whom the order is addressed.

29.12 Undertakings

At any hearing attended by the party against whom the injunction is sought, an offer may be made of an undertaking in lieu of an injunction. Such an offer is almost invariably given without any admission of liability. An undertaking is a promise to the court to do or refrain from doing some stated act or acts. It is enforceable in the same way as an injunction.

When undertakings are given in lieu of an injunction there is sometimes a dispute as to whether the party seeking the order has to give the undertaking as to damages. The practice in the Chancery Division is that a cross-undertaking as to damages will be given unless the contrary is expressly agreed at the time. No similar presumption applies in the Queen's Bench Division or the County Court so any cross-undertaking must be recorded in any order.

Just as a party may apply to vary or discharge an injunction, application may be made to be released from an undertaking given. The application should be made in the usual way, with evidence in support, explaining the basis for the application (eg, that there has been a change in circumstances or that there has been unnecessary delay by the claimant in prosecuting the action).

30 Applications to strike out for want of prosecution

30.1 Introduction

The court has the power to strike out an action for want of prosecution where there has been delay in progressing the action to trial. This chapter deals with High Court applications to strike out for want of prosecution. The procedural timetable previously imposed by CCR O 17, r 11, in the County Court together with the provision for automatic striking out in the event that a hearing date was not requested within 15 months of the commencement of the timetable, means that such applications are rarely made in the County Court. If you are instructed in such an application, the same principles and approach should be adopted as in the High Court. The logistics in terms of reporting to the usher, filling in slips and the documents available to the district judge from the court file will be different. The introduction of the Civil Procedure Rules 1998 with greater control and case management powers vested in the court and tougher sanctions for failure to comply with procedural steps timeously, should lead to the demise of these applications.

30.2 In the High Court

In the High Court the application is made by application notice (CPR, Part 23) to the Master. In the Queen's Bench Division the application will initially be given a date in the general list. These applications should be dealt with in less than 20 minutes. It is highly unlikely that a contested application to strike out for want of prosecution can be dealt with in that time. Your solicitors should have arranged a private room appointment. If they have not done so you should advise them to do so unless you think that it can be dealt with in 20 minutes. There is no point in your turning up and running up the costs in the process if the application should be adjourned to a private room appointment. If it is in the general list you should check that it is in counsel's list. If the application is in the solicitor's list and objection is taken to your presence, the application will be adjourned with your side paying the other side's costs of the adjournment. These points should be checked as soon as the brief arrives on your desk. Do not assume that your solicitor has made all the necessary arrangements. In the Chancery Division the principles canvassed below still apply but the venue is different.

30.3 The test

Before the Civil Procedure Rules, the court would ordinarily only strike out an action for want of prosecution if:

(a) there has been inordinate and inexcusable delay on the part of the claimant or his or her lawyers; and

(b) that delay:

  (i) will give rise to a substantial risk that it is not possible to have a fair trial of the issues in the action; or

  (ii) is likely to have caused serious prejudice to the defendant.

It is not the purpose of this chapter to set out and explain the principles of law applicable to such applications. You will find a useful summary of the relevant principles in *Trill v Sacher* [1993] 1 WLR 1379 at p 1398 onwards, but note, however, that principle (7) is no longer correct in the light of the House of Lords decision, *Roebuck v Mungovin* [1994] 2 WLR 290. You should also read and be familiar with the notes that appear at paragraphs 25/L/1 to 25/L/22 in the White Book (1999 edition).

The extent to which the Civil Procedure Rules 1998 and the ethos underlying them will alter the court's approach has yet to be determined. There is nothing in the Civil Procedure rules of direct application to striking out for want of prosecution which remains an exercise of the court's inherent jurisdiction to control its own proceedings. Nevertheless claimants can probably expect to receive less sympathy than prior to the introduction of the Civil Procedure Rules; see, for example, *Shikari v Malik*, The Times, 20 May 1999.

In *Biguzzi v Rank Leisure plc* [1999] 1 WLR 1926, Lord Woolf gave some guidance on how the Civil Procedure Rules would apply to applications to strike out for want of prosecution. The test set out above will no longer be rigorously applied and the previous authorities are of little value as an indicator of when an action ought to be struck out. The test was reduced to the 'simple' question 'Is there anything unfair in letting the case proceed to trial?'. That question has to be answered with an eye on the overriding objectives and the list of factors set out in CPR, r 3.9. It is likely that a case which would not have satisfied the 'old' test will be struck out under the new test. Equally, the broader range of sanctions and controls over proceedings now given to the court may mean a lesser sanction than strike out might be applied. Each case will turn on its own facts. Although the Civil Procedure Rules will apply to the hearing of the application and result in a decision taken against a CPR background, the conduct of the litigation before the introduction of the Civil Procedure Rules falls to be judged against the rules, practices and procedures applicable at that time.

It will be apparent from the statement set out at the beginning of this section that there were two distinct inquiries that the court had to conduct before striking out an action for want of prosecution. The first relates to delay and the second to the consequences of the delay. These two factors set the structure for the application. You must first ascertain whether there has been delay and, if so, whether it is excusable, when the period(s) of delay occurred and how long the period(s) of delay lasted. It is only after those issues are dealt with that you can look at the effect of the delay that is inordinate and inexcusable to see whether **that delay** gives rise to a substantial risk that a fair trial will not be possible or a serious risk of prejudice to the defendant. Under the Civil Procedure Rules the rigid approach is no longer required and any delay giving rise to prejudice may result in a strike out if that is the only way to do justice between the parties.

Where the delay is substantial it may amount to an abuse of the process of the court with the result that the action may be struck out even if the requirements set out in (b)(i) and (ii) above are not satisfied and the limitation period has not yet expired (see *Grovit v Doctor* [1997] 1 WLR 640 and *Arbuthnot Latham Bank v Trafalgar Holdings* [1998] 1 WLR 1426).

30.3.1 Delay and the limitation period

When your brief arrives on your desk in chambers you need to look at it straightaway. You should check whether or not the limitation period has expired. If it has not, it is unlikely that the court will strike out the action, as there will be nothing to stop the claimant starting a fresh action with the result that the final trial and resolution of the dispute will be even further in the future than would otherwise be the case. The position may be otherwise if the delay can be characterised as an abuse of process. You should check that the evidence before the court includes a suitable chronology from your point of view. You should check whether there is adequate evidence relating to the consequences of the delay alleged by the defendant and whether the evidence can or should be bolstered in any way by a further witness statement. There is no point in sitting down to prepare the brief the day before the hearing only to discover that some further enquiries could have been made or some further evidence could have been put before the court which would have strengthened your position. The majority of applications that fail do so because there is inadequate evidence of the consequences of the delay, or the court is not persuaded that the consequences are so serious that the action should be dismissed. It is difficult to do anything, beyond the power of your own advocacy, to avoid the latter but it is often easy to do something to remedy the former.

30.3.2 A chronology and skeleton argument

If your brief does not contain a suitable chronology, you must prepare one yourself and be ready to give it to the Master at the beginning of the hearing. If you can do so, as a matter of professional courtesy you should send a copy to your opponent before the hearing so that he or she has a chance to consider and agree it. Treat your opponent as you would wish him or her to treat you. A **suitable chronology** means one that presents the history of the action in the best possible light from your client's point of view but without misleading the court. From the defendant's point of view the chronology should ideally show lengthy periods of time between the various stages of the proceedings with not a lot happening in between. Such steps as the claimant takes which are inadequate in terms of progressing the action should be identified. The defendant's chronology is likely to concentrate on the various procedural stages of the litigation process. It should also help the Master to focus on the consequences of the delay that the defendant relies on; so, for instance, if an important witness dies, the date of his death should appear in the chronology, and if allegations raised in the action are only raised for the first time long after the cause of action accrued, the date and nature of the allegations raised should appear in the chronology. On the other hand, if the important witness died before the onset of delays in the prosecution of the action, it is difficult to attribute any prejudice arising from death of the witness to the claimant's delay.

From the claimant's point of view the chronology should give the impression that the claimant has been busy getting on with the action albeit the defendant may not have been aware of the industry involved. The chronology should also highlight those factors which might excuse the claimant's delay. For example, a chronology prepared by the defendant may show that there has been a substantial delay in giving disclosure of documents relating to a claimant's loss of earnings in a personal injury action. The claimant's chronology may well show that this period has been taken up with writing numerous letters to the claimant's employers to obtain the relevant documentary evidence and that the employers are responsible for the delay rather than the claimant or his legal advisers. It is important to retain a sense of proportion; a chronology that refers to each and every letter written by the claimant's solicitors may lose its impact if it is so detailed that the Master cannot quickly achieve an overall grasp of how the action has been progressing.

Any chronology must include the date upon which the cause of action accrued, the date upon which the proceedings were issued and the date upon which they were served. The latter two dates are not the same and may be months apart. From the defendant's point of view the first he or she knows of the commencement of the proceedings will be when the claim form is served upon him or her.

In all but the most straightforward applications you will need to prepare a skeleton argument.

30.4 Before the hearing

Before entering the Master's room, counsel for the defendant should make sure that the application notice and the defendant's witness statements and exhibits are readily available to be handed to the Master at the outset. Counsel for the claimant should also ensure that the claimant's witness statements and exhibits are readily to hand to give to the Master when required. Counsel should also ensure that there is a bundle comprising the writ (issued before the introduction of the Civil Procedure Rules) or the claim form (post-CPR) and any statements of case in the action which can also be handed to the Master. In the High Court none of the statements of case are filed at court and unless you give them to the Master he or she will not be able to see what the issues in the action are. Counsel for the parties should ensure that they have completed the slip identifying the protagonists. The slip is usually to be found in a little box on the outside of the Master's door and should be handed to the Master when the parties enter the room. If the application is in the general list, there will be an usher who will collect the relevant details and hand out a slip to be filled in and returned.

30.5 The hearing

30.5.1 Introductions

Counsel for the defendant who issued the application notice should begin by introducing those who appear before the Master for the various parties. There is no need to introduce your solicitors, just yourself and other counsel present. If one of the parties is represented by a solicitor only, you should introduce him or her too. By convention other counsel are introduced as 'my learned friend' whereas solicitors are simply 'my friend'. You could instead introduce the solicitor as 'Mr Speed of Messrs Wright, Sloe and Stops, the solicitors for the second defendant'.

30.5.2 The opening

Having advised the Master from whom he or she can expect to hear, you should then move on to explain what you are there for. You simply tell the Master what the application is about, eg, 'Master, as you will see from the application notice, this is an application by the defendant to strike out the claimant's claim for want of prosecution'.

You are now embarking on opening the application to the Master. The opening should be neutral and should inform the Master what the case is about and outline the nature of the issues which the application involves. It is often the defendant's first opportunity to lay the foundations for the submissions that he or she will make after the evidence has been dealt with. It also gives counsel for the defendant an opportunity to undermine the claimant's arguments before they are heard by the Master. You should already have a good understanding of what the claimant is likely to say based on his or her evidence. You should not strive to do so to the extent that your opening becomes overtly partisan. If you are representing the claimant and your opponent is making a lot of comments relating to submissions of the parties, you might whisper to him or her in a voice sufficiently loud for the Master to hear that he or she should save their submissions for closing speeches and get on with opening the case.

By the time the opening has finished the Master should be able to embark on reading the evidence with a real understanding of the case and the questions that he or she will have to decide. A good opening should set out in a logical order the information that needs to be fed to the Master to help him or her understand the case, ideally from your point of view. The following sets out the sort of logical progression that is helpful. It is only an example and not a definitive or complete model to be followed come what may.

After finding out who is appearing before him or her and what the application relates to, the Master will want to know what sort of action he or she is being asked to strike out. You should try to work out a way of formulating a short introduction which tells the Master the nuts and bolts of the claim and how it arises, eg:

> In the action the claimant claims damages for personal injury. The claimant was formerly employed by the defendant at his factory in Toytown as a press operator. The defendant is a manufacturer of car body panels. The claimant was injured on 4 March 1995 when he caught his arm in the press he was supposed to be operating. As a result of the accident his arm was amputated at the elbow. He did not return to work after his accident and on 24 December 1995 he was dismissed from his employment with the defendant.

While dealing with the accident you can expand the information available by outlining the parties' allegations and contentions. It is important to establish what these are because the risk that it is not possible to have a fair trial, or the existence of serious prejudice to the defendant will usually relate to the issues that are thrown up in the action and how they will be proved or established at the trial. At this point you might give the Master the particulars of claim and defence so that he or she can see what the pleaded issues are. Again you should be able to set out the issues very shortly, eg:

> The claimant alleges that the accident was caused by the defendant's failure to maintain properly the guards and safety cutout switches on the pressing machine so that it was capable of being

operated when the claimant's arm was still in it. Latterly the claimant has alleged that he and another employee, Mr Cotton, were both trying to remove an extra sheet of metal from the machine when the guards were down and it was ready for action and Mr Cotton inadvertently pressed the button to start the machine. The defendant contends that the machine was in perfect working order at the time of the accident and that the accident was caused by the claimant attempting to retrieve a sandwich from the machine after it had already started its action. Mr Cotton had, as something of a prank, thrown the claimant's sandwiches into the machine. The defendant's health and safety regulations specifically direct employees not to take food onto the factory floor and to keep it in their lockers adjacent to the canteen and rest rooms.

At this point one might begin to set up the points which prejudice the defendant so that the Master can see where the argument is likely to go. As an example the opening might carry on with the following:

The press was inspected the next day by an expert engineer, Mr Flat. His inspection disclosed no fault with the machine at all and he concluded that it was in perfect working order. Regrettably Mr Flat died in a road traffic accident in December 2002. The machinery accident was also witnessed by the defendant's foreman, Mr Snoop, who saw Mr Cotton throw the claimant's sandwiches into the machine. Mr Snoop suffered a stroke in April 2005 and it appears unlikely that he will live for more than another six months.

The Master will need to know how the claim has been conducted and what steps have been taken in the action. At this stage the chronology comes into its own. You should be able to take the Master to it and use it as a skeleton for this part of your opening. You should mark your own copy with the various dates by which things should have been done so that you can, in opening the case, explain to the Master what should have happened and when it should have happened, in contrast with what did in fact happen and when it did in fact happen. Your opening might carry on along the following lines:

Master, if I can take you to the chronology you will see that the accident occurred on 4 March 1995. The claimant's trade union instructed solicitors who wrote to the defendant's insurers on 19 March 1996 intimating a claim for negligence and breach of statutory duty and alleging that the machine and in particular its guards and safety switches were not maintained in proper working order. **Not much happened thereafter until** the claimant issued the writ on 3 September 1997 **some six months before the expiry of the limitation period.** The writ was served on 2 January 1998 **shortly before its validity lapsed.** The defendant gave a notice of intention to defend on 12 January 1998. **Pursuant to Order 18 Rule 1 of the Rules of the Supreme Court the claimant should have served his statement of claim within 14 days, ie, by 26 January 1998. In fact** the statement of claim was not served until 28 November 1998 when **for the first time** references were made by the claimant to Mr Cotton assisting him to remove a sheet of metal from the press and alleging that Mr Cotton started the machine when it was unsafe to do so as the claimant's arm was still within it.

In a perfectly neutral opening the emphasised words might well be omitted. By making those points in opening, counsel for the defendant can begin to create a prima facie impression that the claimant has been laggardly in his conduct of the action to the prejudice of the defendant, without going so far as to give an unduly partisan opening or making submissions which should be saved for closing speeches.

The opening should conclude with a short résumé identifying the period of delay relied on by the defendant and the prejudice that makes it unjust to allow the claim to continue. You should be stating the conclusion you want the Master to reach and not all the arguments that lead to the conclusion. It may help you to arrive at a good formulation if you try to write down in two short sentences the substance of your argument on prejudice. In the present opening you might well conclude with, eg:

There has been four years of delay in the prosecution of the claim. In that time the defendant's expert witness has died and therefore can no longer be called to give evidence at the trial and an important witness of fact, Mr Snoop, has suffered a stroke which has impaired his memory. Given the rate of progress to date it is likely that Mr Snoop will die before the trial of the claim. Had this claim progressed with proper speed the trial should have been over and done with five years ago in 2000.

30.5.3 The evidence

It is then time to move onto the evidence. The defendant's evidence should be read first. Counsel should enquire whether the Master wishes to hear it read out loud or merely to read it for himself or herself. You will often see the Master skimming through the evidence leaving you with the impression that he or she has not read it as carefully as you did in preparing your brief and that he or she may not have appreciated the nuances that appear in it. As part of your preparation you must be thoroughly familiar with the evidence and where the important points are made. You may well be asked simply to take the Master to the meat of the witness statement or to deal simply with the question of prejudice or risk that a fair trial is not possible. Counsel should then give way to counsel for the claimant who should take the Master through the claimant's evidence. Counsel for the defendant can then take the Master through any evidence in reply.

If the Master indicates that he or she wishes to hear you read the witness statements (highly unlikely), you can start by saying, 'Mr Smith says at paragraph. . . as follows' and just read on with the evidence. You should avoid reading aloud as fast as possible in monotone speech. The likely effect is that the Master will not be reading with you and may well doze off. You should modulate the pitch and tone of your voice by placing emphasis where it is required, ie, on the strong points which you wish to push home. You might also slow down a little when you reach a particularly important passage to make sure the Master follows it with you. You should read aloud clearly and distinctly at a speed which allows a half-informed listener to take in what you are saying. The common error is to go too fast: it can be avoided by adopting the approach of telling a story rather than simply reading aloud.

You should not add comments or explanations as you go through your evidence nor should you interject with too many comments about your opponent's evidence. You should sit quietly and patiently awaiting your turn to speak. You might interject if both the Master and your opponent seem to be getting it horrendously wrong but any interjection should be helpful rather than adversarial. That does not mean you switch off. You should be listening to what is being said by your opponent and the Master. You should be watching to see how much of the evidence the Master appears to be absorbing and be alert to points which seem to sway him or her either for or against your opponent.

30.5.4 Closing speeches

Counsel for the defendant goes first followed by counsel for the claimant and then counsel for the defendant in reply. Closing submissions should be structured. You should not just ramble through the evidence without saying what conclusions should be drawn nor why they should be drawn. The structure for your submissions is the structure canvassed above, ie, (1) delay and (2) consequences. The same structure should be followed by both sides.

Counsel for the defendant should be seeking to maximise the periods of delay and undermine the excuses put forward by the claimant. For example, in the disclosure example considered above in dealing with chronologies, the defendant's riposte is that writing letters to the claimant's employer clearly was not achieving the desired end, that a summons for third-party disclosure should have been issued and had the claimant done so the action could have moved on with no undue delay. A measure of the pace at which the action should have progressed can be taken from the interim timetable provided by the various old Rules of the Supreme Court governing the interim stages of the action. RSC O 25, r 8, contained automatic directions applicable to personal injury actions. Failure to follow the timetable amounts to delay which becomes inordinate once it becomes longer than one can reasonably allow. This part of the closing submission should conclude with a realistic appraisal of the period of time which amounts to inordinate and inexcusable delay. There is no point in putting forward an unrealistic suggestion as it may be taken to indicate that the rest of your arguments are similarly misconceived. You should then move on to deal with the prejudice that flows from that delay. This involves identifying the prejudice and then establishing a causal connection between the prejudice and the delay. Using the example opening, counsel for the defendant would argue that prejudice arises from the death of Mr Flat as he is no longer available to give evidence. You would need to acknowledge that there are likely to be reports and notes relating to his inspection that would be admissible under the Civil Evidence Act and go on to point out that the admissibility of those documents as evidence does not help at all with questions which arise outside the scope of the documents, nor does it help with the detail of what Mr Flat saw at the time or adequately deal with points which would otherwise have arisen in cross-examination. The defendant may well be unfairly handicapped at the trial if the claimant has a live, contemporaneous expert witness and the defendant does not. Having established the nature of the prejudice the causal link can be established by pointing out that the trial should have taken place in 2000 and Mr Flat did not die until 2002, ie, after the trial should have taken place in the ordinary course of events.

It is of the utmost importance to keep in mind that there are two things to establish: (i) prejudice or risk of an unfair trial; and (ii) caused by the delay. A good opening accompanied by a well-drafted witness statement raising the right points, which has been well read and digested by the Master, may leave you with little to do beyond recapping the main points where delay has occurred, the adequacy of any excuse put forward and the prejudice that flows from it. If your application is based on serious prejudice within the limitation period accompanied by more than just minimal prejudice arising thereafter as a result of the delay, you must make sure that your closing submissions adequately canvass the serious prejudice that your side has suffered together with the prejudice suffered later.

Counsel for the claimant will probably have little to say on the delay as the facts tend to speak for themselves so far as what was done and when it was done. You may well find that the best way forward is to look at individual stages in the litigation with a view to arguing that the time taken for each stage was not unduly long or, if it was, the time taken was excusable. The best sort of excuse is that it was beyond the claimant's control or it was the defendant's fault. Again you should not simply assert that a particular period of delay was excusable, you must go on to refer to the evidence giving rise to the excuse so that your submissions explain why the delay was excusable. Having dealt with the delay, if there is some delay for which the claimant has to accept responsibility, counsel should deal with the questions of prejudice, risk to a fair trial and whether those factors were caused by the delay. You will need to look at the length of delay which you accept as relevant and also the periods of delay which the defendant contends is relevant. Just because the Master accepts the defendant's submissions as to the relevant period of delay does not mean that the defendant will establish the requisite degree of prejudice arising from that delay. In dealing with these substantive issues you must not lose sight of the fact that there must be **evidence** of the prejudice and evidence that it is caused by the delay. An assurance by the defendant's solicitor that the defendant has been prejudiced by the delay is not likely to be sufficient. In our example the witness statement should deal with the evidence that Mr Flat could have given and explain how the lack of that evidence damages the defendant's case. The claimant's submissions will generally follow this pattern depending on the contents of the witness statements:

(a) there is no inordinate delay;

(b) if there is, it is excusable;

(c) if it is not, there is no sufficient evidence of prejudice;

(d) if there is evidence of prejudice, there is no sufficient evidence that the prejudice is attributable to the delay;

(e) on the evidence of prejudice put forward by the defendant there is not in fact any prejudice caused to the defendant;

(f) on the evidence of causation the prejudice was not in fact caused by the delay;

(g) any prejudice is not sufficiently serious to warrant the striking out of the action;

(h) some lesser sanction such as payment of costs or limitation of interest recoverable is proportionate and just.

Questions of prejudice are rather like peeling the layers of an onion; eg, the defendant says that Mr Flat is no longer available to give evidence; the claimant says that there is no serious prejudice as his report and notes are admissible in evidence, ie, this is not a case where death deprives the defendant of admissible evidence; the defendant says that Mr Flat made no report and took no notes; the claimant says that prejudice is caused by Mr Flat's failure to make proper notes and compile a proper report, therefore there is no prejudice attributable to the delay; the claimant might well say 'instruct another expert' but that may be of no assistance if the machine does not still exist in the same form as at the time of the accident. Under the Civil Procedure Rules the court will take an overview rather than deal with details in this way.

Counsel for the claimant should be alert to look behind the prejudice alleged by the defendant to see whether it exists and what the real cause of it is. If the defendant has had an early opportunity to investigate the circumstances surrounding the accident and has good, contemporaneous witness statements available, it may be difficult to establish that he will be prejudiced by the delay: the witnesses will have plenty of material to refresh their minds about what did or did not happen. Industrial accidents are often well recorded and documented in compliance with the relevant Health and Safety at Work Regulations, rendering the quality of witness recollections at the trial of less significance. On the other hand if no proper investigations were undertaken by the defendant, the cause of any prejudice to the defendant may be his own failings rather than any delay on the claimant's part.

If the Master has been skimming through the evidence, you should make sure that you cover all the evidence fully in your closing submissions by taking him or her to the important passages. Instead of simply saying, '. . . as you will have seen from the claimant's witness statement. . .', you should be more direct: 'Mr Speed states in paragraph 7 of his first affidavit that. . .'; then deal with what he says and then apply what he says to the submissions that you are making. You must take the evidence and use it to support the point you are trying to make.

30.5.5 Judgment

After hearing your submissions the Master will, in the vast majority of cases, give a reasoned judgment there and then. You should take as full a note as possible of the judgment as it is delivered. You may not want to appeal whatever the outcome, however, your opponent may wish to do so. You can hardly agree a proper note of judgment if you did not take one yourself. You should also be listening carefully to the way in which the Master expresses himself or herself in dealing with the various issues in the application. By doing so you increase your prospects of working out what sort of point appeals to that particular Master or does not appeal to the particular Master and the sort of language to use in putting the point across. If you speak the same language as the Master the point is more likely to strike home. An important quality of a good barrister is knowing what sort of argument the court will swallow. As no two judges are the same you need to build up a store of knowledge about individual judges before whom you are likely to appear. It may not help you to win this application but it may help you next time you appear before the same Master.

30.5.6 Costs

Please refer to **Chapter 35.**

30.5.7 The order

The Master will endorse the order he or she makes on the application notice. You should be clear about precisely what has been endorsed on it before you leave the room. If you think you might wish to appeal, you must ask for permission.

If the application fails, the Master will wish to review what needs to be done to get the case to trial as directed in the Civil Procedure Rules. Both sides need to be fully prepared to argue about how the claim should proceed and fully briefed about the time scale required to complete the procedural steps required to get the claim to a trial.

30.5.8 Leaving the room

Before you leave you should ensure that the Master has handed back all the documents handed in, except the witness statements. The witness statements are filed with the court but the exhibits are returned to the custody of the solicitor to whom they belong. Courtesy costs nothing: make sure you thank the Master for dealing with your case, even if you think he or she has got it completely wrong. You should also consider whether an apology is merited from all concerned if the hearing has substantially overrun the allotted time. If it has, you should make a mental note to ensure that next time you give a more accurate time estimate.

30.6 Law and lore

The vast majority of applications turn on their own facts as to delay and prejudice. It is most unlikely that a legal point will arise which requires any great explanation of the law in opening the case to the Master. You may well need to refer to authorities in your closing submissions to underline the points that you are making as to how the legal propositions should be applied. It is prudent to prepare your brief on the basis that the Master will be unfamiliar with the law: it will enhance your understanding of the area and your advocacy. You may draw a deputy Master on his or her first day in court in which case you may have to go back to basics and improve his or her understanding of the law.

There is one area of fertile debate which is partly a matter of law and partly a matter of fact. It relates to the adequacy of the evidence of prejudice and the extent to which the court can infer or rationalise the existence of prejudice from the existence of the delay. The principal reported authorities are *Hornagold v Fairclough Building Ltd* [1993] PIQR 400, *Rowe v Glenister & Sons* [1995] TLR 463, *Slade v Adco Ltd* [1995] TLR 650 and *Shtun v Zaljejska* [1996] 1 WLR 1270. Lore has it that substantial delay, more or less as night follows day, leads to diminution in witness recollections. The law tends to require some evidence of it. Under the Civil Procedure Rules it is likely that lore will prevail. In a perfect world one would hope to adduce evidence of what a witness could say when first proofed and what that witness could say at about the time the application to strike out is made. It leads to an unreal exercise in trying to extract from a witness what it is that they have forgotten and when they managed to forget it. The more balanced approach seems to be to put before the court sufficient material for the court to judge the importance of the 'lost' evidence and the likelihood that it will prejudice the defendant or create a risk of an unfair trial. Whether the evidence is sufficient or not is down to the power of your advocacy.

31

Applications in the Chancery Division

31.1 Chancery Division proceedings

Claims involving Chancery business may be dealt with either in the High Court or in a County Court. CPR, PD 7, para 2.5, defines 'Chancery business' as including any of the matters specified in the Supreme Court Act 1981, Sch 1, para 1. The classes of claim specified in Sch 1, para 1 are those relating to:

(a) the sale, exchange or partition of land, or the raising of charges on land;
(b) the redemption or foreclosure of mortgages;
(c) the execution of trusts;
(d) the administration of the estates of deceased persons;
(e) bankruptcy;
(f) the dissolution of partnerships and the taking of partnership or other accounts;
(g) the rectification, setting aside or cancellation of deeds or other instruments in writing;
(h) probate business, other than non-contentious or common form business;
(i) patents, trade marks, registered designs, copyright and design right;
(j) the appointment of a guardian of a child's estate; and
(k) the exercise of the High Court's jurisdiction under the companies legislation.

The Civil Procedure Rules and Practice Directions supplementing them contain information on Chancery Practice. Additional practical information may be found in the *Chancery Guide* (see *Blackstone's Civil Practice,* App. 3).

31.1.1 Applications

Any procedural application (eg, for directions) should be made to a Master unless there is some special reason for making it to a judge. Otherwise the application may be dismissed with costs. Some applications, particularly for interim injunctions, have to be made to a judge. CPR, Part 23, contains rules as to how an application may be made and it is worth noting that in some cases it can be dealt with without a hearing, or by a telephone hearing. Further details can be found in *Blackstone's Civil Practice,* **Chapter 32**. An application is usually for interim relief although orders may be made which finally dispose of a question or an issue in a proceeding (eg, the vacation of a caution on a register of title, or the grant of a declaration).

31.2 Procedural aspects

Unless an application is to be made without notice, or the court gives permission to the contrary, the documents which must be filed with the Listing Office are the application notice (minimum four copies where the proceedings involve one defendant and additional copies for further defendants), two copies of the proceedings and the judges' application information form (containing details of solicitors, counsel and parties, etc). The application notice must be served a minimum of three clear working days before the hearing (not including Saturday, Sunday or recognised holidays) and must not include either the day of service or the day of the hearing. The normal CPR rules on service apply; see *Blackstone's Civil Practice,* **Chapter 15.**

Applications are generally heard in open court. Where it may be unjust for the application to be heard in public, the judge may exercise a discretion to sit otherwise than in open court.

31.2.1 Skeleton arguments

The general rule is that for the purpose of all hearings before a judge skeleton arguments should be prepared. The exceptions are where the application does not warrant one, for example, because it is likely to be short, or where the application is so urgent that preparation of a skeleton argument is impracticable.

On judges' applications without notice, the skeleton argument should be filed with the papers which the judge is asked to read on the application. In more substantial matters, such as applications by order (see **31.3.1**), they should be filed not less than two clear days before the hearing. In all other applications to a judge, including interim applications, they must be filed no later than 10 am on the day before the hearing. Skeleton arguments should be filed with the judge's clerk, if the name of the judge is known; otherwise filing is done at the Listing Office.

The *Chancery Guide* (Appendix 3) contains guidelines on the content of a skeleton argument. See also *Blackstone's Civil Practice,* at 32.18. Failure to lodge this document in accordance with the *Guide* may result in the matter not being heard on the scheduled date and/or disallowance of the costs of preparation and/or an adverse costs order (see the *Chancery Guide,* para 7.30).

31.2.2 Bundles, time estimates and reading lists

Bundles of documents for use in court will generally be required for all hearings if more than 25 pages are involved (and may be appropriate even if fewer pages are involved). The efficient preparation of bundles of documents is very important. Where bundles have been properly prepared, the case will be easier to understand and present, and time and costs are likely to be saved. The representatives for all parties involved must cooperate in agreeing bundles for use in court. Documents in agreed bundles are admissible as evidence at the hearing unless the court orders otherwise or a party gives written notice objecting to the admissibility of particular documents (PD 32, para 27.2). The court and the advocates should all have exactly the same bundles (*Chancery Guide,* para 7.12). Detailed guidelines on the preparation of bundles are set out in the *Chancery Guide,* Appendix 2. These should always be followed unless there is good reason not to do so.

The general rule is that the claimant/applicant must ensure that one copy of a properly prepared bundle is delivered at the Listing Office at least two clear days before the hearing of an application and at least seven days before a trial. However, the court may direct the delivery of bundles earlier than this. Where oral evidence is to be given, a second copy of the bundle must be available in court for the use of the witnesses. In the case of bundles to be used on Judge's Applications (other than applications by order), the bundles must be delivered to the Clerk to the Interim Applications Judge by 10 am on the morning preceding the day of the hearing unless the court directs otherwise (para 7.16).

Where documents are copied unnecessarily or bundled incompetently, costs of preparation may be disallowed. Where the provisions of the *Chancery Guide* as to the preparation or delivery of bundles are not followed, the bundle may be rejected by the court or be made the subject of a special costs order (para 7.10).

When lodging the agreed bundles there should also be lodged an agreed time estimate, together with an agreed reading list and an agreed time estimate in respect of that reading list. The time estimates and reading list must be signed by the advocates for the parties. Failing agreement as to the time estimates or reading list, then separate reading lists and time estimates must be submitted signed by the appropriate advocate (para 7.17).

If the case is one which does not require the preparation of a bundle, the advocate should check before the hearing starts that all the documents to which he or she wishes to refer and which ought to have been filed have been filed, and, if possible, indicate to the associate which they are (para 7.18).

31.3 Conduct of applications before the judge

31.3.1 General

The interim applications judge is available to hear applications each day in term and an application notice can be served for any day in term except the last. If the volume of applications requires it, any other judge who is available to assist with interim applications will hear such applications as the interim applications judge may direct. Special arrangements are made for hearing applications out of hours and in vacation.

Where the circumstances of a case require a 'short notice' period (less than three clear days' notice to the other side), permission to abridge time may be obtained on an application without notice, usually made after the midday adjournment.

Counsel do not robe on interim applications, although the judge will wear the judicial gown. The traditional practice is that the judge will ascertain at the sitting of the court which of the listed applications will be 'effective', that is, disputed, and if so, what counsel's estimate of length is, or 'ineffective', that is, disposed of by agreement or which the parties wish to be adjourned. The current practice is to concentrate on the time estimate for the application, with the judge not particularly insisting on counsel stating whether their application is 'effective' or 'ineffective'. It is a matter of courtesy both to the court and to other counsel and litigants:

(a) to be present in court when the judge takes his or her seat;
(b) to be ready to say whether the application is 'effective' or 'ineffective' (if required);
(c) to have carefully considered the estimate of length (if the application is to be effective) and to have agreed that estimate with one's opponent;
(d) not to waste the time of the court when the judge is going through the list 'first time round' by explaining the substance of the application instead of simply indicating whether it is effective or ineffective/the time estimate.

Although the judge has a discretion as to the order of hearing applications, he or she will normally deal with ineffective applications first, eg, matters which are to be adjourned or have been settled, or, under the current practice, by taking the shortest applications first and the others in order of their time estimates. Counsel are often 'released' until stated times of the day based on the time estimates of the applications which will be dealt with at earlier stages of the day.

Applications likely to take two hours or more will usually be given an order that they are given a subsequent fixed date for hearing (they are then called 'interim applications by order'). In these cases the judge will, at the first hearing, hear argument for any application for a court order to last until the application is heard fully. The hearing where the main application will be fully argued will be fixed through the solicitors or the clerks to counsel for all parties with the Clerk of the Lists. All other listed, unlisted and applications without notice will be heard in the order determined by the judge. Those affecting the liberty of a subject (eg, for release from committal to prison for contempt, or for *habeas corpus)* are always accorded priority.

Counsel with effective applications may be asked to wait, in case another judge becomes free to hear the matter. The judge may transfer any application as deemed appropriate, irrespective of priority. Counsel should not leave the precincts of the court unless released by the judge until a particular time. Counsel should also ensure that the court staff can easily locate them if a judge becomes free. Any application which at the end of the day is part heard (ie, unfinished), will normally head the list for the next court day.

31.3.2 Time estimates

Time estimates are critical. The applications judge will determine only applications which are estimated to last less than two hours. Counsel will be required to lodge with the Chancery Listing Officer a written time estimate signed by the advocates for all the parties as soon as possible after the application notice has been lodged. An indication may be given that an application by order is to be treated as urgent. If it is apparent that it will be likely to last more than two hours, the only proper course is to inform the court that it is ineffective, and 'second time round' to inform the judge to the effect, 'This application is likely to occupy the court for two days, and I therefore ask your Lordship to stand it over as an interim application by order. Subject to your Lordship's approval, the defendant is to give certain undertakings in the meantime'.

31.3.3 Unlisted and emergency applications

Frequently, counsel is instructed to apply to the court urgently without notice, which means there will not have been time for the application to appear on the court's list. It also happens that instructing solicitors sometimes forget to lodge the papers for applications on notice in accordance with the directions mentioned above. Counsel may in these circumstances ask the judge to hear the matter although unlisted. The judge's clerk should be notified (usually through counsel's clerk) as early in the day as possible, that an application is to be made, and two copies of the proceedings (showing the title of the claim), and the draft of the order to be sought should be made available. If the proceedings have not yet been issued, every effort should be made to issue the claim form before the application is made. If this is not practical, the party making the application gives an undertaking to the court to issue the claim form forthwith. The usual practice is to rise in counsel's place after the judge has worked through the list for the first time, and to say words to the effect, 'I have an unlisted application in the claim of Smith and

Jones [giving the claim number]'. Such an application will only rarely be ineffective, and counsel should go on to indicate the time estimate. Unless the application affects the liberty of the subject or is of exceptional urgency and importance, listed applications will be given priority.

31.3.4 Ineffective applications

An application can only genuinely be described as 'ineffective' if there is no point of disagreement between the parties which requires the decision of the judge. Counsel must ensure that all such points have been dealt with, and not attempt to be heard early in the list under the guise of an ineffective application. The degree of information which the judge will require to have on the substance of an application depends on the nature of the order which the court is to be asked to make. It is usual to indicate in very general terms the nature of the claim (eg, 'This is an application for an injunction to restrain the defendant from dealing with certain land which is alleged to be subject to an option agreement'). Counsel will then usually inform the judge orally of the terms of the order which the judge is invited to make. If the order involves undertakings to the court or submission to an order (other than a purely procedural order) by one of the parties, the judge is likely to wish to know the exact terms of the undertakings. It is therefore not merely a formality to say, 'The parties have agreed *subject to your Lordship's approval* that the application should stand over for 14 days on the defendant's undertaking not to dispose of the land known as [describing it]': the terms of the undertaking or an order in the same terms are subject to the approval of the judge.

31.3.5 Effective applications

The sequence in which effective, ie, disputed, listed applications are dealt with is in the discretion of the judge. Normally the judge will direct that the shorter applications be heard first. Naturally, this must not be abused by underestimating the time which the matter will take. The procedure will then follow this outline:

(a) Counsel presenting the application will open by giving a short account of the facts giving rise to the application.

(b) Counsel for the applicant then makes his or her submissions on the evidence as presented.

(c) Counsel for the respondent makes his or her submissions.

(d) Counsel for the applicant is entitled to reply to the submissions of the opposing party.

31.3.6 Agreed adjournments

If all parties to an application agree to do so, an application can be adjourned for not more than 14 days by attending the Chancery Listing Officer in Room WG4 with signed consents from all parties before 4.00 pm on the day before the listed hearing. A litigant in person who is a party must attend before the Clerk as well as sign a consent. Not more than three successive adjournments may be made and no adjournments are to be made to the last two days of any sitting (*Chancery Guide,* para 5.13). Undertakings previously given to the court may be continued unchanged over the duration of any adjournment. If an existing undertaking is to be varied or a new undertaking given, the adjournment must be dealt with by the judge.

An application may be adjourned to be heard as an application by order without attendance before the judge where the parties are agreed that the application will take two hours or more. The consents signed by all parties should also contain an agreed timetable for the filing of evidence or confirmation that no further evidence is to be filed. Any application arising from the failure of a party to abide by the timetable and any application to extend the timetable must be made to the judge. Interim applications by order will, initially at least, enter the Interim Hearings warned list on the first Monday after the close of evidence. See the *Chancery Guide,* para 5.14.

31.3.7 Drafting of orders

It may often be possible for the court to prepare and seal an order more quickly if a draft of the order is handed in. Speed may be particularly important where the order involves the grant of an interim injunction or the appointment of a receiver without notice. In all but the most simple cases a draft order should be prepared and brought to the hearing.

The court may in any case direct the parties to agree and sign a statement of the terms of the order made by the court. Where a draft or an agreed statement of the terms of an order exists in electronic form, it is often helpful if the draft or agreed statement is provided to the court by email or on disk as well as in hard copy, particularly if the order needs to be drawn quickly. Any disk supplied for this purpose must be new and newly formatted before writing the material on it so as to minimise the risk of transferring a computer virus. The current word-processing system used by the Chancery Associates is Word for Windows 2000. Where a judge directs that a statement of the terms of an order be agreed and signed, the agreed statement should be lodged in Room TM 5.04. Agreed statements will normally be adopted as the order of the court.

Orders will be drawn up by the court, unless the judge or Master directs that no order be drawn. Unless a contrary order is made, or the party concerned has asked to serve the order, a sealed order will be sent to each party.

31.3.8 Use of information technology

The Civil Procedure Rules 1998 contain provisions about the use of information technology in the conduct of cases. No standard practice for its use in Chancery cases has yet evolved although this is likely to change over the next few years. In any case where the solicitors for one or more parties take the view that some form of IT will assist the presentation or management of a case, the solicitor should obtain, at an early stage, directions from the judge who is to try the case. Where no nomination of a specific judge has yet been made, solicitors who wish to use any form of IT should invite the Vice-Chancellor (by request to his or her clerk) to nominate a judge to hear the case including all interim applications. The solicitors for all parties should try to agree a common protocol for the electronic exchange and management of information.

When skeleton arguments or chronologies exist in electronic form, inquiries should be made of the judge (via his or her clerk) as to whether the provision of these documents on disk as well as in hard copy would be welcome. Any disk supplied to a judge should be new and newly formatted to minimise the risk of transferring a computer virus.

The *Chancery Guide* contains specific provisions relating to transcripts, the use of fax and evidence by video link. See the *Chancery Guide,* paras 14.1 to 14.17.

32

The companies court

32.1 Insolvency proceedings: winding-up petitions

32.1.1 Introduction

The Insolvency Service is working on a consolidation of the secondary legislation dealing with insolvency, which is intended to culminate with a new set of Insolvency Rules 2009 planned for implementation in October 2009. This project aims to reduce the regulatory and administrative burdens that exist for users of the insolvency legislation, but is proving to be a complicated task. At the time of writing there is no published draft of the new Rules, so this chapter will make references to the existing provisions in the Insolvency Rules 1986.

A petition for the compulsory winding up of a company incorporated by registration under the Companies Acts may be presented by the company, or its directors, or by any creditor or creditors (including any contingent or prospective creditor or creditors), or by a contributory (ie, shareholder) or contributories, various officials (eg, Secretary of State for Business, Enterprise and Regulatory Reform and the Attorney General), administrators and administrative receivers, or by all or any of those parties, separately or together (Insolvency Act 1986, s 124(1)). A great many junior barristers will find that they are briefed to appear on creditors' winding-up petitions in the Companies Court (see the ***Company Law in Practice*** manual, **Chapter 9**). An inexperienced advocate should beware of believing that such petitions present no difficulties simply because they are very numerous and usually undisputed. Before appearing on the hearing of such a petition, the advocate should study carefully the relevant provisions of the Insolvency Act 1986 and the Insolvency Rules 1986 (SI 1986/1925), which will be referred to in this chapter as 'the Act' and 'IR 1986'. References to forms, by number, are references to the forms prescribed by the IR 1986. The IR 1986 prescribe the form which a petition should take (see Sch 4, Form 4.2). Where written evidence is required, it may take the form of affidavits or witness statements verified by statements of truth (r 7.57(5)). Generally the High Court and County Courts have concurrent jurisdiction and a petitioner may choose in which court to proceed.

32.1.2 Evidence verifying petition

The petitioner or someone with knowledge of the matters giving rise to the petition must file written evidence (in a witness statement or affidavit) verifying the petition (see IR 1986, Form 4.3). The written evidence must state various facts and comply with IR 1986, r 4.12. It must state that the allegations in the petition are true or are true to the best of the deponent's knowledge, information and belief.

32.2 The court

High Court winding-up petitions are listed for hearing before the Registrar of the Companies Court sitting in open court on Wednesday mornings at 10.30 am. Petitions are listed in 30-minute batches, so that a number of matters will be found in the list marked 'not before 11.00' and so on. Counsel must be robed, and the Registrar is addressed as 'Sir'.

32.3 Petitions by creditors

While petitions may be presented by a variety of parties mentioned above, the most common category of petitioners are creditors. To qualify as a creditor within the meaning of the Insolvency Act 1986, the petitioner must establish that a debt is due from the company to him or her which is not bona fide disputed on substantial grounds. Some creditors may be described as 'trade' creditors (meaning that their debts have been incurred in the course of the company's business). Others may be 'judgment' creditors where the company has failed to satisfy a court judgment made against it.

32.3.1 Restraining presentation of the petition

If the company disputes the *locus standi* of the petitioner as a creditor, on the ground that the debt upon which a petition is to be or has been presented is disputed, the company may make an application to restrain the presentation or advertisement of the petition (which occurs after the petition has been served on the company). Such application must be made to the judge by the issue of an originating application (Form 7.1). See ***Company Law in Practice*** manual, **9.6**.

If the company fails to take such preventive steps, it may still dispute the petitioner's entitlement to a winding-up order on the ground that the debt is disputed by giving notice to the solicitors for the petitioner. Because of the danger of spurious disputes being used to defeat creditors, the Companies Court judges have introduced a practice of requiring the company in doubtful cases to make a payment into court of (or otherwise securing the amount of) the debt, pending an application for summary judgment by the petitioner.

32.4 Before the hearing

The following is a checklist of the matters which must have been attended to by the instructing solicitors before the hearing. Counsel should ensure that he or she has copies of these documents in preparing the case for the hearing and that any defects which are found in them, eg, inconsistent dates or sums owed, erroneous title of company in the advertisement, etc are discussed with the solicitor before the hearing. If there has been non-compliance with the rules, remedial action will be required, as indicated after each point.

32.4.1 Petition and verifying evidence

Counsel should have a copy of both of these documents. Problems with the petition, such as insufficient particulars of the debt, or incorrect details dealing with the EC Regulation on the jurisdiction of insolvency proceedings, have to be dealt with by standing the petition over for amendment.

32.4.2 Evidence of service

Service must be proved by written evidence in the form set out in Form 4.4 or 4.5. The text of the witness statement or affidavit should state the date on which the petition was served. It is a strict requirement that it must also specify the method of service used. Service of the petition and verifying written evidence must generally be effected at the company's registered office: IR 1986, r 4.8(2). Permissible methods of service are set out in r 4.8(3), which provides:

> Service of the petition at the registered office may be effected in any of the following ways—
>
> (a) it may be handed to a person who there and then acknowledges himself to be, or to the best of the server's knowledge, information and belief is, a director or other officer, or employee, of the company; or
> (b) it may be handed to a person who there and then acknowledges himself to be authorised to accept service of documents on the company's behalf; or
> (c) in the absence of any such person as is mentioned in sub-paragraph (a) or (b), it may be deposited at or about the registered office in such a way that it is likely to come to the notice of a person attending at the office.

If service by any of the above methods is not practicable, the petitioner may instead either:

(a) effect service at the company's last known principal place of business, under r 4.8(4); or

(b) apply without notice by witness statement or affidavit for an order for substituted service under r 4.8(6), (7);

The Court Manager of the Companies Court is authorised to deal with applications for substituted service.

The witness statement or affidavit of service should exhibit the petition and any order for substituted service (r 4.9).

32.4.2.1 Remedies

If the written evidence of service is defective, the court will have to be asked for an adjournment of the petition either:

(a) to file a fresh witness statement or reswear the affidavit, if the petition was properly served but the written evidence does not correctly state the facts or failed to specify the manner of service; or

(b) to effect reservice, if the petition has not been properly served.

If the company appears at the hearing, it may seek dismissal of the petition on the ground that it has been advertised after defective service. If the company has been properly served and appears at the hearing, a defect in the written evidence will cease to be relevant.

32.4.3 Advertisement

Unless the court directs otherwise, each petition must be advertised once in the *Gazette* and contain certain required information as set out in IR 1986, r 4.11. There is a prescribed form of advertisement (Form 4.6):

> The advertisement of the petition must state—
>
> (a) The name of the company and the address of its registered office, or
> (i) in the case of an unregistered company the address of its principal place of business;
> (ii) in the case of an oversea company, the address at which service of the petition was effected;
>
> (b) the name and address of the petitioner;
> (c) where the petitioner is the company itself, the address of its registered office or, in the case of an unregistered company, of its principal place of business;
> (d) the date on which the petition was presented;
> (e) the venue fixed for the hearing of the petition;
> (f) the name and address of the petitioner's solicitor (if any); and
> (g) that any person intending to appear at the hearing (whether to support or oppose the petition) must give notice of his intention in accordance with r 4.16.

A copy of the advertisement should be included in the brief for counsel for the petitioner. Unless it is the company's own petition, the advertisement must have appeared not less than seven business days after service of the petition, nor less than seven business days (which do not include Saturdays, Sundays or bank holidays) before the hearing date (see IR 1986, r 4.11(2)(b)). This is a most important requirement, as it enables the company to prevent the highly damaging consequences of advertisement by applying for an injunction if the petitioner's debt is disputed. Counsel should ensure that the advertisement complied with r 4.11, that there are no printing errors in the advertisement, and the time requirements have been met.

32.4.3.1 Remedies

If the advertisement rules have not been complied with, the court may dismiss the petition. In the case of premature publication, if the publication is a day early, eg, because of an innocent failure to count a bank holiday, the court may waive the defect. Counsel should point out the premature advertisement, state the reason shortly, and ask that the defect be waived. There is always a serious risk that the petition will be dismissed on this ground.

If a court orders that a petition be re-served due to defective service, counsel should ask whether a second advertisement will also be required. If this is required, counsel may request that the required time periods be abated although this is at the discretion of the court.

32.4.4 Certificate of compliance

In order to assist High Court practitioners, the time laid down by IR 1986, r 4.14 for filing a certificate of compliance and a copy of the advertisement has been extended to no later than 4.30 pm on the Friday before the hearing (PD Insolvency Proceedings, para 3.1). A certificate of due compliance shows the dates of presentation, service, advertisement and hearing (Form 4.7), together with a copy of the advertisement. The present practice is to stand petitions out for 14 days to allow time to file the certificate where this has not been done in time. The Registrar will normally mention this matter as soon as the petition is called on.

32.4.5 List of appearances

Every person including creditors or the company itself intending to appear on the hearing to support or oppose the making of a winding-up order must give notice to the solicitors for the petitioner not later than 4.00 pm on the business day before the hearing (IR 1986, r 4.16). Failure to comply means that person cannot appear without the permission of the court. If the company intends to oppose the petition, its witness statement or affidavit must be filed in court not less than seven days before the hearing (IR 1986, r 4.18). It is the duty of the petitioner's solicitors to prepare a list of the persons who have given such notice (Form 4.10, known formally as the 'list of appearances', informally in court as 'the list', and colloquially from its colour as 'the blue form'). The list must be handed in before the hearing (IR 1986, r 4.17(3)). If it is not handed in, the Registrar will usually simply say when the petition is called on 'There is no list', and decline to proceed further.

32.4.5.1 Remedy

The only help for this is to make sure that the solicitors' representative is seen well before the time for which the petition is listed, and told to hand in the list when the current half-hour's petitions are over. If the list has not been handed in, ask the Registrar to 'take this matter second time round'.

32.5 Substitution

If the original petition is not proceeded with (because the petitioner withdraws), or is not advertised, or in other similar circumstances (see IR 1986, r 4.19(1)), the court may, on such terms as it thinks just, substitute as petitioner any creditor or contributory who in the court's opinion would have a right to present a petition, and who is desirous of prosecuting it. The 'new' petitioner asks for a substitution order (see **32.7**, 'The Hearing', Counsel C below).

32.6 Noting the back sheet

It is helpful to compile the relevant information and the dates on which the required steps were taken for use as a quick guide during the hearing to avoid having to search through a file during the presentation. One example would be as follows:

Re: [name of company]
Trade creditors' petition based on a statutory demand in the sum of £ . . .
List: [enter any creditors, contributories, or others supporting/opposing the petition and the nature of their interest]
Co: [note whether the company will make an appearance]

Relevant dates:

Presented:	[eg, 28/4/09]
Verified:	[28/4/09]
Served:	[7/5/09]
Affidavit:	[8/5/09]

Advert: [28/5/09]
Cert. Comp: [1/6/09]
UCO (Asking for the usual compulsory order)

32.7 The hearing

The following applications may be heard in unopposed petition situations:

(1) Associate:	'Petition number 546, Tyro Advisers Limited.'
Counsel A (for Petitioner):	'This is a trade creditor's petition based on a statutory demand for the sum of £32,459 odd. The company is not represented, and the list is clear (or 'negative'). I ask for the usual compulsory order.'
Registrar:	'Usual compulsory order, main proceedings.'
(2) Associate:	'Petition number 547, D-I-Y Services Limited.'
Counsel B:	'This is a petition based on a statutory demand for unpaid solicitors' fees.'
Registrar:	'This petition was advertised only five business days after service, and r 4.11 has not been complied with.'
Counsel B:	'Sir, I am instructed that my instructing solicitors unfortunately overlooked the fact that seven business days must elapse between service and advertisement, and therefore did not omit from their calculation of the time two weekends and a bank holiday. In those circumstances, I ask that the defect be waived.'
Registrar:	'No. These errors are capable of causing severe damage to a company which may wish to dispute the debt. There has been no effort in this case by the solicitors to cure the error, or to communicate with the court office in lieu of complying with r 4.11. In the circumstances I will dismiss the petition.'
Counsel C:	'I appear for Suppliers Limited, a supporting creditor which has not given notice to the petitioner's solicitors prior to this hearing. My client has a trade debt amounting to £78,968 odd, and my application is for permission to be added to the list out of time and for an order substituting my client as petitioner.'
Registrar:	'I will give you permission to be added to the list out of time on the usual terms. I will also make an order substituting Miss C's client as the petitioner, and adjourn the matter for 28 days for amendment of the petition, re-service and re-advertisement.'

32.8 Notes on the hearing

(a) It is usual to describe the basis of the petition and to show what is alleged to prove the inability of the company to pay its debts (in this case failure to comply with a statutory demand, but other evidence may also be adduced).

(b) The court is told whether the company is represented.

(c) The court should be informed whether there are any supporting or opposing creditors or contributories on the list of appearances, and if so, how many of each and whether any of them have in fact appeared at the hearing. If there are none, the court is told that the list is clear or 'negative'.

(d) The usual compulsory order is set out in Form 4.11. (See **Figure 9.3, *Company Law in Practice*** manual.) The reference to 'main proceedings' (See the Registrar's order in answer to counsel A) is to the EC Regulation on insolvency proceedings, and means the debtor company's main interests are in England and Wales and not in another EU state.

(e) The 'usual terms' on which a creditor is added to the list of appearances out of time are that the applicant's solicitor undertakes not to seek any costs of giving notice or of the application to be added to the list in the event of a compulsory winding up being made. (A substituted petitioner will normally obtain an order for the subsequent costs of amendment, re-service, re-advertisement, and hearing.)

32.9 Opposed petitions

If it becomes apparent that the petition is opposed, the Registrar will adjourn the matter for hearing before the judge because the Registrar only has jurisdiction over unopposed petitions.

32.10 Adjournments

If an order is made, the winding up commences with the presentation of the petition (s 129(2) of the Act). Section 127 avoids dispositions of property of a company made after the commencement of the winding-up, unless the court has otherwise ordered (see ***Company Law in Practice*** manual, **9.7**). For this reason, the court will not permit a petition to remain outstanding for protracted periods (except in the case of petitions by contributories, where a winding up is sought, the company is solvent, and the judge has made appropriate orders under s 127). Even if the petitioner and the company have agreed that the company should have time to attempt to pay the petition debt, the court will only grant an adjournment if there is a good reason, and only on condition that the petition is advertised in time for the next hearing. A second adjournment is unlikely to be granted (PD Insolvency Proceedings, para 2.1).

32.11 Rescission of a winding-up order

An application for the rescission of an order must be made within seven days after the date the order was made (IR 1986, r 7.47(4)). Applications can only be made by a creditor, a contributory, or by a company jointly with a creditor or with a contributory. The application must be supported by written evidence of the company's assets and liabilities. If the petition is unsuccessful, the costs will normally be ordered to be paid by the petitioner.

33 Possession cases

33.1 Introduction

33.1.1 Types of cases included

You may be instructed to act in a claim for the possession of land in a variety of circumstances. A landlord may seek to recover possession of residential or commercial property from persons to whom the landlord has granted a tenancy or a licence or from trespassers. A mortgagee may seek to enforce the charge on the mortgagor's property to sell it to obtain the money owed under the mortgage. Although different considerations apply to each, all are covered by CPR, Part 55 or CPR, Part 56.

This chapter considers the different circumstances. The requirements of Civil Procedure Rule 55 and Practice Direction 55, which apply to all possession cases issued after 15 October 2001, are considered first, highlighting the matters which you must check. The common matters to check in respect of cases of possession by landlords generally (residential, commercial and trespassers) are then considered. There are then three separate sections dealing in turn with specific considerations in respect of trespassers, residential occupiers and commercial occupiers. Mortgage possession cases, being based on a different relationship, that of a lender enforcing the charge on premises, are covered at the end.

33.1.2 Civil Procedure Rules

33.1.2.1 Which court

Proceedings must be issued in the County Court for the district in which the land is situated unless there are exceptional circumstances which justify bringing them in the High Court (CPR, r 55.3(1) and (2)).

If the case is in the High Court, you should check that there is a certificate stating the reasons for bringing it there and that the circumstances do come within those set out in PD 55.3, para 1.3 which may justify starting a claim in the High Court. These include matters involving complicated disputes of fact or points of law of general importance. The value of the property and amount of the financial claim may be relevant circumstances but will not alone normally justify starting the claim in the High Court (PD 55.3, para 1.4).

33.1.2.2 Statements of case

(a) Content

Check that the claim form, particulars of claim, defence and any counterclaim and defence to counterclaim are in the correct form and contain all the information required by the CPR, both generally (CPR, Part 16) and the additional requirements set out in PD 55. Thus, for example, check that the general requirements for possession proceedings set out in PD 55.4 are fulfilled. This includes identifying the land, stating whether it is residential property and the ground on which possession is claimed, and giving full details of any mortgage or tenancy agreement and of every person who, to the best of the claimant's knowledge, is in possession of the property. Note in particular the requirement in PD 16, para 7.3 to attach to the particulars of claim a copy of any agreement on which the claim is based. Any written tenancy agreement should be attached. There are additional requirements in respect of residential occupiers, trespassers and mortgage arrears claims.

(b) Service

Check that the requirements in respect of service have been fulfilled. Note that in possession cases, the particulars of claim must be filed and served with the claim form (CPR, r 55.4). Generally the court will have served the documents and there will be no issue as to service. However, where the parties have elected to serve themselves, check there is a certificate of service. In many possession cases, the defendant occupants do not respond to the particulars of claim and do not appear. It is therefore important that the court is satisfied that they have been properly served. CPR, r 55.8(6) specifically requires the claimant to produce the certificate at the hearing. In cases against trespassers, there are special rules as to service that must be fulfilled (see later).

33.1.2.3 The fixed date hearing

Under CPR, r 55.5(1), on issue of the possession claim form, the court will fix a date for the first hearing. The defendants must be served a certain number of days before the hearing, the number of days varying according to the type of case and property (see CPR, r 55.5). Ensure they were served in time. The aim of this first hearing is to identify whether there is any defence to the claim. If so, the court will use the hearing to give case management directions to prepare for trial. If not, the court may decide the claim at this hearing.

(a) If the defendant does not appear

If you are instructed to appear at such a first hearing, it may be that the defendant has not filed a defence. If acting for the claimant you must be ready to prove your case at the first hearing. This means having the evidence to do so. Under CPR, r 55.8(3), where a claim has not yet been allocated to a track, any fact that needs to be proved may be proved by evidence in writing. Thus, you may find that you are instructed to appear on the basis of the statements of case and witness statements with any documents annexed to the statements of case or exhibited to the witness statements. Check you have all relevant documents.

(b) Where the defendant does appear

Even if no defence has been filed, the defendant may turn up at the hearing. Failing to file a defence does not preclude him or her from taking part in the proceedings, although it may be taken into account when the court decides costs, eg, of an adjournment. If acting for the landlord, you will need to determine from the defendant or the legal representative whether the defendant does intend to defend. If he or she does, the court is unlikely to hear the case that day, partially because the defendant is unlikely to be ready to proceed and partially because the court will not have time to hear it as usually a large number of cases are listed. However, you should attempt to determine what the defence is and check whether an adjournment will be sought or case management directions can be agreed. If instructed on behalf of the defendant, you will need to take careful instructions from your client to determine whether or not there is a defence and, if so, whether you wish to seek an adjournment to have time to consider the case in more detail or whether it would be appropriate for case management directions to be given.

(c) The risk of 'consent orders'

If the defendant does not contest the case or, although taking issue with some of the allegations, is prepared to agree to a possession order (eg, on payment of money to him or her to leave), be aware of the dangers of 'consent orders' in possession cases. A tenant cannot contract out of statutory protection given by the Rent Act 1977 or the Housing Acts 1985 or 1988. The court cannot make a 'consent order' against such a tenant unless there is either an express admission that the Acts do not apply or it is established by evidence or admission that a ground under the Act is made out and, if appropriate, it is reasonable to make a possession order. An order made without such concession or establishment is a nullity and can be challenged by judicial review even where both parties were legally represented and consented to the order (see *R v Bloomsbury & Marylebone County Court, ex p Blackburne* (1985) 275 EG 1273). In addition, where you are acting for the defendant who may become homeless and apply to the local authority for housing, be aware that consenting to an order may be interpreted by the local authority as becoming homeless 'intentionally' thereby depriving him or her of any call on the local authority's duty to rehouse those in 'priority need'.

(d) Track allocation and case management directions

Where no order is made at the first hearing, unless an adjournment is granted, the case will be allocated to either the fast track or the multi-track (cases will only be allocated to the small claims track if both parties agree—CPR, r 55.9(2)). In deciding which is the appropriate track, the court will take into account the usual factors set out in CPR, r 26.8 and those in CPR, r 55.9, which include the importance to the defendant of retaining possession and to the claimant of vacant possession. The court will also make appropriate case management directions including the usual ones in respect of disclosure, witness statements and experts (where relevant).

33.1.2.4 Preparing for a contested hearing

Where you are instructed to appear for one of the parties in a contested hearing (the most usual type of case in which counsel is instructed), you will need to check that all the case management directions have been complied with (eg, disclosure completed, witness statements exchanged, directions in respect of experts fulfilled). You also need to check that you have a copy of the trial bundle, which does include all the necessary documents, eg, statements of case, witness statements, expert(s) reports where relevant and relevant documents. Ensure as well that relevant witnesses and experts have been warned to attend and, where necessary, compelled to attend by witness summons.

You need to check that the evidence covers all the necessary allegations made by your client. Thus, if acting for the landlord, ensure the evidence does cover all the matters that he or she must prove to establish the right to possession and to rebut any defence raised. If acting for the defendant, check that the evidence is focused on rebutting the landlord's allegations and proving any positive defence raised by your client. Although the matters to be checked depend on the type of case you have, there are some matters common to all possession claims which are set out below.

33.2 Possession by landlord—common matters to check

33.2.1 Landlord's title

The landlord must prove his or her title to the land. This means proving that he or she has the interest in the land that gives him or her the right to seek possession. Well-drafted statements of case should state what the landlord's title is (eg, freeholder or leaseholder). Frequently there is no issue between the parties as to title. However, where there is a dispute as to the landlord's title or where the defendant does not attend the hearing, s 67 Land Registration Act 2002 renders office copies of the register and documents filed at the Land Registry including charges admissible to the same extent as the originals.

The landlord must also show that he or she has the immediate right to obtain possession against the named defendant. This means that there is no interest between the landlord and the person against whom he is seeking possession. Thus, for example, a landlord has no right to obtain possession directly against a sub-tenant. If he or she wishes to get possession against the sub-tenant, he or she must seek possession from his own tenant. Generally (although not always), if the landlord does get possession against his or her own tenant and that tenancy ends, the sub-tenancy will also end and entitle the landlord to possession against both the tenant and the sub-tenant. Check that the landlord is not attempting to take action directly against a sub-tenant without seeking possession from the tenant.

33.2.2 Tenancy or licence

The occupant's status may be disputed as protection is often afforded to tenants but not to licensees. In construing the agreement between the landlord and the occupant the court will consider the substance of it and be astute to detect 'sham' terms or agreement. You therefore need to ensure that you are au fait with the current law on the factors which determine the difference between a licence and tenancy, consider carefully the written agreement (if any) and/or what was agreed orally and the circumstances in which the letting was made and have your arguments ready. Where proceedings are brought under the specialised proceedings for 'trespassers' (see below), you need to check that the occupancy is one which permits this procedural method to be used (see below).

33.2.3 Nature of premises and use by occupant

Check the type of premises that form the subject matter of the proceedings. The nature of the premises and the use by the occupant determine the type of statutory protection that might be afforded to the occupant. The form of security and requirements to be fulfilled to gain security are different for residential and business tenants. There are different provisions in respect of proceedings against trespassers in residential and non-residential premises (CPR, r 55.5(2)). Mortgagors of residential premises have more protection against possession being granted than those of commercial premises.

Where statutory protection is claimed but disputed on the basis of use by the occupant, you may need to check the agreed use under the tenancy agreement and the actual use by the occupant from the start of the tenancy to determine what, if any, statutory protection exists at the time of the proceedings. There is much case law on this and on what level of 'business' use can bring a tenant out of protection under the Acts covering residential premises.

33.2.4 Other terms of the agreement

Check the terms of the agreement between the landlord and the occupant; in particular, check the provisions for ending the agreement. Statute generally adds to the protection of the occupant but does not reduce any protection afforded by the agreement. Thus, even where tenants have statutory protection, the landlord will generally have to show that he or she has complied with the terms of the agreement as well as the statutory provisions.

33.2.5 Terminating the right to occupy

Check whether the tenancy is a fixed-term or periodic tenancy as different considerations apply to terminating them.

33.2.5.1 Fixed-term tenancies

Where the landlord claims that a fixed-term tenancy has expired, check that it has. Even where the period set out in the tenancy agreement has expired, the tenancy does not terminate but is continued by statute if it is a residential tenancy which comes within the Housing Act 1985 or Housing Act 1988 (a statutory periodic tenancy will arise) or a commercial tenancy which comes within the Landlord and Tenant Act 1954 (a continuation tenancy will arise).

The landlord has the power to terminate the tenancy before the fixed term has expired only if the tenancy agreement contains a provision enabling him or her to do so. Where the landlord purports to end the tenancy during its currency, you need to check whether the landlord is exercising a right under a 'break' clause or under a 'forfeiture' clause.

(a) Break clauses

A break clause is one that entitles the landlord (or less frequently the tenant) to end the tenancy before the end of the fixed term in certain circumstances, usually either at a particular point in the tenancy (eg, at the end of the seventh year of a 21-year agreement) or on the happening of a specified event (eg, the landlord's need to redevelop). Check that the circumstances come within the clause and that any procedures required by the agreement to terminate the tenancy have been strictly followed. Thus, for example, it may require that a particular period of notice be given to end on a particular date (eg, three months' notice expiring at the end of the seventh year of the tenancy).

(b) Forfeiture

A forfeiture clause is one that entitles the landlord to end the tenancy for breach by the tenant. Forfeiture is an ancient remedy of a landlord which is extremely complex with much relevant case and statutory law that may require some research on your part if you know nothing about it. It is too complex to deal with in any detail in this manual and the following is an outline of the basic points to check in such a case. First, check that the tenancy agreement/lease contains a forfeiture clause, that it enables the landlord to forfeit in respect of the breach alleged by the tenant and that any procedure required by the agreement has been followed. Check that the landlord has not done anything after knowing of the breach which could be construed as waiving the breach. If the breach of covenant alleged is anything other than non-payment of rent (or a few other limited exceptions), check that a notice under s 146 of the Law of Property Act 1925 has been served prior to forfeiture proceedings being commenced and that the notice fulfils the necessary requirements. If the allegation is that the tenant is in breach of repairing obligations, check that the notice fulfils the requirements of the Leasehold Property (Repairs)

Act 1938. Finally, check what relief from forfeiture may be claimed by the tenant or subtenant and whether this is likely to be granted. At present, the court's construction of the Housing Act 1988 is that where the landlord claims possession during the fixed term, the claim is under the statute and not for forfeiture. The tenant therefore cannot apply for relief from forfeiture. The position under the Housing Act 1985 is unclear as, although the concepts are the same, the wording of some of the relevant provisions is different. There are no provisions in the Rent Act 1974 which prevent forfeiture of a protected tenancy or the tenant claiming relief.

33.2.5.2 Periodic tenancies

Many of the proceedings in which you will be involved will relate to periodic tenancies, where no fixed term was agreed by the parties. At common law such tenancies continue to renew themselves each period unless one of the parties terminates the tenancy by service of notice to quit. Statutory intervention renders any common law notice to quit ineffective and substitutes its own procedure which the landlord must follow prior to instituting proceedings in respect of residential tenancies which come within the Housing Act 1985 and the Housing Act 1988 (see below). Statutory intervention also alters the position in respect of commercial premises under the Landlord and Tenant Act 1954, which requires certain statutory notices to be served and, until they are, generally the tenancy continues. In respect of other tenancies (eg, those which have no statutory protection or which come within the Rent Act 1977), the common law rules apply and you need to check that a proper notice to quit has been served by the landlord seeking possession.

In respect of notices to quit, you need to check three things. First, check that the period of notice is sufficient. At common law this is generally a full period of the tenancy (eg, a monthly tenancy requires a full month's notice). The only exception is a yearly tenancy where only a half year's notice is required. In addition to fulfilling the common law requirements, where the Protection from Eviction Act 1977 applies (ie, in respect of dwellings), the notice to quit must give a minimum period of four weeks from the date of service of the notice (a notice under the Protection from Eviction Act 1977 must also contain prescribed information to be valid). Second, check that the notice expires on the anniversary of the commencement of the tenancy (eg, a monthly tenancy commencing on the 10th of the month may only be terminated by a notice to quit which expires on the 9th or 10th of the month as it takes effect at the very end of the 9th/start of the 10th). Finally, check that notice has been effectively served on or before the date from which time runs on the notice.

33.2.6 Against whom is the claim brought

In addition to checking that the landlord has the immediate right to possession (see **33.2.1**), you need to check that all relevant parties have been joined. Although the general rule is that when the landlord terminates the tenancy and obtains a possession order, all rights dependent on that tenancy die with it and the possession order is effective against all occupants, this is not always the case. A subtenancy may survive if it comes within the provisions of s 137 of the Rent Act 1977 or s 18 of the Housing Act 1988. In addition, occupants may have claims under other provisions, eg, matrimonial rights. It is therefore usual to join all adult occupants of the premises as defendants. Special rules apply to seeking possession against squatters where the number of occupants and/or their names may not be known to the landlord (see below).

33.3 Trespassers

There are special procedures available where there is a clear-cut case by the landlord that either the occupants entered and remained without his or her consent or any licence granted by the landlord has been terminated. The procedures cannot be used against tenants or ex-tenants and are not appropriate where there are genuine issues about the status of the occupant. They are most commonly used against squatters (ie, those who entered and remained as trespassers). Generally such proceedings involve residential premises, although the procedure also covers commercial premises.

33.3.1 Correct court

Check that the case is in the correct court. It must be issued in the County Court for the area in which the land is situated. If the case is brought in the High Court, check that there is a certificate stating the reasons for bringing it there, and that the circumstances do come within those set out in PD 55.3, para 1(3), which may justify starting a claim in the High Court. Note in particular that a claim against trespassers may be brought in the High Court where there is a substantial risk of public disturbance or of serious harm to persons or property which properly requires immediate determination.

33.3.2 Procedure appropriate?

CPR, Part 55, contains specific provisions for obtaining possession of land against trespassers, squatters and licensees whose licences have been determined. The provision enables possession to be obtained quickly and on the basis of the claim form, particulars of claim and witness statements. This procedure is intended to be used in straightforward cases. It is not appropriate to use it where there are real issues as to the status of the occupier, eg, whether he or she is a licensee or tenant. In such case, the normal procedure should be followed. The first thing you need to check is whether this procedure is appropriate.

33.3.3 Procedure followed

Frequently the owner will not know the names of some or all the occupants. In such a case, the claim must be brought against 'persons unknown' in addition to any named defendants (CPR, r 55.3(4)).

In many cases, no defendants will appear at the hearing. However, the court will be astute to ensure that the requirements of the CPR have been fulfilled. The matters you must therefore check before the hearing are:

(a) the claim form and particulars of claim contain all the relevant information. A new form of particulars of claim (N121) relates specifically to trespassers. Ensure that the matters required by PD 55.4, para 2.6 are included;

(b) service has been properly effected. Although the normal rules of service apply to named defendants, 'persons unknown' must be served by the method set out in CPR, r 55.6. This involves attaching copies of the documents to the main door or some other part of the land so they are clearly visible and inserting another set through the letter slot in a sealed transparent envelope addressed to the 'occupiers'.

33.3.4 Costs

In a very large number of cases, there are no named defendants. Thus, even where possession is granted, no order can be made as to costs as there is no named defendant against whom to make it. If there are named defendants, you need to take instructions as to whether or not you should seek an order for costs against them, if a possession order is granted.

In some cases, the defendants will appear at the hearing. Where they are not named, they should be joined as named parties, if they want to contest the case. If acting for the defendants, you need to advise them that this exposes them to the risk of being ordered to pay costs.

33.3.5 Contested cases

If the defendant(s) raise a triable issue, the court may deal with it there and then, provided the issue is simple and clearly still within the ambit of the procedure for trespassers. In any other situation, eg, a point is raised as to the status of the occupier who may or may not have been a tenant, the court will adjourn the application and direct that it be dealt with as an ordinary possession case and give directions accordingly.

33.4 Residential possession cases—ordinary proceedings

Having determined that the case before you involves possession against an occupant of residential premises, you then need to determine more precisely what, if any, protection the occupant may have against possession being obtained by the landlord. There is a long history of statutory intervention into the landlord and tenant relationship in respect of residential premises. The three current principal statutes have provisions:

(a) setting out the qualifying conditions which the occupant must satisfy to gain protection of the Act and specifying categories or circumstances which exclude protection of the Act even if the occupant satisfies the qualifying conditions;

(b) specifying the basis on which possession may be granted by the courts and the procedure which must be followed to obtain possession;

(c) implying terms into the agreement which may be relevant to the possession proceedings and provisions by which the tenant may seek to control the level of rent charged (in the Rent Act 1977 and the Housing Act 1988 only).

Some of these provisions are identical across the statutes. Some are different either radically or marginally. The following sets out those matters which you must check carefully, whatever type of protection the occupant has. It also indicates where differences occur between the statutes and where more care must be taken in particular statutes than in others.

In determining which statute might apply, check who the landlord is and the date of the tenancy. The three main types of landlord are local authorities (Housing Act 1985), housing associations (may be either Housing Act 1985 or Housing Act 1988) and private landlords (may be Rent Act 1977 or Housing Act 1988). The date that determines which Act applies in respect of housing associations and private landlords is 15 January 1989. Unless caught by one of the transitional provisions, tenancies granted on or after that date are covered by the Housing Act 1988. Housing Association tenancies granted before that date are covered by the Housing Act 1985 and private tenants by the Rent Act 1977.

33.4.1 Status of occupant

The statements of case should make it clear whether or not the occupant's status is in dispute. If the landlord is claiming a status that denies statutory protection, identify the basis of the landlord's allegations. Is it that the occupant fails to fulfil the qualifying conditions of the relevant Act or that the occupant comes within one of the categories specifically excluded from protection or both (ie, pleading in the alternative that the occupants fail to fulfil the qualifying condition but, even if they do, they come within one of the excluded categories)? Check the specific provisions in the statute on which the landlord relies. In considering any case which might be used to argue the construction of the provision, check whether it related to the particular provision on which this landlord relies or a similar one in a different statute. There are small but significant differences in the wording of the statutes, and a case which appears to be 'on all fours' with your case may in fact have been decided on the basis of a different provision and therefore may be distinguished.

Where the occupant does not qualify for the protection of any statute, the landlord merely needs to prove the general matters set out above (**section 33.2**). Where, however, the occupancy does attract statutory protection, you need to go on to check the matters set out below.

33.4.2 Procedural steps followed

33.4.2.1 Housing Act 1985 (HA 1985)

Where the Housing Act 1985 applies, the landlord must serve a notice under HA 1985, s 83, within a specified period before issuing proceedings, the period required depending on the grounds claimed for possession. The notice may be invalid because it is defective or the landlord may have issued prematurely. Check that the notice is in the prescribed form and contains all the relevant information, in particular the grounds on which the landlord relies, the particulars of those grounds and the date after which proceedings may be issued. Check that the notice was served in sufficient time to give the tenant the required period of notice prior to issue and that the proceedings were not issued before the stated date. Although the courts have the power to dispense with service of the notice, many judges are reluctant to do so. There is a growing body of case law on this and, if the point is taken, you need to ensure that you are up to date on the way in which the courts are dealing with this issue.

33.4.2.2 Housing Act 1988 (HA 1988)

Where possession is sought against a tenant with protection of the HA 1988, you need to check whether the tenancy is assured shorthold or assured, as the procedure to be followed differs.

(a) Assured shorthold

If the tenancy was granted on or after 28 February 1997, it will be an assured shorthold unless it is caught by transitional provisions or it was expressly agreed or stated that it was an assured tenancy. Many Housing Associations will so expressly state, but private landlords rarely do.

If the tenancy was granted before 28 February 1997, the landlord must prove that it satisfies the requirements in s 20 of the Housing Act 1988 to be an assured shorthold, ie, that it was for a fixed term of at least six months with no power for the landlord to determine earlier than that (a forfeiture clause does not count as such a power) and proper notice in the prescribed form was served on the tenant before/at the time of entering the tenancy agreement.

If the tenancy is an assured shorthold, the landlord has an automatic right to possession provided he has served the requisite notice under s 21 of the Housing Act 1988 on the tenant. The court has no power to waive this notice. Although there is no prescribed form for this, the notice must be in writing. A landlord cannot rely on this ground during a fixed term unless there is a clause in the tenancy agreement allowing him to do so. Notice can be served during any fixed term provided it is of at least two months' duration and expires at or after the end of the fixed term. Notice in respect of a periodic tenancy (either as granted or as a statutory periodic tenancy arising at the end of the fixed term) must expire at least two months after service and end not earlier than the date on which the tenancy could have been determined by notice to quit at common law. It must also expire on the last day of the tenancy. So check the notice to ensure it is correct and that proceedings were not issued before the date stated in the notice.

(b) Assured

Where the landlord seeks possession on one of the grounds under the Housing Act 1988 because either the tenancy is not an assured shorthold or the landlord does not rely on that automatic right, a notice under s 8 of the Housing Act 1988 must be served on the tenant. This procedure is the same as that under s 83 of the Housing Act 1985 so you will need to check the matters referred to in **33.4.2.1**. Note the court has no power to waive the notice if Ground 8 is relied on by the landlord (see **33.4.3.1**).

33.4.2.3 Rent Act 1977

Common law rules about the termination of tenancies apply to tenancies within the Rent Act 1977 (there is no statutory intervention equivalent to that in the Housing Act 1985 and Housing Act 1988 regarding notices). You will therefore need to check that the contractual (protected) tenancy has been properly terminated prior to commencement of proceedings—ie fixed-term expired or periodic tenancy determined by notice to quit—see **33.2.5**. Check also whether any notice of increase of rent has been served as this may act as a notice to quit provided it fulfils the requirements of notice to quit. Once the contractual (protected tenancy) is terminated the tenant remains in occupation as a statutory tenant. There is no requirement for the landlord to serve a further notice before issuing proceedings.

33.4.2.4 Form N119

Check that the particulars of claim are in the form specified (N119).

33.4.3 Grounds on which possession sought

There are similarities across all three Acts as to the grounds on which possession may be obtained (although they are called 'grounds' under the Housing Acts 1985 and 1988 and 'cases' under the Rent Act 1977). In addition, all three Acts differentiate between mandatory grounds (ie, those where the landlord need only prove the ground) and discretionary grounds (ie, where the court must also be satisfied that it is reasonable to grant possession). It is important to note whether the ground(s) relied on are mandatory or discretionary for two reasons:

(a) if a mandatory ground is proved, the court must order possession. No further test is applied and the court has no discretion not to make an order. However, where a discretionary ground is proved, the court must also be satisfied that it is reasonable to make a possession order. You will need to be prepared to bring evidence on and argue reasonableness. Although each case turns on its facts, there is much case law on the factors which can be taken into account. The court's decision on reasonableness may be difficult to disturb on appeal.

(b) where a court grants possession on the basis of a mandatory ground, it has limited powers to delay the order—it must grant an outright order. It cannot postpone the date by which the tenant must give up possession for more than 14 days unless there is exceptional hardship, when the date may be extended to six weeks. Where the court grants possession on the basis of a discretionary ground, it has very wide powers to suspend the order and frequently does so on conditions. The most common situation where this happens is where an order is granted on the basis of rent arrears. The order may be suspended on payment of current rent plus X off the arrears. So long as the tenant keeps to the conditions, the tenancy continues. Breach of the conditions of the suspended order ends the tenancy and brings the right to remain in the premises to an end. Where discretionary grounds are relied on, you will need to be ready to argue both whether or not the order should be suspended and any conditions.

The grounds under all three Acts divide into different categories, the most common of which are covered below.

33.4.3.1 Rent arrears

This is the most common ground for possession. There is one in the Rent Act 1977 (case 1), one in the Housing Act 1985 (ground 1), and three in the Housing Act 1988 (grounds 8, 10 and 11). All are discretionary except Ground 8 in the Housing Act 1988, which is mandatory. Check the precise wording of the case/ground relied on. They are all differently worded. What precisely must be proved in respect of the arrears?

Check that the rent claimed to be in arrears is due. Check that s 48 of the Landlord and Tenant Act 1987, which requires the landlord to furnish the tenant with his address in England and Wales at which notices may be served on him by the tenant, has been fulfilled. Any rent or service charge is treated as not due until the landlord complies with the section. There is a developing area of case law on what is good notice. So if this is a matter in dispute, you will need to check the current position. Check that any rent increases have been in accordance with the tenancy agreement and, where dealing with a Rent Act tenant, check that any increase has been in accordance with the provisions of the Act. Check whether any of the rent claimed is, in fact, statute barred, remembering the general rules on appropriation of payments.

Check that the claim form and particulars of claim comply with the requirements under the CPR in respect of claims for possession, which include rent arrears as a ground. Check that there is a schedule of rent as specified in the CPR. At court ensure that you are clear precisely what rent is due at that date.

Check whether there is any potential defence to the rent claim, eg, a counterclaim by the tenant for damages for disrepair which amounts to a set off.

Even if rent arrears are proved, for all but Ground 8 under Housing Act 1988, the court must also be satisfied that it is reasonable to grant possession and this is likely to be argued. There is a wide range of factors which the court will consider when determining whether or not it is reasonable. Frequently tenants in arrears are eligible for housing benefit but are not in receipt of it. This is a factor the court will consider when deciding whether or not it is reasonable to grant the order and, if an order is granted, whether or not to grant an outright or a suspended order. Check whether the tenant is eligible for benefit, has applied and, if so, the reasons for any delay in the processing of the claim. Finally, be ready to argue the conditions on which a suspended order should be granted. If acting for the tenant, check that the tenant can realistically pay off the arrears in addition to the current rent. Ensure that the tenant is aware that failure to keep the payments up will mean that the landlord can execute the order by getting the bailiffs in and that there will be no further hearing at that point unless the tenant applies to suspend or set aside the possession order.

33.4.3.2 Nuisance/annoyance

This ground is a discretionary ground under all three Acts. The grounds are similar across the Acts but there are some differences in the wording used. Check the precise wording of the case/ground on which you rely. All three impute the tenant with responsibility for the acts of a limited range of other people that differs across the acts. Where the allegation is nuisance or annoyance, check the wording of the ground/case as to who must be affected as this also differs across the Acts. Where the allegation is of a relevant conviction, check what convictions come within the ground as this also varies across the Acts.

33.4.3.3 Other tenant's default

All three Acts include as a discretionary ground for possession if any obligation of the tenancy has been broken or not performed. You will need to check which term it is alleged has been broken, the tenancy agreement as to the wording, and what evidence there is to prove breach. Check also whether the tenant is alleging waiver of breach by the landlord (ie, the landlord with knowledge of the breach acquiesces to it). You need to be clear both on the law on waiver and the facts of your case that may be used to argue it.

The court must be satisfied that it is reasonable to make an order and can suspend any order made on conditions. Be ready to argue both of these.

33.4.3.4 Condition of dwelling house/furniture has deteriorated

A discretionary ground across all three Acts, it is slightly differently worded. Check the precise wording of the ground on which you rely. Also be prepared to argue reasonableness and whether or not the order should be suspended and, if so, conditions to be attached.

33.4.3.5 Landlord requires the premises

All three Acts have several grounds under which the landlord can obtain the premises because he or she requires them for some purpose. These differ considerably across the Acts. The Housing Act 1985 relates to public sector landlords so has a broad range of grounds under which the landlord can claim possession for various purposes or types of people (eg, those with special needs). The Housing Act 1988 and Rent Act 1977 have more limited numbers of uses available as grounds but include grounds to enable the landlord to gain possession to house him or herself and/or his or her family (not available under Housing Act 1985 for obvious reasons).

In all cases where the landlord is seeking possession on the basis that the landlord requires it for some purpose, you must check the ground on which the landlord relies and ensure that all requirements can be proved. Generally these include requiring the landlord to prove that:

(a) the tenant was given notice at the start of the tenancy that possession may be required. The court may or may not have the power to dispense with this notice;

(b) the purpose for requiring possession is that specified in the ground. Check precisely what must be proved on this. For example, the landlord may require the premises for his or her own occupation. Some grounds require the landlord to have lived in the premises previously, some do not. Some require the landlord to show reasonableness of requiring the premises, while some do not.

33.4.3.6 Suitable alternative accommodation

The Rent Act 1977 and Housing Act 1988 include as a separate ground that suitable alternative accommodation is or will be available. The Housing Act 1985 does not include this as a separate ground but does require suitable alternative accommodation to be provided in addition to proving some of the grounds (eg, where the landlord requires premises for an alternative use).

All three Acts contain some guidance on the factors the court will take into account when considering whether the accommodation offered is suitable. Although the wording differs, the main considerations under the Rent Act 1977 and Housing Act 1988 are:

(a) the security of the alternative accommodation is reasonably equivalent to that enjoyed by the tenant in the current premises. So you need to check the status of the occupancy being offered, eg, a licence will not suffice;

(b) the accommodation is reasonably suitable for the tenant and his or her family. There is much case law on this particular aspect and some difference between the Rent Act 1977 and the Housing Act 1988. If this is an issue, you will need to check both what is offered and the case law on factors that the court will consider in deciding what is reasonably suitable.

33.4.4 Preparation for hearing

Having checked the points above which are relevant to your case, plan both your submissions and questioning of witnesses so that you are focusing on the main issues which will be of concern to the judge. Remember, witness statements stand as evidence-in-chief. If you wish to add to them or amplify them you will need to get the permission of the court. Consider whether a skeleton argument would be useful. Where appropriate, be ready to argue not just the grounds, but also reasonableness and the type of order.

Generally possession hearings are held in public. However, where possession is sought on the grounds of rent arrears, the hearing is now listed in private. Check the local practice as to whether you should appear robed or not but, when in doubt, come prepared to be robed.

Local authority and large housing association landlords have large numbers of possession cases for rent arrears. They generally get the procedure right but may not be very precise on the rent due. As social landlords, they are also generally reasonable when it comes to discussing the possibility of a suspended order and the conditions to be imposed. Private landlords are generally less used to possession proceedings and may be less willing to discuss the possibility of settling the case on the basis of a suspended order.

33.4.5 Costs

In cases which last less than one day, the court will summarily assess costs and you must be ready to address the court on them. PD 43–48, para 13.5, requires a written statement of costs to be prepared in Form N260. This is the starting point for the judge's assessment of costs. You should have a copy of the schedule and understand the basis of the figures contained in it. The court can call for evidence in deciding the figure, for example, looking at counsel's brief to see the brief fee. Ensure your brief is marked!!

Be alert to PD Costs, para 8.7(2) and (3), which provides that the court should consider recording whether the hearing was fit for counsel, in particular where the paying party asks for the court to express a view or where the judge thinks the hearing was not fit for counsel.

Detailed assessment of costs is a more complicated process done by a costs officer at a separate assessment some time after the hearing. Generally the paperwork and representation at such hearings is done by the solicitor.

33.5 Possession in commercial cases

The Landlord and Tenant Act 1954 Part II gives the occupants, if they qualify, the statutory protection of the right to apply to the court for a new tenancy at the end of their old one. The landlord can oppose the grant of the new tenancy on particular grounds.

33.5.1 Tenancy without statutory protection

Tenancies of business (commercial) premises attract the statutory protection of the Landlord and Tenant Act 1954 Part II if they fulfil the requirements of the Act and are not excluded. A landlord may seek possession in respect of business premises alleging that the occupant cannot claim statutory protection. The main reasons by which the occupancy may not come within the Act are:

(a) that it is a licence (the Act only protects tenants);

(b) the tenant does not occupy for the purposes of a business carried on by him or her (the tenancy is held by one person and the business is run by another; a typical example would be a tenancy in the name of an individual with the business run by a company of which the individual is the majority shareholder); or

(c) the tenancy is for a short term, certainly not exceeding six months unless the tenancy contains provisions for renewing the term or for extending it beyond six months from its beginning.

If any of these are alleged, you must check both the law and facts carefully to ensure that the ground on which the landlord claims lack of protection is in fact made out.

33.5.2 Tenancy with protection under Part II of the Landlord and Tenant Act 1954

Where a tenant seeks this protection, by applying for a new tenancy under Part II Landlord and Tenant Act 1954, CPR Part 56 applies.

33.5.2.1 The possession claim

A tenancy with protection of the Act is automatically continued (the 'continuation tenancy') after the expiry of the contractual term until a statutory notice is served by the landlord or the tenant. On termination of the continuation tenancy, the tenant is entitled to a new tenancy under the Act unless the landlord can prove one or more of the grounds for opposing the new tenancy set out in the Act. When instructed in a case where the tenancy does come within the Act, the two main things you must check are:

(a) The notice procedure has been properly followed. The requirements of the notice and service are detailed and there is much case law on whether or not the proper procedure has been followed. If the tenant has failed to follow the procedure as set out in the Act, he or she loses the right to claim a new tenancy.

(b) If the notice procedure has been properly followed, the landlord will be required to prove one of the grounds set out in the Act for opposing the grant of a new tenancy. There is some similarity between these grounds and those in the Acts giving protection to residential tenants in that they are based on some fault of the tenant, the landlord's own need for the premises, or an offer of suitable alternative accommodation. There is no easy division between mandatory grounds and discretionary grounds as under the statutes giving protection to residential tenants. Check the precise wording of the ground relied on and the evidence required to prove it.

33.5.2.2 Additional matters

Where instructed in a case to which Part II of the 1954 Act applies, you must also be prepared to argue:

(a) the terms of any new tenancy which may be granted. If the landlord loses in his opposition to the grant of a new tenancy and the parties cannot agree the terms, the terms will be determined by the court;

(b) compensation for the tenant if the landlord is successful in opposing the grant of a new tenancy. This is only relevant to some grounds. Check whether the ground relied on is one which can attract compensation. In addition, the tenant may be making a claim for compensation for any improvements to the premises carried out by him or her.

33.6 Mortgage cases

Possession proceedings by a mortgagee may be taken against a leaseholder or freeholder of residential or commercial premises. A mortgagee's right to possession arises out of the nature of the mortgage itself, the mortgagee taking possession of the property to sell it to recoup the money secured by the charge. Despite the fact that the basis of these proceedings is very different to that of a landlord seeking to obtain possession of premises let to tenants, such claims also come with CPR, Part 55. Thus, the matters set out under **33.1.2** apply with specific rules in respect of mortgage possession cases where appropriate, eg:

(a) the particulars of claim must contain the information specified in PD 55.4, para 2.1 plus that specified in PD 55.4, para 2.5.

(b) where the mortgagee seeks possession of land which includes residential property a notice must be served on the property not less than 14 days before the hearing and a copy of it produced at the hearing (CPR, r 55.10).

33.6.1 Matters to check

The law in this area is complex and in need of reform. It is too complex to deal with in any detail in this manual and the following is an outline of the basic points to check in the most common type of case. Generally mortgage possession cases are taken by institutional lenders which have a mortgage by way of a legal charge on the property. When the borrower defaults on the mortgage, the lender has various statutory powers in respect of the property and those powers are contained in the mortgage agreement (deed). Although the mortgagee can enforce the security through various methods, eg, foreclosure or suing the mortgagor on the personal covenant to pay, the most common method is to obtain possession to sell the property with vacant possession to recover the money owed to them. In such cases the main things to check are as follows.

First, check that the mortgagee has a valid charge on the property and check the terms of the agreement itself. The mortgage deed should be available (usually exhibited to the witness statement made on behalf of the mortgagee). Most mortgages are legal charges that give the lender a notional lease on the property. The mortgagee is therefore entitled to take possession of the property once the deed is executed. No proof of default by the borrower is needed. Check the type of charge and that you are clear as to all the terms of the loan (including inspecting any collateral agreements between the mortgagor and mortgagee).

Second, check whether there are any other parties with a claim on the property that may interfere with the mortgagee's right to possession and have a right or wish to be joined as a defendant or notice of the proceedings. Two common examples are tenants and spouses of owners. There may be tenants in occupation who were granted tenancies before the property was mortgaged to which the mortgagee's interest is subject as an unregistered interest which may override a registered disposition under the Land Registration Act 2002. The property may be the matrimonial home of a couple where the non-owning spouse has registered a right to occupy under matrimonial legislation (Matrimonial Homes Act 1967 or 1983 or the Family Law Act 1996). Check that the above requirement under CPR, r 55.10 to serve notice on the property has been fulfilled. The notice should be addressed to the occupiers notifying them of the possession proceedings, case number, hearing date and the name and address of the claimant, the defendant and the court. Check also that relevant information required by PD 55.4, para 2.5 in respect of such occupiers has been included in the particulars of claim.

Third, what type of mortgage forms the basis of the proceedings? The two main types are capital repayment/instalment mortgages (the mortgagor paying both capital and interest by regular instalments) and interest-only endowment mortgages (the mortgagor paying the interest on the loan and investing sufficient money regularly into a fund to be able to pay off the capital at the end of the period of the mortgage). Ensure you understand the underlying concepts of the type of mortgage in question. Also, check when and how payments (capital, interest and any other payments) are to be made and that the relevant information required by PD 55.4, para 2.5 about the mortgage is included in the particulars of claim. Check what the alleged arrears are and how they arose. This information should be set out in the schedule of arrears required by PD 55.4, para 2.5(3). Is there any dispute over the arrears?

Fourth, check whether the court's powers under the Administration of Justice Acts 1970 and 1973 or the Consumer Credit Act 1974 may be exercised. Both of these are complicated provisions and the most common one you may encounter is the Administration of Justice Acts.

(a) *Administration of Justice Acts 1970 and 1973*

Where the mortgagee under a mortgage of land which includes a dwelling house claims possession (but not foreclosure), the Administration of Justice Acts empower the court to adjourn the case or suspend the possession order if it appears that the mortgagor(s) are 'likely' to be able to pay any 'sums due' under the mortgage or remedy any default consisting of a breach of any obligation under the mortgage within a 'reasonable' period.

The court may impose conditions, eg, of payment, on such adjournment or suspension. In respect of claims for possession for arrears, there are two main things to check:

(a) what are the 'sums due': this includes the capital, interest and any other 'further amounts'. Be clear precisely what is included in your case.

(b) is the mortgagor 'likely' to be able to pay within a 'reasonable time': what proposals are there? what is the mortgagor's financial position? what period of time is likely to be 'reasonable' in the circumstances?

(b) *Consumer Credit Act 1974*

The provisions of the Consumer Credit Act 1974 will apply in place of the Administration of Justice Acts where the mortgage is a 'regulated agreement' as defined by the Act. Basically this includes those agreements where an individual is given credit which does not exceed £25,000 and the agreement is not exempt. Most loans secured on land for the purchase of land, the provision of a dwelling or business premises or repair, improvement, etc, of a dwelling or business premises where the lender has already lent for such purchase or provision, are exempt. This would not catch, for example, a loan to buy a boat secured on the property. Note that it covers both residential and business premises. The particulars of claim should make clear whether or not this Act applies (see in particular PD 55.4, para 2.5(4)). If these provisions do apply, you will need to check:

(a) that the agreement was 'properly executed' in compliance with the formalities of the Act. These requirements are complex, as are the effects of a failure to comply rendering the agreement 'improperly executed', which include in some circumstances an inability to enforce the agreement;

(b) that the mortgagee has followed the proper procedure to enforce the agreement by serving a default notice in the prescribed form;

(c) whether the mortgagor has or should apply for a 'time order' whereby the court may extend the time for payment.

Finally, in dealing with costs, generally the mortgagor will be entitled to costs even without a costs order. Where the court does make an order as to costs, eg, for detailed assessment on the standard basis, this will be subject to any term in the mortgage agreement as to costs, which many mortgage deeds contain. The terms of the agreement may entitle the mortgagor to costs that are greater than would be allowed under an assessment on a standard basis and will usually also provide that the costs can be added to the security. Where costs are likely to be an issue, whether acting for the mortgagor or the mortgagee, check whether or not you should be asking the court to deal with costs (eg, if acting for the mortgagee do you wish to ask the court to restrict the mortgagor's claim for costs). If so, you need to check both the terms of the agreement and the law, in particular the powers of the court to override the contractual provisions.

33.7 Practical tips on documents and dress in claims for possession from tenants

33.7.1 Documents

1. The court bundle—see **33.1.2.4**.
2. Proof of landlord's title—see **33.2.1**.
3. The tenancy agreement—see **33.2.2**.
4. If forfeiting the lease—copy of S146 notice (if served—see **33.2.5.1(b)**).
5. If statutory tenancy protected by:

   Housing Act 1985—copy of S83 notice—see **33.4.2.1**;

   Housing Act 1988—copy of S20 Notice if relevant—see **33.4.2.2(a)**;

   —copy of S8 notice—see **33.4.2.2(b)**;

   Rent Act 1977—copy of notice to quit (if needed)—see **33.4.2.3**.
6. If ground is rent arrears—see **33.4.3.1**:

   Schedule of arrears;

   Notice by landlord under S48 LTA 1987—if needed.
7. If ground is that landlord requires premises—see **33.4.3.5**:

   Copy of notice served—if needed.
8. If commercial tenancy—see **33.5**:

   Copies of relevant notices served under LTA 1954.
9. Costs—schedule in Form N260.

33.7.2 Dress

Check with the court—practice varies;

If in doubt, take your robes.

34

Application for a preliminary reference to the European Court of Justice

34.1 References to the European Court of Justice: Article 234 EC

When a matter of European Community law arises before any court or tribunal, it may be possible to have the proceedings stayed in order that the particular matter be referred to the European Court of Justice (ECJ) for a determination of the relevant point of European law. Article 234 (ex 177) of the EC Treaty establishes the jurisdiction of the ECJ in these matters. In particular, it provides that the ECJ has jurisdiction to give a preliminary ruling concerning the interpretation of the EC Treaty and the validity and interpretation of EC legislation.

Note that jurisdiction is limited to examining EC law and that there is no provision for the ECJ to determine the validity or interpretation of English law (or any other national law). It is common, however, for questions to be referred in which the ECJ is asked whether a particular piece of national legislation is compatible with the EC Treaty or with EC legislation. In such cases, the ECJ usually answers the question by reference to the meaning to be attributed to the relevant EC law. Technically, it is then for the referring national court to apply that meaning to its own national law. The delimitation of jurisdictions in these cases is therefore relatively clear: it is for the ECJ to determine the true meaning and effect of EC law, while it is for the national court to apply that meaning in the context of the proceedings before it. Accordingly, the ECJ is not, in this context, a court of appeal. Rather, Article 234 EC provides a means of cooperation between the national court and the ECJ to ensure that EC law is properly and effectively applied.

The mere fact that a question of EC law arises does not, of course, mean that the issue should be referred to the ECJ. Every national court is required to interpret and apply EC law in the normal course of events. Generally speaking, it is only where a particular difficulty arises which cannot confidently be solved by the judge that a reference should be considered.

34.2 Which courts can make a reference?

Article 234(2) EC provides that where a question of EC law is raised before any court or tribunal of a Member State, that court or tribunal may, if it considers that a decision on the point is necessary to enable it to give judgment, request the ECJ for a ruling thereon. The definition of court or tribunal is a question of Community law, so that the classification of the body for the purposes of English law is not directly relevant. The court or tribunal must be a public body exercising official authority and it must have a judicial function. References have been made from the House of Lords, Court of Appeal (Criminal and Civil Divisions), High Court, Crown Court, County Court, magistrates' courts, VAT tribunals, Employment Appeal Tribunal, employment tribunals, Social Security Commissioners and the Special Commissioners for Income Tax. It is arguable that certain professional bodies exercising disciplinary powers may be considered as tribunals. Arbitration tribunals are not competent to make a reference to the ECJ since they are not public bodies and have no connection with the exercise of official authority.

Under the Brussels Convention on jurisdiction and the enforcement of judgments in civil and commercial matters, a reference may only be made from appellate courts. This is therefore in the United Kingdom limited to the House of Lords, the Court of Appeal and the High Court sitting in an appellate capacity.

The Rome Convention on the law applicable to contractual obligations has been in force in the United Kingdom since 1991. However, a protocol attached to the Convention which provides for the possibility of making a reference to the ECJ (and which limits references to appellate courts) has not yet entered into force.

The application of Article 234 EC was modified by the Amsterdam Treaty in relation to Title IV matters. Title IV governs visas, asylum, immigration and other policies relating to the free movement of persons and the Council is required to adopt various legislative measures governing these matters. However, Title IV also covers other measures concerning judicial cooperation in civil matters, administrative cooperation, and measures in the field of police and judicial cooperation. Measures in the field of judicial cooperation in civil matters having cross-border implications will include improving and simplifying the system for service of judicial documents, cooperation in the taking of evidence and the recognition and enforcement of decisions in civil and commercial cases. Article 68 (ex 73p) EC provides that Article 234 will apply to Title IV such that, where a question on the interpretation of Title IV or on the validity of Community legislation based on Title IV is raised in a national court against whose decisions there is no judicial remedy under national law, that court must, if it considers that a decision is necessary to enable it to give judgment, request the ECJ to give a preliminary ruling. The ECJ will have no jurisdiction to rule on any measure or decision taken pursuant to Article 62(1) (ex 73j) EC relating to the maintenance of law and order and the safeguarding of internal security.

34.3 Which courts must make a reference?

Article 234(3) EC provides that where a question of EC law is raised in a case pending before a court or tribunal against whose decisions there is no judicial remedy under national law, that court or tribunal must refer the matter to the ECJ.

In the United Kingdom, this is generally limited to the House of Lords. Although it is necessary to obtain leave to appeal to the House of Lords, the Divisional Court and the Court of Appeal have specifically stated that in the absence of such leave being granted, those courts may not be considered as falling within Article 234(3) EC. Thus, even though the clear intention of Article 234 EC seems to be that a party has the right to seek a reference at some stage in the appeal procedure even though the relevant court may not deem it necessary to enable it to decide the matter, the appeals procedure involving the House of Lords may frustrate that. It is not possible to go back to the Court of Appeal after the House of Lords has refused permission and then argue that the Court of Appeal has become the court to which Article 234(3) EC refers. See further **34.5**.

Where the question at issue involves the validity of EC legislation (such as a regulation or directive) it is not possible for the national court to decide that the legislation is indeed invalid, no matter how strong the arguments to that effect. The court has two possibilities open to it. It may decide, having regard to the arguments, that the legislation is valid and continue the proceedings on that basis. Alternatively, if it is of the opinion that the legislation is invalid (or that there is a strong argument to that effect), it must refer the matter to the ECJ, since only the ECJ has competence to declare EC legislation invalid. See for example, *R (International Air Transport Association and European Low Fares Airline Association) v UK Department of Transport* (C-344/04), judgment of 10 January 2006 (The Times, 16 January 2006).

34.4 In what circumstances is a reference to be made?

Generally, a reference is only to be made if an answer is necessary to enable the court to give judgment. Accordingly, it is common practice for English courts to seek to decide the action on the basis of English law issues which do not raise questions of EC law.

The Court of Appeal has laid down guidelines for the exercise of the discretion to refer (contained in Article 234(2)) in rather general terms. If the facts have been found and the EC law issue is critical to the court's final decision, the appropriate course is ordinarily to refer the issue to the ECJ unless the national court can with complete confidence resolve the issue itself. In considering whether it can with complete confidence resolve the issue itself the national court must be fully mindful of the differences between national and EC legislation, of the pitfalls which face a national court venturing into what may be an unfamiliar field, of the need for uniform interpretation throughout the EC and the great advantages enjoyed by the ECJ in construing EC legislation. Other factors which might be considered are the delay and costs involved, the difficulty of the point of law and the presence of similar actions before the ECJ.

A lower court might also be mindful of the fact that its decision may be appealed with a reference being sought at the appeal stage. However, if the parties have made clear that they will seek a reference at each stage, it might be more sensible to impress on the judge in the lowest court that it would save time and costs if he or she were to refer the matter immediately.

34.5 Exceptions to the requirement to refer under Article 234(3)

There are three exceptions to the general requirement to make a reference under Article 234(3) EC for a court from whose decisions there is no judicial remedy. First, no reference is necessary if the question raised is materially identical to a previous question already referred to the ECJ. Second, a decision for interim measures which depends on a question of EC law need not be the subject of a reference even if it is final, as long as this does not bind the court which hears the substantive action and provided that either party can ensure that proceedings in the main action are actually instituted.

Third, the national court need not make a reference if the matter is *acte clair*. The extent of this exception is not wholly clear and there has been some suggestion in recent years that it should be relaxed. However, in general it means that a reference is unnecessary where the answer is so obvious as to leave no scope for any reasonable doubt as to the manner in which the question raised is to be resolved. Before it comes to that conclusion, the court must be convinced that the matter is equally obvious to the courts of the other Member States and to the ECJ. This must involve consideration of the different language versions of the particular EC legislation. Even where the different language versions are entirely in accord with one another, it must be borne in mind that EC law uses terminology which is peculiar to it and that legal concepts do not necessarily have the same meaning in EC law and in the laws of the various Member States. Finally, every provision of EC law must be placed in its context and interpreted in the light of the provisions of EC law as a whole, regard being had to the objectives of EC law and to its state of evolution at the date on which the provision in question had to be applied.

34.6 It is the court (not the parties) which makes the reference

The decision of whether or not to make a reference is solely for the court. If the parties suggest that a reference is desirable, it is likely that the judge will agree. However, it is quite common for one party to oppose the reference and for the other to be in favour. In those circumstances, the party seeking the reference must make representations to the judge seeking to convince him or her to take this action. It is, however, not unknown for a judge to decide of his or her own motion (and even against the wishes of the parties) that a reference should be made. In those circumstances, this is solely a matter for the discretion of the judge and the parties (subject to a right of appeal) cannot resist the decision to refer.

34.7 At what stage in the proceedings should the reference be made?

A party which is seeking to have a matter referred to the ECJ should make this plain to the judge at the earliest opportunity. Apart from courtesy, it means that the judge can possibly cut the time in the national court considerably.

Before the reference is made, it is necessary for the facts to be established although the relevant facts may, of course, be agreed between the parties. In most civil matters this should not pose too much of a problem. A statement of agreed facts can then be drawn up and handed to the judge.

Criminal cases pose special problems, since once the jury is sworn in it is difficult, from a practical point of view, to make a reference to the ECJ with the consequential delay of up to two years before the jury is called on to decide the factual issue. On the one hand, the defendant may wish to argue that, even if the facts alleged against him or her are proven, there will still be no offence committed since EC law precludes a prosecution in those circumstances. This may be either on the basis that the relevant English law conflicts with EC law or that, for instance, an EC Regulation which is central to the prosecution is invalid. In that case, the facts may be deemed to be agreed solely for the purpose of the reference. It is preferable for the question of EC law to be determined at that stage, with a reference if necessary, before the issue is put to a jury. Accordingly, the issue of EC law should be raised by means of a motion to quash the indictment before the jury is chosen. This approach has the added advantage that the defendant, particularly if he or she is of previous good character, does not suffer the ignominy of being found guilty at first instance only to be vindicated on appeal. On the other hand, once the trial has started and the jury is in place, the House of Lords has said that it can scarcely be a proper exercise of the court's discretion to make a reference. Instead the trial must proceed, leaving the possibility of a reference for the appellate court.

There are no hard-and-fast rules about making submissions on the point of EC law in the national court prior to the reference being made. Clearly, if the parties have agreed that a reference is desirable, counsel should immediately suggest this course of action to the judge. However, since the reference is solely at the discretion of the judge (except in the case of courts of last instance) it may well be that the judge will require argument on the point before he or she is satisfied that a reference is appropriate. From the point of view of the parties, this may well also be desirable since it gives an idea to each side as to the submission which will be made before the ECJ. (Having said that, the parties are not limited to repeating in the ECJ only those arguments put to the national court.)

34.8 Procedure for making the reference

Much of the procedure for making the reference to the ECJ is carried on behind the scenes rather than in open court. References from the High Court and Court of Appeal are now governed by CPR Part 68. Similar rules apply to criminal proceedings in the Crown Court and in the Court of Appeal (see Criminal Procedure Rules 2005, 5.75.1, SI 2005/384). There are no specific rules laid down for references from magistrates' courts or other tribunals which, therefore, take their power to refer solely from Article 234 EC as incorporated by s 2(1) of the European Communities Act 1972 (see for example, *Stone's Justices' Manual 2008* at 1–1430).

Under CPR Part 68, a request for a ruling by the ECJ must be set out in a schedule to the court's order. PD 68 states that the order for reference itself should 'as clearly and succinctly as possible' identify the question(s) for the ECJ. In a schedule to the order, the court should set down:

- the full name of the referring court;
- the identities of the parties;
- a summary of the nature and history of the proceedings;
- the salient facts, stating clearly whether these are proved, admitted or assumed;
- the relevant national legal rules;
- the parties' contentions on the questions;
- an explanation of why a ruling by the ECJ is sought;
- the identity of those provisions of EU law on which the ruling is sought.

Further reference should be made to Practice Form 109; also to *Blackstone's Civil Court Precedents* C[817], which contains a useful precedent for a preliminary reference.

34.9 Costs and public funding

Costs will usually be reserved until the reference has returned from the ECJ. Usually costs will follow the event. Public funding is generally extended to cover the cost of proceedings before the ECJ.

34.10 Proceedings before the European Court of Justice

The proceedings before the ECJ fall into separate parts, only two of which involve the lawyers for the parties. First, the parties submit their written observations. Second, the parties subsequently make an oral presentation at the ECJ in Luxembourg. Third, the Advocate General gives his Opinion and, finally, the ECJ gives its decision. Lawyers are directly involved only in the first two stages. There is no need for lawyers or the parties to be present at the ECJ either when the Advocate General's Opinion is given or when the judgment is handed down.

Written observations are the most important part of the proceedings. These should be clear and concise. There is, however, no prescribed format for written observations and each counsel has his or her own style. Unlike English court proceedings, it is inadvisable to recite large chunks of case law. Rather, the precise dictum relied upon should be set out, with other references to the cases being made in footnotes. It is quite permissible for reference to be made to academic articles or books in order to substantiate arguments. As a general rule, written observations should not be overly long, although this depends on the complexity of the case. Twenty pages of argument should usually be quite enough! Another unusual aspect of the written stage is that all parties submit their observations at the same time rather than one after the other. Accordingly, there is no opportunity at this stage to know precisely what is being argued by the other side. Needless to say, this may call for some ingenuity since counsel then have to put themselves in the position of second-guessing the other side. It is also possible for Member States to intervene in the proceedings; they need not show any direct interest.

Guidance notes are given by the ECJ to all counsel prior to the oral hearing. This is a short hearing with counsel for each side having a maximum of thirty minutes. It is not an opportunity to put the entire case. Instead, the essence of the argument should be quickly put, concentrating on the strongest points. It is also the only opportunity counsel has for rebutting the arguments put by the other parties. Questions may be asked by the judges, although sometimes no questions are asked.

Some months later the Opinion will be given followed some months after that by the judgment. In all, the delay between reference and judgment is usually about 18 months.

35 Applying for costs in a civil case

35.1 The principal costs orders

This chapter deals with making an application for an order for costs. The following are the principal costs orders:

- Claimant's costs.
- Defendant's costs.
- Costs in the case/application.
- Claimant's costs in the case/application.
- Defendant's costs in the case/application.
- Costs thrown away.
- Costs of and caused by.
- 'Bullock' order.
- 'Sanderson' order.
- Costs reserved.
- No order for costs, ie, each party is to bear its own costs.

For an explanation of the various orders see the ***Civil Litigation*** manual, **Chapter 36** and CPR, Part 44, PD Section 8. The CPR costs regime seeks to relate the level of costs payable to the value of the dispute, in an effort to avoid the position in which the parties spend many thousands of pounds on costs of the litigation with the result that the costs incurred are out of all proportion to the value of the claim. It also seeks to provide a more balanced approach to defining the 'winner' and 'loser' to avoid the situation where a party who has been largely unsuccessful recovers all of his costs on the basis that he has succeeded on something. The CPR costs regime makes provision for the summary assessment and speedy payment of costs incurred in connection with fast track trials and other hearings, whether applications or disposal hearings, listed for one day or less. What might be termed a 'pay as you go' approach was intended to bring home to the parties and their advisers that there are costs consequences in making applications to the court. The requirement for your client to write out a cheque for his opponent's costs at an early stage concentrates minds on the costs that are being incurred in the litigation as it proceeds instead of when the big bill arrives at the end of it. From an adviser's point of view it concentrates the mind on dealing with the case in a way that avoids applications to the court. In practical terms, losing an application can bring about a reappraisal of a party's position and fundamental change of attitude to the litigation as a whole. For example, a party who applies for summary judgment and fails will begin to wonder whether things really are as straightforward as he had first thought and will have to pay his opponent's costs of the application at the same time.

The CPR costs regime also allows the parties to seek, and the court to order, a payment on account of costs where a detailed assessment of the costs has been ordered. A payment on account will allow a party who has obtained a favourable costs order to recoup some of the money already spent on the litigation without waiting for the detailed assessment to be concluded many months later. It also helps to set a benchmark for the amount of the costs which might be awarded in a detailed assessment. If the paying party cannot pay a payment on account that the court has ordered, the receiving party may save himself further wasted costs on concluding a detailed assessment before he discovers that he is unlikely to see any of the money.

35.2 How does the court decide what order to make?

The court's order will be influenced by the submissions the parties make as to what order should be made in all the circumstances of the case. Those submissions should be shaped by the desired outcome that is best suited to your client's needs given the circumstances of the case. Generally speaking, your client's needs will be financial. If an order for costs is made in your client's favour, your client will want to recoup as much as he has had to spend on his own lawyers (including you) as quickly as possible. If your solicitor client has conducted the case on credit terms, he too will want to see money flowing in his direction sooner rather than later. If your client has a costs order made against him, he will usually want to pay as little as possible as slowly as possible. For the 'pay later loser', summary costs assessments are an anathema. If your opponent is a 'pay later loser', a substantial summary costs order on an interim application may help to weaken his resolve to see the litigation through to the end of the trial. It may also weaken the resolve of those who support the conduct of the litigation through funding arrangements or legal expenses insurance. It may also help to drain him of money needed to pay his lawyers to see the matter through to the end of the trial.

Your submissions on an application for costs should also be shaped by the way in which the court reaches its decision about the right order to make. You need to know how the court reaches its decision. If you understand the way in which the decision will be made, you can apply your advocacy skills to directing the way in which the court should reach the decision best suited to your client's needs.

The court exercises a discretion in awarding costs for or against a party to the litigation. The only rule of law is that the order made must be a just one in all the circumstances of the case. There are guidelines that govern the exercise of the court's discretion. The most important guideline is that costs generally follow the event, ie, the loser will ordinarily be ordered to pay the winner's costs (see CPR, Part 44, r 3(2)(a)). In most simple applications it is clear who is the winner and who is the loser. At trial, if judgment is given in the claimant's favour, generally the claimant will be considered the winner and vice versa. Regrettably it is not as simple as that, for the claimant may recover relief which is either a small proportion of that which he set out to recover at the beginning of the action or the trial, or a sum which is less than the defendant has paid into court as a Part 36 payment in satisfaction of the claimant's claim. If the claim relates to relief that cannot be measured in money terms, 'win' or 'lose' may be measured by reference to whether the claimant has obtained some or all of the relief he sought in the claim or whether the relief obtained by the claimant is more or less advantageous that the defendant was prepared to concede.

In deciding what order to make as to costs, the court will have regard to all the circumstances of the case. It may make different orders in respect of different parts of the case, whether defined in time or in issues, to ensure that the order made is a just order in all the circumstances of the case—see CPR, Part 44, r 3(6). The principles to be applied are set out in CPR, Part 44, r 3(2) to (5) together with a list of the principal matters that the court will consider in the exercise of its discretion. The list is not a comprehensive list. The Court of Appeal set out the basic principles governing the exercise of the court's discretion in *Johnsey v Secretary of State for the Environment* [2001] EWCA Civ 535. The matters set out in CPR, Part 44, r 3 together with the overriding objectives and the principle of proportionality set the agenda for the arguments that might be raised in an application for a costs order. Given that the court has a discretion to exercise, anything is possible provided the court can be persuaded that the order suggested is fair and reasonable in all the circumstances of the case in question. The range of orders that can be described as fair and reasonable in any one case can be wide depending on the circumstances of the case. No two cases are the same and no two judges are the same. The same case might produce a different order depending on the judge that hears it. The arguments that can be raised in any given case are dependent on the outcome of the case, how the case has been conducted both before and after the commencement of the proceedings, the conduct of the hearing or trial and the practical result achieved. The court will be unwilling to order costs to be paid to a party whose conduct has caused the costs to be unnecessarily incurred. A failure to comply with CPR will generally result in an order for costs against the defaulting party. Unreasonable conduct by a party, eg failing to accept a reasonable settlement proposal made without prejudice save as to costs, or failing to agree an order the court was highly likely to make, will almost certainly result in an adverse costs order against that party whether in terms of an order to pay the other party's costs or an order depriving that party of costs that would otherwise have been recovered.

Where a party succeeds on some issues but fails on others the court may make an order that reflects both the success and the failure. The order may be issue based or it may simply be an award of a proportion of the party's costs. The nature of the order may be heavily influenced by the relative success or failure whether in terms of the final outcome or the way in which disputed issues of fact are resolved for or against the parties. For example, in a five-day trial, if four days were devoted to an issue on which the claimant lost and one day to an issue on which the claimant won, the court might simply order the claimant to pay the defendant's costs of issue 1 and order the defendant to pay the claimant's costs of issue 2. Where there has been partial success the court should seek to make an order for the payment of a percentage of the winner's costs rather than an issue-based order (see *English v Emery Rheinbold and Strick Ltd* [2002] 1WLR 2409 and CPR, Part 44, r 3(7)). This can give rise to considerable difficulty. In the example considered above the claimant's success on issue 2 may result in an award of damages in the same amount as would be awarded if successful on issue 1. In real terms one might well consider the claimant had won the war in obtaining damages but lost a substantial battle along the way. One might also consider that the defendant had scored a substantial victory on the first issue given the proportion of the total costs incurred devoted to the resolution of the issue on which the defendant succeeded. A detailed assessment on an issue basis is likely to result in the costs payable to the defendant by the claimant outweighing those payable by the defendant to the claimant in a case where the claimant was obliged to argue both issues, because the defendant failed to agree to pay the claimant the sum the court awarded in damages. One must also bear in mind that a percentage apportionment should not simply reflect the fact that the claimant has succeeded in part but must also reflect the fact that the defendant too succeeded in part, with the consequence that an issue-based approach would see money in costs flowing from the claimant to the defendant to set off against money flowing from the defendant to the claimant. In the example considered above it is not possible to state definitively what the right order is. There will be a range of orders each of which will differ from the others and all of which are unappealable. An order for the defendant to pay the claimant's costs of the claim would be a harsh order from the defendant's point of view but unlikely to be altered on appeal. Equally an order for the defendant to pay as little as 60% of the claimant's costs of the claim would be harsh on the claimant but unlikely to be altered on appeal. Where the apportionment might fall within that band may be determined by the extent to which the factual issues raised in issue 1 were resolved in favour of the claimant.

Proportionality also has an important role to play. The court must ensure that the costs awarded are proportionate to the value of the claim whether in monetary terms or importance to the parties. Proportionality arguments tend to be taken by the paying party to reduce the amount of costs payable, particularly where there is a summary assessment.

35.3 Part 36 offers and Part 36 payments

A defendant's Part 36 payment or Part 36 offer can turn a successful party into an unsuccessful party so far as costs orders are concerned. If the claimant fails to recover more than the sum paid into court by the defendant, the claimant will ordinarily be ordered to pay the defendant's costs from the last date for acceptance of the Part 36 payment or offer—see CPR, Part 36, r 20. If the defendant has made a Part 36 offer rather than a Part 36 payment, you need to consider whether the defendant could properly make a Part 36 offer—see CPR, Part 36, r 2 and r 3. A Part 36 offer made when a Part 36 payment should have been made does not count for the purposes of Part 36 but does still count for the purposes of CPR, Part 44, r 3. An ineffective Part 36 payment should not be raised in the submissions on costs made by the claimant unless it was so derisory that it reflects badly on the defendant's conduct of the action where it might support a submission for costs to be assessed on an indemnity basis rather than the standard basis. The defendant may raise it as part and parcel of a submission inviting the court to depart from the general rule that costs follow the event. In that event the claimant can deal with the points made in his reply to the defendant's submissions.

Part 36 allows a claimant to make a claimant's Part 36 offer to encourage the defendant to settle. If a claimant does better than his Part 36 offer the court should award enhanced interest at up to 10% above base rate from the last date for acceptance of the claimant's Part 36 offer, enhanced interest at up to 10% above base rate on the claimant's costs incurred after the last date for acceptance and award costs on an indemnity basis from that date onwards—see CPR, Part 36, r 21. Enhanced interest on the costs can be a valuable order from the claimant's point of view. Costs carry interest from the date of the order for their payment rather than the date on which the amount payable is finally determined. The costs of preparing for and conducting the trial tend to be the larger part of the claimant's costs, so interest at 10% above base rate can impose a substantial additional burden on the defendant and provide a substantial additional bonus to the claimant. *Little v George Little Sebire & Co* The Times, 17 November 1999, indicates that the starting point is to award enhanced interest at 10% above base rate and then consider whether a lower figure should be adopted. That approach may be wrong given that the wording of CPR, Part 36, r 21 seems to give the court a general discretion as to the rate at which enhanced interest is to be paid.

Where there is an effective defendant's Part 36 payment or offer or an effective claimant's Part 36 offer the court should make the orders that flow from those events unless it is unjust to do so. The burden of persuading the court that it is unjust to do so falls on the party making that assertion. If you are representing the party that should receive the benefit of the orders that the court should make, you should not indulge in detailed submissions about whether it is unjust to make those orders. You should not do much more than bring the court's powers to the judge's attention and make a bald assertion that there is nothing in the circumstances of the case that makes it unjust to make the order that CPR, Part 36, directs the court to make. You should leave your opponent to raise the issue in detail if he wants to and deal with it in reply to your opponent's submissions.

Where a Part 36 payment is made but not accepted in time, the moneys in court cannot be paid out again without an order of the court. While the money has been with the court, interest will have accrued on it. The court must at the conclusion of the case make an order for the money in court and interest accrued on it to be paid out to one or other of the parties. The usual order where the claim fails is for all the money and any accrued interest to be paid out to the solicitors for the defendant. The usual order where the claim succeeds is to order the money (or so much as is required to satisfy the judgment) together with any interest accruing on that sum after the date of the order to be paid out to the solicitors for the claimant and for the balance of the money in court (if any) together with interest accrued up to the date of the order to be paid out to the solicitors for the defendant. Do not forget to ask the court to make the required orders.

35.4 Summary or detailed assessment

When you receive your brief you will need to decide whether the court is likely to conduct a summary assessment of the costs at the end of the hearing. If the hearing is listed for a day or less, the court will summarily assess the costs unless there is a good reason not to do so. A good reason not to do so is where the effect of requiring an impecunious party to pay there and then may well stifle what might turn out to be a good claim at trial. Another good reason is that something in the funding arrangement between the receiving party and his solicitor breaches the indemnity principle or renders the funding arrangement unenforceable. A good reason often given by a busy district judge is that the statement of costs appears to claim too much in amount for too much work with insufficient time to go through the details of the statement of costs in order to adequately deal with the amount payable on a summary basis. If the assessment of the costs is likely to be difficult or complicated, the court should order a detailed assessment. The court will not summarily assess the costs payable if:

(a) you do not intend to apply for an order for costs against your opponent at the conclusion of the hearing. For example case management hearings often do not give rise to an application for costs unless the hearing has been occasioned by the default of one of the parties. In those circumstances the court will, unless there is a good reason not to, order the costs of the hearing to be costs in the case; or

(b) your lay client's costs of the litigation are publicly funded by the Legal Services Commission (see CPR, Part 44, PD para 13.9); or

(c) your lay client is a child or a patient, unless your instructing solicitor has waived any right to seek further costs from the lay client over and above that which the court might summarily assess (see CPR, Part 44, PD para 13.11).

Please note that in both instances if you lose the application the court will summarily assess the costs payable by your client if a costs order is made in favour of your opponent. As a consequence your preparation for the hearing needs to cover the arguments you will seek to advance against a summary assessment of the costs payable and on quantification of the amount payable in the event that a costs order is made against your client. CPR, Part 44, r 5 sets out the factors the court will take into account in deciding the amount payable. The list of factors provides a framework for your submissions. You will also obtain some assistance from the *Guide to the Summary Assessment of Costs* published by the Supreme Court Taxing Office. Costs estimates provided in the parties' Allocation Questionnaires can prove to be a useful tool to reduce the costs of the action sought on a summary assessment. For some reason the final bill always seems to be more than estimated at the outset and it is often difficult to explain why it was necessary to run up more in costs than originally estimated.

If you intend to seek an order for your opponent to pay the costs of a hearing where a summary assessment is likely, your solicitors must provide a statement of costs setting out the costs incurred in connection with the hearing. There is a practice form for the statement of costs (N. 260). The form itself need not be used so long as the statement, in whatever form it is produced, contains the required information. The statement of costs must be served on your opponent *and* filed with the court not less than 24 hours before the hearing. You need to check that the statement contains the right information, has the right certificate as to the amount the party is liable to pay his solicitor and has been served in time. If this has not been done, you face the risk that the court may simply decide to make no order for costs or to assess the costs summarily in the sum of £0. The court has a discretion to exercise: it follows that it must exercise its discretion judicially and that it is just in the circumstances of the case to make such an order. The court is unlikely to do so if there is a good reason for the failure to comply with the requirements or if the failure to comply has not resulted in any injustice to your opponent. If this issue is likely to arise, you need to prepare the arguments you will put forward before the hearing starts, not at the end of the hearing when you will have little or no time to think about it.

If a summary assessment is to be made, you will need to make sure you are properly briefed by your instructing solicitor about the time spent in working on the application (or the case if it is a final hearing), the grade of fee earner chosen to undertake the work and the rates at which the time has been charged. You will not help your lay client or your instructing solicitor if you cannot provide any explanation beyond what appears in the statement of costs in the event that one or more of the items listed in the statement of costs is challenged by your opponent. You may also face the ignominious position of arguing that your own brief fee is a reasonable one in all the circumstances and that your opponent's is not. You also need some instructions from your solicitor about your opponent's statement of costs: if you lose the application, the argument will be about whether your opponent's costs are reasonable. You need to be in a position to say more than 'Having regard to the matters set out in CPR, Part 44, r 5 the costs sought are ridiculous and out of all proportion to the costs one would expect to see in an application such as this'. You need to be able to go on and say 'because' and set out a reasoned argument. For example 'the time apparently devoted to reading the documents is excessive given that the relevant documents occupy no more than 20 pages and the claimant's solicitors were able to read them in one hour rather than the three hours claimed in the defendant's statement of costs'. As to the latter point some circumspection is required. The party making an interim application will generally have a little more to do in preparation than the party responding to it.

It may be that both sides' statements of costs seem reasonable to you. That does not mean they will seem reasonable to the court. You should *always* be in a position to justify the amount you seek in costs if asked to do so.

If the case is one in which the court is not likely to make a summary assessment of the costs incurred, you will not have to deal with the nitty-gritty of how much has to be paid at the end of the hearing. You still have to deal with the costs order that the court might make.

35.5 Preparation

You will not have time to prepare your submissions after judgment has been given. You must therefore prepare your submissions on costs before the hearing. You will not know whether you have won or lost until judgment is given. You must therefore prepare submissions to cater for either event. In your preparation you must consider how you would argue the submissions on costs if you were acting for the other side. If you do this, it will help to concentrate your mind on the submissions you need to make to answer what the other side may have to say against you. Make a note of exactly what wording you wish the court to use in making its order for costs. If the order is precise, ie the words used express exactly what the order is to mean, it avoids the risk of someone seeking to place a different interpretation on the order at a later date, eg at a detailed assessment hearing. It is highly unlikely that anyone who was present when the order was made will be in attendance when the detailed assessment takes place with the consequence that the costs judge will be guided solely by the words in which the order is expressed.

35.6 Making the application

35.6.1 When should the application be made?

The application should be made after the pronouncement of the judgment or order that the court proposes to make. An application for costs should not form part of your closing submissions or final speech.

35.6.2 Who should address the court first?

As costs generally follow the event the successful party should address the court first as the party applying for a costs order. The usual order of speeches is application by successful party, response by unsuccessful party, final comments in reply by successful party. If your opponent is speaking, *do not* interject or interrupt: wait until it is your turn. Make a note of the point made that you dispute. If you draw a margin down the side of the page in your notebook, you can note your opponent's point on one side and your response to it on the other. It is very tempting to try to puncture your opponent's balloon by a well-timed and pithy interjection which may put your opponent off the train of his submissions. If the temptation becomes irresistible remember that your opponent is likely to do the same to you. If you are going to do this you should make sure that it is a 'killer' comment and not one that will simply result in a riposte from your opponent. You will simply end up with something approaching a slanging match which will be difficult for the court to follow and your point will be lost in the wash. Do not assume that the court will ask you to respond to your opponent's submissions. When your turn comes, stand up and start to make your submissions in response. If the court does not want to hear from you the court will tell you.

In many cases the court will invite counsel for the successful party to state what order for costs is sought and then turn to counsel for the unsuccessful party to ask whether there is any reason why the order sought should not be made. You may also find that in cases where there is likely to be little dispute about what order the court should make, the court may simply state what order it proposes to make and ask whether there are any objections. If the court does not ask for objections but you have some, you have the burden of explaining that the order suggested should not be made, set out the order that should be made and explain your reasons for the order you suggest should be made. In giving your reasons you must also explain why the order put forward by the court should not be made. In these situations the normal order of speeches can get somewhat muddled. If you are the unsuccessful party you might allow your opponent the opportunity to speak first but if you do not accept the suggested order is right, you should seize the initiative and make sure your submissions form the first substantial speech the court hears. You want to try to deflect the court from following the course it has suggested before your opponent has had an opportunity to buttress the court's initial view with his submissions. If your opponent is saying little or nothing beyond assenting to the order suggested, your submissions will be the first substantial speech with the consequence that you are likely to have the final word after your opponent has responded to your submissions—assuming of course that your submissions weigh sufficiently with the court for it to call on your opponent to respond to them.

In some cases it will not be clear which of the parties has been successful. In that event the party that goes first is the party that made the application that the court has heard. If it is a trial the claimant goes first.

You may well find that the court will ask one or other of you what order for costs should be made. In that event, the order of speeches will be determined by the court. If the court wants to hear from the unsuccessful party first the successful party will have to wait until the submissions made on behalf of the unsuccessful party have been completed. Notwithstanding the order of speeches set out above, most courts will allow the parties a full opportunity to respond to points that have been made even if it means allowing you to speak three or four times rather than once or twice. That does not mean that your submissions can be delivered in instalments.

35.6.3 Making the application

If you are counsel for the successful party you should state precisely what order for costs you want the court to make. The order requested should be the most favourable that you can *realistically* invite the court to make. You should then go on to set out the reasons why the court should make the order you have just set out. Most courts will want to know what you want and why you want it, not the other way round. If the order you want is unusual or the factual basis is complicated, it may be better to introduce the application by giving a brief résumé of the factual matters which the court should have in mind, before stating precisely what order you seek. Then explain the reasons which justify making the order you have just stated at greater length, referring again to the factual matters which support your argument. By so doing you can steer the court towards thinking about the matters you consider highly relevant from the outset, and then reiterate those matters in your reasons. If you adopt this approach, you must be careful to ensure that the court knows at an early stage what order you want the court to make, otherwise your submissions will be made in something of a vacuum and not in the context of the order you want the court to make.

In structuring your application you should bear in mind that there are four principal questions to be considered. The first is what order should be made in principle, ie which of the orders listed above is the right order to make. The second is whether the amount payable should be determined on a standard or an indemnity basis. The third is the means by which the amount payable should be determined, ie summary assessment or detailed assessment. The fourth is the time by which the costs must be paid by the paying party. If there is an effective Part 36 offer or Part 36 payment, it will have an impact on the first and second questions. If the case is one in which you will be inviting the court to make a summary assessment of the costs payable, it will be convenient to deal with the first and second questions first and then deal with the question of quantifying the amount payable and time by which it must be paid after the court has decided which party is to be the paying party and which party is to be the receiving party. If you are making the application, at the outset you should state that you propose to deal with matters in that way subject to any view the court may have. If you will be inviting the court to order a detailed assessment, all three questions can be canvassed in one instalment and question 4 will be irrelevant.

In a simple case your application may amount to saying little more than:

> On the question of costs I invite your Honour to order the defendant to pay the claimant's costs of the claim such costs to be determined, if not agreed, by a detailed assessment on the standard basis. In the light of the judgment given in the full amount of the claimant's claim the claimant's claim has clearly succeeded. In the circumstances there is no reason why the court should not make an order for the defendant to pay the claimant's costs in accordance with the general rule set out in CPR, Part 44, r 3, paragraph (2).

In the example considered above, with a five-day trial and two issues you may want to say a little more given that the defendant is likely to suggest that the case is one in which the court should depart from the general rule given the defendant's success on issue 1. You should not argue in full all the points that you think you can make in answer to the defendant's likely argument, because you want to hear how the defendant puts his submissions before you respond to them in your final speech in reply to those submissions. In that way your submissions can be tailored to meet the argument the defendant actually raises rather than the argument you think he might be about to raise—the two might not be the same! The most important point for your side is that the defendant forced you to argue the whole of the case by not offering to settle or compromise on the issue on which the claimant won so you might seek to put down a marker for that along the lines of:

> The defendant has fought the claimant's claim vigorously but with no practical benefit given the judgment given by your Honour for the full amount of the claimant's claim. The claimant was obliged to pursue his claim to trial on both issues in the case when the defendant could, and should in the light of your Honour's judgment, have conceded issue 2 and settled the claimant's claim long ago.

If the claimant made a Part 36 offer to settle at less than the sum awarded by the court, you will have to introduce the making of the offer and the consequences that flow from it. One might do so as follows:

> The claimant made a Part 36 offer on 1st February 2005 in the sum of £20,000 after witness statements had been exchanged and at a time when the claimant's position in the case was fully known to the defendant. The time for acceptance of the claimant's Part 36 offer expired on 21st February 2005. Your Honour has given judgment against the defendant in the sum of £25,000. In the circumstances your Honour has a discretion pursuant to CPR, Part 36, r 21, paragraph (2) to order the defendant to pay interest at a rate not exceeding 10% above base rate from 21st February 2005 and a discretion pursuant to paragraph (3) to order the claimant's costs to be assessed on an indemnity basis from 21st February onwards and to order the defendant to pay interest on those costs at a rate not exceeding 10% above base rate. Paragraph (4) directs the court to make those orders unless it considers it unjust to do so. There is nothing in the circumstances of the case which makes it unjust to do so and, in the light of your Honour's judgment, the defendant clearly should have accepted the claimant's Part 36 offer in February 2005. Base rate is currently 4% pa. In the circumstances I invite your Honour to order that the defendant pay the claimant additional interest pursuant to CPR, Part 36, r 21, paragraph (2) at the rate of 14% p.a. from 21st February 2005. Interest on the damages awarded from 21st February 2005 until today amounts to the sum of £xxx. I also invite your Honour to order that the claimant's costs be determined by a detailed assessment on the standard basis to 21st February 2005 and on an indemnity basis thereafter and to order the defendant to pay interest at the rate of 14% per annum from today on the claimant's costs incurred after 21st February 2005.

If the defendant has made an effective Part 36 payment, you should bring it to the attention of the court. A formulation of words appears below. If there is something in the case which makes it unjust to order the claimant to pay the defendant's costs, you need to set out the reasons why the court should conclude that it is unjust to make such an order. Much depends on the circumstances. If for example the claimant failed to better the Part 36 payment only because of some last-minute evidence produced by the defendant, one might justifiably conclude that at the time the Part 36 payment was made it was properly rejected by the claimant. It may be that there is some change in circumstances between the last date for acceptance of the Part 36 payment and the trial which has made the Part 36 payment effective at trial when it would have been ineffective when made.

You can then move on to deal with any interim payment on account of the costs which will become payable after the detailed assessment as follows:

> I invite your Honour to make an order for the payment of a sum on account of the costs payable to the claimant pursuant to CPR, Part 44, r 3, paragraph (8). In this case the claimant has incurred solicitors' costs of approximately £10,000, and disbursements including court fees, counsels' fees and expert witnesses' fees of approximately £7,500. The claimant's costs total in round figures £17,500 inclusive of VAT. The court should ordinarily make an order for payment on account in the sum that the claimant will almost certainly collect. The position is set out in the notes at paragraph CPR 44.33[23] on page 765 of the Green Book. Some allowance should be made for the fact that there is a risk that some part of the claimant's costs may be disallowed at the detailed assessment I have invited your Honour to order. Making a generous allowance in the defendant's favour I respectfully invite your Honour to order the defendant to pay £10,000 on account of the claimant's costs within 14 days.

You will note that the sample submissions set out above clearly direct the court to the relevant rules, explain the nature of the court's powers and provide a justification for the exercise of those powers in the claimant's favour. You should flag the relevant rules in your civil procedure text book with a Post-it note so that you can quickly turn to the relevant page and direct the court to the provision in question.

35.6.4 Responding to the application

When you find yourself in the position of responding to the application (remember that in the vast majority of hearings someone will be representing a losing party and at some time or other it will be you) what you can say depends on the circumstances of the case. In the simple straightforward case canvassed above, you may only be able to say that there is nothing you can usefully add or some other gracious submission to the inevitable order against your client and leave the judge to make the order sought. Otherwise your response should follow the same format as outlined above, ie set out the order you invite the court to make, the reasons why it should make that order and the reasons why it should not make the order sought by your opponent. It may be that you can find something in the circumstances relating to the manner in which the claim was conducted which has resulted in the costs incurred by the claimant being unnecessarily increased. For example, lengthy witness statements served by the claimant for witnesses who were not called at the trial. In that event our response might be along the following lines:

> Accepting as one must that the claimant has succeeded in his claim, nevertheless the right order to make in this case is an order for the defendant to pay a proportion of the claimant's costs for the following reasons. In the first place, much time has been spent on dealing with matters that have not materially advanced the claimant's case as it has progressed to trial and have not advanced the case as presented to your Honour in this court at the trial. Lengthy witness statements were served for four witnesses, none of whom have been called by the claimant. Their witness statements were not thought sufficiently useful to find their way into the trial bundle [. . . *add anything else with each new reason prefaced by 'in the second place' . . . 'in the third place' and so on*].

Listing your reasons in this way will help you to focus your submissions and give the judge a list of separate identifiable reasons to consider rather than a monologue covering many unconnected points in one lump. Your response should end with something along the lines of:

> In the light of the factors I have outlined I respectfully suggest that the proper order to make is an order for the defendant to pay 85% of the claimant's costs of the claim.

In these circumstances there is a lot to be said for leaving the actual figure for the proportion of the costs until the end of your submission. If you give a figure at the outset, there is a chance that the judge's instant reaction will be that there is no way he is going to deprive the claimant of that much in costs and your reasons will then be shut out as the judge's mind closes against you in an outbreak of premature adjudication. If you give your reasons first, there is a chance that the judge will have turned his mind to accepting that some reduction has to be made before he is faced with considering the figure that you put forward. You will also have a chance to assess the judge's reaction to your submission as an indicator for where to pitch the figure for the apportionment of the costs. This might help you to put forward a figure within the range in the judge's contemplation (in which case he is more likely to think your submissions are sound) rather than a figure which is outside the range in the judge's contemplation (in which case there is an increased chance that he will think your reasons are as unsound as your figure).

In the five-day, two-issue trial example set out above your response should pick up from the submission made by the successful party that costs follow the event pursuant to CPR, Part 44, r 3, paragraph (2)(a). Paragraph (2)(b) goes on to state that the court may make a different order. You might say something along the following lines:

Although CPR, Part 44, r 3, paragraph 2(a) provides for the unsuccessful party to pay the successful party's costs, paragraph 2(b) provides that the court may make a different order in the light of the circumstances set out in paragraphs (4) and (5) and all the circumstances of the case. In this case the court should properly make an order for the claimant to pay the defendant's costs on issue 1 and an order for the defendant to pay the claimant's costs of the case save for the claimant's costs of issue 1. The defendant was clearly the successful party in relation to issue 1. Given the time devoted to dealing with this issue the defendant should clearly be considered to be the successful party so far as the trial is concerned notwithstanding the judgment given for the claimant arising out of issue 2 which occupied only one of the five days devoted to the trial. Issue 1 was an issue on which the claimant was bound to fail for the reasons set out in the court's judgment. Those reasons were as apparent to the claimant before the trial as they are after judgment. In the circumstances the claimant could not reasonably have pursued issue 1 in the way that he has. [*One might add depending on what happened before trial.*] From the outset the defendant's solicitors have made it clear to the claimant that this aspect of the claim would fail for the reasons given in the judgment. At the CMC the defendant specifically invited the claimant to abandon issue 1 at an early stage in the action. Your Honour may be assisted by the correspondence between the parties dealing with this. [*Hand in the relevant correspondence and then take the judge through the letters to ensure the point is driven home.*] The trial of the action could and should have been devoted to resolving issue 2 alone. Had the claimant adopted that course the costs incurred by both parties would be much reduced beyond those which have in fact been incurred and valuable court time would not have been devoted to dealing with issue 1. If one turns to CPR, Part 44, r 3, paragraph 4(a), the court *must* have regard to the conduct of the parties. In this case the claimant has pursued a claim in respect of issue 1 that was bound, as it has done, to fail. Subparagraph (b) requires the court to have regard to whether a party has succeeded on part of his case even if he has not been wholly unsuccessful. In this case the defendant has succeeded on that part of his case relating to issue 1, that part being by far the larger part of the case. [*You can then proceed through the various matters raised in subparagraphs (4) and (5) one by one as each one gives you an opportunity to strike the same nail in different ways and build up the appearance of a welter of points which all drive the court towards making an order for the claimant to pay the defendants costs of issue 1. Given that four days have been effectively wasted from the point of view of the claimant and the court you can also draw on the overriding objectives in CPR Part 1, saving expense and allocation of the court's resources, before finally concluding with something along the lines of:*] In all the circumstances of the case the just order to make is an order for the claimant to pay the defendant's costs of issue 1 and for the defendant to pay the claimant's costs of the case save for the costs of issue 1.

If your clients have made an effective Part 36 payment, you must bring it to the attention of the court, if your opponent has not already done so, and set out in your submissions what consequences flow in terms of the order the court should make and the reasons why that order should be made. Something along the following lines should suffice:

On 1st March 2005 the defendant made a Part 36 payment in the sum of £20,000. The time for acceptance of the defendant's Part 36 payment expired on 21st March 2005. In this case your Honour has given judgment for the claimant in the sum of £15,000. Part 36, r 20, paragraph (2) directs the court to order the claimant to pay the defendant's costs after 21st March 2005 unless the court considers it unjust to do so. There is nothing in the circumstances of the case to support any submission that it is unjust to order the claimant to pay the defendant's costs after 21st March 2005. In the circumstances I invite your Honour to order the defendant to pay the claimant's costs up to 21st March 2005 to be determined, if not agreed, by detailed assessment on the standard basis to 21st March 2005 and to order the claimant to pay the defendant's costs thereafter to be determined, if not agreed, by a detailed assessment on the standard basis.

If the claimant has made an effective Part 36 offer, your submissions in response should focus on whether it is unjust as a matter of principle to order the defendant to pay enhanced interest and costs and whether it is unjust as a matter of fact to order interest at 10% above base rate as opposed to some lower figure. CPR, Part 36, r 21(5) provides some factors to consider in that regard.

35.6.5 Replying to your opponent's submissions

If it is your application, you should have the final word. It is not an opportunity to restate all the submissions you have already made. You should deal only with matters which the unsuccessful party has raised in answer to your submissions. Before you sit down you should ask the court whether there are any other points on which the court requires assistance. It may be that there is something troubling the judge which you and your opponent have not dealt with. The court may have in mind a different order from those suggested by the parties. If you ask and something is raised, you can at least have a go at making some submissions about the order the court is contemplating before, rather than after, it is pronounced by the court. You must also be prepared to suggest a less favourable order than that which you initially asked for if your opponent's submissions have been well received. For example on an interim application for a claimant who has been partially successful you might set out to persuade the court to make an order for the defendant to pay the claimant's costs. If your opponent appears to have persuaded the court that no order for costs is the appropriate order, you might want to suggest that the order should be claimant's costs in the case, which is something of a halfway house between claimant's costs and no order for costs.

35.6.6 Word of warning

The above sample speeches are merely examples, not a stereotype. You must find your own words to use to set out what order you want the court to make and the reasons that justify the court making that order. You also need to monitor carefully the court's response to the points that you make. In the five-day, two-issues example, sooner or later the court is likely to point out to the defendant that the effect of the order proposed is that the claimant will effectively make no recovery in money terms for his costs notwithstanding the fact he has recovered all that he sought from the defendant. If this point is made strongly by the court, the defendant should consider adapting his submission so that the final submission as to the appropriate order is one for the payment by the defendant of a stated percentage of the claimant's costs only. You should always be prepared to put forward a different order if the response from the court appears unfavourable. 'Unfavourable' means the order you seek is not going to be made as opposed to the court simply testing the argument you have advanced.

35.7 Making the order

After the parties' submissions are concluded the court will make its decision as to what order for costs to make. In simple cases the court will simply pronounce its order. You must take a careful note of exactly what order is pronounced so that you can endorse it on your brief and report it accurately to your instructing solicitor afterwards. If the court decides that it is unjust to make the orders provided in CPR, Part 36, r 20 or r 21, it must give reasons for that decision. You should ensure that the court does so. Do not be tempted to say nothing about absent reasons in the belief that it will help you to appeal that decision. In more complicated cases the court will deliver a mini-judgment solely on the issue of costs setting out the court's reasons for the order that it makes. This should help to give you some insight into the court's decision-making processes which you can usefully use on future occasions. Generally speaking the points that carry weight will be reflected in the court's expressed reasons. If you made points that are not reflected in the reasons or are rejected in the reasons given, you should give careful consideration to whether the point can be presented more attractively or more effectively should the occasion arise again in the future.

35.8 Costs on interim applications

35.8.1 Generally

The same procedure applies as explained above. In the vast majority of interim applications the 'event' against which success or failure is judged is the relief sought in the application and the court will proceed to make an order for costs against one or other of the parties. At this stage there is no determination as to which party is successful in the action and which is not, so there is more scope for making an order for costs in the case or reserving the costs to the trial judge. If the application relates to something the court would have to deal with sooner or later in the exercise of its case management function, the most likely order is costs in the case. If the reality is that your client will win at trial, its effect will be little different from an order for costs in any event. The only thing you will miss out on is a summary assessment and prompt payment.

Almost all interim applications will give rise to a summary assessment of the amount of the costs payable if one or other party intends to seek an order for the costs of the application in any event. You need to have a list of the points to attack in your opponent's statement of costs and a list of the points to support your statement of costs. The paying party will have to pay the assessed sum within 14 days unless some other period is ordered at the time the order is made. You need to make sure your client will be able to pay within 14 days and, if not, you need to have an explanation which covers why your client cannot pay within 14 days, what period of time is required and an argument to put forward in support of the period of time you wish the court to allow for your client to pay. If you are the receiving party, you need to know whether there is any good reason why the court should not allow further time beyond 14 days for payment of the costs as that too has a part to play in the court's decision.

35.8.2 Applications for an injunction

If the application is fought and an injunction is granted or refused, there is an event against which success or failure can be gauged. If it was an obvious case for the grant or refusal of the injunction, the successful party has a good argument to put forward for an order for costs in any event against the other party. It may, however, be that there is a risk that the claim will fail at trial in which event the interim injunction should not have been granted. That possibility will support an argument that the costs of the injunction application should be costs in the case or costs reserved to the trial judge. If the party seeking the injunction is successful and has before issuing the application sought undertakings from the unsuccessful party which have been refused, there is a powerful argument for ordering the unsuccessful party to pay the costs of the application, based on success coupled with the unsuccessful party's conduct in refusing to give undertakings which would have avoided the need to make the application.

35.8.3 Applications for permission to amend and extensions of time

In these instances the applicant is seeking the indulgence of the court and, in consequence, the applicant will usually be ordered to pay the costs of the application. For example, where the claimant applies for and obtains permission to amend his particulars of claim from the district judge the defendant's submission will be along the following lines:

> Sir, this application is the result of the claimant's failure to properly set out his case at the outset when the particulars of claim were drafted. There is no good reason for the claimant's failure to properly set out his case at the outset. As a consequence of the amendment the defendant will now incur further avoidable costs in the amendment of his defence to meet the new allegations now raised rather late in the progress of the action by the claimant. In the circumstances the court should order the claimant to pay the defendant's costs of the application and the costs of and occasioned by the amendment of the particulars of claim.

The submission can be fleshed out with references to CPR, Part 44, para 3(4) and (5).

The claimant might avoid such an order if he can show that the amendments are due to circumstances arising after the service of the particulars of claim, eg where the defendant's own defence raises matters which provide the basis for the amendments the claimant seeks to make, for example by asserting that some other person is liable to the claimant. The claimant might also be in a position to argue that it was obvious that permission to amend would be granted. In this type of application the applicant is able to protect himself against the costs of the hearing, if not the application itself by asking the other party to consent to the amendment or extension of time before issuing the application. It strengthens the applicant's position when it comes to arguing that the costs have been incurred by the other party's unreasonable conduct in fighting the application rather than the applicant's need to seek the court's indulgence and does not weaken the applicant's position on costs should the application fail.

Where a court order is required, even if the other party consents to the relief required by the applicant, the applicant will usually have to bear the costs of issuing the application and preparing the evidence in support of it. If the respondent contests the application and loses at the hearing, the respondent is at risk of having to pay the costs of the hearing in any event. If the respondent's arguments regarding costs are skilfully presented and heap sufficient blame on the applicant, it should be possible to secure an order which avoids the respondent having to pay the claimant's costs even if he does not succeed in obtaining an order which might provide for the payment of his costs by the applicant.

35.8.4 Applications to set aside a judgment or for relief from sanctions

The applicant will almost invariably be ordered to pay the respondent's costs unless there is a good reason to explain why the need to make the application arose. Unless the explanation involves some fault on the part of the respondent, the applicant will be ordered to pay the costs of the application. If the applicant is able to satisfy the court that a default judgment was entered in circumstances where the proceedings did not come to the applicant's attention through no fault of his, it may be possible to persuade the court to order costs in the case: things do go wrong from time to time without fault on the part of either party to the claim.

35.8.5 Applications for 'unless' orders

This type of application will arise only where the respondent is in breach of a provision of the CPR or an existing court order. In the ordinary course of events the respondent will be ordered to pay the costs of the application whether the applicant is successful or not, given that the cause of the application being made is the respondent's own default. In the unlikely event that the application is dismissed it may be possible to persuade the court that the respondent's success justifies some relief in respect of costs. That relief is unlikely to extend beyond an order for the applicant's costs in the case, ie if the applicant wins at trial he will recover the costs of the application and if the applicant loses at trial he will not have to pay the respondent's costs of the application.

35.8.6 Applications for summary judgment

There are three potential outcomes on an application for summary judgment—(1) judgment for the claimant or dismissal of the claim, (2) a conditional order or (3) dismissal of the application. In terms of success, (1) counts as success for the applicant, (3) counts as success for the respondent and (2) is a partial success for the applicant in that an advantageous order has been obtained against the respondent and a partial success for the respondent who lives to fight another day. The court is likely to treat the applicant who obtains a conditional order against the respondent as the successful party from a costs point of view given that it must be satisfied that it is possible but improbable that the claim or defence will succeed at trial before a conditional order can be made. The general rule applies: the successful party's costs of the application should be paid by the unsuccessful party.

Where the outcome is judgment for the claimant or dismissal of the claim the action is at an end and the successful party is entitled not only to the costs of the application but also the costs of the action. If the claim is for a specified sum of money in excess of £25, the successful applicant is only entitled to fixed costs in respect of the cost of the action in the amounts set out in CPR, Part 45. If the claim relates to relief other than a specified amount of money, eg damages or declaratory or injunctive relief, the court should summarily assess the costs of the application and the costs of the claim with the consequence that the applicant needs to provide two separate statements of costs—one dealing with the costs of the application and the second dealing with the costs of the claim—and counsel for both parties need to be ready to make submissions relating to the summary assessment of the costs in both statements at the end of the hearing.

The best order that an unsuccessful applicant might achieve is costs in the case on the basis that at trial his claim or defence may well succeed on the merits even if not established to the level required for summary judgment in the application. To succeed in this you will have to find an argument that deflects the court from the view that success or failure is to be measured by the outcome of the application or an argument that some other factor in the circumstances surrounding the application justifies 'a different order' in the words of CPR, Part 44.3(2)(b). An example of something which might assist the unsuccessful applicant is where the application is dismissed because of some point which arises very late in the service of the evidence before the hearing or at the hearing. An application based on statements of case as they stood at the date the application was issued that would have succeeded but only fails because a draft amended statement of case is produced at the last minute resulting in the dismissal of the application may also suffice.

35.8.7 Applications to adjourn or amend at trial

Usually the application is made because the applicant is not ready for the trial or hearing. Unless the applicant can show that he is not ready because of some factor outside his control he will usually be ordered to pay the costs of the application to adjourn and the costs occasioned by the adjournment of the trial or hearing. If the applicant is not ready because of some default on the part of another party in the case, it can be argued that the conduct of that party is the cause of the adjournment of the trial with the consequence that the other party should pay the costs incurred by the application and adjournment.

Applications to amend or adjourn made at the trial itself can provide a significant tactical advantage in the litigation because the burden of costs which may have to be paid as the price of securing an adjournment or amendment can be very significant. If a party succeeds at trial only because the court has allowed a late application to amend the statement of case at the trial itself, there is scope for persuading the court that the successful party should pay the costs up to the date of the amendment and recover no or limited costs thereafter—see for example *Beoco v Alfa Laval* [1995] QB 137. An application to amend at trial if granted may prejudice the position of the other party to such an extent that the trial has to be adjourned in order to permit that party to deal properly with the case in the light of the amendment permitted. In that event although the application to adjourn will be made by the party prejudiced by the amendment, the costs thrown away by the adjournment will be paid by the party whose amendment has resulted in the adjournment of the trial.

35.9 Procedural default

As CPR, Part 44, r 3(6) makes plain, different orders may be made with respect to different parts of a claim or application depending on the circumstances of the case. The CPR provides rules governing the making of applications to the court and the evidence required both in terms of content and formalities. You will quickly learn that there are no boundaries when it comes to the ingenuity of humankind to turn the simplest procedural task into something of unachievable difficulty. If you represent the paying party, that unachievable difficulty represents an opportunity to reduce the amount you may have to pay. You can always argue that, where something has not been done properly in accordance with the rules, the receiving party should not recover the costs of doing it, eg where a witness statement does not have a signed statement of truth it ought not to be admitted in evidence and if it is, the party preparing it ought not to recover the costs of its preparation from the paying party. A degree of circumspection is required in taking this type of point. For example, a complaint that the witness statement referred to above does not have margins of the requisite width is not likely to carry much weight but does carry a substantial risk of creating irritation on the part of the court with the wrong party, ie you.

35.10 Reserved costs

Where the court has made an order for reserved costs on a previous occasion the costs have to be dealt with by the trial judge. If you want the costs reserved to be paid by your opponent, you must bring the order reserving the costs to the attention of the trial judge and set out in your submissions the reasons that justify the court making the order you seek in respect of those costs. If nothing is said about reserved costs or no order is made by the trial judge in relation to those costs, they become costs in the case (a different rule applies in family proceedings). It follows that if the court orders the costs of the case to be paid by your opponent, you do not need to refer specifically to the reserved costs or seek a separate order in respect of them. If you represent the party ordered to pay the costs of the case, you must raise the question of what order should be made in respect of the reserved costs in the event that you wish the court to make an order which absolves your client from paying them or provides for them to be paid to your client. Whether this is achievable depends on the circumstances in which the reserved costs order came to be made and the circumstances of the case as a whole. For example, if the claimant applied for permission to amend and there was some doubt as to whether the amendment was actually required, the court might have granted permission to amend and reserved the costs to the trial judge. If the claimant won at trial and the amendment proved to be unnecessary, the defendant might then wish to argue that he should not have to pay the costs of the unnecessary amendment and the application for it at worst and, at best, that the claimant should pay his costs of the application and amendment in any event.

Most trial judges display a marked reluctance to deal with reserved costs in any way other than as costs in the case on the ground that they cannot adequately inquire into the circumstances at the time the reserved costs order was made. If you want them to be dealt with differently, you have to make sure you clearly explain why that outcome would be unjust and will have to ensure that the judge has a clear understanding of the reasons why the court reserved the costs on the occasion on which that order was made.

35.11 Small claims track costs

CPR, Part 27, r 14 restricts the costs recoverable in claims on the small claims track to fixed costs, court fees and witness expenses. The court may, pursuant to r 14(2)(d), order a party that has behaved unreasonably to pay further costs which have to be summarily assessed. Whether a party's behaviour is unreasonable depends on what was done and the consequences of it for the other party and the court. The following may be held to amount to unreasonable behaviour:

- pursuing a claim or defence which enjoyed no reasonable prospect of success;
- limiting the value of the claim so as to avoid the costs consequences attaching to fast track or multi track claims;
- failing to comply with pre-action protocols;
- filing a defence solely in order to avoid a judgment;
- failing to comply with the court's orders;
- making unnecessary applications;
- causing a late adjournment of the hearing;
- failing to attend the hearing;
- failing to negotiate properly by refusing reasonable settlement offers or obstructing negotiations.

If you are seeking costs on the ground of unreasonable behaviour, your submissions should clearly set out the behaviour that is relied on and explain why that behaviour was unreasonable. You should be in a position to demonstrate that avoidable costs have been incurred on the part of your client or that the ethos of small claims track disposal (simple, speedy and cheap) has been undermined by your opponent's behaviour. If your opponent's behaviour has inconvenienced the court, your prospects of success will be increased.

If the claim has a value in excess of the small claims track limit but was allocated to the small claims track with the parties' consent, normal fast track costs rules apply.

35.12 Fast track costs

Cases allocated to the fast track have their own costs regime for trial costs as set out in CPR, Part 46. Pre-trial costs and disbursements such as expert witness fees fall to be dealt with in accordance with the normal rules by summary assessment and with a greater emphasis on proportionality than in multi-track cases. Solicitors' costs of attending the trial are limited to £250 and that may only be awarded if the court considers that it was 'necessary' for the solicitor's representative to attend to assist the advocate—see CPR, Part 46, r 3(2). 'Necessary' is not the same as 'desirable' or even 'useful'. If your solicitors have sent a representative, you should do your best to make sure that the representative does as much as possible so that you can, at the end of the case, mount a convincing submission that the attendance was necessary in the light of what the representative has done in the course of the hearing. It will also be useful to find some reason for referring to notes taken by your solicitor's representative whilst you were on your feet and unable to take your own note.

The trial costs regime provides for a fixed fee for advocates at trial graduated according to the value of the claim. In this instance it is possible for the court to award a greater fee than your clerk may have agreed for your services. In so doing CPR, Part 46 ignores the indemnity principle that is the fundamental foundation of costs orders and allows your client the opportunity to earn a modest profit from your success. The fee fixed by r 2 may be decreased pursuant to r 3(7) if the receiving party has behaved unreasonably or improperly during the trial or increased pursuant to r 3(8) if the paying party has behaved improperly during the trial. There is no explicable reason for the inclusion of 'unreasonably' in r 3(7) and the failure to include it in r 3(8). The one thing that can be said is that improper behaviour must mean something other than unreasonable behaviour. Unreasonable behaviour is likely to flow from a failure to conduct the trial in a sensible, practical and pragmatic manner. Improper behaviour is likely to flow from conduct which undermines the effective conduct of the judicial process in a fair and just manner. Quite what behaviour is intended to attract the operation of the punishment provisions in r 3(7) and (8) is unclear. Equally it is a little unclear whether the 'party' refers simply to the lay client or whether it also encompasses the party's legal representatives, including you. It probably does not include your conduct of the trial, with the consequence that the obstreperous client who refuses to answer the questions put to him can be punished for his temerity, but the client whose advocate asks contentious but irrelevant questions cannot (at least in the absence of express instructions to ask the questions). It cannot be unreasonable or improper to give evidence that the court finds unreliable or unacceptable in giving judgment. It probably will be unreasonable or improper conduct if the court finds that the evidence was given deliberately with knowledge that it was untrue. It will probably not be unreasonable or improper for one party to accuse the other of lying in his evidence; it probably will be unreasonable or improper behaviour to use the witness box as a platform for launching an unjustified diatribe against the other party that is not associated with any of the matters which fall to be decided in the claim. The references to behaviour 'during the trial' also create difficulty. The emphasis is on what happens during the trial, not what happened before the trial started, with the consequence that unjustifiable intransigence in the agreement of evidence or documents in the run-up to the trial date falls outside the scope of the punishment provisions, even though the consequence is that a witness attends trial when it is unnecessary. For example, in a personal injury claim the claimant's claim will be supported by medical evidence. If the defendant has no medical evidence but refuses before trial to agree the claimant's medical evidence, the medical expert may need to be called to give evidence with the result that he attends on the day of the hearing. If, when he is called, counsel for the defendant asks no questions of him because he has no instructions as a basis for challenging any part of the evidence, it is easy to conclude that the defendant has behaved unreasonably resulting in the unnecessary appearance of the witness at the trial. During the trial, however, counsel for the defendant has acted reasonably and perfectly properly: he has no basis for challenging the witness's evidence and has not delayed or lengthened the trial by asking irrelevant questions. Although the matter has yet to receive authoritative consideration, it may be that a substantial failure to conduct the trial in line with the trial timetable template will amount to unreasonable or improper behaviour for the purposes of the punishment provisions.

Where both parties succeed to some extent the court has power to apportion the fixed fee for the advocate between the two parties—see CPR, Part 46, r 2(2). You then have the opportunity to argue with your opponent as to which of you should have the larger share of the cake.

35.13 Appeals

Success and failure in an appeal are measured by whether the appeal has been allowed or dismissed. An appeal allowed in part may count as a partial success. Where the appeal is allowed the appeal court will substitute its own order for the order appealed by the appellant. The court's decision as to which party should pay the costs of the appeal falls to be decided on the same principles, and your submissions should follow the same structure, as set out above. The appeal court will also deal with the costs order made at the time the order appealed against was made. If the appeal is successful, the appeal court will make the order that should have been made at the application or trial which resulted in the order appealed by the appellant. The costs order made on that occasion must also be revised to reflect the position as it should have been had the correct order been made at the end of the application or trial. That means your costs submissions on the appeal should include those which you would, in the light of the substantive order made by the appeal court, have made at the application or trial.

35.14 Publicly funded costs

At the end of any case in which a party is publicly funded, counsel for the publicly funded party must obtain an order for the detailed assessment of that party's costs pursuant to CPR, Part 47, r 17 or r 17A as appropriate. Without such an order the court has no power to assess the costs which should be paid to you and your solicitor for representing the lay client. It is prudent to ask for such an order at each interim application which comes before the court.

If the publicly funded party is ordered to pay any part of the costs of the action, a costs protection order in accordance with s 11 of the Administration of Justice Act 1999, the Community Legal Service (Costs) Regulations 2000 and the Community Legal Service (Costs Protection) Regulations 2000 *must* also be sought. There is a Guidance Note issued by the Senior Costs Judge of the Supreme Court which deals with the position and sets out what should and should not be done. You will find a copy of the Guidance Note at para 48.14 in the White Book 2009. You must be familiar with the rules and regulations that apply. If you are not, you will not be able to assist the court and run the risk of failing your client in what has become a technically complicated area of law and practice. Costs protection bites on the amount of the costs that the publicly funded party should pay with the consequence that the court should make an order for costs to be paid by the publicly funded party if that is the just order to make in the absence of public funding for that party (question 1 of the four questions canvassed above in **35.6.3 Making the application**). A publicly funded party can only be ordered to pay such amount in costs as the court considers to be a reasonable amount to pay in all the circumstances. That is not the same as a reasonable amount for the receiving party to receive. The judge may decide the amount at the end of the trial or he may leave it to be dealt with by the costs judge. If a costs order has been made in your client's favour against a publicly funded party, you face the choice of inviting the court to decide what amount is reasonable there and then or leaving that question for later determination by the costs judge. If the issue is left for later determination, the publicly funded client will have to provide a full appraisal of his means which may not be available to the trial judge. If you represent the publicly funded party, you need to have some information ready about your client's means in case the court decides to deal with ascertaining a reasonable amount there and then. If your client is totally bereft of means, you might try to persuade the court to assess the reasonable amount at £nil. It will probably discourage the receiving party from taking any further steps in connection with the assessment and recovery of costs after the hearing.

You will find a model order for this type of case at para 48.14.19 of the White Book. The model form caters for summary and detailed assessments of the amount payable. You must use this form of order. The old form of order commonly employed—'Costs not to be enforced without the permission of the court'—is meaningless in the current regime.

The current regime does not appear to have effected any change in the area of set off. The non-publicly funded party can set off against costs or damages payable to the publicly funded party, costs which the publicly funded party has been ordered to pay to him—see *Lockley v National Blood Transfusion Service* [1992] 1 WLR 492. In an interim application where the non-publicly funded party is successful, the court should be invited to make an order permitting him to set those costs off against any costs or damages he may be ordered to pay to the publicly funded party. The model order can be adapted to meet the circumstances of the case. Para 1 of the model order will deal with the order made on the application. Para 2 will be something along the lines of 'The [*publicly funded party*] pay the [*non-publicly funded party*]'s costs of this application summarily assessed in the sum of £[*amount*] enforceable by way of set off against any costs or damages the [*non-publicly funded party*] may be ordered to pay to the [*publicly funded party*]'. Para 3 will be something along the lines of 'The [*publicly funded party*] (a party in receipt of services funded by the Legal Services Commission) do pay to the [*non-publicly funded party*] after any set off pursuant to paragraph 2 above an amount to be determined by the District Judge'.

Costs protection only applies during the currency of the public funding. If the party receives public funding part-way through the action or loses public funding before the end of the action, the periods in which he was not a publicly funded party attract the normal orders with no protection. If public funding is revoked rather than discharged, the publicly funded party is treated as if he were never publicly funded at all for any part of the action. If you represent the non-publicly funded party, you need to make sure you clarify whether a certificate was revoked or discharged as it has an important impact on your client's position and the submissions you may need to make.

35.15 Funding arrangements

Funding arrangements are defined in CPR, Part 43, r 2(1)(k) and include agreements such as conditional fee agreements. Funding arrangements have provided another fertile area for argument by counsel which rather reflects the importance of costs issues in litigation. The successful party may also recover as an additional liability (see CPR, Part 43, r 1(o)) some or all of the uplift for success and insurance premiums in connection with the litigation costs. Like publicly funded costs, you must be familiar with the law and practice in this area. If the funding arrangement does not comply with the relevant regulations or the relevant procedure has not been followed, the unsuccessful party may escape any liability to pay anything in costs to the successful party.

CPR, Part 44, r 3A and B apply. From counsel's point of view, the funding arrangement should only become relevant at the end of the case where a summary assessment is conducted. If a detailed assessment is ordered, the enforceability of the agreement and the amount of the additional liability payable will be dealt with at the detailed assessment. If there is some doubt over the enforceability of the funding arrangement, it may deflect the court from making an order to the payment of an amount on account of the costs payable. If your opponent has a funding arrangement, you will know of its existence but will not be entitled to see the agreement until the end of the case and after the court has decided to summarily assess the costs. You will not have time to go off and research the rules and regulations at that juncture. You may be able to persuade the court that the existence of the funding arrangement is a good reason to order a detailed assessment rather than conduct a summary assessment. In principle the existence of a funding arrangement should not deflect the court from conducting a summary assessment—see CPR, Part 44, PD para 14.

If you represent the party who has entered into a funding arrangement, you need to make sure your solicitors have provided you with the bundle required by CPR, Part 44, PD para 14.9. The submissions of both parties to the court in the quantification of the amount payable on a summary assessment at the end of the case will have to cover the reasonableness of the amounts claimed in respect of any additional liability under the funding arrangement. The principal areas of contention are the amount of the insurance premiums and whether the success fee represents a proper assessment of the risk in the litigation. That may change as the litigation progresses: for example the uplift may be set at 100% based on liability being in dispute. If liability is subsequently admitted, the success fee is grossly unreasonable for the period after the admission is made. Some guidance on these issues can be gleaned from *Callery v Gray* [2001] 1 WLR 2112, *Callery v Gray*

(*No. 2*) [2001] EWCA Civ 1246, *Halloran v Delaney* [2002] EWCA Civ 1258 and *Claims Direct Test Cases* [2003] EWCA Civ 136.

35.16 Contractual entitlement to costs

In some cases, for example, mortgage possession claims, there may be a contractual entitlement to costs. Generally speaking where a party has a contractual entitlement to costs the costs payable are those stipulated by the contract and the amount is likely to be more generous than the court will allow in the application of the general principles applicable to litigation costs. CPR, Part 48, r 3 applies where the court assesses the amount payable pursuant to the contract. See also the notes at para 48.3.1 in the White Book. In those cases you should not seek an order for costs in the proceedings. You should try to ensure that the order records your entitlement to costs in accordance with the agreement between the parties.

35.17 Costs against solicitors and counsel

The court has power under s 51 of the Supreme Court Act 1981 and CPR, Part 44, r 14 to order costs against a solicitor or counsel personally. The court will only do so if costs have been wasted. Wasted costs are those incurred as a result of any improper, unreasonable or negligent conduct or those incurred prior to such conduct as the court considers unreasonable for a party to pay. For example the claimant may fail to appear at an interim application made by the claimant as a result of some negligent oversight on the part of the solicitor or counsel, with the consequence that the defendant's costs of preparing for the application and attending the hearing are wasted. Examples of relevant conduct are a failure by the solicitors to brief counsel in sufficient time for counsel to deal with the hearing or where counsel fails to devote adequate time to preparing for the hearing. If the party in default is publicly funded, an order for costs against solicitors or counsel personally may be the only order that will in practical terms result in payment to the other party. That factor can result in the court adopting an over-protective approach to the legal adviser who acts for a publicly funded client. It will result in the court looking carefully to see whether there is a proper basis for such an application rather than an attempt to find someone solvent to pay the costs in question. Before such an order can be made the court must be persuaded that the legal adviser in question has failed to conduct the proceedings with reasonable competence and expedition or has acted improperly, unreasonably or negligently. The procedure to be followed is set out in CPR, Part 44, r 7. The court must first be satisfied that there is a good reason for the legal adviser to show cause why a wasted costs order should not be made. Guidance as to the applicable principles can be found in *Ridehalgh v Horsfield* [1994] 3 WLR 462, *Filmlab Systems International v Pennington* [1995] 1 WLR 673, *Horsham District Council ex p Wensum* [1995] 1 WLR 680 and *Medcalf v Mardell* [2003] 1 AC 120. Applications should be made only where there is a very good prospect of success and the default on the part of the legal adviser can be clearly established without long-drawn-out further investigation by the court. Unless the application is going to be simple, straightforward and short the court will probably refuse to entertain it and you will have gained nothing from attempting to make it.

You must not on any account threaten an application for a wasted costs order for the purpose of intimidating the other side. It is a contempt of court and likely to attract a highly unfavourable reaction from the judge should he get to hear of it. As a matter of personal courtesy you should tell your opponent if such an application is to be made but make it clear that you are not seeking to dissuade the party's legal advisers from fulfilling their duty to their client.

CPR, Part 44, r 14 also allows the court to disallow costs where there has been a default on the part of a legal adviser. The court is more likely to exercise this power to prevent a legal adviser recovering payment for poor or shoddy work falling below the standard reasonably expected of him.

36 Employment tribunals

36.1 Introduction

This chapter considers some basic points of advocacy for a hearing before an employment tribunal. Industrial tribunals were renamed employment tribunals on 1 August 1998 by s 1, Employment Rights (Dispute Resolution) Act 1998. This is not intended to be an exposition of the principles of employment law, for which you should use the ***Employment Law in Practice*** manual.

You should familiarise yourself with the rules which govern the constitution and powers of the employment tribunal in England and Wales. The current rules are to be found in the Employment Tribunals (Constitution and Rules of Procedure) Regulations, 2004, SI 2004 No 1861, as amended by the Employment Tribunals (Constitution and Rules of Procedure) (Amendment) Regulations 2004, SI 2004 No 2351—both of which came into force on 1 October 2004. Most cases are governed by the rules set out in Sch 1. A large number of statutes give jurisdiction to the employment tribunal to determine questions. This chapter is concerned with the most common claims numerically, namely unfair dismissal claims, redundancy claims and contract claims.

You should note that almost 25 years after the statutory power was enacted so that employment tribunals can hear contractual disputes arising out of a contract of employment, on 12 July 1994 the necessary statutory instrument was passed. The Employment Tribunals Extension of Jurisdiction (England and Wales) Order 1994, SI 1994 No 1623 enables most contractual employment disputes with a value of less than £25,000 to be heard and determined by the employment tribunals.

36.2 Some expressions explained

You may encounter a number of expressions with which you may not be familiar. The main ones are:

ET1	The number given to the form used as the Applicant's Originating Application (claim)
ET3	The number given to the form used as the Respondent's Notice of Appearance (defence)
Compromise agreement	A binding agreement settling a complaint complying with the statutory requirements of s 77(4A), Sex Discrimination Act 1975; s 72(4A), Race Relations Act 1976; s 288(2B)(c), Trade Union and Labour Relations (Consolidation) Act

	1992; s 9(3)(a), Disability Discrimination Act 1996; or s.203(3)(c), Employment Rights Act 1996
Constructive dismissal	A resignation by the employee which amounts in law to a dismissal (as being the acceptance of a serious breach of contract by the employer)
COT3	An ACAS settlement form
ACAS	The Advisory, Conciliation and Arbitration Service, which receives a copy of every claim for unfair dismissal and has a statutory responsibility to attempt to achieve a settlement of the claim
Preliminary hearing	An initial jurisdictional hearing
Pre-hearing assessment	An obsolete type of hearing designed to sift out weak cases (replaced by the pre-hearing review)
Pre-hearing review	The current sifting process designed to eliminate weak cases
Recoupment	The system by which certain state benefits may be reclaimed from part of the compensatory award in an unfair dismissal claim

36.3 Steps prior to any hearing

The overriding objective of the Tribunal is (as in CPR) to deal with cases justly, reg 3 of the Regulations. There is now an express obligation on the parties to assist the Tribunal to further the overriding objective. Time limits are to be calculated in accordance with reg 15 of the Regulations. There is a new power to issue a default judgment: Sch 1, r 8.

The general power to manage proceedings under r 10 includes the following important powers:

(a) to provide further information—r 10(2)(b);

(b) to disclose documents or information—r 10(2)(d); and

(c) to require written questions to be answered—r 10(2)(f).

When an application is made in proceedings and the other party is legally represented, the party applying for any order must provide details of the application to the other party and confirm in writing to the Tribunal that they have done so: r 11(4). This important requirement should avoid the previous practice of applying without notice for orders which, if granted, were often reviewed or set aside on a later application by the other party.

Case management orders can be made by the Tribunal of its own initiative, r 12. There is a new power to impose a sanction for breach of an order or practice under r 13. The sanction can include awarding costs of preparation time.

If you are instructed before any proceedings are issued, you should consider whether a binding compromise agreement can be negotiated which avoids the need for a claim to be made. The criteria for such an agreement are set out in the statutory provisions listed under the explanation of the term 'Compromise Agreement' (see **36.2**).

36.4 Listing of hearings

Except where a shorter period of time has been agreed with the parties, every party must receive at least 14 days' notice of the date fixed for hearing (r 14(4)).

The notice of hearing is accompanied by information about the documents required for the hearing, the facilities available at the particular employment tribunal and a map showing the location of the tribunal.

36.5 Addressing the employment tribunal

The employment tribunal can consist of a chairman sitting alone or, more normally, a panel of three persons. Tribunals will occasionally sit with two persons (provided one is a chairman) if the parties consent, in which case the chairman has the casting vote. The chairman (who is legally qualified) tends to deal with most points which arise during the hearing (after consulting the other members where necessary).

The parties normally sit at tables facing the tribunal, with the witnesses using a smaller table nearer the tribunal or in the centre between the representatives. In most tribunals the applicant will sit on the right (looking towards the employment tribunal) and the respondent will sit on the left.

In London the members of the employment tribunal are normally present in the room used for the hearing when the parties are brought in by the clerk. In some tribunals outside London the parties and public are shown in first, in which case you should stand when the tribunal members arrive.

Although witnesses stand to take the oath or to affirm at the beginning of their evidence, all other steps take place with everyone seated, incuding counsel addressing the tribunal. The chairman and members if addressed individually are 'Sir' or 'Madam'; they can conveniently be referred to collectively as 'the tribunal' or 'this tribunal' or through the chairman as 'you and your colleagues'. When your witnesses have finished their evidence, at the point at which you would normally ask the judge whether he or she has any questions, you should ask 'Do you Sir/Madam, or your colleagues have any questions for this witness?'. The chairman will normally ask each member in turn whether they have any questions (often they do have questions) and will then ask any questions of his or her own.

36.6 Adjournments

The employment tribunal has a general power to adjourn any hearing. The power must be exercised in the interests of justice in the individual case and the CPR overriding objective has been introduced into tribunals. There is no power to impose conditions upon an adjournment (such as one party paying costs) although an order for costs may be made in the normal way; see **36.10.9**.

Two particular situations involving adjournments require special mention: first, where there are also other proceedings between the same parties (eg, a wrongful dismissal claim); and second, where there are criminal proceedings pending.

36.6.1 Other claims

In unfair dismissal cases the compensation powers of the employment tribunals are severely limited by statute. An employee may therefore wish to bring a wrongful dismissal claim as well as a claim for compensation for unfair dismissal. A very long line of cases exists which considers when the employment tribunal claim should be adjourned pending the determination of the wrongful dismissal claim; see, for example, *O'Laire v Jackal* [1991] ICR 718 and *Bowater plc v Charlwood* [1991] ICR 798, which identify some of the factors which ought to be considered.

Two changes in the law may affect the way in which employment tribunals exercise this discretion in the future: first, the changes in employment tribunal jurisdiction to include contractual claims have yet to be considered in this context; and second, the effect of the Civil Evidence Act 1995 has yet to be considered.

Since July 1994 the employment tribunals have had power to determine contractual claims under the Employment Tribunals Extension of Jurisdiction (England and Wales) Order 1994. You should look at the text of the order for its full terms. The most important qualifications are that the claim must be made within three months of the effective date of termination or the last day worked (although there is a limited power to extend time) and there is a limit on damages of £25,000. Although there are as yet no reported cases on this aspect it seems that employment tribunals might now refuse to adjourn an unfair dismissal claim pending wrongful dismissal proceedings, if the wrongful dismissal proceedings could also have been brought before an employment tribunal. This might be particularly appropriate where a tactical decision had been made to have two sets of proceedings, for example, in order to obtain legal aid for the wrongful dismissal claim.

One reason why employment tribunal claims are adjourned is that employment tribunals are not bound by the strict rules of evidence (r 11(1) of the 2001 Rules). Since a decision reached by an employment tribunal will give rise to an estoppel *per rem judicata* in a subsequent court hearing, the preference was to have the court hearing first. In *O'Laire v Jackal* a decision by the employment tribunal was described by Browne-Wilkinson LJ, a former President of the Employment Appeal Tribunal, as 'plainly wrong', yet the High Court and Court of Appeal were bound by it. The difference which used to exist over admissibility of evidence has been considerably reduced now that the Civil Evidence Act 1995 has been brought into force. It may be that applications to adjourn employment tribunal proceedings will be made less often or with less success.

36.6.2 Criminal proceedings

Employment tribunals often have to decide whether to adjourn proceedings for compensation for unfair dismissal pending criminal proceedings against the employee. The fact that the employee has been charged with a criminal offence certainly does not mean that his or her dismissal will always be fair (even if the offence arises out of or at his or her work). However, a conviction will often affect an award of compensation for unfair dismissal. The employment tribunals have a wide discretion to adjourn pending criminal proceedings and frequently do so despite the decision in *Bastick v James Lane (Turf Accountants) Ltd* [1979] ICR 778 in which the decision not to adjourn was upheld on appeal. Perhaps the crucial words in the decision of the Employment Appeal Tribunal in that case are (at p. 784) that:

> we are bound to conclude that, although it would have been perfectly reasonable to come to the opposite conclusion, nevertheless the conclusion which this chairman reached is not so unreasonable a conclusion as to lead us to a finding of perversity.

Truly a case of being damned by faint praise.

The common decision to adjourn also avoids the difficulty highlighted in *Ladup Ltd v Barnes* [1982] ICR 107. In that case the employment tribunal found a dismissal unfair when the employer dismissed on learning that the employee had been arrested and charged with growing and possession of cannabis plants. The employment tribunal awarded compensation. Later the employee was convicted of possession of cannabis. The employment tribunal refused to review its decision (see **36.12.1** for an explanation of review). The Employment Appeal Tribunal allowed the appeal against the refusal to review the decision and found that the employee had contributed towards his dismissal 100%, thus extinguishing his compensation.

36.7 Preliminary hearing

Unfortunately a preliminary hearing is often confused with a pre-hearing review or pre-hearing assessment. They are quite different procedural creatures. A preliminary hearing is normally ordered where there is a legal or jurisdictional issue to be determined before any consideration of the merits of the claims. A pre-hearing review (formerly known as a pre-hearing assessment) is an initial consideration of the merits of the claim (see **36.8**).

A preliminary hearing can be ordered at any stage prior to the hearing of the Originating Application (at the request of one or more parties or by a chairman). Slightly more unusually a preliminary issue may be directed to be considered at the beginning of the main hearing under an employment tribunal's general power to regulate its own procedure. It is imperative that the legal or jurisdictional issue is carefully defined so that all relevant evidence is given and submissions are made. So, for example, if the jurisdictional issue is whether a claim for compensation for unfair dismissal is made within time, it should be decided if the subsidiary question, ie, to grant an extension of time, if necessary, is to be heard at the same time (as would be normal), or only after a decision has been made as to whether the claim was in fact in time.

The most common examples of preliminary hearings are:

(a) A hearing to determine whether the claim has been brought within the relevant statutory time limit and, if not, whether time should be extended under the relevant power.

(b) A hearing to determine whether the applicant is an employee within the meaning of s 230(1), Employment Rights Act 1996 (unfair dismissal and redundancy claims).

(c) A hearing to determine whether the applicant has the necessary length of service to qualify to bring the claim.

If the disputes of fact which have to be resolved at the preliminary hearing are inextricably linked to the merits of the case, an employment tribunal may refuse a separate preliminary hearing. A common example would be where there is confusion as to the exact date of dismissal which is relevant to determine whether the claim is brought within time and whether any extension of time should be given. In such a case it is easier to hear all the evidence and determine all the issues together.

A preliminary hearing can be heard by an employment tribunal chairman sitting alone.

The practice of holding preliminary hearings has existed for more than 20 years. It was first recognised by the Rules in 1993. The Rules suggest that written representations and oral argument can be used but make no express reference to oral evidence being heard. In practice oral evidence is required at most preliminary hearings before the legal or jurisdictional issue can be properly decided and a number of decisions have criticised attempts to short-circuit the need to make proper findings of fact; see, for example, *BL Cars Limited v Brown* [1983] ICR 143. An unusual example of a case where oral evidence was not taken can be found in *Janstorp International (UK) Limited v Allen* [1990] IRLR 417, where the employment tribunal decided whether wages in lieu of notice fell within the statutory definition of 'wages' in the Wages Act 1986 without hearing evidence and the Employment Appeal Tribunal gave guidance on situations where a case might be decided without hearing evidence. It is occasionally possible to agree facts for the purposes of a preliminary issue but the employment tribunals are not strictly bound by that agreement and Mummery J has warned of the dangers which exist if the facts are agreed hurriedly at the door of the hearing or during the hearing. Errors can have most unfortunate consequences: *Waters v Metropolitan Police Commissioner* [1995] IRLR 531.

The procedure at a preliminary hearing is similar to that at a main hearing. The party upon whom the burden of proof lies will normally go first. The burden is usually upon the applicant employee to show that the employment tribunal has jurisdiction to hear and determine the claim. The applicant's representative will briefly outline the basic facts indicating the extent of the preliminary issue. The applicant's evidence will then be given, cross-examination will take place and, if necessary, any re-examination or questions from the employment tribunal. Any witnesses for the applicant will then be heard. Thereafter any witnesses for the respondent will be heard. The respondent's counsel will address the employment tribunal and finally the applicant's counsel will have the last word.

The employment tribunal will often give a brief decision very quickly to be followed by written reasons in short or extended form (see **36.10.6**).

36.8 Pre-hearing review

In 1980 pre-hearing assessments were first introduced in the hope that hopeless cases would be weeded out. The procedure never worked as intended and it fell into disuse.

In 1993 the current weeding-out process known as a pre-hearing review was introduced, now to be found in r 18.

A pre-hearing review may be ordered by the employment tribunal of its own motion or at the request of a party. It may be conducted by a full employment tribunal or a chairman sitting alone.

If the employment tribunal decides that a party's contentions have no reasonable prospect of success, then a party may be ordered to pay a deposit of up to £500 as a condition of the case proceeding to a full hearing. Account must be taken of the means of the party being ordered to pay the deposit. The decision is recorded in a summary form and sent to the parties with a warning that if the claim continues, costs may be awarded against the party ignoring the warning. If the deposit condition is not complied with, the Originating Application or Notice of Appearance (or certain specified parts of it) may be struck out.

If the claim continues to a full hearing after a pre-hearing review, no member of the employment tribunal may sit on the employment tribunal which hears the substantive claim. If the person against whom the order is made pays the deposit it will then be returned if the claim is withdrawn before the main hearing, or in the unlikely event of the claim succeeding, or if the claim continues but an award of costs is not made against the party paying the deposit.

This sifting process seems to be used against more applicants than respondents.

At a pre-hearing review the employment tribunal considers the pleadings and the contentions of the parties, but does not make detailed findings of fact and rarely hears any oral evidence. If you represent the party against whom the hearing has been convened, you should be prepared to explain the basis of your case clearly and succinctly. Since the employment tribunal does not make a detailed inquiry into disputed facts at this stage, it should be asked to accept the facts asserted as correct at that stage. Although it is not often necessary to cite authority, if the contention which you rely upon is not well known, citing the relevant authority may be essential.

36.9 Directions hearings

The employment tribunals now make wide use of directions hearing and case management discussions held under Rule 17 (which are similar to case management conferences in the courts). These can be held by telephone. The case management discussion is not a pre-hearing review.

The old practice of asking for directions and obtaining orders by letter, without notice to the other side, has been abandoned. When asking for any order by letter, the Tribunal will want to know whether the other party has been given notice of the application and will not make an order unless the other party has had an opportunity to make representations.

As with case management conferences in a court, the case management discussion is intended to increase judicial control over the proceedings. At a case management discussion you should be familiar with the facts and the issues that have to be determined in the case, as well as each of the orders or directions that may be required. The Tribunal will record the result of the discussion including any admissions made as to the issues to be determined. The Tribunal will often wish to fix the hearing date or dates during the discussion so that the directions and timetable can be given in the light of the time available before that hearing. It is therefore important to attend with dates to avoid for the advocate, the party and any witnesses.

36.10 The substantive hearing

The preparation for the hearing should include attempting to agree a bundle of documents for the hearing. If agreement cannot be reached, each side should prepare at least six copies of its paginated bundle (three for the members of the employment tribunal, one for the witness and one for each party). An agreed bundle means that the parties accept that the documents are to be placed before the employment tribunal, not that the contents of each document are admitted to be accurate.

If there is a claim for reinstatement or re-engagement, the respondent should be in a position to give any evidence opposing the making of such an order at the main hearing.

It is becoming increasingly common to prepare written witness statements for each witness. This is not compulsory but saves considerable time, particularly if they are exchanged in advance of the hearing. The witness can then read the witness statement as his or her evidence-in-chief. If this practice is adopted, the employment tribunal generally limits supplementary questions to matters arising on exchange of witness statements and more recent events.

There is a power for the employment tribunal to receive written representations or submissions provided that they are given not less than seven days before the hearing (r 10(5)). This is not the same as admitting written evidence.

The hearings are held in public. There is a limited power to hear part or all of the claim in private under r 16. There is also a very limited power to impose reporting restrictions and to prevent the identification of a person affected by a sexual harassment allegation. In England and Wales the witnesses normally remain in the tribunal room throughout the case and hear the evidence of earlier and later witnesses.

36.10.1 Non-attendance

If one party does not attend, the clerk normally tries to contact the party to see if there is any reason for the non-attendance (such as not receiving the notice of hearing). You should also ask if any written submissions have been submitted by the absent party.

If the party absent is the one with the burden of proof, then the other party may ask for a finding in its favour without hearing evidence. If the employment tribunal adopts the approach and the finding is in favour of the employee, the employment tribunal will still have to calculate the redundancy payment or determine the remedy for an unfair dismissal. If, for example, the employer admits dismissal but does not attend to establish an acceptable reason for dismissal, the applicant may seek a finding of unfair dismissal. The statutory presumption that a dismissal was for redundancy in s 163(2), Employment Rights Act 1996 applies only to a claim for a redundancy payment and not to claims for unfair dismissal and so would not assist the absent employer.

36.10.2 Opening

At the substantive hearing the first issue is which side opens the case. In unfair dismissal or redundancy claims, if dismissal is admitted, the respondent employer will go first. The respondent must still establish the reason for dismissal even though there is no longer any burden of proof in relation to fairness. If dismissal is not admitted, then the applicant employee will go first and must show that there was an actual or constructive dismissal. In contract claims the applicant will go first.

It is important that it is established whether the entire case is to be heard at once or whether the question of liability is to be separated from the question of remedy. Many employment tribunals prefer to consider remedy separately after deciding liability, even if both aspects are dealt with on the same day. If the remedy of reinstatement or re-engagement is sought by the applicant, separate subsequent consideration of remedy is usually directed as detailed evidence may have to be heard on the availability of other jobs. If no indication is given by the employment tribunal on this point, a ruling should be sought well before the applicant begins giving evidence about his or her losses resulting from dismissal. When this aspect is being considered you should ensure that it is clear whether or not liability includes any finding of contribution towards dismissal and/or any deduction for the risks of a fair dismissal at some future point.

The opening can often be extremely brief. Employment tribunals are regularly critical of overlong openings by counsel. It is useful to indicate the correct basic facts or the extent of the dispute about those basic facts such as dates of employment, rates of pay, job description, place of work. Any amendments to the ET1 (the Originating Application) or the ET3 (the Respondent's Notice of Appearance) should be made at this stage. If the respondent's business is not obvious from its name, or well known, a brief explanation of the business may assist the tribunal. It is often helpful to give some indication of the size and administrative resources of the respondent in opening, mentioning the size of the business and/or the number of staff employed at the applicant's place of work and generally. Finally, it is often much quicker to take the employment tribunal through the bundles of documents in opening rather than ask each witness to 'produce' documents which it has been agreed should be placed before them.

36.10.3 The taking of evidence

Evidence is usually taken on oath or affirmation (r 9). Before the hearing the clerk will normally check who is giving evidence and how they wish to take the oath so that the necessary form of oath and appropriate holy book will be ready. As in court a separate oath will be taken by any interpreter. As in court the oath should be taken standing and whilst everyone else is silent (never use this time to take last-minute, spoken instructions).

Witnesses are normally released once their evidence has been taken. However, you should ask the employment tribunal to release a witness before allowing a witness to leave.

If more than one claim is being heard at the same time, the evidence which is relevant and admissible on each claim may require careful consideration. The most common problem is where claims for wrongful dismissal and claims for unfair dismissal are heard together.

(a) At the liability stage of a claim for unfair dismissal the employment tribunal is focusing on the knowledge and actions of the employer up to and at the time of dismissal. No account should be taken of subsequently discovered facts (until remedy is considered): *Devis (W) & Sons v Atkins* [1977] AC 931. Thus, for example, evidence coming to light after dismissal supporting an allegation of misconduct is not admissible in the unfair dismissal claim.

(b) In a wrongful dismissal claim, as in most contract claims, the tribunal is concerned to determine whether the employee was justifiably dismissed summarily. Subsequently discovered misconduct and subsequently discovered evidence can be relied upon by the employer to justify the dismissal: *Boston Deep Sea Fishing & Ice Co v Ansell* (1888) 39 Ch D 399.

36.10.4 Submissions of no case to answer

Although it is possible to make a submission of no case to answer at the end of the evidence from the party with the burden of proof, such a practice should only be used in exceptionally plain and obvious cases. Before making a submission take care to determine whether the employment tribunal will regard you as having elected to call no evidence if you make a submission (as would be the case in a civil trial but not in a criminal trial).

36.10.5 Closing submissions

Employment tribunals often criticise lengthy closing speeches and excessive reference to authority. The party with the burden of proof should have the final say. You can usually assume that the employment tribunal will be familiar with the leading cases. If the law in your case is more complex, then you may need to cite authority, in which case you may find a written skeleton argument extremely useful. If you are citing authorities, let the clerk to the tribunal know in the morning so that copies can be obtained for the employment tribunal.

36.10.6 The liability decision

If time permits, the employment tribunal will give a decision on liability very shortly after hearing closing submissions. A written decision will then be sent to the parties at a later date signed by the chairman. The old practice of having reasons given in summary or extended form has been abolished. The mandatory requirements for orders, judgments and reasons are now to be found in rr 28 to 30.

36.10.7 The remedies issue

If the claim is for a redundancy payment, the calculation of the correct payment should be a matter of simple mathematics, applying the formula in s 162, Employment Rights Act 1996.

If the claim is for unfair dismissal, employment tribunals are obliged to consider an order for reinstatement or re-engagement and only thereafter to award compensation. In practice orders for reinstatement or re-engagement are extremely rarely sought and even more rarely made by a tribunal. If re-engagement or reinstatement is sought, employment tribunals will normally hear evidence from both parties. If only compensation is sought, the tribunal will normally only hear evidence from the applicant about efforts to find a new job and any temporary or permanent position found.

If employment tribunals announce that a dismissal is unfair, it is quite common for the parties to be recommended to attempt to reach a settlement because the financial benefits of settlement can be considerable (see **36.11**).

36.10.8 Interest

In awards of a redundancy payment or compensation for unfair dismissal no interest is included in the award. However, interest will run in repect of an unpaid award from 42 days after the date of the decision—the period allowed for lodging an appeal (see **36.12.2**).

36.10.9 Costs

Costs are rarely awarded by an employment tribunal. The power to award costs is set out in r 38. The power is used where a party has acted vexatiously, abusively, disruptively or otherwise unreasonably. However, note that an employment tribunal must award costs if the respondent asks for an adjournment to oppose the making of an order of reinstatement or re-engagement, provided that the wish to make such a claim was communicated to the respondent at least seven days before the hearing (as would be the case if it is sought in the ET1).

If costs are awarded they may be a specific sum of up to £10,000 fixed by the employment tribunal, any sum agreed between the parties, or assessed costs.

If, on a pre-hearing review: (i) a party was ordered to pay a deposit as a condition of continuing to participate in the proceedings; (ii) the party paying the deposit has lost;

and (iii) no award of costs has been made under the general power, an employment tribunal must consider whether to award costs on the grounds that the party continued the proceedings unreasonably in persisting with the case. However, an employment tribunal must not make an award unless the document recording the decision at the pre-hearing review and the eventual decision are substantially the same.

The application for costs is normally made at the end of the hearing. If no decision is announced at the end of the hearing, the question of costs would have to be considered at a further hearing (involving additional expense) or by written representations. The Employment Appeal Tribunal has suggested that to avoid a further hearing a party could indicate that, if successful, he or she wished to apply for an order for costs. In practice that is rarely a sensible approach as: (i) it is not until the basis of the decision is known that the application for costs can properly be formulated by labelling the conduct frivolous, vexatious or merely unreasonable; and (ii) the employment tribunal could not be informed of the decision at any pre-hearing review before they have arrived at their own decision.

36.11 Settlement

Employment tribunals frequently encourage parties to settle claims 'at the door of the court'. If a liability decision is announced, a further opportunity is often given for settlement before the employment tribunal rules on the remedy. In addition to the usual benefits of settlement, there is one factor peculiar to claims before employment tribunals which you should bear in mind. The factor is the effect of recoupment of state benefits received by the employee after termination.

The position is governed by the Employment Protection (Recoupment of Jobseekers' Allowance and Income Support) Regulations 1996. In short if an applicant is awarded compensation for unfair dismissal, an employment tribunal has to calculate the period covered by past loss and the net award made for that period (known as the prescribed element). The Secretary of State is then informed of the decision and will reclaim any benefits paid in that period up to the amount awarded. Thus the applicant actually receives less than the sum awarded to him but the respondent pays out the amount awarded, diverting some part to the Government.

If a settlement is reached, there is no recoupment of benefit. In this respect the approach in employment tribunals is quite different from the approach in personal injury actions. In many unfair dismissal cases the sum which will be recouped will be a substantial part of the compensatory element of the award.

An example may assist. If the employee has been unemployed for, say, six months prior to the hearing and has received £4,000 in recoupable benefit, the position is as follows:

(a) If the employment tribunal awards compensation of £5,000 for the six-month period of loss, and further compensation (including a basic award) of, say, £5,000, the respondent will have to pay out £10,000 but the applicant will only receive £6,000 of that sum.

(b) If the case is settled, there is no recoupment of the benefits of £4,000 received. Thus, an agreed settlement of £8,000 payable to the applicant will mean that both parties are better off by £2,000.

If you reach a settlement at the hearing, you should ensure that it is binding and enforceable. There are a number of ways of making the settlement binding. Many chairmen have their own preferred way and some will seek to impose their preferred approach on the parties. The most common methods are a consent order or a type of 'Tomlin' order.

(a) A simple consent order for payment can be made by an employment tribunal. There will be no recoupment because there is no prescribed element to which a recoupment notice can be applied.

(b) Employment tribunals do not favour the normal 'Tomlin' form—where the proceedings are stayed indefinitely—as they are anxious to close their files. A common practice is therefore to order that the claim is dismissed on withdrawal by the applicant at some future date, unless either party notifies the employment tribunal that the claim should be released. If, for example, the settlement payment is to be paid in 21 days, it might be convenient for the case to be dismissed on withdrawal by the applicant in 42 days' time if a request for a further hearing has not been made within 35 days. If the payment is received, no request is made and the claim ends in 56 days. If the payment is not made in 21 days (or even shortly thereafter), the applicant would request a further hearing well within the 35 days allowed.

36.12 Further steps

There are two ways of challenging a decision of an employment tribunal: by review and by appeal.

36.12.1 Review

A review is a reconsideration of the decision by an employment tribunal. The power to grant a review is found in rr 33–36. It is rarely exercised. An application by a party for a review must be in writing made within 14 days of the date the decision was sent to the parties. The employment tribunal has power to review its own decision of its own motion without time limit. The grounds for a review are very limited and are that:

(a) the decision was wrongly made as a result of an administrative error;

(b) a party did not receive notice of the proceedings leading to the decision;

(c) the decision was made in the absence of a party;

(d) new evidence has become available since the conclusion of the hearing to which the decision relates, provided that its existence could not have been reasonably known of or foreseen at the time of the hearing; or

(e) the interests of justice require such a review.

36.12.2 Appeal

An appeal against the decision of an employment tribunal lies on a point of law to the Employment Appeal Tribunal: Part II, Employment Tribunals Act 1996. The procedure is governed by the Employment Appeals Tribunal Rules 1993 (SI 1993 No 2854) as amended. The Notice of Appeal normally has to be lodged within 42 days of the date on which the written decision of the employment tribunal was sent to the parties. There is a detailed and extremely useful EAT Practice Direction which you should study.

37

Remands/adjournments

Among the first court appearances you are likely to undertake during your second six months' pupillage are an application for a remand in the magistrates' court, an application to stand a case out of the list in the Crown Court, or an application to adjourn a hearing in the County Court/High Court or in a tribunal. Often the case will not actually be your case but that of a member of chambers. As you progress in practice, however, you will continue to find that there are many occasions when it is necessary to apply for a remand or adjournment in cases of your own and often you will consider such an application appropriate even where your instructing solicitor has not briefed you specifically for that purpose. Sometimes, unforeseen circumstances arise at a court or tribunal hearing which make it necessary to make or respond to such an application with little notice.

37.1 Preparation

Before you make an application for a remand or adjournment, investigate the reasons for the case not being ready to proceed. The most common grounds for applying for a remand/adjournment are insufficient time to prepare the case (eg, investigations incomplete; client only recently instructed solicitors; public funding just granted; late service of affidavit or witness statement, late disclosure of documents); or the court or tribunal or one of the parties is not in a position to proceed (eg, witness unavailable; pre-sentence report required; lack of court time).

Consider the history of the case; if it is not your case, try to speak to counsel whose case it is. Have there been any previous adjournments in the case? For what reason? Has there been any delay on your client's/solicitor's part? Can you explain the delay? Always ensure you have clear instructions on these matters and have advised your solicitors where it may be necessary to lay the blame for undue delay at their door. Ensure you have a chronology of the progress of the case clear in your mind.

Advise your client of the reasons for an application to adjourn being appropriate and the consequences this may have for him or her, eg, on the question of costs. In some cases, the client may instruct you to proceed even if you are not fully prepared, eg, he or she may prefer to proceed with the witnesses that have attended rather than risk the costs of an adjournment or the agony of further delay simply to secure the attendance of another witness. (It is sensible to invite your client to endorse this instruction on your brief.)

Consider the steps, if any, that have been taken to notify the other party and the court or tribunal of the application to adjourn the case. Be in a position to explain the absence of any notice. Inform your opponent at the earliest opportunity of your intention to apply for an adjournment. Discover whether your application is likely to be/will be opposed.

Look at the merits of your application. Will your opponent be prejudiced by an adjournment or can any prejudice be compensated, eg, by an order for costs? Will you be prejudiced by a refusal to adjourn? How vital is it to your case? If you have time, make a note of the main points of your argument.

Consider how long you realistically need to be ready to proceed with the case.

Apply your mind to any orders or directions you want the court or tribunal to make pending the adjourned hearing (whether you are making or responding to the application), eg, permission to amend a statement of case; permission to file further witness statement(s); specific disclosure of documents; an interim injunction to maintain the status quo or to protect your client; continuation of any existing order(s) such as an interim injunction; an interim order to provide for your client, eg, order for maintenance or contact with his or her children; the grant of bail or the continuation of an existing surety. Where appropriate, try to agree any orders/directions with your opponent.

Ask yourself what order for costs you want the court or tribunal to impose in the event of your/your opponent's application for an adjournment being successful, eg, an order for the costs thrown away; costs reserved. Advise your client of any risk that he or she will be ordered to pay the costs (or your solicitors if the fault lies with them).

Never assume that the court or tribunal will accede to your request for an adjournment. Be prepared to proceed if your application is refused **but** never assume an obligation to do a case in such circumstances when you do not feel professionally qualified to do so. If you face such a possibility when the brief is one delivered to another member of the Bar and you are simply making the application because he or she cannot be at the hearing, you must discuss the matter with them beforehand and make your position clear to them. If the brief is one which has been delivered to you, then you should not hesitate to discuss your position with your former pupil supervisor or a senior member of chambers. It may be necessary later to speak directly to your instructing solicitor. Always remember, the interests of the client come first.

37.2 Making the application

When your case is called on for hearing, inform the court or tribunal at the outset that you have an application to make for a remand/adjournment/the case to be stood out of the list (as appropriate) and indicate if your application is opposed/unopposed.

Set out the reasons for your application in a succinct manner. If appropriate, refer the court or tribunal to any affidavit or document which is relevant to the application for an adjournment. Explain any delays—be honest. Deal with the merits of your application and the manner in which any possible prejudice to the other party can be met, eg, an order for interim relief, an order for costs.

Be as brief as possible and do not repeat your arguments! Do not try to argue the merits of your substantive case. Remember that at this stage you are applying for an adjournment.

Tell the court or tribunal how long you will need before you are in a position to proceed with the hearing of the case.

It will then be your opponent's turn to address the court or tribunal. If resisting such an application, he or she will emphasise any delay on the part of the applicant and the inconvenience and/or prejudice his or her client will suffer as a result of the delay which cannot be met in any other way, eg, by an interim order or an order for costs.

You may then have a further opportunity to address the court or tribunal in response to your opponent's submissions. Do not use this as an opportunity to repeat your arguments.

If the application to adjourn is either unopposed or succeeds, indicate to the court or tribunal the orders or directions which you seek in the interim and whether any or all of them are agreed subject to the court's or tribunal's approval.

Make or respond to the application for costs. Make any appropriate application for legal aid assessment (this is often not granted until the final hearing).

38

Bail application

The following is a checklist for the preparation and conduct of a bail application. Reference should be made to the ***Criminal Litigation and Sentencing*** manual for the procedure.

38.1 Preparation

The first and most important step is to discover what are the objections to bail. These may be fairly obvious, eg, your client may have allegedly committed the offence while on bail for another offence; or may have a history of absconding; he or she may be charged with a serious offence such as supplying drugs or a series of offences such as burglary.

If not apparent, then ask the prosecuting advocate what are the objections to bail. Get to court early enough to have the opportunity to speak to him or her; in the magistrates' court, he or she is likely to be dealing with a considerable caseload.

Ensure you have an up-to-date copy of the defendant's antecedents (especially their convictions, if any); if you don't have it, ask the prosecution for a copy. Never rely solely on a client's description (or recollection) of his or her past record.

Consider with your client whether he or she wants you to make a bail application and advise on the prospects of success. Some clients are realistic and appreciate when their prospects of obtaining bail are hopeless; others anticipate a custodial sentence and prefer to serve part of their eventual sentence on remand (see Criminal Justice Act 2003, s 240(3)). Consider whether it is the right time to make a bail application or whether it is appropriate to wait, eg, until you have been served with advance disclosure of the prosecution case, have fuller instructions or there is a surety at court.

Consider the strength of the prosecution evidence. If advance information has not yet been served on the defence, consider the nature and extent of the charge(s), the amount of any money involved, the gravity of any alleged injury; ask the prosecutor for basic information such as whether there are any eyewitness accounts, whether the evidence is circumstantial, whether the defendant is alleged to have confessed.

Take as full instructions from the client as time permits upon the circumstances of the alleged offence(s), and his or her tentative plea.

Go through the client's previous record in detail, establishing the circumstances of any serious or similar offences to the present charge(s), whether he or she pleaded guilty in respect of any past offences, the reasons for any previous failure to appear, whether he or she has ever been convicted of committing an offence while on bail.

Find out the client's present circumstances; job, home ties, responsibilities, the potential/probable effects of a continued loss of liberty.

Look at whether there has been any change in the client's circumstances since the time of the alleged offence, eg, has he or she moved from the area, changed his or her group of friends? Is any change likely in the future?

Discuss any possible conditions that can be put forward to meet the objections to bail and whether your client is prepared to abide by them. Consider practical solutions to the objections, eg, if the defendant has no fixed abode, is a place in a bail hostel or other accommodation a possibility? Speak to the probation officer at court about this; if necessary, ask for your case to be put back on the list for this purpose. Note that bail hostels will not normally consider a defendant with a drug habit or convictions for violence. If possible, discuss any proposed conditions with the prosecutor in advance to determine whether such conditions would meet the objections. (If so, the bail application will become effectively 'unopposed' and offering the 'agreed' conditions to the court will be likely to succeed.)

Consider whether any surety is (or is likely to be) available, the amount any proposed surety is/would be prepared to offer; if the proposed surety is at court, ensure he or she understands the meaning of standing as a surety and the likely consequences in the event of the defendant absconding. Consider whether a proposal to lodge security at court is a practical option (normally more appropriate in the case of a foreign defendant or where a risk of leaving the country is involved).

38.2 Making the application

In making your application for bail, keep it as brief as possible and to the point. Do not repeat yourself, wander off on a tangent or lecture the court upon your client's rights to bail. Deal with your points in a logical sequence, making your strongest points first and last. Do not make weak points which will detract from the strength of your other submissions.

Deal with the objections in two ways. *Step 1*: undermine/cast doubt on their validity. Show the court that there are no 'substantial grounds' for the objection(s). *Step 2*: propose how such objections (if still of concern, in that there may be a 'real risk') could sensibly be met.

For example, if the objection is that the defendant is likely to commit offences while on bail, draw the court's attention to such matters as the weaknesses in the prosecution case, your client's intention to plead 'not guilty'; the fact that he or she has always pleaded guilty in the past, or has no history of committing offences while on bail; the dissimilarity between the present charge(s) and his or her previous offences; the amount of time that has elapsed since his or her last conviction; the fact that he or she has an address to stay at away from previous associates or has moved since the time of the alleged offence(s). Suggest possible conditions such as: a condition of residence, a curfew, restriction to/from a particular location.

Or, if the objection is that he or she is likely to interfere with witnesses: draw the court's attention to the fact that there is no suggestion the defendant has ever done so before; and/or that no threats or pressure are alleged to have been made/applied in this case; point to the lack of any close connection between the defendant and the witness (eg, family relationship, neighbour) that would enable him or her to influence the alleged victim/witness if he or she were released on bail. Suggest possible conditions such as: prohibiting the defendant from contacting or interfering with any witness; restricting his or her entry into the areas where the alleged victim/witness lives.

Or, if the objection is that the defendant is likely to abscond: highlight such matters as the fact that the defendant has never done so before; or explain the circumstances of any failure to appear in the past (eg, dates mixed up; went to the police/court as soon as he or she realised); and/or point to the fact that he or she has in the past attended court even where he or she has pleaded guilty or anticipated a custodial sentence; address the court upon the weaknesses in the prosecution case and/or the unlikelihood of a custodial sentence even if the defendant were to plead guilty/be convicted; emphasise the defendant's community ties, employment, secure home, family responsibilities as indicators of the unlikelihood of his or her absconding. Suggest possible conditions such as: (daily) reporting to the nearest police station; condition of residence; residence at a bail hostel; surrendering his or her passport; providing a surety; lodging security.

There are some cases where it is simply not possible to undermine the objections. If the defendant has a history of absconding, it is useless to argue that 'she has learned her lesson and has asked me to assure the court that she will not abscond again'. That will get you nowhere! If you cannot deal with the objection(s) in this way, be realistic about it. Concentrate your efforts upon persuading the court that there are (stringent) conditions which could be imposed to ensure the defendant's good behaviour and attendance at court.

Having dealt with the objections to bail, it may assist to point out the likely consequences of a continuing loss of liberty upon the defendant, eg, losing his or her job; mortgagee possession proceedings in respect of his or her home; children will be taken into care.

If you call any proposed surety, establish his or her relationship to the defendant; then ask questions designed to elicit that he or she understands the meaning of what he or she is proposing and the consequences if the defendant fails to attend the trial (eg, 'Do you understand that you will be liable to forfeit such a sum if the defendant absconds?'); establish the amount of money he or she is proposing to pledge and the manner in which he or she would raise that sum in the event of the defendant absconding (it should be otherwise than by selling/mortgaging his or her home, such as from savings in the building society), eg, 'Are you worth £x after all your debts are paid?'; 'How would you raise that sum if ordered to do so?'; confirm that he or she is still prepared to stand as a surety to ensure the defendant's surrender to bail (eg, 'Are you still prepared to stand surety in the sum of £x?').

If bail is granted, ensure your client understands the nature and extent of any conditions imposed and the likely consequences if he or she breaches them.

If bail is refused by the magistrates, obtain a copy of the magistrates' certificate recording their reasons for the refusal (see the Bail Act 1976, s 5(6A)). Consider with your client whether he or she wishes you to renew the application before the magistrates on the next or a subsequent court appearance or whether he or she wishes to appeal to a Crown Court judge for bail. You must know the procedure on the application itself and also that relating to appeal. Advise your client realistically of the prospects of such an appeal.

38.3 Procedure

Bail applications

The following diagram charts the procedure in a magistrates' court when the magistrates, having asked the defence whether there is an application for bail, receive an answer in the affirmative.

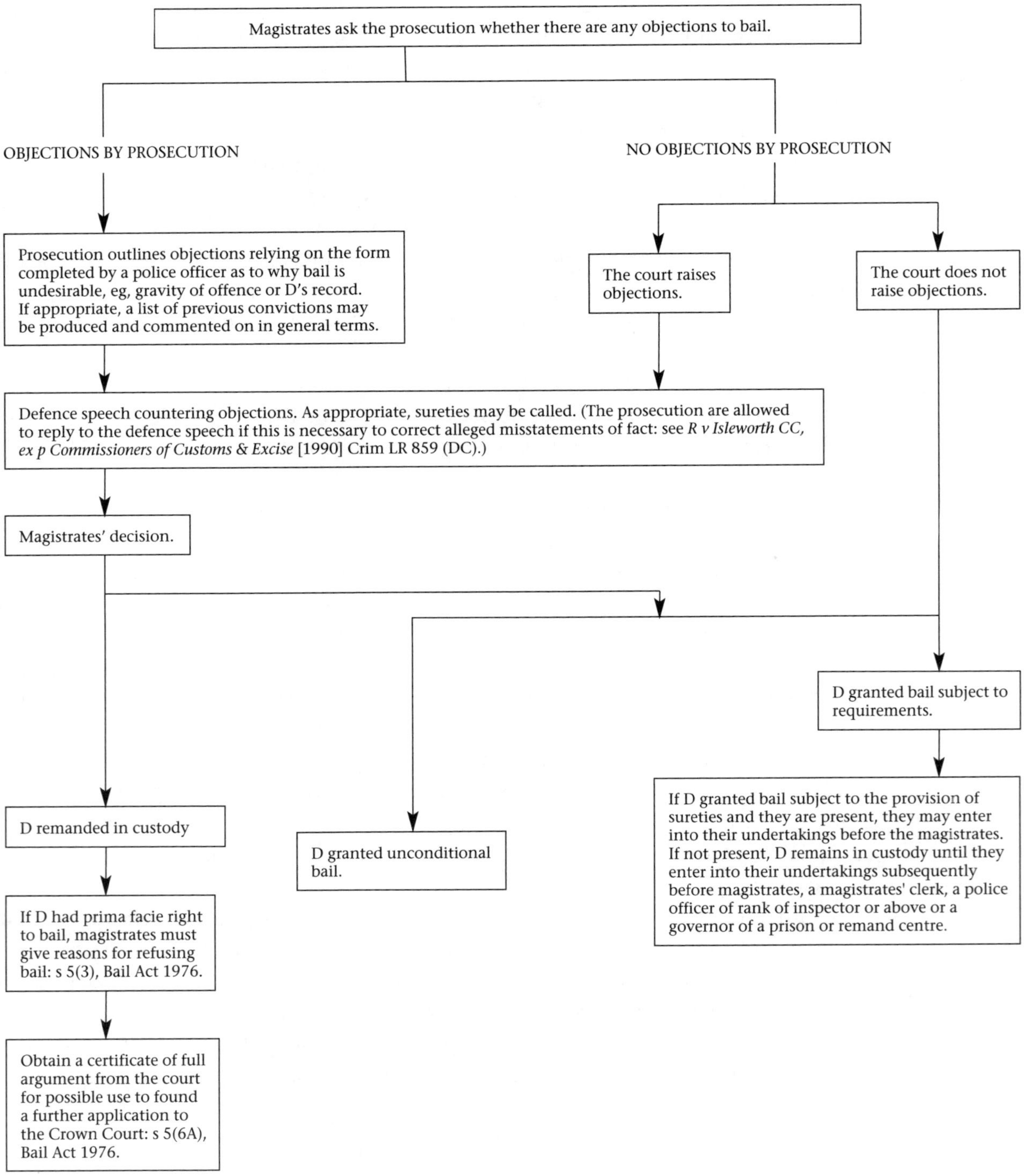

39

Conducting a 'trial within a trial'

39.1 Defence

If you are likely to require a 'trial within a trial' (also known as a 'voir dire') to challenge the admissibility of some part of the prosecution evidence in the Crown Court, you will probably have been aware of this before the start of the trial at the Plea and Case Management Hearing. The first thing to do is what you are being paid for—think. In particular, think about what you are trying to accomplish by challenging the evidence. The same good tactical reasons exist for not making an unfounded challenge to the evidence—juridical irritation and possible jury confusion—as exist for a submission. There is also the crucial point that if you put prosecution witnesses in the witness box on a trial within a trial, you may simply allow them to rehearse their evidence and so look better in front of the jury. Bear in mind that any witness is likely to be nervous when they give evidence for the first time and that as a general rule it is better that they appear nervous in front of the jury rather than in front of the judge. On the other hand, it may be a good idea to give your defendant a taste of giving evidence. As with a submission, tactics become much easier with experience, so don't be afraid to ask other barristers in your chambers/the robing room or whom you know socially for advice, provided you do so on an advocate-to-advocate basis.

Mark the witness statements clearly, showing which parts of the evidence you believe are inadmissible. See the prosecutor as soon as possible and tell him or her the parts of the evidence to which you object. This is essential because otherwise he or she may open the evidence to the jury (ie, refer to it in the opening speech). See if you can agree with the prosecutor that some or all of the evidence is not given—in nine cases out of ten you will be able to agree. For example, no prosecutor will (or should) seek to rely on evidence which is clearly inadmissible hearsay. Mark clearly those parts which remain in dispute after you have talked to your opponent.

Mark clearly for your own use the sections of the Police and Criminal Evidence Act 1984, *Archbold, Blackstone's Criminal Practice* and any other texts on which you rely (see eg *Blackstone's Criminal Practice*, 2009, D15.41–D15.49). Take two unmarked copies of the authorities with you to court. Give a copy to the prosecution and hand one in to the court clerk or associate in advance.

Explain to your client what you are going to do and why. Take instructions on whether or not you are going to call your client on the trial within a trial, remembering to explain that he or she can only give evidence on admissibility, not on guilt or innocence. Think about what you will do if the evidence is ruled admissible and make the decisions arising in advance. For example, try to decide in advance whether or not your client will give evidence in front of the jury.

Agree with the prosecutor the appropriate moment at which to raise the issue of admissibility. This will usually be when the relevant witness is about to give the disputed evidence. In any event, ask for the jury to retire in the same way as when making a submission, ie, 'Your Honour, there is a point of law I wish to raise in the absence of the jury', coupled with a sensible time estimate of how long the trial within a trial will last. As with a submission, err on the side of caution with your estimate. You cannot assume that all will go smoothly.

In conducting the trial within a trial remember to stick to the point of the exercise, which is solely the exclusion of the disputed evidence. Direct your questions to that issue only, and do not make 'jury points', such as minor inconsistencies between witnesses, to the judge. Not only will he or she be unimpressed but you will lose the element of surprise. Any appeal to the judge's supposed emotions is wasted—the judge is there only to consider a point of law.

Again, remember that you may not succeed in excluding the evidence and accordingly, try to keep questions in reserve to ask in front of the jury. If you can, plan a different line of cross-examination altogether, so as to retain at least some element of surprise, whether or not the evidence is excluded.

Make a list of the points that you wish to make to the judge. Either put these in reverse order of merit, or deal with your best points first and last. Both methods are acceptable and it is often a question of style which one you choose. Always remember that you are only concerned at this stage with admissibility. As much as possible, cross-reference your points to the authorities on which you rely. Do not be afraid to modify your list according to the evidence—for example, the absence of a caution being given may look like a fine point on the papers, but if the police say that they gave one and forgot to write it down, be prepared to embarrass them in front of the jury rather than bang on about it before the judge—be flexible and think tactically.

A judge will usually make it plain whether or not he or she has taken your point. If he or she has, do not belabour it but move onto the next point.

When you have run out of things to say, stop talking.

If at any stage you need time to take instructions or simply to think about your next move, then request it.

39.2 Prosecution

It is always a good plan to put yourself in the position of the defence and accordingly try to anticipate likely challenges to admissibility. If you see a likely trial within a trial on the papers, then plan your response in the same way—set out your arguments, mark the statements, flag and photocopy authorities.

Always ask the defence before a trial whether they object to your opening any part of the evidence. Try to agree with the defence what parts of the evidence are inadmissible. Make sure that you do not open those parts or allow your witnesses to refer to them.

There may be cases where you cannot open the facts to the jury without the disputed evidence—for example where the only evidence is a confession which the defence says is inadmissible. If so, ask for the jury to retire as soon as they are empanelled and tell the judge why. Give the best time estimate you can as soon as you can.

Remember, in conducting the trial within a trial, you may not cross-examine the defendant on the truth of the evidence—do not ask if the disputed confession was true! As with the defence, keep your questions and submissions brief and to the point, and if you cannot think of anything more to say, sit down.

39.3 Checklist

For the **defence**:

- Think about tactics and what you are trying to achieve by challenging the admissibility of the evidence. Plan your attack accordingly. Mark those parts of the evidence you object to.
- Mark all authorities and take photocopies where required.
- Discuss your plan with your client. Decide what you will do if the evidence is ruled admissible.
- Tell the prosecutor which parts of the evidence you object to and disclose any authorities to him or her.
- When the prosecution are about to put in the disputed evidence, ask for the jury to retire.
- In conducting the trial within a trial, be brief and keep to the point. Remember that you may fail, and so try to keep something in reserve.

For the **prosecution**:

- Think about likely questions of admissibility and mark the statements accordingly.
- If you have the chance, mark all authorities and take photocopies.
- Ask your opponent if he or she objects to any part of the evidence being opened. If you need to, ask for the jury to retire after being empanelled.
- In conducting the trial within a trial, concentrate solely on admissibility and be as concise as possible.
- If evidence is ruled inadmissible and you need time to consider your next move, request it.

39.4 The trial within a trial

The most common example of a trial within a trial is where the defence considers, or the judge questions, whether a confession upon which the prosecution seeks to rely is inadmissible. The procedure in such cases is as follows:

At the plea and case management hearing or immediately before the trial, defence counsel informs the prosecution that he or she intends to object to the admission of the confession.

At the trial the judge exercises his or her discretion to raise the issue of the admissibility of the confession.

If the prosecution case depends wholly or largely on the confession and therefore they cannot sensibly open their case without referring to it, the issue is raised immediately after the jury is empanelled. N.B.: If subsequently the judge rules the confession inadmissible, the prosecution will often offer no evidence.

If the prosecution case does not depend wholly or largely on the confession, counsel for the prosecution makes no reference to it in his or her opening speech and at that point in the trial when he or she would otherwise have adduced evidence of it, indicates to the judge that a point of law has arisen which does not concern the jury.

↓

The judge requests the jury to retire to their room: see *R v Davis* [1990] Crim LR 860 (CA).

↓

Defence counsel represents that, or the judge questions whether, the confession was or may have been obtained by oppression or in consequence of anything said or done likely to render unreliable any confession which might be made in consequence thereof: Police and Criminal Evidence Act 1984, s 76(2) and (3).

↓

The prosecution call the person(s) to whom the confession was made, typically an officer (and any other person who can give relevant evidence on the question of admissibility), to give evidence on a special form of oath known as a *voir dire*. The officer will give evidence of the circumstances in which the confession was made. If there is a contemporaneous note of the interview (containing the confession) signed by the accused (or transcript of a tape recording or visual recording with sound of an interview), it will be produced before the judge. Defence counsel may cross-examine.

↓

The accused (and any other person who can give relevant evidence) may then be called and cross-examined. N.B.: The accused should not be asked if the confession was true: PACE 1984, s 76(2).

↓

Submissions by counsel on the question of admissibility.

↓

The judge gives his or her decision on the evidence heard and the question of admissibility (PACE 1984, ss 76 and 78) and recalls the jury.

↓

Confession ruled inadmissible: the prosecution continue with their case, without referring to the confession, or offer no evidence – see above.

Confession ruled admissible: prosecution adduce evidence of the confession.

↓

Defence counsel may cross-examine the prosecution witness(es) to whom the confession was made and adduce evidence with a view to reducing the weight to be attached to the confession by the jury.

39.5 Example of a trial within a trial in *R v Lewis and others*

IN THE CROWN COURT SITTING AT LEWES

R v Lewis and others

Instructions to counsel for the prosecution

Counsel has herewith:

1. Bundle of witness statements
2. Antecedent history of the accused

Counsel is instructed:

(i) to prosecute in this matter and

(ii) to settle the appropriate indictment.

Case Summary

On 17.4.09 a branch of the South Downs Building Society was held up at gunpoint by two masked men. One kept watch by the door, observing both the people inside the branch and passers-by. The other demanded money from a cashier. On obtaining a hold-all containing £15,967, the two men fled on foot. They were pursued by a passer-by and one of the men stopped and shot the pursuer, a Mr Goodbody. They then made good their escape, using a car parked nearby.

The prosecution case theory is that three of the accused, namely Lewis, Duke and Ella, were involved in the actual robbery with Ella as the driver of the escape vehicle, a stolen Audi motor vehicle. The fourth accused, Peterson, stored the vehicle in his garage for several days prior to the robbery.

Original charge

Against Finlay LEWIS, Arthur DUKE, Gerald ELLA and Leonard PETERSON.

You are charged that, on the 17th day of April 2009, you did rob Mary Penny of £15,967, contrary to the Theft Act 1968, s 8(1).

STATEMENT OF WITNESS

Statement of: Mary Penny

Age: Over 18

Occupation: Building society cashier

[Usual declaration omitted]

Dated: 4th May 2009

Signed by: *M. Penny* Signature witnessed by: *D. Law DS 494P*

I am a cashier for the South Downs Building Society. I work in the Churchill Square Branch. I have been there for about 4 years.

I remember the 17th of April 2009. I was at work that morning. At about 10 am two men entered the branch. Both were wearing dark-coloured donkey jackets which had orange fluorescent material on the top half. They had on dark balaclava helmets with 'Porky Pig' masks. They were both carrying what looked like sawn-off shotguns.

One of the men shouted for everyone to get on the floor. There was some screaming and the same man shouted to shut up.

He came to my window and said 'fill this with money and nobody will get hurt'.

He produced a nylon holdall and passed it through the window. I looked at the manager who indicated that I should do as the man asked.

I emptied the contents of the tills into the bag. This was both cash and cheques. Then I gave it back to the man at the counter.

All this time the other man had just stood by the entrance door, pointing his gun at the staff and customers.

The man with the holdall joined the other one by the door. One of them shouted 'Nobody move and you won't get hurt' and they both ran out. I think it was the man with the holdall who shouted.

I had pressed the silent alarm as the man approached my window and about two minutes after the men left, several police officers arrived.

I would describe the man with the holdall as about 6 feet tall and medium build. His voice was unusual. He had an accent. Irish is how I would describe it.

I saw his hands when he gave me the bag—they were white.

On the 26th of April I attended an identification parade at Brighton Police Station where I saw a number of men. They all looked about the same height and build as the man with the holdall.

They each said the words 'fill this with money and nobody will get hurt'. I picked out the 5th man. I am sure he was the man with the holdall.

I did not get a good look at the second man. I think he was about 2 inches shorter than the other one, again medium build. I would not recognise him again.

The whole incident lasted for about 5 minutes.

I did not see the face of either man. I did not see their hair, they were both wearing balaclava helmets. Their jackets were not tight on them. They could have been slimmer than medium build.

I saw no distinctive features on either man. The voice was distinctive.

I would call it Irish. I have no Irish relations or friends. I have not been to Ireland on holiday. I have never been to Scotland.

I can recall the voice of the man with the holdall. I am sure that the man I picked out at the identification parade had the same voice. I am not mistaken. I am not an expert on voices or regional accents.

Signed by: *M. Penny* Signature witnessed by: *D. Law DS*

STATEMENT OF WITNESS

Statement of: Reginald Goodbody

Age: Over 18

Occupation: Retired grocer

[Usual declaration omitted]

Dated: 30th May 2009

Signed by: *R. Goodbody* Signature witnessed by: *D. Law DS 494P*

On 17.4.09 I was in Brighton, to do some shopping, my wife was with me.

We started looking around the shops in Churchill Square. Just after 10 o'clock we were going past a small parade of shops when two men ran out of the South Downs Building Society premises there. I was about 20 yards away from them. They ran towards me and my wife. They had a bag and guns. They were wearing balaclava helmets. They had workmen's jackets on—black I think, with orange patches.

I realised they had robbed the Building Society and I put up my arms to try and stop them. One got past me but I caught hold of the bag that the other one was carrying.

We got into a bit of a struggle over the bag. I think people were coming out of the Building Society by now.

The other man ran back and shouted at me to let go. When I said No, he deliberately took aim and fired. He shot me in the leg with his gun. I fell over and let go of the bag. Both of them ran off.

The one I was struggling with was about my height and build. I am 6 feet tall and weigh about 13 stone. The other one was about the same. I can't recall him clearly. I would not recognise either of them again. Their features were quite obscured by their helmets.

I went to hospital in an ambulance with my wife. It was the Royal Sussex Hospital in Brighton. I was there for 8 days. My leg was badly damaged by the shot from the gun. I lost some blood and quite a bit of muscle and flesh in my calf.

I now have to walk with a stick. I find my mobility is very restricted. I attend the hospital physiotherapy department every week to build my leg up.

The one with the bag shot me. The gun did not go off in the struggle—I am quite sure.

Signed by: *R. Goodbody* Signature witnessed by: *D. Law DS*

STATEMENT OF WITNESS

Statement of: Brenda BROWSE

Age: Over 18

Occupation: Housekeeper

[Usual declaration omitted]

Dated: 11th May 2009

Signed by: *B. Browse* Signature witnessed by: *D. Law DS 494P*

On the 17th of April 2009 I left my home to meet a friend in Brighton. We had arranged to meet by the Oxfam shop, just along the road from Churchill Square. I got there early, at about 9.30 am. There were several cars parked around the area but I did not take any notice of them. I went to a cafe over the road for a cup of tea.

While I was in the cafe, I could see the road ahead—Mountfort Road. There was a dark blue Audi parked there with a man sitting behind the wheel. The car was there the whole time I was in the cafe. At about 10 o'clock, as I was about to leave, two men came running along the road, shouting something. The man in the car started the engine and the two men leaped into the car. It tore off down the road, towards the junction by the cafe and straight over without waiting to see if anyone was crossing the road.

I was astonished by this behaviour and made a note of the car registration number. It was EF02 JPO.

I would not recognise the two men who jumped into the car again but both were wearing workmen's jackets with orange fluorescent patches like Council workmen wear. I think they both had dark hair.

The man in the car was quite slim with dark wavy hair, fair-skinned and in his early twenties. I would recognise him again.

I am willing to attend court to give evidence.

Signed by: *B. Browse* Signature witnessed by: *D. Law DS*

STATEMENT OF WITNESS

Statement of: Brenda BROWSE

Age: Over 18

Occupation: Housekeeper

Dated: 15th May 2009

Further to my statement of 11th May 2009, on the 15th of May 2009 I was asked to attend Brighton Police Station. I was met by Inspector Charger who explained that there was going to be a parade where the man I saw in the Audi might be. He explained that the man might not be there and I was to look at all of the men very carefully. He said only if I was sure I saw the same man, I should stop and point him out.

I was escorted into a waiting room by a WPC and eventually taken to a larger room with several men lined up against one wall. I went to one end of the line and walked along it. The seventh man was the one I had seen driving the Audi on the 17th of April. I was quite sure and I pointed him out. He did not do anything. The Inspector asked me to leave the room as the parade was now over.

I was then brought to a room where I wrote this statement.

Signed by: *B. Browse* Signature witnessed by: *D. Law DS*

STATEMENT OF WITNESS

Statement of: David LAW

Age: Over 18

Occupation: Detective Sergeant 494P, Brighton CID

[Usual declaration omitted]

Dated: 18th May 2009

Signed by: *D. Law* Signature witnessed by: *A. Libby, DC 675P*

On 17th April 2009 at 12.10 pm, as a result of information received, I went to 33 Dials Lane in Brighton where I found a navy blue Audi which appeared to have been abandoned in a hurry. The doors were wide open. Under the driver's seat were some shotgun cartridges. The registration number of the vehicle was EF02 JPO.

I had reason to believe that this vehicle had been used in an armed robbery which had occurred earlier that day in Brighton and I requested that a Scenes of Crime Officer attend the location in Dials Lane.

On 11th May 2009, I went to a private house at 72 Power Station Row, Southwick. The door was opened by a woman who identified herself as Sharon Ella. I asked her if I could speak to Gerald Ella—she replied that he was not in. Subsequently, I attended the rear of the house where colleagues had apprehended Gerald ELLA, while he was climbing over a fence in the garden of number 72.

I said to him, 'Are you Gerald Ella?' He replied, 'What if I am?' I said to him, 'I have reason to believe you were involved in an armed robbery on the South Downs Building Society in Brighton on the 17th of April, specifically as the driver of the getaway vehicle.' He replied, 'You've got a very good imagination for a copper'.

I then told him that his fingerprints had been identified on the getaway vehicle, the navy blue Audi. He seemed to be about to fall down so I grabbed him and said, 'I am arresting you for your part in the South Downs robbery on the 17th of April 2009. You do not have to say anything. But it may harm your defence if you do not mention when questioned something which you later rely on in court. Anything you do say may be given in evidence.' He made no reply and was taken to Brighton Central Police Station under escort.

He was later seen by myself and DC Libby in an interview room at Brighton Central at 10.25 pm on the 11th. He was reminded of the caution and I then asked him if he was prepared to talk to us about the robbery. He indicated that he did not wish to talk to us and he was returned to his cell at 10.28 pm.

I was present at 7.35 am on the 12th of May 2009 when ELLA was charged with robbery, the charge was read over to him, he was cautioned and made no reply.

At 2.40 pm on the 12th of May I interviewed Arthur DUKE at Brighton Central Police Station where he was in custody. The interview was tape-recorded and concluded at 3.02 pm.

At 6.00 am on the 13th of May 2009 I went to 22 Bramber Street, Brighton. There I saw a man I now know to be Finlay LEWIS. I said to him, 'Are you Finlay Lewis?' He said, 'Yes, why?' I told him that he had been implicated in the robbery of the South Downs Building Society in Brighton and he replied, 'Someone's a grass. I'm saying nothing till I see my solicitor.'

After a brief search of the premises, I told LEWIS that he was under arrest for robbery and cautioned him. He replied 'I'll be wanting a word with my solicitor.' He was then taken to Brighton Central Police Station and booked into a cell.

I saw LEWIS again at 2.10 pm that day in the interview room, together with DC Libby. The interview was tape-recorded and ended at 2.25 pm.

At 4.45 pm on the 13th of May 2009 LEWIS was charged with robbery, the charge was read over to him, he was cautioned and made no reply.

Signed by: *D. Law* Signature witnessed by: *A. Libby*

STATEMENT OF WITNESS

Statement of: Alan LIBBY

Age: Over 18

Occupation: Detective Constable 675P, Brighton CID

[Usual declaration omitted]

Dated: 18th May 2009

Signed by: *A. Libby* Signature witnessed by: *V. Worthy PS 11 1P*

At 6.00 am on the 12th of May 2009, I went to a private flat at 344 Lewes Road, Brighton, together with several other officers. The door was answered by a man I now know as Arthur DUKE. I said to DUKE, 'I have reason to believe that you were involved in an armed robbery last month on a Brighton building society. Have you got anything to say?' He replied, 'You've got the wrong man this time.' I asked if we could look round his flat and he said 'Yes'.

On the floor of a wardrobe in the bedroom I found a balaclava helmet. A shoebox in the same wardrobe contained six shotgun cartridges. Hanging in the wardrobe was a navy-blue donkey jacket with an orange fluorescent upper half. I said to DUKE, 'Where did you get this jacket?' He said, 'I've had it for a while now. I wear it if I get any building-site work.' I then showed him the balaclava and cartridges and said, 'How do you explain these then?' He did not reply.

I said, 'I am arresting you for robbing the South Downs Building Society in Brighton on the 17th of April this year.' I cautioned him and he made no reply. He was taken to Brighton Central Police Station.

At 2.40 pm on the same day, I was present when DS Law interviewed DUKE at Brighton Central Police Station. The interview was tape-recorded. I produce the master tape as exhibit AL/1 and the record of the taped interview (ROT I) as AL/2.

At 5.25 pm on the 12th May 2009 DUKE was charged with robbery, the charge was read over, he was cautioned and made no reply.

On the 12th of May at 10.50 pm, I went to 65 Brighthelmstone Street where I saw a man I now know to be Leonard PETERSON. I said to him, 'Are you Lennie Peterson?' He said, 'That's right. Who are you?' I showed him my warrant card and explained that I was investigating the robbery of the South Downs Building Society.

I said, 'I have reason to believe that you garaged the car for the gang before the robbery. What have you got to say?' He said, 'I know nothing about it.' I said, 'It's right that you've got a lock-up garage at the back of the house, isn't it. That's where the car was kept.' He replied, 'Who's been talking out of turn?'

I said, 'The car was stolen on the 10th of April—that's a week before the robbery. It had to be kept somewhere, out of sight. I think you warehoused it for the gang. For all I know, you stole it, too.' He said, 'Look, I'm no car thief. Gerry ELLA asked me to keep it safe for him until he needed it. He brought it round on the 10th and took it away on the 17th. That's all I know.'

I told him he was being arrested for the robbery and cautioned him. He made no reply and was then taken to Brighton Central Police Station.

At 7.30 pm on the 13th of May 2009 at Brighton Central Police Station PETERSON was charged with robbery, the charge was read over to him, he was cautioned and replied, 'I've been very silly and it's all for nothing. What can I say?'

On the 13th of May at 2.10 pm, I attended an interview of Finlay LEWIS by DS Law in an interrogation room at Brighton Central Police Station. The interview was tape-recorded and I produce the master tape as exhibit AL/3 and the record of the taped interview (ROT I) as AL/4

Signed by: *A. Libby* Signature witnessed by: *V. Worthy*

Extracts from record of taped interview of Arthur Duke by DS LAW, produced by DC Libby (AL/2): —

Q. Do you want us to wait for your lawyer?

A. No, let's get it over.

Q. As I mentioned on the way here, we've found some fingerprints on the Audi and it looks like they are yours.

A. Oh yeah?

Q. I'm serious. Those prints place you in the car. Take them together with what we found in your home . . .

A. All right. It was never meant to end up the way it did.

Q. What do you mean?

A. The old man. Finlay's always been stupid but that tops the lot.

Q. So it was Finlay that shot Mr Goodbody?

A. Yes.

Q. Is that Finlay LEWIS?

A. Yes. I should never have agreed to take part in it. Finlay had it all set up before I got invited. His original partner had to drop out—he's on remand in Brixton at the moment.

. . .

A. Finlay had Gerry ELLA and Len PETERSON lined up. He knew Gerry from Wandsworth and Len was a friend of Gerry's.

. . .

A. I kept watch while Finlay played the hard man with the cashier. Everything went smooth as silk until the old man grabbed Finlay's bag. I couldn't believe what they were doing. Just as I went back to help, Finlay's gun went off and the old boy went down. I don't know whether it was an accident or not.

Extracts from record of taped interview of Finlay LEWIS by DS Law, produced by DC Libby (AL/4):—

Q. I am refusing to delay this interview so that you can have your solicitor present because I believe that delay may prevent recovery of the stolen money.

A. No reply.

...

Q. . . . First, I must remind you that you are under caution . . .

Q. This was a very serious offence. I tell you now—I'm more worried about the guy that got shot than the money. Have you got anything you want to say?

A. No reply.

Q. Look I'll be straight with you. We've got a confession from Arthur and he's dropped you right in it.

A. I don't believe you.

Q. Listen to this. (Plays part of Duke's interview.)

A. Well, it seems like you know it all. Why bother talking to me?

Q. We need to get your side of things, to see how everything fits together.

A. There's no point in holding back now—so much for honour among thieves. It was Arthur's idea—he's planned it for weeks before he spoke to me. We decided that we needed a driver and I knew Gerry from our time in Wandsworth.

Q. You mean Gerry ELLA and HMP Wandsworth in South London?

A. That's right.

. . .

Q. Who got the car?

A. That's down to Gerry. I don't know where it came from—he just got it for the day. The first time I saw it was when I got in it after the job.

Q. Who did what in the shop?

A. I asked for the cash while Arthur kept everyone calm.

Q. With a sawn-off?

A. You don't want heroes in a situation like that.

Q. Like Reg Goodbody?

A. Is he the old boy? He never should have interfered. He got what was coming to him.

Q. From you?

A. No way. That was Arthur. I could have got the bag away from the old man but Arthur got impatient with him.

. . .

Q. So where's the money now?

A. Money? That's rich. Lots of it was cheques. The rest, well, I'll need a nest egg for when I get out, eh?

Q. So you won't tell me where it is?

A. No reply;

. . .

Summaries of the antecedent histories of the accused men:—

Finlay LEWIS (Age 40) Born Stornoway, Outer Hebrides.

18 previous convictions including 2 for wounding (s 18 OAPA) and 3 for armed robbery. Last conviction was at Portsmouth Crown Court for robbery in May 2002. Sentenced to 10 years' imprisonment. Released June 2008.

Arthur DUKE (Age 43) Born Catford, London.

8 previous convictions, mainly for offences of dishonesty, 1 recorded for robbery. Last conviction was at Winchester Crown Court in February 2003 for a fraud on the Department of Social Security. Sentenced to 6 years' imprisonment. Released April 2007.

Gerald ELLA (Age 26) Born Worthing, West Sussex.

6 previous convictions, all for theft of cars, except the last one. In 2001 a 3-year term of imprisonment was imposed by Inner London Crown Court. In September last year, Brighton Magistrates' Court fined him £250 and banned him from driving for 1 year for driving while unfit through drink or drugs.

Leonard PETERSON (Age 55) Born Brighton.

16 previous convictions, all for petty offences of dishonesty. Imprisonment has been ordered in the past, but the last conviction was in 1992 and resulted in a conditional discharge.

At the trial of Lewis and Duke on charges of robbery and wounding with intent, Miss Vaughan, counsel for the prosecution, addresses the judge:

Miss Vaughan: Your Honour, at this stage there has arisen a matter of law which need not trouble the jury.

His Honour: Members of the jury, counsel and I will be spending some time discussing matters of law and I would therefore ask you to retire to your room while these discussions take place.

The jury then retire.

Trial within a trial (on Duke's interview):

DS Law is called and gives evidence-in-chief that he interviewed Duke and that a record was made.

Miss Vaughan: What did you actually say to Mr Duke regarding the fingerprints?

DS Law: I told Duke that we had his fingerprints from the Audi.

Miss Vaughan: What reason did you have for telling him this?

DS Law: At that time I thought that there was a strong possibility that some of the prints we found might belong to Duke.

Miss Vaughan: Can you assist by stating at what stage you became aware of the result of any checks made regarding the fingerprints?

DS Law: Some time after that interview occurred, I was informed by our forensic laboratory that none of the prints taken from the car matched Duke's fingerprints.

Miss Vaughan: Please wait there, officer, there may be some questions from Counsel for the defence.

Cross-examination of DS Law by Mr Good, counsel for defence.

Mr Good: At the time when you told Duke you had his fingerprints, you knew very well that that was not true, didn't you?

DS Law: When I told Duke we had his prints, I genuinely thought that was the case.

Mr Good: It was in fact a deliberate lie which you had told, wasn't it?

DS Law: It was not a deliberate lie.

Mr Good: You needed to lie because you had no evidence against Mr Duke, had you?

DS Law: I didn't need to lie, he knew what we'd found at his place.

Mr Good: Would you not agree that your conduct could be described as a deliberate deceit of my client?

DS Law: I would describe it as unfortunate, that's all.

Summary of defence submissions

Mr Good submits that DS Law obtained the confession by deceit, as he had deliberately lied to Duke about the fingerprints, knowing full well that they were not Duke's; that the officer needed to lie to obtain a confession, as there was no direct evidence against the defendant; that the evidence ought to be excluded under s 76(2)(b) of the Police and Criminal Evidence Act 1984 (PACE) as the prosecution had not proved beyond reasonable doubt that the confession was not obtained in consequence of anything said or done which was likely to render unreliable the confession obtained; that alternatively, the confession should be excluded under s 78 of PACE as the admission of the evidence would have such an adverse effect on the fairness of the proceedings that the court ought not to admit it.

Summary of the prosecution submissions

Miss Vaughan submits that DS Law did not lie to the defendant; that he genuinely, albeit mistakenly, believed that the fingerprints were Duke's; that the prosecution had proved beyond reasonable doubt that the confession was not obtained in consequence of anything said or done which was likely to render it unreliable; and that alternatively, the confession should not be excluded under s 78 of PACE, as the admission of the evidence would not have an adverse effect on the fairness of the proceedings.

The defence then replies and the judge delivers a reasoned ruling.

40

Making a submission of no case to answer

40.1 Defence

Whether in the magistrates' court or the Crown Court, you should have some idea in advance as to whether or not you will be making a submission of no case to answer for the defence. This will be based on the papers rather than the evidence. The following guide is written on the premise that you have some time to prepare the submission. On occasion you may wish to make a submission at short or no notice because, for example, the prosecution witnesses have not come up to proof. Usually, you will find that you can deal with the matter on your feet (without authorities or extensive preparation), but if you need time to prepare, request it. Most judges, district judges or magistrates will be sympathetic if you have been taken by surprise, and there is no point in making a muddled or flustered effort which will do neither you nor your client justice. The court will probably give you up to about 15 minutes.

Always think about whether or not you should make a submission. As a general rule, in case of doubt—have a go, but bear in mind that there are good reasons **not** to make an ill-founded submission, especially in the Crown Court. It is never wise to irritate the judge unnecessarily, and if your submission is hopeless (known in the trade as a 'try-on') he or she will assuredly be irritated. Also, jurors who have already sat on at least one trial may guess why they are asked to leave court, and there is a danger that they will draw an adverse conclusion if the submission fails. In other words, 'Well, if the judge thinks there's such a good case against them . . .'.

All that having been said, if in doubt, make the submission. The decision is a question of judgement that will become much easier with experience.

40.2 Prosecution

In responding to a submission, remember what you are there for—you are not there to obtain a conviction at all costs, but to put the case for the Crown fairly. If the submission is a good one in your opinion, then be prepared to say so, or indeed to save the defence the trouble by saying to the court that you cannot ask for a conviction on the evidence. For example, if your only identification witness describes the perpetrator as a four foot six inch, red-headed man and the defendant is a six foot tall and bald man, then do not tell the judge that this is a question of fact for the jury to decide—give in gracefully.

40.3 Organising the case

Whether prosecuting or defending in whatever court, organisation of your case is crucial. If you can, have all authorities flagged and marked for your own benefit. It is a good idea to have *Turnbull* [1977] QB 224, *Galbraith* [1981] 1 WLR 1039, *R v Shippey* [1988] Crim LR 767 and the criteria in *Archbold* and *Blackstone's Criminal Practice* flagged, whatever the case (see eg *Blackstone's Criminal Practice*, 2009, D15.51–D15.67). Obtaining copies of *Galbraith* and *Turnbull* in full is also a good investment. If you have prior notice and intend to rely on case authority and/or texts then, in the magistrates' court, if the authorities are in anything other than *Archbold, Blackstone's Criminal Practice* or *Stone's Justices' Manual,* take at least two photocopies—one for your opponent and one for the clerk to the justices or court legal adviser. It is a good idea to provide the bench with copies as well. Do not mark these copies. Hand them in when you make the point arising from the authorities and read from the authorities yourself.

In the Crown Court there may be a more extensive library for the judges with at least the *All England Law Reports* and *Criminal Appeal Reports,* but it is still a good idea to come armed with your own photocopies. Certainly, if the report or texts that you intend to rely on are at all obscure, you should try to get copies for the judge and your opponent; failing which, take photocopies. In any event, take your authorities with you. Hand the copies into the court clerk as soon as you can, flagged at the appropriate points. All of this will save time and is likely to make the court more disposed to listen to what you have to say.

You may well decide to make a submission of no case upon reading the papers in advance of trial or committal. In such cases a skeleton argument should be prepared, served on the prosecution and filed at court in advance of the hearing.

40.3.1 Structuring your submission

If you have time, write down the points you intend to make for your own benefit either in reverse order of merit or by listing your best points first and last. Always try to end your submission with a strong point so that it sticks in the minds of the tribunal. Conversely, if you are responding to a submission, deal with your opponent's best points first and his worst point last, for the same reason. Sometimes this may not be possible because of the need to go through the evidence chronologically, but always bear in mind that you should try to end on an upbeat note, with a point in which you have confidence.

In the Crown Court, submissions are to be made in the absence of the jury, so you will ask for the jury to go out. An acceptable form of words is 'Your Honour, there is a matter of law arising which would be more conveniently dealt with in the absence of the jury'. A less pompous way of putting it can be 'Your Honour, there is a matter of law I wish to raise; perhaps this would be a good time for the jury to have a break for refreshments'. This may also help to ingratiate you with the jury, if you can carry it off.

It will help all concerned if you can give a realistic time estimate at this stage, such as, 'The matter will probably take five minutes/hours/days'. Err on the side of caution, as submissions have a habit of expanding themselves no matter how brief you intend to be.

40.3.2 The client

Apply your mind in advance to what you are going to do if the submission fails in whole or in part. If it does fail, you are likely to be faced with what I think is the most difficult decision you have to make as an advocate: whether or not to call your client to give evidence. Remember that a submission you are certain will succeed may still fail. Calling your client will depend on the circumstances of the case, but you do not want to make the decision on your feet if you can possibly avoid it. At the end of the day, if you are completely confident that you have made a good submission and there genuinely is no case to answer, then it may be that the proper course is not to call the defendant. This is, of course, subject to clear and informed instructions from the defendant.

Note: you must explain all this in advance in plain English to your client and get his or her instructions on giving evidence. In the end, it is the client's decision as to whether or not he or she will give evidence. You can only advise him or her—the client is not obliged to take your advice. In a marginal case (eg, your instructions say the client will testify and he or she then decides not to), have the client sign your brief with a note saying, 'I have had the advantages and disadvantages of giving evidence explained to me and I do/do not wish to give evidence'.

40.3.3 The tribunal

Adapt your submission or response to a submission to the tribunal you are addressing. Lecturing a Crown Court judge or a district judge on the burden or standard of proof will lessen his or her respect for your judgment and may affect his or her view of your best points. It is also likely to irritate. On the other hand, you may be faced with lay justices who feel that they 'want to hear more'. As a general rule, in the Crown Court or before a district judge, be as brief as you can. Before lay justices in the magistrates' court, start from first principles and build your submission up stage by stage.

40.3.4 Responding to a submission

On the prosecution side, you are likely to have less time to prepare your response to a submission. If your opponent tells you that he or she is making a submission, ask him or her if he or she has any authorities on which he or she wants to rely and if he or she has copies. If so, ask to read them. Again, keeping *Galbraith* and *Turnbull* with you is a good investment. Prepare a skeleton argument and serve and file it in response to your opponent's skeleton.

40.4 Checklist

For the **defence**:

- Think about whether or not to make a submission.
- After doing any necessary research, write a rough list of your points in one of the ways suggested above.
- Where appropriate, prepare, serve and file a skeleton argument in advance of the hearing.
- Think about what you intend to do if the submission fails.
- Take instructions from your client—explain clearly what you are going to do and discuss whether or not he or she will give evidence.
- If possible, have all texts and authorities on which you intend to rely marked clearly.

- Take photocopies of all such texts ready to hand into the court. You will need at least two of each—one for the court, one for your opponent.
- Modify your list of points based on the evidence.
- In the Crown Court, ask for the jury to go out while you make the submission. Give a realistic time estimate.
- If you need time to prepare, **request it.**
- Provide your opponent with copies of your own authorities and references and hand the other copies into the court.
- Make your submission—remember, no jury speeches at this stage and modify your submission according to the court. Refer clearly to any authorities on which you rely.
- If your submission succeeds, good. If not, then if you need time to consider your next step, **request it.**

For the **prosecution** if you think there is likely to be a submission of no case:

- Consider whether you should oppose it.
- If you decide to oppose it, write a list of your points in one of the ways suggested above.
- Prepare a skeleton argument in response, serve and file.
- Mark all the authorities on which you intend to rely and take photocopies.
- Revise your list of points according to the evidence.
- If you need time to consider your response, **request it.**
- Disclose all authorities to your opponent and give him or her copies. Hand in your other copies into the court.

40.5 Procedure on submission of no case to answer (jury trial)

(a) Defence counsel indicates that there is a matter of law to be decided in the absence of the jury.

(b) The judge asks the jury to retire.

(c) Defence counsel outlines the submission, citing appropriate authorities. It is usually argued that the case should not proceed as there is either no evidence of an essential element of the case, or the evidence taken at its highest is so tenuous that a jury properly directed could not convict on it: *R v Galbraith* [1981] 1 WLR 1039.

(d) Prosecuting counsel responds to the submission.

(e) Defence counsel replies.

(f) The judge delivers a reasoned ruling.

41

Prosecuting a plea of guilty in the Crown Court

41.1 Preparatory steps

(a) Ensure you have a copy of the indictment. This is often settled after the brief has been sent to counsel and can therefore be missing from the brief.

(b) If the defendant is in breach of any sentence, such as a suspended sentence of imprisonment, conditional discharge or probation order imposed on an earlier occasion, ensure you have details of the original offence(s) in respect of which such sentence was imposed.

(c) If there are other offences to be taken into consideration (TICs), ensure the appropriate form has been prepared (this is normally done by the officer in charge of the case) and signed by the defendant. A copy of this form should be handed to the clerk of the court before the case is called on for hearing.

(d) Ensure you have an up-to-date copy of the defendant's antecedents. The court and defence counsel should also have copies in advance of the trial/listed plea. You will be required to give the antecedent information to the court (see below).

(e) Obtain instructions from the CPS representative at court as to the amount of any costs order you should seek.

41.2 The hearing

(a) This may be a plea and case management hearing (PCMH) or the case may have been listed for a trial, following not guilty pleas entered at a PCMH. The defendant will be arraigned and plead guilty to some or all of the counts on the indictment. If you are instructed to proceed with the other counts, it will be necessary to empanel a jury to try those matters. If the plea to some of the counts is acceptable, introduce yourself and your opponent to the court and inform the judge either that you are instructed to offer no evidence on the other matters or invite the judge to leave such matters 'on the court file'. Then proceed to stage (b) below. If the defendant pleads guilty to all the counts on the indictment, start by introducing yourself and your opponent.

(b) Briefly outline the facts of the offences. The judge is likely to have read the committal papers in any event. There is no need to go into great detail, simply deal with the salient facts either in a chronological or the most convenient order. This usually involves a summary of the way in which each offence was committed, any aggravating or mitigating features, the amount of any money or the nature of any injury involved, brief details of the arrest, the defendant's response to the arrest/charge, any important replies during an interview and acknowledging, where appropriate, that the defendant frankly admitted his or her guilt or cooperated with the police.

(c) If there are any TICs (offences which the defendant asks the court to 'take into consideration' when passing sentence), it is normal to mention this to the judge either before or when dealing with the brief facts. The judge will have or be given a copy of a schedule of the TICs by the clerk. Either the judge or the clerk (at his or her direction) will read out the offences and ask the defendant if he or she admits each of the offences and wants them taken into consideration when sentence is passed. As soon as the defendant confirms that this is the case, deal **briefly** with these other offences. It is usual to deal with them together, for example, by mentioning the fact that they are all similar offences committed over X period and involving £Y.

(d) You will then have to take the judge through the defendant's antecedents—see p 35: for a copy of these. Check that the judge has a copy.

Q: 'Does Your Honour have the antecedents of Jane Forrester dated 10 June 2009?'

In dealing with the antecedents, it is usual to read out each part of the relevant information. The order in which you deal with the defendant's history is as follows:

(i) Date of birth/birthplace, etc.

Example

'The defendant was born on 21 December 1984 in London and is now aged 24 years.'

(ii) Previous convictions.

Example

'There are a number of matters recorded against the defendant including offences of dishonesty.'

Q: 'Where would Your Honour like me to start?' (This is to enable the judge to determine which of the previous convictions are relevant.)

A: 'Deal with the last three matters—from June 2004.'

'On 2 June 2004, at the West London Magistrates' Court, for an offence of theft, the defendant was fined £400 and ordered to pay costs of £75.'

'On 9 September 2005, at the same court, for two offences of obtaining property by deception, the defendant was also fined £300 in respect of each matter and ordered to pay costs of £80.'

'Finally, on 5 January 2009, at this court, for three offences of theft, the defendant was sentenced to a period of one month's imprisonment on each count concurrent, such sentence being suspended for a period of one year.'

At this point, ask for the breach of the suspended sentence to be put to the defendant. Upon the judge's direction, the clerk will then put the fact of the conviction and sentence to the defendant and ask the defendant whether they agree with it. If the defendant does not (this is rare), it will be necessary to put the case back in the list in order to produce strict proof of the conviction, ie, a certificate of the conviction (see the Police and Criminal Evidence Act 1984, s 73). If the defendant admits the details, the clerk will inform the defendant that, as the current offences were committed during the period of the suspension, the defendant may now be dealt with again in respect of the original offences.

(iii) Give the court brief details of the facts of the original offences. If your information is sparse, and an officer is present, he or she may be able to assist the court with more detail.

(iv) Proceed with the rest of the antecedents, ie, education, employment, home circumstances.

(e) Make any application for costs that you are instructed to make and any application for a compensation or destruction order (usual in a drugs case).

Example:

'Your Honour, there is an application for a destruction order in respect of the drugs which form the subject of the charge and a further application for costs in the sum of £120.'

(f) Finish by informing the court that you have closed your case.

'That is the case for the prosecution.'

(g) It is now the turn of defence counsel to mitigate on his or her client's behalf.

(h) The judge will then proceed to sentence. See ***Criminal Litigation and Sentencing*** manual, **Chapter 13**. Be ready to assist the judge on his or her powers of sentence and be prepared to remind him or her tactfully if he or she exceeds those powers.

Antecedents of: Jane FORRESTER Dated: 10.6.2009

Charged with: Possession of controlled drugs, intent to supply (x 2)

Date and place of birth: 21.12.84 (aged 24); London

Nationality: British

Date of arrest: 1.6.09/On bail

Summary of convictions: 2 findings of guilt as a juvenile

8 previous convictions recorded

Education: Attended Bishop's Rock Comprehensive School; left aged 16 with no formal qualifications.

Employment since leaving school: Many occasional jobs of short duration.

Presently unemployed, not claiming benefit.

Address, home conditions: 264 Bath Street, Streatham, London

Lives with parents and receives £100 p.w. from them.

No financial commitments.

Convictions recorded against: Jane FORRESTER CRD No 40457/01

Charged in name of Jane FORRESTER

Date	Court	Offences	Sentence	Release Date
1.4.02	West London M.C.	Soliciting	Fine £20	
2.6.04	West London M.C.	Theft	Fine £400; Costs £75	
9.9.05	West London M.C.	Obtain prop by deception (x 2)	(1) and (2) Fine £300; Costs £80	
5.1.09	Inner London Crown Court	Theft (x 3)	(1)—(3) 1 month's imprisonment concurrent. Suspended 1 year	

41.3 Procedure before sentencing—a flow chart

The procedure before sentencing, once an accused, D, has either pleaded guilty or, having pleaded not guilty, is found guilty, is as follows:

D pleads guilty

D found guilty

The court may adjourn, eg, to obtain reports or to await the outcome of a co-accused's trial. If the court adjourns for reports, there is still a prima facie right to bail: s 4, Bail Act 1976.

Prosecution summary of the facts of the case. Note: (i) counsel for the prosecution should take a neutral stance and not suggest any particular sentence; (ii) if there is a substantial conflict between prosecution and defence as to the facts of the offence, the judge may allow both sides to call evidence on the matter (a *Newton* hearing) and then reach a decision as to what happened.

The antecedents. The prosecution adduces evidence of D's character and antecedents using a copy of written antecedents prepared by the police. This covers such matters as age, education, past and present employment, domestic circumstances, income, date of arrest, remands in custody or bail and previous convictions. If the antecedents are not in dispute, the information is normally given by prosecuting counsel. Exceptionally, the evidence is given by an officer who takes the *voir dire* oath. If so, the normal rules of evidence are relaxed but the defence are entitled to cross-examine and if they challenge any of the officer's assertions, the prosecution must then provide strict proof.

Reports. The judge reads any reports prepared on D, eg, pre-sentence reports, medical and psychiatric reports and assessments for suitability for community service.

Mitigation by defence counsel on behalf of D.

Sentence, taking into account any other offences which D wishes to be taken into consideration.

42 The plea in mitigation

42.1 Introduction

A plea in mitigation can be made:

(a) either after a plea of guilty, following the prosecution's presentation of the case and defendant's antecedents; or

(b) after conviction, following the verdict/s and the presentation of the defendant's antecedents.

The objective of a plea in mitigation is to ensure that a sentence is passed by the court which is appropriate both in the circumstances of the offence(s) and to the circumstances of the defendant. The aim is to obtain the most lenient punishment which can reasonably be imposed. It should be remembered that very few crimes carry with them a sentence fixed by law and so in most cases there is discretion in the court to decide which of a number of possible sentences is appropriate (for example, whether to imprison or fine) and within a particular sentence, a discretion to decide where, within the upper and lower limits, the particular sentence should be fixed.

42.2 Preparing to make a plea in mitigation

Always begin your preparation by checking on the sentencing principles which apply to the particular crime. You should use the Guideline Judgments Case Compendium on the website of the Sentencing Guidelines Council (at <http://www.sentencing-guidelines.gov.uk/docs/complete_compendium.pdf>) to find the guiding cases. Your aim should be to identify the type of sentence or order which would normally be imposed (see ***Criminal Litigation and Sentencing*** manual and ***Blackstone's Criminal Practice, Section B,*** which sets out guidance on sentencing tariffs; also see the website of the Sentencing Guidelines Council for information).

Having identified the type of sentence, you should then identify any aggravating features which would normally encourage a court to take the view that a sentence at the higher end of the scale would be appropriate and then see whether you can dissociate the defendant from those features. The following list of features will often be seen as aggravating: ringleader, planned or premeditated act; serious injury caused; use of weapon; unprovoked; large sum of money involved; breach of trust; reoffending soon after a court order is made; elderly/young victim; poor response to supervision; lack of concern for injured victim; lack of remorse; and offence committed while on bail.

Your next task is to identify whether there are any mitigating factors which should be brought to the attention of the court. The following list of features will often be seen as mitigating: minor role; spontaneous; provoked; minor injuries; property recovered; severe domestic or emotional stress; little or no damage to the victim; dependent children; has the care of an ill or disabled spouse; exceptional help to others; previous good character; offence out of character; long time since previous offence; out of trouble since offence; pleaded guilty; good response to supervision; full confession; gave himself or herself up; recently married; secure job; cured of addiction to drugs or alcohol; paid compensation prior to hearing; compensation offered; other restitution made or offered to victim; expression of remorse; suffered loss or injury due to the offence; mental disorder; good work record; consequences unintended; low intelligence; signs of reform; in financial problems not of own making; offence committed out of loyalty; parity with co-defendants needed; in some sex offences—willing victim; offender forgiven by the victim; and that it is a long time since the offence was committed.

42.2.1 Holding a conference with the client

You should aim to arrive at court in plenty of time to obtain the information that you need to present the plea in mitigation. You may only get the papers in the case a short while before you are due to appear in court but you should always see your client in conference before starting to mitigate in court. If, for whatever reason, you have not had enough time to get full information, you should ask the court to put the case back in the list to be dealt with later that day. If you try to make a plea in mitigation with inadequate or incomplete preparation, this may raise professional conduct issues for you; it is also likely to jeopardise your client's human rights. Where the court is told that your preparation time has been inadequate, it should consider seriously whether to adjourn the hearing (see European Convention on Human Rights, Article 6(1) and (3)(b) and (c); *Goddi v Italy* (1984) 6 EHRR 457, *T and V v UK*, unreported, 16 December 1999, and *cf. F v UK* (1992) 15 EHRR CD 32).

During the conference with your client you should seek to establish the following facts and/or make the following assessments of your client:

(a) Your client's age (if relevant); and

(b) Whether your client's actual age should be ignored because he or she appears to be immature or is mentally disabled. You should also consider whether to apply to have the case adjourned for reports to be prepared.

(c) Your client's background: whether there are any circumstances which might excuse or explain the offence; your client's past character (you should get a form listing any previous convictions (usually on form MG16) from the Crown Prosecution Service and take your client through it); whether this offence is similar to or different from previous offences; whether there are any underlying problems, for example, drug or alcohol addiction; past instances of generosity or kindness.

(d) Your client's involvement in the crime: was your client a principal actor in the offence or did he or she take a minor role in it; was the offence premeditated or did it happen on the spur of the moment; what, if any, pressure was your client subject to; was it an isolated incident or does your client's criminal conduct extend over a long period; was your client influenced by another offender; if so, was he or she unable to resist that influence because of age or experience; quantify how much damage was done, or money taken and establish whether any offences are being taken into consideration.

(e) Your client's present situation: here you are looking for evidence of your client's stability, a regular home, job and people who will be supportive to the defendant; compare the situation as it is now with the time when the offence was committed; ask what your client has done to help himself or herself—acts showing contrition are more important than words, so establish whether your client has made any attempt at restitution. When a fine is a possibility you need to obtain considerable detail about your client's financial situation in order to help the court fix the fine at a proper level. So, you need to know your client's income after tax etc, your client's outgoings out of income and his or her capital. You also need to take your client's instructions on how much time he or she will need to pay any fine imposed and the level of weekly instalments he or she could meet.

(f) You may want to call one or two character witnesses to speak on behalf of your client. This can be useful sometimes. You should only call people who know your client well and who can say something about him or her which is relevant in either dissociating your client from the aggravating features of the offence or enhancing the mitigating factors in the case.

(g) Prepare your client for what will happen by giving him or her realistic advice as to the likely sentence which will be imposed and by describing the procedure in court.

42.2.2 Reading and understanding the pre-sentence report

Make sure that you have got any reports (usually from the court probation service), have read them and that you have noted the comments made about the defendant's background, the background to the offence and any recommendation on sentence. Note that you should comply with a request not to show a report (for example, a medical report or one relating to the defendant's mental health) to the defendant and that you should always ensure that material which is given to you in confidence is dealt with on that basis.

42.3 Presenting the plea in mitigation

42.3.1 The length of the plea

It is very important to keep your plea in mitigation short. In an ordinary case, aim to keep your submission to no more than 10 minutes.

42.3.2 Witnesses

After a guilty plea the defendant's instructions may be that his or her view of the circumstances of the offence are different from the case put by the prosecution; in these circumstances the court may decide to hear evidence to determine which version of the facts to accept (*R v Newton* (1982) *77* Cr App R 13; ***Criminal Litigation and Sentencing*** manual, **13.4.2). However, in most circumstances, the need for this ought to be removed by the use of a written 'basis of plea' document—the content of this should be agreed by counsel for the prosecution and defence before the guilty plea is entered.**

Any witnesses as to character may be called before making the substance of (or during) your plea. You can call your witness in the following way:

> 'Your Honour, before I address you in mitigation on behalf of Ms Smith, I should like to call Mr Jones. Mr Jones please.'

You should ask witnesses to identify themselves and explain their relationship to the defendant. Then ask any questions which will provide relevant information to be used later on in your plea. For example, if you are seeking to establish that Ms Smith's criminal act is completely out of character, you will want to call a witness who can say, based on the witness's long and detailed knowledge of her, that this act was completely out of character. You could try to elicit this kind of information from the witness with one or more of the following questions:

'Do you know Ms Smith?'
'When did you first meet her?'
'How did you come to know her?'
'As her (employer, etc) . . . have you had the opportunity of assessing her character?'
'How would you describe her character?'
'What are her responsibilities at work?'
'From what you know of Ms Smith, do you regard her involvement in this offence as in or out of character?'

42.3.3 Introducing the pre-sentence report

Usually the pre-sentence report will have been handed to the judge or magistrates before the plea in mitigation starts and it is sometimes necessary for the court to adjourn while the report is read. However, before you can refer to the contents of the pre-sentence report you will want to be sure that the judge or magistrate has a copy of it and has had a chance to read it. You can introduce the report in the following way:

> 'Your Honour, a pre-sentence report has been prepared, dated . . . which I shall refer to in the course of my plea in mitigation. Has Your Honour had an opportunity to read the report?'

42.4 The content of the plea in mitigation

42.4.1 Summary

You should start your plea with a summary of the main points you intend to make. You could say:

'The substance of my plea in mitigation is . . .' or
'I shall seek to persuade Your Honour that . . .' or
'Your Honour, the defendant accepts that this was a serious offence and has fully admitted his part in it. I do not propose to address Your Honour on the circumstances of the offence but will seek to persuade Your Honour that . . .'

42.4.2 Sentencing policy

You may then want to bring in the matters of sentencing policy which will bear upon the case. For example, you could say:

> 'In my submission, as Your Honour will appreciate, the guidelines state that sentences at the higher end of the scale are reserved for offences where . . .' (state the aggravating features).

Next you will want to explain (if you can) to the court why the defendant can be dissociated from these aggravating features, and how the evidence (what the prosecution have said, and what any witnesses have said) supports your contention. For example,

> 'I hope that Your Honour will accept that on the prosecution's case, the defendant can be dissociated from any aggravating features and that as a matter of principle, a sentence at the lower end of the scale is appropriate.'

In the early days, however, you may be concerned more with the appropriate type of sentence, rather than the scale.

42.4.3 Mitigating factors

You should then make specific, albeit brief reference to the mitigating factors which are relevant. For example, that the defendant pleaded guilty, confessed immediately or was previously of good character. Where relevant you should tie in your submissions on these issues with any evidence which has been given to the court, for example, the testimony of the antecedents officer, any witnesses as to the defendant's character and any statements in the pre-sentence report. The pre-sentence report should be referred to by page number and where on the page the paragraph appears, so that the court is able to follow the points you are making. You should then round off this part of your submission with a plea for a sentence at the lower end of the scale if that is appropriate. For example,

> 'It is my submission that when all these factors are borne in mind, a sentence at the lower end of the scale is justified.'

If your client has indicated genuine remorse to you, you should refer to what the client has said to you in conference. For example,

> 'Your Honour, in conference Ms Smith told me how terribly sorry she is for what she has done and she has asked me to repeat this to the court.'

If you can also point to concrete signs of remorse—eg, helping the police, wherewithal to pay compensation—that will carry much more weight with the court.

42.5 Conclusion

You will then be in a position to conclude your plea. For example,

> 'In conclusion, Your Honour, my submission is that, both as a matter of principle and on account of the particular facts of this case, a financial penalty would be appropriate which can justifiably be put at the lower end of the scale.'

or:

> 'Your Honour, the defendant appreciates that a custodial sentence is justified in this case and I do not propose to seek to persuade Your Honour otherwise. However, this is a case where, I submit, there are some mitigating features which could enable Your Honour to take a lenient view and (impose a short period of imprisonment) or (suspend any sentence of imprisonment) . . .'.

42.6 Warning

Always make sure that you have properly prepared your submissions in a plea in mitigation and that they are realistic. There is no point in suggesting to the court that a case is not appropriate for a sentence of imprisonment if the sentencing guidelines make it clear that a sentence of imprisonment should be imposed. Equally there is no point in dwelling on aspects of the defendant's background which are no longer relevant to mitigating the defendant's conduct, for example, when the defendant is 45 years old, revealing that his or her parents divorced when he or she was 8 years old! You will also be in some difficulty if you try to tell the court that the defendant is really sorry for what he or she did, when the plea in mitigation follows conviction after a not guilty plea.

The Court of Appeal has emphasised on several occasions that it is the duty of both prosecuting and defence counsel to know what sentences may in any particular case be lawfully passed, so as to correct the judge if need be and avoid unnecessary appeals on the basis that the sentence was not one that the judge had power to impose.

42.7 Further reading

Hyam, M. *Advocacy Skills,* Blackstone Press (OUP), 4th edn, 1999.

APPENDIX
A CRIMINAL CASE: *R v HEATH*

<u>BRIEF FOR THE PROSECUTION</u>

R

v

KEVIN HEATH

Counsel has herewith:

(1) Indictment
(2) Committal statements
(3) Defendant's antecedents and previous convictions
(4) Witnesses' previous convictions
(5) Statement of Defence in accordance with the Criminal Procedure and Investigations Act 1996.

Counsel is instructed in the prosecution of the above-named Defendant who faces the two counts shown on the indictment.

The facts emerge clearly from the statements. The reviewing lawyer takes the view that a plea to s 20 GBH would not be acceptable.

Counsel will note that two of the prosecution witnesses have previous convictions. The defence must be told of these, whether or not they ask for them, in accordance with the decision in *R v Collister and Warhurst* (1955) 39 Cr App R 100 and the Attorney General's Guidelines on Disclosure, although of course their use in the trial will be dependent on getting permission from the judge under CJA 2003, s 100.

IN THE CROWN COURT AT CROYDON

THE QUEEN

V

KEVIN HEATH

INDICTMENT

Kevin HEATH is charged as follows:

COUNT 1 STATEMENT OF OFFENCE

Causing grievous bodily harm with intent contrary to section 18 of the Offences Against the Person Act 1861.

PARTICULARS OF OFFENCE

Kevin Heath on the 24th day of December 2008 unlawfully caused grievous bodily harm to John Bull with intent to do him grievous bodily harm.

COUNT 2 STATEMENT OF OFFENCE

Inflicting grievous bodily harm contrary to section 20 of the Offences Against the Person Act 1861.

PARTICULARS OF OFFENCE

Kevin Heath on the 24th day of December 2008 unlawfully and maliciously inflicted grievous bodily harm on John Bull.

Date: 17 March 2009

John Collison
Officer of the Crown Court

STATEMENT OF WITNESS

Statement of: JOHN BULL

Age of witness: Over 18

Occupation of witness: Publican

This statement consisting of one page, signed by me, is true to the best of my knowledge and belief and I make it knowing that, if it is tendered in evidence, I shall be liable to prosecution if I have wilfully stated in it anything which I know to be false or do not believe to be true.

Signed : *J. Bull*

Signature witnessed by: R. Maybury *Statement dated*: 28th December 2008.

I am the landlord of The Cutpurse public house and have been so for 5 years.

On Wednesday, 24th December 2008 I was serving behind the bar throughout the evening together with Tracey CROFT, my permanent barmaid, and a number of part-time staff.

Being Christmas Eve the pub was very busy and in general the atmosphere was noisy but pleasant.

At about 9.00 pm I had reason to speak to a youth who I know as 'Ferret'. He is in his early twenties, about 5′7″ with dark hair and a pointy face. He had been in the pub since opening time and at this time he was being difficult and abusive towards Tracey who was serving at the part of the bar near the pool table. He was waving a pool cue around. I told him to pack it in or go home. I have had trouble with him in the past and banned him from my pub in June last year following a fight in my garden. I know he has been in trouble with the police plenty of times and is always playing 'Jack the Lad'.

All was well until about 10.30 when a group of carol singers arrived to sing in the public bar. This was by invitation and is something of which I am particularly fond.

The carol singers were grouped around the door. They had just begun to sing when they were interrupted by foul chanting from near the pool table. Although I could not at this stage actually see who was doing it, I had no doubt who was responsible. I felt very angry and upset and decided to take swift action as I am entitled to do by law. I went along the bar to the pool table where I could see Ferret and his friends chanting and yelling and once again Ferret was waving his pool cue about. I could see other people were getting upset. I called to him 'Alright you foul mouthed lout, shut it, and out'. I then left the bar by the hatch and went to eject him. At this Ferret came over to me and said, brandishing the cue, 'I'm going to stuff this . . .' I said 'Don't mess with me Ferret' and fearing an attack took the cue from him and threw it behind the bar, turning away from Ferret as I did so. As I turned back I heard the words 'You've had this coming, fat man'. After that, everything went blank, although I dimly remember hearing screaming.

I woke up in hospital and found out that I had been hit in my face with a glass beer mug. I have cuts to the left side of my face from my eye to my chin which needed 50 stitches. I am in considerable pain.

At no stage did I provoke this attack. I am 61 and weigh 16 stones.

I made a sketch of the layout of the Public Bar which I produce as JB/1.

I am willing to attend court and give evidence, if required.

Signed by: *J. Bull* Signature witnessed by: *R. Maybury*

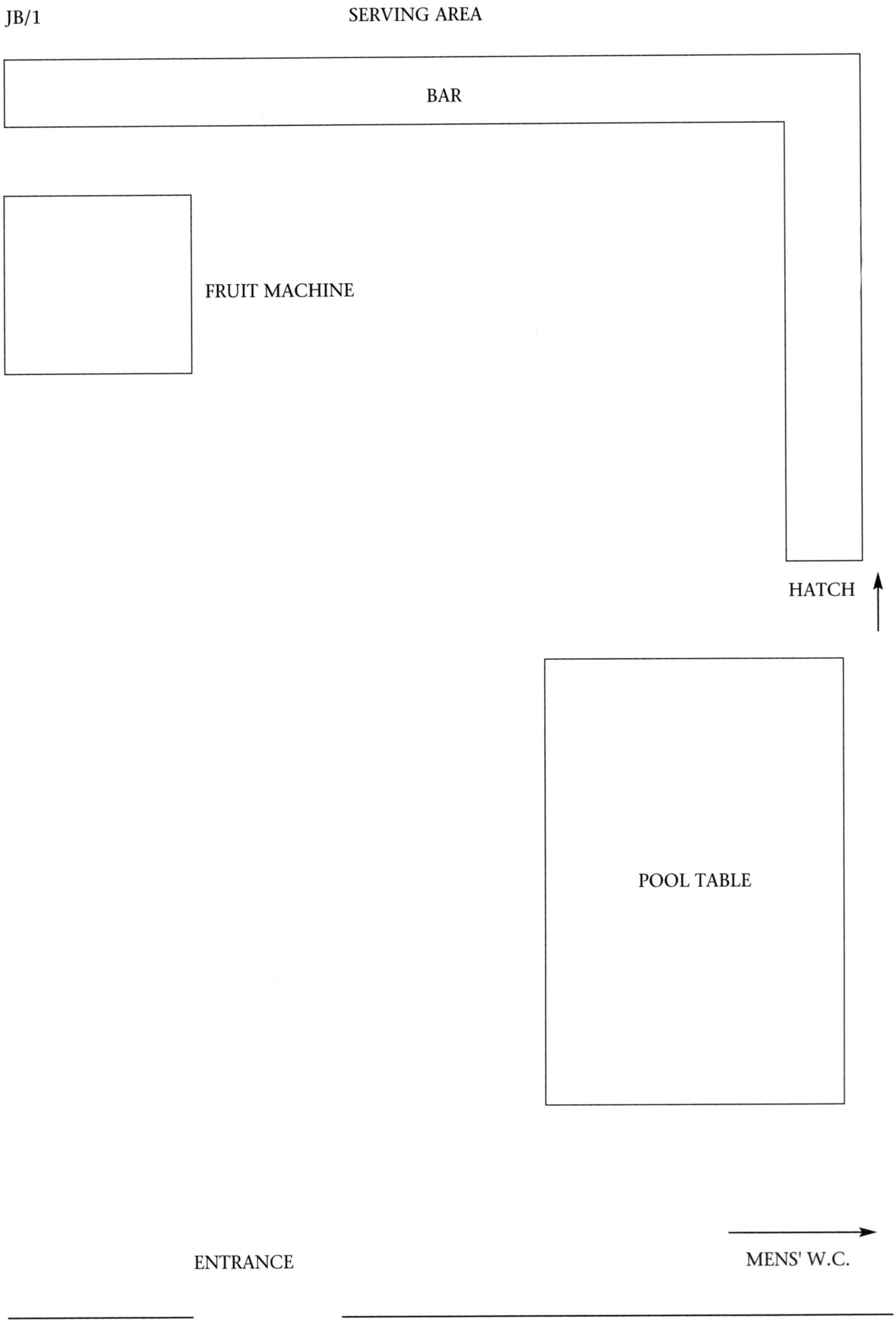
JB/1
SERVING AREA
BAR
FRUIT MACHINE
HATCH
POOL TABLE
ENTRANCE
MENS' W.C.

STATEMENT OF WITNESS

Statement of: TRACEY CROFT

Age of witness: Over 18

Occupation: Barmaid

This statement consisting of three pages, signed by me, is true to the best of my knowledge and belief and I make it knowing that, if it is tendered in evidence, I shall be liable to prosecution if I have wilfully stated in it anything which I know to be false or do not believe to be true.

Signed: *T. Croft*

Signature witnessed by: *R. Maybury* Statement dated: 25th December 2008.

I am 19 years old and am a member of the bar staff at The Cutpurse public house. I have worked there since about December 2006.

I was working in the evening on Christmas Eve 2008 together with John Bull, the proprietor and my boss, and several part-time staff. It was very crowded and busy. Lots of people were buying drinks for me and John Bull. John had a Happy Hour promotion during the early evening to get people in, and everyone had a bit of a laugh when we did the karaoke competition. It was a really good atmosphere.

Among the regulars is a young man who is usually called Ferret, although I think his real name is Kevin. I do not know his last name. He has been a regular in the pub since I have worked there except for a period earlier this year when John Bull banned him. John does not like him. He has told me he thinks Ferret is mouthy and a show-off. I am not sure how long he was banned but he has certainly been coming to the pub regularly since early autumn.

Ferret was in the pub on Christmas Eve. I cannot remember when I first saw him but I think it was fairly near opening time at 6 o'clock. I served him a number of drinks. I can't remember exactly how many times I served him but I think it was about five times.

Each time I served him a pint of Tennent's, which is his normal drink. Over the course of the evening he seemed to me to get louder and more noticeable among the general crowd in the pub, making loud comments which were slightly rude and using swear words.

Before the fight, the only time I heard John Bull speaking to Ferret that evening was a couple of hours earlier. Ferret had been over with his mates by the pool table. However at that point he was playing the fruit machine and I was serving near it. I do not remember whether or not he had a pool cue in his hand at this point. He came over and asked for some change which I gave him. While he was waiting, he made some comments about my dress. I can't remember exactly what he said. The comments were a bit silly, about how sexy it was, why didn't I show off my legs more often, etc.

He was talking a bit loudly but I thought it was just good-humoured banter and high spirited. I didn't take offence at all and didn't really respond or say anything. John was serving fairly close to me at the time and seemed to take offence. He stopped serving other customers and turning to Ferret told him to 'Sod off'. He seemed quite cross when he said it but then turned away to serve someone else. Ferret seemed quite cross too. He just stopped and looked at John. Although Ferret had asked for change for the fruit machine, he didn't go back there. He turned and muttered something under his breath which I didn't catch. He then walked back over to the pool table area. He said something to the people he was with when he got back there and they all looked over at John. Ferret seemed angry still and kept looking over at John. John was just ignoring him. I did too.

The carol singers arrived a couple of hours later. I can't remember the exact time. John had told me he had booked them and was really looking forward to it. He also said at some point in the evening that if there was any trouble from Ferret and his lot then either they'd be out or he'd sort them out. I can't remember which one it was (they'd be out or he'd sort them out) nor exactly when he said it, although I think it was after the incident about my dress.

Shortly after the carol singers started, I could hear people singing along with them but using different words which were rude and I thought disgusting and obscene. At this point I was serving up at the end of the bar away from the pool table nearer the fruit machine. The singing was coming from over near the pool table area. John Bull was serving not far from me. He looked really angry. He went very red. He went round behind the bar to the part by the pool table and shouted to Ferret to get out. I can't remember the exact words he used. John then went out from behind the bar towards the pool table and Ferret.

It all happened very quickly. I can't remember the exact order of things. While John was yelling and going towards Ferret I ran around behind the bar towards the pool table area to see what was happening.

The pub was quite crowded but, once John yelled and went out from behind the bar towards Ferret, people moved quite quickly away from the pool table area where John and Ferret were. While I was running around behind the bar towards the pool table end, I couldn't see much. By the time I got up to that end, it was fairly clear. There was no one in my way and I would have been no more than 6–8 feet away.

I could see John and Ferret moving towards each other. Ferret had a pool cue in his hand. John got hold of it too and there was a bit of a struggle over it. John eventually got the cue away from Ferret and broke it in two and then flung it over the bar. Although I can't be sure, I think Ferret was holding the cue in one hand only until John Bull grabbed it and then I think both of them had both hands on it until John actually got it away from Ferret. John did break it in two before he threw it behind the bar but I can't describe it any more than that. It all happened very quickly, in a couple of minutes or less.

As John turned to throw the pool cue over the bar, Ferret picked up an empty beer glass which was on the pool table. It was a straight glass, not a mug. As John turned back towards Ferret, Ferret said something which I couldn't hear and lunged towards John with the glass. They were only about two or two-and-a-half feet apart. I screamed 'look out' but it was too late. Ferret just put the glass in John Bull's face. He was holding onto the glass and just thrust it into his face and suddenly there was a lot of blood. I think the glass broke at this point. I can't remember exactly how Ferret was holding it. I think he was holding it vertically.

Again it all happened very quickly, but I think I remember seeing the blood at the same time as John Bull fell to the ground. I could see that the blood was coming from his face. There was a lot of screaming and shouting after that. I heard Ferret shouting 'He had it coming, he fucking had it coming' over and over again. He sounded frightened. His girlfriend was shouting at him, calling him 'You fucking idiot'.

Ferret had tried to run off but Dave Dray and some other men were holding onto him. I waited by John Bull until the ambulance and police came. I could see that he had been cut very badly and I did what I could to stop the blood. I couldn't work out what had happened and I do remember saying What happened? What happened—I was confused and frightened.

John is a lot bigger than Ferret, who is about the same size as me. I am 5′7″ tall.

I know Ferret but only as a customer of the pub. He can be quite funny at times but at other times he can be quite loud and disturb the atmosphere. John Bull is a good employer. I am the only permanent bar staff he has. All the others are temporary who come and go quite quickly.

I am willing to attend court and give evidence, if required.

Signed: *T. Croft* Signature witnessed by: *R. Maybury*

STATEMENT OF WITNESS

Statement of: DAVID DRAY

Age of witness: Over 18

Occupation of witness: Builder

This statement consisting of one page, signed by me, is true to the best of my knowledge and belief and I make it knowing that, if it is tendered in evidence, I shall be liable to prosecution if I have wilfully stated in it anything which I know to be false or do not believe to be true.

Signed: *D. Dray*

Signature witnessed by: *R. Maybury* Statement dated: 25th December 2008.

On Christmas Eve 2008 I was in The Cutpurse pub in New Addington, Croydon. I am a regular there and have been drinking there for at least 15 years. Everyone was very merry and we were all having a good drink. John Bull, the landlord had put on a good night—there was a Happy Hour from 6–9pm and then there was an hour of karaoke with drinks as the prizes which began at about 7 pm, and he had also arranged carol singers to come in. The pub was decorated and was packed out. I was there with my wife and my son Joe and his girlfriend, Sanchia.

At about 11.00 pm the carol singers arrived. Shortly after they started I was in the men's having a pee. When I came out I looked over the pool table and saw some sort of scrap going on between big John and some little guy. I now know the little one is Kevin Heath, but I didn't know his name on that night. I recognised him from the pub but no more than that.

I saw Kevin Heath get a clout round the ear and John took his pool cue away from him. Kevin had been waving it around and it looked dangerous to me. I think John got it off him to stop trouble. I had stepped toward the two of them as soon as I saw this as it looked as if there was going to be trouble. I was no more than 10 feet away. I had a clear view. As John turned round to put the pool cue behind the bar the other one picked up his beer mug and smashed it into John's head. John fell like a stone. I didn't have time to call out any warning, it all happened so fast.

Kevin tried to run past the table and toward the door, but I grabbed hold of him as what he done was out of order. A couple of other men there helped me out and we held him until the police arrived. When we were waiting some women started shouting at Kevin, one was saying something like 'You idiot, you idiot, what have you done now?', someone else was crying and it had gone very quiet. Tracey Croft who works at the Cutpurse was holding John Bull still and trying to stop blood coming from a cut to his face. She looked up at me and Kevin and was saying 'What happened?, What happened?' She was crying. Everyone was shocked at what had happened.

When the police came they took my details and I was asked to attend Croydon Police Station to make this statement. I am willing to attend court if required.

Signed: *D. Dray* Signature witnessed by: *R. Maybury*

STATEMENT OF WITNESS

Statement of: IAN MICHAEL FIRM

Age of witness: Over 18

Occupation of witness: Police Constable 2212

This statement consisting of one page, signed by me, is true to the best of my knowledge and belief and I make it knowing that, if it is tendered in evidence, I shall be liable to prosecution if I have wilfully stated in it anything which I know to be false or do not believe to be true.

Signed: *I. M. Firm*

Signature witnessed by: *R. Maybury* Statement dated: 3rd February 2009.

On Wednesday, 24th December 2008 I was on duty in full uniform in a marked police vehicle. At 11.20 pm as a result of information received I went to The Cutpurse public house, New Addington. It was very crowded when I arrived. Lying on the floor between the pool table and the bar was a man I now know to be John BULL. He appeared to be unconscious and was bleeding heavily from wounds to the left side of his face and I proceeded to give Mr Bull first aid. Shortly after this the ambulance arrived and Mr Bull was taken to hospital.

As a result of enquiries I spoke to a youth who I know to be Kevin HEATH. I noticed that he had blood on his right hand and spots of blood on his jacket. He was slightly dishevelled and his breath smelt strongly of drink, although he was not drunk.

I said to HEATH 'From what I have been told you hit the landlord, is this true?' And I then cautioned him. He replied 'He went for me'. I then told HEATH I was arresting him on suspicion of causing grievous bodily harm. After caution, he was taken to Croydon Police Station by other officers.

After the pub had been cleared I briefly examined the public bar area. Behind the bar near the pool table I found 2 pieces of pool cue which I produce as Exhibit IMF/1. Between the bar and the pool table I found a broken pint beer mug with jagged edges which appeared to have blood on it. This was placed in a bag and sealed. I produce this as Exhibit IMF/2.

Signed by: *I. M. Firm* Signature witnessed by: *R. Maybury*

STATEMENT OF WITNESS

Statement of: RONALD MAYBURY

Age of witness: Over 18

Occupation of witness: DS Croydon CID

This statement consisting of one page, signed by me, is true to the best of my knowledge and belief and I make it knowing that, if it is tendered in evidence, I shall be liable to prosecution if I have wilfully stated in it anything which I know to be false or do not believe to be true.

Signed: *R. Maybury*

Signature witnessed by: *S. Gent* Statement dated: 26th December 2008.

At 9.30 am on Christmas Day 2008 I was on duty at Croydon Police Station. There I saw a man I now know to be Kevin HEATH. I reminded him that he was under caution to which he replied 'I know all that—let's get on with it'. In the company of DC Tibbs I then interviewed HEATH in the interview room at the police station between 9.32 and 10.00 am. The interview was tape-recorded using two tapes. At the conclusion of the interview I sealed one of the copies and signed over the seal. I produce this as my Exhibit RM/1. I later prepared a written summary of the interview, which I produce as my Exhibit RM/2.

Later that day at 11.30 am HEATH was charged with wounding John BULL with intent to do him GBH. The charge was read over to him, he was again cautioned and replied 'No I've really done it this time though haven't I?'

Signed: *R. Maybury* Signature witnessed by: *S. Gent*

IN THE CROWN COURT AT CROYDON

THE QUEEN

V

KEVIN HEATH

DEFENCE
STATEMENT

Defence Statement under the provisions of Section 5 Criminal Procedure and Investigations Act 1996

1. Nature of the defence

At 6 pm on 24 December 2008, the accused went into The Cutpurse public house with his friends, including his girlfriend, Sharon Wood, and her sister Debbie. They spent a pleasant evening talking, playing pool and enjoying a social drink, aside from an incident at about 9 pm when the landlord of the pub, John Bull, was aggressive and intimidating towards the accused. The accused had been engaged in an informal conversation with one of the pub staff, Tracey Croft, when John Bull intervened and told the accused to sod off. The accused did not react and simply returned to his group of friends at the pool table. When a group of carol singers arrived around 10.30 pm, several people in the pub joined in with their singing in an irreverent and light-hearted fashion. The accused was simply one of these; he had no intention to annoy or upset anyone who was present. Those people in the vicinity of the pool table all seemed to enjoy the singing. The landlord of the pub seemed to have decided to eject the accused immediately and violently, running around the bar and shouting at the accused as he moved towards him. This instant decision was disproportionate to any need to restore order and the selection of only the accused as the recipient of the landlord's attention was quite deliberate on his part. The landlord had displayed an aggressive and hostile manner to the accused earlier that evening. The landlord clipped the accused around the head as soon as he came within reach, he then took the accused's own pool cue from him, with considerable force and violence, breaking it in two in an act of extreme aggression before recklessly flinging it away. As the landlord turned back to confront the accused once more, the accused felt that he had no alternative but to defend himself. He punched out towards the landlord, a much bigger man. The hand that he punched with had been holding his beer glass and still was, with the result that the glass smashed on impact with the landlord's face.

2. Issues taken with the prosecution case

The accused takes issue with the prosecution case that he deliberately or recklessly intended to cause grievous bodily harm to the landlord.

3. Reasons why the accused takes issue with the prosecution case

The accused takes issue with the prosecution case because he is not guilty of these offences—he acted at all times in self-defence and used only reasonable force. He was unable to retreat away from the assault on himself due to the press of people behind him and the proximity of the pool table. He admits that he struck the landlord the blow that knocked him unconscious and that he had a beer glass in his hand but had not armed himself with the glass and sought only to fend off the anticipated continuation of the assault upon him.

4. Points of law

(i) Exclusion of police interview under s 78 Police and Criminal Evidence Act 1984, relying on breach of s 58 PACE and breach of PACE Code C
(ii) Admission of evidence of the bad character of a prosecution witness, John Bull, under s 100 Criminal Justice Act 2003

5. Alibi

The accused does not deny being present at the time of the incident.

6. Disclosure

Please disclose the following items on the Schedule of unused material which are capable of assisting the defence case or undermining the prosecution case

[not included here]

7. Declaration

I, Kevin Heath, have read and understood this defence statement. I agree with its contents and confirm that it is consistent with my instructions. I understand that if I give evidence which conflicts with it, the prosecution may apply it in evidence and use it to cross-examine me.

Signed: *Kevin Heath* (Accused)

Dated: 11 April 2009

Keymon & Keymon

147 Sutton Place

Croydon

Solicitors for the accused

0127	RM	How many do you drink on average when you go to the pub?
0131	KH	About 5/6 a night.
0144	RM	How many did you have last night before you hit John?
0150	KH	About 3/4.
0157	RM	Pints?
0163	KH	Yeah.
0170	RM	Any shorts?
0174	KH	No.
0181	RM	What were you doing before John, the publican came up to you?
0194	KH	Drinking with my mates.
0200	RM	Which ones?
0211	KH	I don't know—there were lots of them around.
0223	RM	So you must have had a pint glass in your hand?
0229	KH	Well, yeah.
0237	RM	So you must have realised when you punched out that you would hit John with the glass?
0242	KH	Well—no.
0250	RM	Come off it, you don't just forget you're holding a pint glass.
0265	KH	Well I did.
0273	RM	Do you know Tracey Croft?
0278	KH	Yeah.
0288	RM	Well?
0294	KH	Yeah—she's my bird—well sort of anyway.
0304	RM	Does John fancy her?
0310	KH	Yeah he does a bit.
0321	RM	I put it to you that you are jealous of John because of Tracey and . . .
0323	KH	*(interrupted)* Bollocks.
0335	RM	I'll continue, you are jealous and when John told you to get out of the pub in front of your mates you felt small and decided to do him.
0342	KH	Rubbish.
0351	RM	Please let me finish.
0360	KH	Sorry.

RECORD OF TAPE RECORDED INTERVIEW

Person Interviewed:	Kevin HEATH	Exhibit no: RM/2
Place of Interview:	Croydon Police Station	No of Pages: 3
Date of Interview:	25th December 2008	
Time Commenced:	9.32 am	Time Concluded: 10 am
Duration of Interview:	28 minutes	Tape Reference No: RM/1/1234
Interviewing Officer(s):	DS Maybury	
Other persons present:	DC Tibbs	

Tape Counter	*Person Speaking*	*Text*
0001	RM	(Introductions) I must remind you that you are under caution. You do not have to say anything. But it may harm your defence if you do not mention when questioned something which you later rely on in court. Anything you do say may be given in evidence. Do you understand?
0008	KH	Yeah.
0015	RM	Do you object to being interviewed without a solicitor being present?
0025	KH	Well, I ain't going to get one this morning, am I? Anyway, I've done this a few times before.
0038	RM	Well, if you change your mind at any point, stop and tell me.
0049	KH	Yeah OK.
0055	RM	Now, what do you know about the glassing in The Cutpurse last night?
0066	KH	Well, not much really. That fat bastard of a landlord went for me with a pool cue. He hit me over the shoulder with it and it broke. He looked really angry as if he was going to do me again with the thick end of the cue so I punched out at him. He dropped like a stone, the girls started screaming and the geezer I know as Wally grabbed me and said that's out of order, you're staying here until Old Bill get here.
0081	RM	Were you drunk when you hit Big John Bull?
0089	KH	No—well merry really.
0096	RM	Are you a regular drinker?
0101	KH	Yeah.
0110	RM	What's your tipple?
0119	KH	Lager top.

BRIEF FOR THE DEFENCE

R

v

KEVIN HEATH

Counsel has herewith:

(1) Indictment [see prosecution brief]

(2) Prosecution Statements [see prosecution brief]

(3) Proof of Kevin Heath

(4) Previous convictions of Kevin Heath [see prosecution brief]

(5) Statement of the Defence disclosed to Prosecution [see prosecution brief]

Instructing Solicitors act for Kevin Heath who faces an indictment alleging s 18 Grievous Bodily Harm with s 20 GBH in the alternative.

Mr Heath admits his presence at The Cutpurse on Christmas Eve but says that he hit the landlord in self-defence in the form of a pre-emptive strike.

As Counsel will appreciate, there is quite a lot of background history to this matter, including the fight with Mr Bull in the summer of 2008 for which he received a sentence of 28 days' imprisonment. Mr Heath remains adamant that on the previous occasion, as on this, he was the victim and not the aggressor. Instructing Solicitors are aware of rumours concerning Miss Croft and Mr Bull. Mr Heath is an old client, though inclined to be headstrong and tends to 'want his say' in the witness box.

Instructing Solicitors do not know whether or not any of the prosecution witnesses have previous convictions. No doubt, any such convictions will be disclosed in due course.

If convicted, Mr Heath would be willing to undertake a community order. The Rev. Thanet is prepared to give character evidence on his behalf. Would Counsel please use his best endeavours on behalf of Mr Heath.

CALL KEVIN HEATH of 21 Tree Avenue, New Addington

Who will say:

On Christmas Eve I was in The Cutpurse with Sharon and her sister, Debbie Wood. I used to go there quite a lot until one day last summer when I was having a bit of a laugh with Tracey Croft in the garden (Sharon does not know this). John, the landlord, came over and turned nasty and smacked me in the mouth. I tried to defend myself but I got nicked and was found guilty by the Magistrates, even though I wasn't. I got a prison sentence for this and John banned me for 3 months. On Christmas Eve I got to the pub about seven. I was drinking pints of Tennent's. I suppose I had about 7 or 8 pints.

About 9.00 pm I was over playing the fruit machine. I asked Tracey for some change and made a couple of comments about her dress which was very low cut. Sharon was over at the pool table. Next thing John came over and told me to 'sod off' and leave Tracey well alone. Although I felt angry I just turned and walked back to the pool table. I never picked up a pool cue like he said. I didn't even swear at him. It's ridiculous the way he carries on—he must be almost 60 but Tracey is a young girl, not 20 yet.

When the carol singers came I was over near the pool table with Sharon and Debbie and a couple of others. When they started I suppose we were taking the mick a bit. Suddenly John was barging through everyone yelling at me to get out. I did have a pool cue in my hand, it's my own. John just came up to me, hit me round the left ear with his right hand. I tried to block him with the cue but he broke it in two and turned away and threw the bits behind the bar. As he turned back I thought he was going to attack me, so I picked up my pint mug and hit him across the head with it. I never said anything to him.

After this I panicked and tried to run off but some big geezer held onto me. The police came and I was arrested. I was then taken to the Police Station.

Since being charged I have seen Tracey Croft and she won't give evidence against me.

PERSONAL CIRCUMSTANCES

I am 25.

I have a number of previous convictions.

I live with my girlfriend, Sharon Wood, and she is expecting a baby in six months' time.

I do casual work as a roofer and take home £100 a week.

INDEX

A

B

C

T

U

V

W

Y